LITERACY ACROSS THE COMMUNITY

This volume explores and evaluates community-based literacy programs, examining how they bridge gaps in literacy development, promote dialogue, and connect families, communities, and schools. Highlighting the diversity of existing literary initiatives across populations, this book brings together innovative and emerging scholarship on the relationship between P20 schools and community-based literacy programming. This volume not only identifies trends in research and practice, but it also addresses the challenges affecting these community-based programs and presents the best practices that emerge from them.

Collaborating with leading scholars to provide national and international perspectives, and offering a clear, bird's-eye view of the state of community literacy praxis, chapters cover programming in a multitude of settings and for a wide range of learners, from early childhood to incarcerated youths and adults, and including immigrants, refugees, and indigenous communities. Topics include identity and empowerment, language and literacy development across the lifespan, rural and urban environments, and partnership programs. The breadth of community literacy programming gathered in a single volume represents a unique array of models and topics, and has relevance for researchers, scholars, graduate students, pre-service educators, and community educators in literacy.

Laurie A. Henry is Professor of Literacy in the Department of Literacy Studies and Dean of the Seidel School of Education at Salisbury University in Maryland, USA.

Norman A. Stahl is Professor Emeritus of Literacy Education at Northern Illinois University, USA, a Council of Learning Assistance and Developmental Education Associations (CLADEA) National Fellow, and a member of the Reading Hall of Fame.

LITERACY ACROSS THE COMMUNITY

Research, Praxis, and Trends

Edited by Laurie A. Henry and Norman A. Stahl

Routledge
Taylor & Francis Group

NEW YORK AND LONDON

First published 2021
by Routledge
52 Vanderbilt Avenue, New York, NY 10017

and by Routledge
2 Park Square, Milton Park, Abingdon, Oxon OX14 4RN

Routledge is an imprint of the Taylor & Francis Group, an informa business

Library of Congress Cataloging-in-Publication Data
Names: Henry, Laurie A., editor. | Stahl, Norman A., 1949– editor.
Title: Literacy across the community : research, praxis, and trends /
edited by Laurie A. Henry, Norman A. Stahl.
Identifiers: LCCN 2020031815 (print) | LCCN 2020031816 (ebook) |
ISBN 9780367468613 (hardback) | ISBN 9780367468620 (paperback) |
ISBN 9781003031550 (ebook)
Subjects: LCSH: Literacy programs.
Classification: LCC LC149 .L54 2021 (print) |
LCC LC149 (ebook) | DDC 374/.0124–dc23
LC record available at https://lccn.loc.gov/2020031815
LC ebook record available at https://lccn.loc.gov/2020031816

ISBN: 9780367468613 (hbk)
ISBN: 9780367468620 (pbk)
ISBN: 9781003031550 (ebk)

Typeset in Bembo
by Newgen Publishing UK

Visit the eResources: routledge.com/9780367468620

CV 03.18.2021 1720

DEDICATION

We write this text on literacy programs serving a multitude of communities at a time in our nation's history where we face both the specter of virulent disease sweeping across the landscape along with economic disparity fueling the unforgiving consequences of intolerance if not inhumanity. In ever so many ways the concept, construct, and strength of community matters more than ever for the women and men, girls and boys comprising each community's human element as the cornerstone of any community.

Authors of books such as this one routinely dedicate their good works to parents, caregivers, spouses, partners, children, and important mentors. Such an action is appropriate. We do indeed have such individuals in our lives for whom we are thankful on a daily basis. But today is another time.

Today we believe that as the co-editors of a text that focuses directly on communities that any dedication can only be directed to all those individuals who have stood tall and vigilant in the face of the twin ravages of disease and prejudice to protect the rest of us community members. It is our nurses, doctors, EMT personnel, essential workers, and teachers among others who have allowed us and the many co-authors to complete this project.

It is through their endeavors across the past months and, unfortunately, so likely to be into the future that community-oriented literacy programs and projects such as those presented in this text can, will, and must flourish. To each and every individual stepping forward into harm's way to protect others, we will be forever appreciative and thankful.

CONTENTS

Editor Biographies   *xi*

Contributor Biographies   *xii*

Foreword: Professional Literacies and Helping in the
*   Community: The Limits of Dash-Literacies*   *xxvi*
*   James R. King*

Acknowledgments   *xxxi*

Introduction   1

PART I
Language and Literacy Development   **9**

1   The Language and Literacy Practices of Emergent Bilinguals
    in a Community-based Writing Program   11
    Stephanie Abraham, Kate E. Kedley, and Kate Seltzer

2   Heritage Language and Literacy Education in East Asian
    Community-based Heritage Language Programs   24
    Kwangok Song

3   Bilingual Family Literacy Challenges   35
    Matthew Knoester

4 Nurturing Multiple Literacies: The Role of Community
and Creativity in an Intergenerational ESOL Class 47
Lily Applebaum, Mara Imms-Donnelly, and Emily Rose Schwab

5 A University/School Partnership Practicum with Culturally
Diverse Students and Teachers 59
Joyce C. Fine

PART II
Unique Populations **71**

6 Fostering Young Children's Literacy in Home and Community
Settings: A Dialogic Approach to Developing Culturally
Relevant and Sustaining Practices 73
*Pauline Harris, Alexandra Diamond, Bec Neill, Elspeth McInnes,
Cynthia Brock, and Ufemia Camaitoga*

7 Literacy Learning in "Unofficial" Spaces: Prospective Teachers'
Tutoring Initiative for Homeless Youth 89
Heidi L. Hallman

8 Family Literacy through Separation and Trauma: Integrated
Perspectives for Fathers 102
*Angela M. Wiseman, Qiana R. Cryer-Coupet, Ashley A. Atkinson,
and Stephen M. Gibson*

9 Incarcerated Languages and Literacies: Attempting Liberatory
Language and Literacy Pedagogies in a Prison Setting 114
Jim Sosnowski and Luz Murillo

10 Sponsoring Older Adults' Improvement of Metaliteracy
Using iPads 128
*Julie A. Delello, Annamary L. Consalvo, Rochell R. McWhorter,
and Gina Doepker*

PART III
Unique Settings and Contexts **143**

11 Community-Based Programs in Rural Settings 145
Pamela J. Farris, Mary E. Gardner, and Teri Reed-Houck

12 Literacy at the Public Library: An Intergenerational
Book Club 157
Molly K. Ness

13 Beyond Visual Literacy: Listening, Speaking, Reading, and
Writing in the Art Museum 171
Meredith Lehman, Sabrina Mooroogen Phillips, and Ray Williams

14 Doing Pedagogic Work to Illuminate the World: Participatory
Literacy in a Community Museum 184
Suriati Abas

15 Health Services in the Literacy Landscape 197
Sue Nichols

PART IV
Identity Development and Empowerment **209**

16 Identity Matters in Service-Learning Literacies: Becoming
Authentic and Agentic within Role Affordance 211
James R. King, Steven Hart, and Deborah Kozdras

17 Empowerment in Digital Literacy Acquisition Programs:
Learners Who Become Tutors 223
Jill Castek and Gloria E. Jacobs

18 Art Museums, Literacy, and Intrinsic Motivation 235
Mike Deetsch and Kate Blake

19 PluggedInVA: Harnessing the Transformative Power of a
Learner-centered Workforce Development Program 246
Kate Rolander and Susan L. Watson

20 Women Tutoring Women: A Community of Learners 258
*Heidi R. Bacon, Patricia L. Anders, Nadia R. Granados,
and Kelly L. Murphy*

PART V
Partnership Programs   271

21 Literacy Demands of Handbooks of Three National
    Youth Organizations   273
    Corrine M. Wickens, Donna E. Werderich, and Carol S. Walther

22 Behind the Fence: A Reading Partnership with the
    Department of Juvenile Justice   289
    Mary E. Styslinger

23 The Evolution of the MILE Reading Mentoring Program:
    The Role of Collaboration in a Teacher Education–Juvenile
    Corrections Partnership   301
    *Joanna C. Weaver, Timothy J. Murnen, Meggan K. Hartzog,
    and Cynthia Bertelsen*

24 STEM Stories: Connecting STEM and Literacy in an
    Afterschool Program   315
    *Mary-Kate Sableski, Margaret Pinnell, Shannon Driskell,
    Todd Smith, and Suzanne Franco*

25 A Sustained Program of Community Engagement in
    After-School Literacy Activities   330
    Kristen L. White and Judith Puncochar

26 The Power of Literacy for Community Engagement:
    Partnering with Youth Community-Based Organizations   342
    *Crystal Chen Lee, Jose A. Picart, Nina Schoonover, and
    Kelsey Virginia Dufresne*

Index   *357*

EDITOR BIOGRAPHIES

Laurie A. Henry is a Professor of Literacy in the Department of Literacy Studies and Dean of the Seidel School of Education at Salisbury University in Maryland. Her research interests focus on the new literacies of Internet-based reading, writing, and communicating and social equity issues related to the digital divide. She has extensive knowledge in adolescent and adult literacy and was the 2011 recipient of the J. Michael Parker Award for contributions in adult literacy research from the Literacy Research Association.

Norman A. Stahl is Professor Emeritus of Literacy Education at Northern Illinois University. He has been the President of the Literacy Research Association, the Association of Literacy Educators and Researchers, the College Reading and Learning Association, and Chair of the American Reading Forum. He is a CLADEA National Fellow and the Historian of the Reading Hall of Fame. Scholarly interests include literacy history, postsecondary literacy, and research methods.

CONTRIBUTOR BIOGRAPHIES

Suriati Abas is a visiting Assistant Professor of Education at Hobart and William Smith Colleges. Her research interests include linguistic landscapes, new literacies and literacy within school and in out-of-school contexts. She has published in several peer-reviewed journals and book chapters. Her most recent co-authored chapter, entitled "What do we bring to 'THE TABLE'? – A Visual Autoethnography of Underrepresented Asian TESOL Practitioners in the US," focuses on transnational literacies. She has taught children's literature and courses on linguistic landscapes, literacy theories, and methods for teaching reading and writing in schools.

Stephanie Abraham is an Associate Professor of Language & Literacy Education at Rowan University. She investigates the language and literacy practices of racialized, multilingual children both in and outside of school. In turn, she works with educators, across a variety of settings, to design and implement critical, multilingual pedagogies for these children. Her research has been funded by the National Endowment for the Humanities, the Fulbright Organization, and the Spencer Foundation. She has published in *Equity and Excellence in Education*, *Critical Education*, and *Discourse: Cultural Studies in the Politics of Education*.

Patricia L. Anders is the Jewell Lewis Distinguished Professor Emerita of Reading in the Teaching, Learning and Sociocultural Studies Department of the College of Education at the University of Arizona. Her research focuses on literacy teaching and learning, especially with adolescents and on literacies in communities. Since achieving emerita status, she is enjoying her garden and reviewing for the *Journal of Adolescent and Adult Literacy* and *Reading Research Quarterly*.

Lily Applebaum has worked and lived in Philadelphia since graduating from the University of Pennsylvania with a BA in English and Environmental Studies in 2012. She works at the Kelly Writers House, a literary arts non-profit center that serves as a community and programming space for Penn students, the greater literary community of Philadelphia, and via the Internet, the world. Through her work at the Kelly Writers House, she learned about alternative learning spaces and pedagogies, and brought this experience to her ESOL volunteer work and then teaching work beginning in 2016 at the community-based center described in this chapter. She hopes to continue teaching ESOL in an intergenerational classroom setting and via other non-traditional pedagogies in the future.

Ashley A. Atkinson is a Doctoral Candidate at North Carolina State University in Teacher Education and Learning Sciences. Her program area is Literacy and English Language Arts Education, and her research broadly centers on children's literature, family literacy, and trauma-informed teaching. Her dissertation focused on trauma-informed practices with middle grades literacy classrooms. Prior to pursuing her PhD, she was a middle grades English teacher and an instructional coach.

Heidi R. Bacon is an Associate Professor of Language, Literacies, and Culture in the School of Education at Southern Illinois University Carbondale where she teaches courses in literacy, action research, and qualitative methods. Her research focuses on adolescent, adult, and community literacies and social justice and has been published in the *Journal of Latinos and Education*, *Linguistics and Education*, and *English Teaching: Practice & Critique*.

Cynthia Bertelsen is an Associate Professor in the School of Teaching and Learning and serves as the Coordinator of the Graduate Reading Program at Bowling Green State University. Her research interests focus on the teaching and learning of all children, especially young children; teacher leadership, preparation and professional development; and literacy intervention and assessment.

Kate Blake is a museum educator with over ten years of gallery teaching experience. She earned her Master of Arts degree in Art History from Bowling Green State University. Most recently Kate was the Assistant Director of Education at the Toledo Museum of Art (TMA), where she oversaw the museum's visual literary curriculum and school and teacher programs. Career highlights include organizing *Drawn to Learn*, a 2019 visual literacy conference for educators and establishing TMA's *Teacher Leader* program. Kate has spoken on the use of visual literacy to support classroom and gallery education at numerous state, national, and international conferences.

Cynthia Brock is Professor and the Wyoming Excellence in Higher Education Endowed Chair in Literacy Education at the University of Wyoming. She is interested in literacy learning opportunities of children from diverse backgrounds.

Ufemia Camaitoga is an Early Childhood Education Consultant and National President of Fiji Early Childhood Teachers Association. She is actively engaged with forging early childhood partnerships across organizations and people.

Jill Castek is an Associate Professor in the Teaching, Learning, and Sociocultural Studies Department at the University of Arizona. Her work examines the development of literate capacities, both in print and digital forms, in schools, libraries, and adult learning settings. She possesses a strong commitment to improving instructional practice through teacher development and learner engagement with an emphasis on digital inclusion. Dr. Castek is active in designing and implementing instruction through partnerships with a range of educational and community-based organizations.

Annamary L. Consalvo is an Associate Professor of Literacy at The University of Texas at Tyler, where she teaches undergraduate and graduate courses. Research interests include the teaching of writing, disciplinary and adolescent literacies, and ways in which multiliteracies inform teaching and learning. Her work has appeared in *English Journal, Journal of Language and Literacy Education, Teaching and Teacher Education* and elsewhere including the NCTE blog, "Writers Who Care."

Qiana R. Cryer-Coupet is an Assistant Professor of Social Work at North Carolina State University. Dr. Cryer-Coupet's program of research focuses on parenting practices and their impacts on family health and well-being across the lifespan. Her current research explores the roles of fathers in families, particularly among those engaged in kinship care or who have been impacted by family traumas such as paternal incarceration, experiences of homelessness, and paternal substance use disorders. This line of research was inspired by her social work practice experience with relative caregivers and their families. Dr. Cryer-Coupet teaches research methods, program evaluation, and human behavior courses in the Master of Social Work program.

Mike Deetsch joined the Toledo Museum of Art (TMA) staff in 2013 as Assistant Director of Education. In 2015 he was named the Emma Leah Bippus Director of Education and Engagement, overseeing the docent program, art classes, youth programming, public programs, the Glass Studio, and visitor engagement. Prior to joining the staff at TMA, Deetsch served as a Senior Museum Educator at the Brooklyn Museum, the Exhibition and Programs Director at the Lexington Art League, and the Student Programs Manager at the Kentucky Historical Society. In 2012 he was selected to participate in the Getty Leadership Institute's NextGen program. Deetsch received his MS in Art Education from the Pratt Institute and a BA in Art History from Hanover College.

Julie A. Delello is an Associate Professor in the College of Education and Psychology at The University of Texas at Tyler. She also serves as the Director of the Center for Excellence in Teaching and Learning at the university. She received her PhD in Curriculum and Instruction with a specialization in Science and Technology from Texas A&M University. Dr. Delello has authored numerous publications and her professional interests focus on academic innovations, visual media technologies, artificial intelligence, STEM explorations, gerontechnology, and social media platforms for authentic learning.

Alexandra Diamond is Lecturer in Early Childhood Development in Education Futures at the University of South Australia. Her PhD study focuses on very young children's language socialization in a rural Indo-Fijian community.

Gina Doepker is an Associate Professor in the College of Education and Psychology at The University of Texas at Tyler. She also serves at the Program Coordinator for the Master of Education in Reading Degree program. She received her PhD in Literacy Education from The Ohio State University. Dr. Doepker's publications and professional interests relate to literacy, literacy education, students that struggle with reading and writing, as well as using children's literature including comic books to support students' literacy development.

Shannon Driskell, Professor of Mathematics Education at the University of Dayton, focuses her research on teaching and learning mathematics with technology.

Kelsey Virginia Dufresne is a Doctoral Student in the Communication Rhetoric and Digital Media program at North Carolina State University. Focusing on visual media studies and digital and public humanities, she is interested in pedagogy and media accessibility as an English educator. With the Literacy and Community Initiative, she works directly with the Juntos Hispanic Literacy Group as the project's coordinator and instructor in promoting community outreach, collaboration, and advocacy.

Pamela J. Farris is Distinguished Teaching Professor Emeritus, Literacy Education, Northern Illinois University. She was also Professor of Literacy in the School of Teaching and Learning at Illinois State University. Dr. Farris taught grades K-6 in Greencastle, Indiana before pursuing her doctorate in reading and language arts education at Indiana State University. A prolific writer, Dr. Farris has published 25 books and over 200 professional articles. Her textbooks include *Language Arts: Process, Product and Assessment in Diverse Classrooms*; *Elementary and Middle School Social Studies: An Interdisciplinary Multicultural Approach*; and *Teaching, Bearing the Torch: Introduction to Educational Foundations*. She is co-author of a guide for college faculty members entitled *To and Fro the Ivory Tower: Life in Academia*. Dr. Farris has presented at conferences on three continents and throughout the United States and Canada. She chaired the Midwest region of Children's and Teachers' Choices for the International Literacy Association. In addition, she was named to the Illinois Reading Hall of Fame.

Joyce C. Fine is an Associate Professor and Literacy Program Director at Florida International University. She was awarded the University Excellence in Teaching Award and a Community Engagement Faculty Senate Award. She was on the International Reading Association's National Commission on Excellence in Reading Teacher Preparation and on the Task Force on Teacher Preparation. She served as President of the Organization of Teacher Educators in Reading and Chair of the American Reading Forum. She was awarded a Service Award from the American Reading Forum and a Knowledge Award. Dr. Fine has researched and published many articles and chapters on reading comprehension and writing strategies and mentored doctoral students. She is the Associate Editor of *Literacy, Practice, and Research*.

Suzanne Franco, Professor of Research & Statistics in the College of Education at Wright State University, also serves as an evaluator for education projects.

Mary E. Gardner currently serves as Director of the Jerry L. Johns Literacy Clinic and an Instructor of Reading Methods in the Department of Curriculum of Instruction at Northern Illinois University. She is a reading specialist who taught in the Oregon, Illinois elementary school for 29 years. She received her BA in Elementary Education from Western Illinois University and her MS in Literacy Education from Northern Illinois University. Mary was named Outstanding Reading Teacher by the Illinois Reading Council. She has served in a variety of roles for the Illinois Reading Council and as President of the Northern Illinois Reading Council.

Stephen M. Gibson is a Doctoral Student at Virginia Commonwealth University with a focus in developmental psychology. Broadly, his research is focused on investigating the impact of African American parental socialization strategies on the development of children's racial identity. Currently, Stephen's research explores the intersection of emotional, academic, and racial socialization strategies of African American parents. Prior to pursuing his PhD, Stephen attended North Carolina Central University, where he received a Bachelor's in Psychology and then he went on to receive a Master's in Educational Psychology at North Carolina State University.

Nadia R. Granados has worked as a Postdoctoral Research Associate at the University of Utah and currently teaches courses in Teaching, Learning and

Sociocultural Studies in the College of Education at the University of Arizona and the Mary Lou Fulton Teachers College at Arizona State University. Her research focuses on biliteracy, bilingualism, dual language education, community literacies, literacy processes, academic literacies, and women's literacies and has been published in the *Bilingual Research Journal* and the *Journal of Literacy Research*.

Heidi L. Hallman is a Professor in the Department of Curriculum and Teaching at the University of Kansas. Her research interests include studying "at-risk" students' literacy learning as well as how prospective English teachers are prepared to teach in diverse school contexts. Dr. Hallman is co-author of *Secondary English Teacher Education in the United States*, winner of the 2018 Richard Meade award for research in English language arts education, and *Reconceptualizing Curriculum, Literacy and Learning for School-age Mothers*, as well as author of several journal articles and book chapters. At the University of Kansas, Dr. Hallman teaches undergraduate and graduate courses in teacher education.

Pauline Harris is Professor and Chair, Early Childhood Research, in Education Futures at the University of South Australia. She is an active leader and researcher in literacies, diversity, and inclusion.

Steven Hart is Professor in the Literacy, Early, Bilingual and Special Education Department and Coordinator of the Minor in Urban Civic Education at California State University–Fresno. He teaches courses on literacy foundations, literacy assessment, disciplinary literacies, and service-learning pedagogy. Dr. Hart continues to work for educational justice and social change through his research investigating how critical literacy and service-learning can converge to frame culturally and linguistically sustaining literacy education for diverse student populations.

Meggan K. Hartzog is an Assistant Teaching Professor at Bowling Green State University, teaching in the Physical Education, Health Education and Human Development and Family Studies Departments. Her research draws on personal experiences teaching in a juvenile detention center to discuss the impetus for a reading/mentoring program in a local juvenile residential center in this chapter. She is invested in providing opportunities for all students to receive a quality education through skill development.

Mara Imms-Donnelly is a graduate of Colgate University with a BA in Spanish. After graduating from Colgate in 2017, she served as an AmeriCorps VISTA volunteer for two years at a community-based center where she taught Adult ESOL and designed arts-based curricula for participants of many ages, which aimed to deepen their critical understanding of social issues present in our lives. She is currently completing her MS Ed in Reading/Writing/Literacy at the University of Pennsylvania. Mara lives in Philadelphia, and she is particularly interested in critical and arts-based literacies, community-based education, and intergenerational learning. In her free time, she likes to cook (and eat!), garden, play soccer, spend time outside, and make art.

Gloria E. Jacobs is a research associate within the Literacy, Language and Technology Research Group at Portland State University, Portland, Oregon, USA. As part of this group, she conducts qualitative investigations into the digital literacy practices of underserved adults. The goal of her research is to better understand the implications of the digital world for adult learners.

Kate E. Kedley is an Assistant Professor in the Department of Language, Literacy, and Sociocultural Education at Rowan University. Dr. Kedley's research centers around critical literacy and education, public engagement, LGBTQ and young adult literature, language education, and social and educational movements in Honduras. Kate has published work in journals such as the *English Journal, Sex Education*, and the *Journal of Lesbian Studies*.

James R. King is an Emeritus Professor of Literacy Studies at the University of South Florida. He continues research in media literacies, literacy teacher education, text analysis, and postsecondary reading.

Matthew Knoester is an Associate Professor of Educational Studies at Ripon College. His research interests are critical literacy, bilingualism, democratic education, social contexts of education, and authentic assessments. He is co-author most recently of *Beyond Testing: Seven Assessments of Students and Schools More Effective than Standardized Tests*, a recipient of the Critics' Choice Book Award from AESA.

Deborah Kozdras is the Associate Director of the Stavros Center at the University of South Florida, where she provides professional development to K-12 educators. Prior to her work at the Stavros Center Deborah worked for 11 years as an elementary educator. While working on her PhD in Curriculum and Instruction with a focus in Literacy at the University of South Florida, she was the recipient of a Carnegie Predoctoral Fellowship from the National Academy of Education. She has presented both research and practical workshops at national and international conferences and has published a variety of articles, book chapters, lesson plans, and educational blogs. Her research interests lie in interdisciplinary literacies used in problem solving and decision-making.

Crystal Chen Lee is an Assistant Professor of English Language Arts and Literacy in the Department of Teacher Education and Learning Sciences at North Carolina State University. Her research lies at the nexus of literacy, community engagement, and marginalized populations. She was an American Association of

University Women (AAUW) Dissertation Fellow for her work on critical literacy among African immigrant girls in community organizations. She is the founding director and Principal Investigator of The Literacy and Community Initiative (LCI), a project that investigates and promotes literacy among currently under-served students in community organizations. The mission is to amplify student voices through student publications, advocacy and leadership: www.fi.ncsu.edu/projects/lci/.

Meredith Lehman is currently Head of Museum Education at the Mildred Lane Kemper Art Museum at Washington University in St. Louis, where she over-sees academic and public programs that support cross-disciplinary learning in the arts, social and emotional learning skills, and cultural proficiency. She taught Francophone language and literature courses in higher education for eight years, developing curriculum that uses object-based learning to engage students. Dr. Lehman's scholarly focus is on the connections between visual art and litera-ture and how works of art support language acquisition.

Elspeth McInnes is Associate Professor of Sociology in Education in Education Futures at the University of South Australia. Her research focuses on young children's well-being and development in families and education services.

Rochell R. McWhorter is an Associate Professor of Human Resource Development in the Soules College of Business at The University of Texas at Tyler. She also serves as the Campus Faculty Liaison for Service-Learning. She received her PhD degree in Human Resource Development from Texas A&M University and currently serves as an Associate Editor of the *Advances in Developing Human Resource Development* journal and has authored numerous journal articles and book chapters. Her publications include topics such as qualitative case study method-ology, virtual human resource development, virtual scenario planning, real-time group meetings, gerontechnology, and eService-Learning.

Luz Murillo is an Educational Anthropologist who studies the biliteracy devel-opment of indigenous, immigrant, and Latinx children, families, and teachers. A native of Colombia, she earned her doctoral degree in Language, Reading & Culture at the University of Arizona. Professor Murillo has taught courses in reading/writing/literacy, language and culture, and ethnography for bilingual educators at universities in the United States, Mexico, and Colombia. Her research has been published in English, Spanish, and TexMex in journals like *Anthropology & Education Quarterly*, *Language Arts*, *Journal of Adolescent and Adult Literacy*, and *Lectura y Vida*. Currently, she runs the Biliteracy Enrichment after-school program at the Centro Cultural Hispano de San Marcos, where Texas State students gain hands-on experience in Spanish and English literacy.

Timothy J. Murnen is an Associate Professor of Literacy Education at Bowling Green State University in Ohio, USA. His research interests focus on literacy education, literacy with at-risk youth, teacher education, and pedagogy for teaching the Holocaust. He has been published in *AERJ*, *Pedagogies*, and *The Reading Teacher* among other venues.

Kelly L. Murphy (formerly *Allen*) is an instructor in Elementary Education at Towson University. She currently teaches graduate courses on the reading process, assessment/instruction in the Towson Reading Clinic. Her research focuses on reading assessment/instruction, family and community literacy, miscue analysis, retrospective miscue analysis, and eye movement miscue analysis. She is also a parent and family literacy educator, has facilitated and coordinated community literacy programs, and serves as a board member for NCTE's Literacies and Languages for All conference.

Bec Neill teaches across the child protection and digital technologies curricula in Education Futures at the University of South Australia and has a professional background and degree in Information Systems. She is a systems thinker and maternal feminist who explores the relations between culture, people, and technology using systems-thinking concepts and practices.

Molly K. Ness began her teaching career as a Teach For America corps member and sixth-grade teacher in Oakland, California. She earned a doctorate in Reading Education from the University of Virginia. Since 2006, she has been a Teacher Educator and Associate Professor at Fordham University. She is the author of four books and multiple articles in peer-reviewed journals. Her research focuses on reading comprehension, teachers' instructional decisions and beliefs, dyslexia, and word knowledge. In 2019, Molly began the End Book Deserts podcast to bring attention to the issue of book access and equity.

Sue Nichols is a Literacy Researcher and Teacher Educator at the University of South Australia. She has had a long interest in literacy practices in out-of-school contexts, which she has studied using ethnographic, geosemiotic, networking and discourse analytic methods. Sue has produced a number of authored and edited books including *Resourcing Early Learners: New Networks, New Actors* (2012) and *Learning Cities: Multimodal Explorations and Placed Pedagogies* (2017). She enjoys collaborating with colleagues from a range of disciplines including health, communication and consumer studies to achieve a fuller understanding of the role of literacy across social contexts.

Sabrina Mooroogen Phillips is the Associate Director of Educator Programs and Resources at the Art Institute of Chicago, where she designs resources and virtual and in-person experiences around teacher self-care. As a former elementary teacher, she worked with fifth and sixth graders at schools in England, Thailand, Egypt, and Qatar, exploring the bilingual learner's experience in multiple contexts. Sabrina's art-historical expertise centers on late colonial Indian art, specifically the works of women artists of the time. She is currently pursuing a doctorate in Education and Social Justice at Lancaster University, UK, with a focus on critical race theory and whiteness in educator programming, including professional development and initial teacher training.

Jose A. Picart is a Professor of Counselor Education and Deputy Director of the Friday Institute for Educational Innovation in the College of Education at North Carolina State University. After completing an ACE Fellowship, he served 15 years as a senior university administrator as a Vice Provost and Interim Dean. His research investigates psychosocial development of youth and positive youth development programs in community-based organizations. As co-founder and co-Principal Investigator of the Literacy and Community Initiative, he explores how engaging in literacy activities helps promote youth social and emotional development.

Margaret Pinnell, Associate Dean for Faculty and Staff Development in the School of Engineering at the University of Dayton, has been involved in research related to K–12 STEM for ten years.

Judith Puncochar is a Professor of Educational Psychology at Northern Michigan University (NMU). She teaches pre-professional teacher candidates and professional educators in research methods, assessment, and educational psychology. Dr. Puncochar obtained her doctorate from the University of Minnesota in 1996 and served as Interim Director of the Human Relations Program for 14 years. She joined NMU faculty in 2004. She has been co-principle investigator or contributing author to more than two million US dollars in science and mathematics education grants. She co-authored *Empowering Higher Education in Indonesia* to advance an expansion of General Education coursework in Indonesian undergraduate education. She has served as NMU Academic Programs Assessment Coordinator, American Association of University Women of Marquette President, and Higher Learning Commission peer corps reviewer.

Teri Reed-Houck recently retired from Oregon Community Unit School District 220, having taught in public education for over 30 years. She is a reading specialist who taught in early elementary grade classrooms as well as Learning Disabilities. Dr. Reed-Houck pursued a doctorate in literacy at Northern Illinois University out of a desire to more effectively assist students who struggled with learning to read. She devoted her career to the early detection and prevention of reading disabilities. Dr. Reed-Houck developed an innovative, flexible Title 1 service delivery system that resulted in the effective long-term reduction of at-risk readers from grades one to four and included a successful summer reading program.

Dr. Reed-Houck received two Those Who Excel Awards for Excellence for the Summer Reading Program and Meritorious Service as a Classroom Teacher. She served on the Executive Board of the Northern Illinois Reading Council for 19 years. Dr. Read-Houck has presented at numerous conferences and provided staff development in the areas of Readers' and Writers' Workshops, Working with Struggling Learners, and Ending the Learn-Forget Cycle.

Kate Rolander is the Workforce Education Specialist at Virginia Commonwealth University, where she coordinates the state's career pathways programs for adult education, facilitates virtual teacher leadership groups, and supports research on adult learning and English language acquisition. Kate has taught English to speakers of other languages at community colleges in Arizona and Virginia, at Northern Arizona University, and in local community-based organizations in Virginia. Her research and professional interests in adult education focus on the intersections of identity and community dialogue with learner motivation and engagement and how instructional design can respond to these intersections.

Mary-Kate Sableski, Assistant Professor of Literacy and Special Needs at the University of Dayton, focuses her research on diverse children's literature.

Nina Schoonover is a Doctoral Candidate studying Literacy and English Language Arts Education in the Department of Teacher Education and Learning Sciences at North Carolina State University. Her research focuses on arts integration, visual and sensory literacies, and equitable English teaching practices. For the Literacy and Community Initiative, she served as the project coordinator at Bull City YouthBuild, working alongside the students to write and publish their stories.

Emily Rose Schwab is currently a Rhode Island-based literacy educator working with learners across ages. After working as a family literacy educator in her early career, she joined the Reading/Writing/Literacy program at the University of Pennsylvania. There she worked as a member of the Community Literacies research project for four years, where she had the honor of working in a community-based center in South Philadelphia. Her research interests include ethical community partnering, practitioner inquiry, and the interconnections between care, imagination, justice, and literacy education.

Kate Seltzer is an Assistant Professor of Bilingual/TESOL Education at Rowan University. A former high school English teacher in New York City, Dr. Seltzer currently teaches pre- and in-service teachers of bilingual students. She is co-author of the book, *The Translanguaging Classroom: Leveraging Student Bilingualism for Learning*, and her research has been featured in a number of journals including *English Education, Research in the Teaching of English*, and *TESOL Quarterly*.

Todd Smith, Associate Professor of Physics at the University of Dayton, focuses his research on education, fundamental nuclear and particle physics, electro-optics, and nanotechnology.

Kwangok Song is Assistant Professor of Literacy Education in the Department of Curriculum and Teaching at the University of Kansas. Her research explores the intersections of language, literacy, learning, and sociocultural contexts. Specifically, her research centers on the influence of ideologies on immigrant families and communities' language and literacy practices and bilingual children's language practices in literacy learning.

Jim Sosnowski's research interests focus on the impact that language ideologies have on shaping classroom practices and policies in adult language and literacy classrooms. He earned his doctoral degree in Curriculum and Instruction with a focus on Language and Literacy at the University of Illinois at Urbana-Champaign. He is currently the Co-Coordinator of Language Partners, a peer-taught, prison-based adult language and literacy program, which is part of the Education Justice Project, a higher education in prison program.

Mary E. Styslinger is a Professor of English and Literacy Education at the University of South Carolina where she directed the Midlands Writing Project for over a decade and served as the secondary program coordinator. She is passionate about interweaving literacy into the English curriculum and serving marginalized and at-risk youth. A past high school English teacher, she is the author of *Workshopping the Canon* (NCTE) and editor of *Literacy Behind Bars* (Rowman & Littlefield). She has published articles in *English Journal*, *Voices from the Middle*, *Language Arts*, *Journal of Adolescent and Adult Literacy*, *English Teaching: Practice & Critique*, and *Kappan*.

Carol S. Walther is an Associate Professor of Sociology at Northern Illinois University. Her research interests focus on social inequalities, specifically race, ethnicity, gender, and sexualities. She previously participated in 4-H as a youth in Indiana, is a lifetime member of Girl Scouts of USA, and a current member of Boy Scouts of America.

Susan L. Watson is an ESOL Specialist at Virginia Commonwealth University, where she coordinates ESOL teacher professional development for adult education programs across the state. Prior to her role as ESOL Specialist, Susan was an ESOL teacher for adult basic education in the Virginia Community College System. She is an active member of TESOL International and serves on their Standards Professional Council. She is also a member of EU Speak, an international group of scholars who work to improve the education opportunities for immigrant- and refugee-background adults. Susan presents original work at local, state, and national level conferences. Her research interest is language and literacy learning for adults who are learning to read and write for the first time in English as a new language.

Joanna C. Weaver is an Assistant Professor in the School of Teaching and Learning at Bowling Green State University. She serves as the Adolescence to Young Adult Integrated Language Arts Coordinator. Her research interests focus on literacy across the teaching continuum, reflective practice, and teacher preparation and professional development. She has been published in the *Journal of Adolescent and Adult Literacy*, *The Reading Teacher*, the *Journal of Empowering Teacher Educators*, and the *Journal of Education and Human Development* among others.

Donna E. Werderich is an Associate Professor in Literacy Education in the Department of Curriculum and Instruction at Northern Illinois University. Her research interests include English language arts education, teaching of writing, and teacher education. She is also a member of Boy Scouts of America.

Kristen L. White is a former classroom teacher with over a decade of experience working with grades K–8. Kristen has a PhD in Curriculum, Instruction, and Teacher Education with a language and literacy specialization from Michigan State University. She is an Assistant Professor of Education at Northern Michigan University. Interested in equity in early childhood contexts, Kristen's research examines the construction of young children's literate identity/ies.

Corrine M. Wickens is an Associate Professor in Literacy Education in the Department of Curriculum and Instruction at Northern Illinois University. Her research interests focus upon critical literacies, adolescent literacy, and gender and sexualities. She is also a lifetime member of Girl Scouts of USA.

Ray Williams (MA art history, UNC-Chapel Hill; EdM Harvard Graduate School of Education) is currently Director of Education and Academic Affairs at the Blanton Museum of Art, University of Texas at Austin. He has been a leader in the field of museum education for many years, recognized for his work using works of art to support learning about world religions; encourage immigrants preparing for the US Citizenship Exam; and foster empathy and communication skills. He is committed to the importance of sharing stories – both traditional and personal – and to the transformative power of art.

Angela M. Wiseman is an Associate Professor of Literacy Education at North Carolina State and a Docent Professor of Multiliteracies at the University of Tampere, Finland. Her research focus includes family literacy and visual qualitative research methods. Her current research project is a family literacy program for parents with substance-use disorder, who have also experienced homelessness and incarceration. In addition, she focuses on using qualitative visual methods to analyze children's artifacts and picture books. From 2016 to 2019, she served as the co-editor of the *Journal of Children's Literature*. Dr. Wiseman teaches qualitative research methods and language arts methods in the college of education.

FOREWORD: PROFESSIONAL LITERACIES AND HELPING IN THE COMMUNITY

The Limits of Dash-Literacies

James R. King

UNIVERSITY OF SOUTH FLORIDA

We have a surfeit of literacies. We have disciplinary-literacies, service-learning-literacies, project-based-literacies, out-of-school-literacies, maker-literacies, design-learning-literacies, and problem-based-learning-literacies. With this text, *Literacy Across the Community*, there are more to add to the list. Each of these locations for literacy presents its own circumstances, and requires a productive expansion of literacy, in order to respond to the needs of the specific actors and enactments. These various scenarios often implicate literacy within the desire to help others. We often read that, with sufficient gains in literate competence, people seen as "at-risk" will, somehow, be made better for their literacy gains. Are they "made better?"

Specifically, these various, dash-laden labels for reading/writing/learning share important commonalities, indicating the connectivity between literacy and its instantiating social contexts. Even in their situatedness, these dash-learning situations create "as if" spaces where participants inhabit created roles to accomplish the work required. An additional "as if" is the degree to which any literacy project sponsors authentic roles from the perspectives of the participants. The work of these projects, the completion of which creates and enhances the participants' senses of identity, is literacy work. While there may be differences found in how such different "as if" learning contexts operate, a commonality is that each claims to enhance literate capabilities, with literacy acting as a proxy for general self-improvement. And each instantiation of literacy intends to help its participants. So, from a perspective of literacy practices, I cautiously group them together as "dash-literacies," or literacy modified by a delimiting adjective, and separated by a dash. Literacy in this sense is rendered broadly, and includes communication of messages in a variety of modes. In these dashed spaces, motivation and personal investment form identities for language/literacy learning. From a positionality of desire to help, literacy calls on its professionals to make space for participants' acquisition of self-recognized growth and command of broader fields of knowledge.

There have been many dash-literacy initiatives. Briefly examining one may make my points more concretely. Wineburg (1991), Moje (2008), as well as Shanahan and Shanahan (2008) have redefined secondary and post-secondary literacies along disciplinary practices, or as disciplinary-literacies (arguably, a dash-literacy), where learners are engaged with knowledge and literacy practices of delimited, professional fields. The idea is that thinking, speaking, and writing like a biologist allows learners to participate in the professional discourse of biologists. However, fashioning literacy practice as a simulation of "real expert literacy" may miss the mark in ways community literacies may hit. First, the disciplinary literacies reconstituted for classroom use may not sufficiently emulate literacy habitus of expert professionals in the real world (Geisler, 1994). That is, reading "like a scientist" in a biology class may not sufficiently emulate the literacy practices of field biologists (Heller, 2010). In contrast, literacies within a community-based project also require certain levels of expertise, but the focus on simulacrum, precision, and accuracy is less important than perhaps the messages made, or the tasks completed. After all, the intent in a community project is community action, not mimicking a professional functioning in a professional role. In contrast, community action could also be a form of disciplinary literacy, although unevenly recognized by the academy. The number of "organizers" and "community activists" is large and a realistic field of employment in some places. In fact, it more readily may be recognized as "non-profit work" in a (non-)valued and classed work context. Second, any specific instance of disciplinary literacy conjured by the teacher in a school-based disciplinary enactment may fail to engage students who may perceive their teacher's siloed disciplinary efforts as more "schoolwork." Community-based literacies have the chance to make it right, by starting with the perceived (and often stated) needs of the participants. In this way, relying on the social needs recognized inside these literacy projects may more likely be recognized by the participants as valuable in the completion of the task(s) within the dash-literacy contexts, thus creating roles with higher social prestige. Accuracy may be subordinated, more likely judged by readers looking for message and results over specific rhetoric and grammars. And finally, community literacies may offer learners more authentic roles to inhabit. Participation roles that emerge within a grounded community-based project may also be grounded in the social context at hand. The larger point is that any instantiation of dash-literacy must be examined for its intentions and outcomes.

As you will read, different projects may require particular literacy practices, adopting different embedded roles, and activating these components within given projects, may require that these practices are adapted and shifted. That is to be expected and appreciated. The flexibility of various dash-literacies adapts to the varying social, contextual, and rhetorical needs. In addition, within the scenarios presented in this text, the rhetorical goal must be the use of particular language and literacies in ways that are validated by the particular audience of experts. Within the situated roles, identity is more fluid, a socially and linguistically mediated construct that considers the multiple, different positions individuals may occupy within a given project. Further, in positioning themselves within an ongoing project, students fabricate new identities within the needs of the context. The constructed and intentionally bounded contexts of socially delimited and disciplinary-based learning projects, like these, are ones that likely host a variety of authentic roles, each needed in the conduct and completion of the planned project. The richness and fluidity of figured worlds (Holland et al., 1998) within community-based literacy projects and the participatory space they provide is what is needed to create opportunities for students' uptake and use of identities. Figured worlds intersect with dash-literacies, explaining the opportunities for students to construct unique and new identities, or roles. As all members involved in a project interact, their individual identities within the project (role affordances) morph in relation to one another to construct a shared sense of identity, which forms the common bonds (or agency) that represent membership in the group.

With co-authors, I have expressed some ethical concerns regarding project leaders' dual roles of curator and evaluator (Chapter 16). I argue that *all* apprenticeship experiences in learning contexts are convened in delimited, as-if contexts, and therefore purposefully do not replicate the complexity (value, importance) of similar work in the professional contexts of the discipline under scrutiny. Rather, the quality, complexity, importance, or significance of the work undertaken in an apprenticeship is always subordinate to the teaching/learning, and taken together, they always comprise the "gold ring" of aspiration. That is because the foremost purpose of the interaction is the pedagogy or tuition for the learner, as monitored by the mentor. Synergistic interaction of different yet contributing roles may be one part of the co-construction of students' and teachers' identities within a given project. In addition, the social context is also heavily influenced by differences in inherent positioning and power that these roles exhibit. However, it may be that in community-based literacies there can be some slippage between what are clearly the power-based demarcations that separate teachers from their students in school-based literacies.

Young people (both "competent" and academically "at-risk") increasingly manage their identities as they assemble different literate competencies and deploy strategic aspects of identities (as shifting roles and positions depending on emergent need). Individuals inhabit and deploy these identities when they participate in a Discourse community (Gee, 1996, 1999), such as a community surrounding and contextualizing a disciplinary dash-literacy project. The tension between executing a credible role, creating a quality product, and performing adequately as a student member of a class is a contest/conflict for the literate performer, who acts within a hybrid, or third space (Gutiérrez, 2008).

These hybrid literacies, constituted from borrowed, repurposed legacy practices, can be understood as completely unique literacy events constructed specifically for and within the community-learning context at hand. Such infusion of literacy is different from the skill-based, decontextualized instruction from much inside-of-school practice. It is up to facilitating teachers (whom I have been calling curators; Persohn, 2020) to name the various literate strategies *as* they occur within and across disciplinary boundaries. In naming, the strategy becomes an object/process the students may choose to use again, and intentionally, a transferable strategy. So, this is a different approach to teaching, as the learning is *emergent*. Teachers curate the process in order to capitalize on a potential strategy *when it emerges*. I use Persohn's (2020) curating to mean the selection and negotiation of possible semiotic representations within power-based relationships and contexts. From a language resources perspective, curating certainly involves rhetorical dimensions. The deployment of the various, possible semiotic resources may be driven by teachers' more nuanced understandings of audience, or by perspective taking, or for social consequence purposes when constructing the message, as she curates outcomes from a community-based, literacy-rich, authentic project.

What remains problematic, and largely unexamined, is the role of the curators, mentors, and researchers in our intents to help. We intend to help through literacy expansion, with the thought that increasing literacies (of various kinds) axiomatically leads to greater opportunity for the learner. Most of us who work in literacy have heard cautions like Dippo's (1990) that we can't be in the business of "empowering them," as empower is clearly not a transitive verb, and the change must always be the business of the one who intends to do so. But, when curators provide opportunity structure, it does not necessarily take over the learners' self-determination. However, project leaders' desire for success, successfully helping others, may get in the way. Where does that leave our desire to "help them" through literacy? These psychodynamics of teaching (Felman, 1997) have been buried in the hustle and bustle of the project, the community event that hosts the helping. However, the burden of our intents is still waiting to be unpacked. We have explored success narratives and victory narratives (Cary, 1999; Nespor & Barber, 1995), but narratives won't disturb the surface, nor look beneath our desire to help. We may witness (Dutro, 2009; Fine, 2006), but what does it mean to stand and watch the results of our own intervention? Is it about our own self-esteem as potential change agents? Or, more pragmatically, is it about squeezing a manuscript from the life work of our participants? Dash-literacies must be critically re-read, as we all present our good work with people we hope will change toward "the literate."

References

Cary, L. (1999). Unexpected stories: Life history and the limits of redemption. *Qualitative Inquiry, 5*, 411–427. https://doi.org/10.1177/107780049900500307

Dippo, D. (1990). Stravinsky's rag. *Qualitative Studies in Education, 3*, 185–188. https://doi.org/10.1080/0951839900030206

Dutro, E. (2009). Children's testimony and the necessity of critical witness in urban classrooms. *Theory Into Practice, 48*, 231–238. https://doi.org/10.1080/00405840902997519

Felman, S. (1997). Psychoanalysis and education: Teaching terminable and interminable. In S. Todd (Ed.). *Learning desire: Perspectives on pedagogy, culture, and the unsaid* (pp. 17–44). Routledge.

Fine, M. (2006). Bearing witness: Methods for researching oppression and resistance – A textbook for critical analysis. *Social Justice Research, 19*, 18–108. https://doi.org/10.1007/s11211-006-0001-0

Gee, J. (1996). *Social linguistics and literacies: Ideology in discourses* (2nd ed.). Falmer.

Gee, J. (1999). *An introduction to discourse analysis: Theory and method.* Routledge.

Geisler, C. (1994). *Academic literacy and the nature of expertise: Reading, writing and knowing in academic philosophy.* Lawrence Erlbaum Associates.

Gutiérrez, K. (2008). Developing a socio-critical literacy in the third space. *Reading Research Quarterly, 43*, 148–164.

Heller, R. (2010). In praise of amateurism: A friendly critique of Moje's "Call for Change" in secondary reading. *Journal of Adolescent and Adult Literacy, 54*, 267–273. https://doi.org/10.1598/JAAL.54.4.

Holland, D., Lachicotti Jr., W., Skinner, D., & Cain, C. (1998). *Identity and agency in cultural worlds.* Harvard University Press.

Moje, E. (2008). Foregrounding the disciplines in secondary teaching and learning: A call for change. *Journal of Adolescent and Adult Literacy, 52*, 96–107. doi.org/10.1598/JAAL.52.2.1

Nespor, J., & Barber, L. (1995). Politics of narrative. In J. A. Hatch & R. Wisniewski (Eds.), *Life history and narrative* (pp. 49–62). Falmer.

Persohn, L. (2020). Curation as methodology. *Qualitative Research.* https://doi.org/10.1177/1468794120922144

Shanahan, T., & Shanahan, C. (2008). Teaching disciplinary literacy to adolescents: Rethinking content-area literacy. *Harvard Educational Review, 78*(1), 40–59. https://doi.org/10.7763/haer.78.1.v62444321p602101

Wineburg, S. S. (1991). On the reading of historical texts: Notes on the breach between school and the academy. *American Journal of Educational Research, 28*, 495–519. https://doi.org/10.3102/00028312028003495

ACKNOWLEDGMENTS

We would like to acknowledge the work of the educators and researchers who shed light on the disparities and injustices that our communities face; those who are impassioned to lift up and empower individuals through the community-based literacy programs they support; those who address inequalities by providing greater access to education for all.

INTRODUCTION

It has been nearly two decades since Glynda Hull and Katherine Schultz released their seminal volume entitled *School's Out: Bridging Out-of-School Literacies with Classroom Practice* (2002). These authors set two goals for the work. The first goal was based on a question, "Why does literacy so often flourish out of school?," that was to be answered by a presentation of the histories, descriptions, and analyses of literacy projects from across the country. Then an additional goal focused upon two questions: Could research on literacy and out-of-school learning help us think again and anew about literacy teaching and learning in the schoolroom – in formal educational settings? And, if so, how?

Are these questions of equal value in the third decade of the twenty-first century? Indeed, we live in a very different world from when *School's Out* was released in 2002. At the turn of the century humanity held expectations of the vast potentials of a golden future built upon the promises of technology, medical breakthroughs, a global economy, and a period of relative peace. Now technology offers us as many problems as promises, a medical renaissance seems more a myth in a reality shaped by pandemics, the global economy has been shattered by the needs of nation states, and world peace seems to once again be nothing but a pipe dream. But regardless of the state of the world, the concept, the construct, and the promise of community remains and may be stronger than ever. Hence, we believe the questions raised by Hull and Schultz are still of value to literacy theorists, researchers, and practitioners today.

We place great value in the Igbo proverb from Nigeria in which they hold a long-time belief, "It takes a village to raise a child," in which the upbringing of a child is the responsibility of the community. Community-based literacy practices the world over embrace this notion as a myriad of service providers engage in the literacy development of individuals of all ages. This volume presents scholarship related to the praxis of community literacy initiatives across age groups (from children to adults), from the United States and within international settings, and includes a variety of populations (e.g., early childhood, incarcerated youth, mature adults) and ethnic groups (e.g., immigrants, refugees, indigenous).

The purpose of this edited volume is to present current trends in research and praxis in the field of community literacy, investigate challenges and solutions to community-based programs, and document implications for P20 education. The aim of the edited volume is to collaborate with both established scholars and emerging scholars in the field to provide national and international perspectives that unpack community-based literacy programs as a means to promote dialogue and build bridges between family, community, and schools. Community-based literacy programs are widely conceived to include family and adult literacy, faith-based and non-profit offerings, and programming supported by a variety of agencies (e.g., governmental, workplace-based, libraries, museums, etc.).

We seek to fill a gap in the scholarship related to the praxis of community literacy initiatives across populations (from children to adults), including a variety of ethnic groups (e.g., immigrants, refugees, indigenous, etc.). We initially sought out original contributions from scholars in the field who are internationally recognized for their research in a particular area of community literacy research. Following these targeted invitations for contributions, we initiated a Call for Proposals to seek contributions from emerging scholars in the field as well as those conducting research who were not familiar to us. We feel this volume is different than other volumes in regard to our focus on the relationship between P20 schools and community-based programming. Our innovative approach for this book is the boundary crossing nature of the chapters in that we do not focus solely on one type of community literacy initiative but address it in a more inclusive fashion to demonstrate the importance of a multitude of programs that support literacy development across the ages.

The chapters herein provide a focus on the relationship between P20 schools and community-based literacy programming. This introductory chapter provides an overview of the importance of community-based literacy programs and how these programs can help bridge gaps in literacy development. The following chapters include a focus on research-based best practices from a variety of researchers, who in most cases are also program providers, that highlight the expansive forms and formats of the praxis of community-based literacy initiatives from respected scholars in the field.

Literacy and Language Development

As one examines the varied sociological, pedagogical, linguistic, and historical constructs that define the parameters of *community* or are part and parcel of either its contextual or the geographical components, one finds that language, or more so a multitude of languages with the interrelationship to a culture, or more so a multitude of cultures, serves as the defining factor of a particular community. This perspective has been with us whether it was in any decade of the nineteenth or twentieth centuries, or now in the third decade of the twenty-first century. Language and culture are paramount whether imported from another land, evolved in place over the years, or viewed as an expected norm reflecting the standards of the status quo for a community that may or may not exist in reality. Section One examines programs and approaches focusing on language that are beyond those found in the traditional public, private, or charter school environments.

Abraham, Kedley, and Seltzer (Chapter 1) employ a spatiolinguistic framework to examine the language and literacy practices of racialized, emergent bilingual children in a bilingual (English and Spanish) after-school, community-based writing program found in urban Philadelphia. In undertaking an ethnographically grounded case study, the authors draw upon a conceptual framework of the constructs of spatial justice and translanguaging. Song (Chapter 2) purports that maintaining a Heritage Language is essential for immigrants and their descendants to perpetuate intergenerational and familial communication and solidarity. This chapter thus examines a community-based Heritage Language program's contribution to immigrant descendants' engagement in cross-cultural and multilingual literacies.

Family literacy and at-home literacy are ultimately components of literacy instruction found in the community. Knoester (Chapter 3) describes how he delivered at-home instructional support to his two English-speaking youngsters who were enrolled in a dual-immersion (Spanish–English) public, urban elementary school as they struggled to understand, speak, read, and write in Spanish. If the family is a key component of the community, equally so are faith-based organizations and services. Applebaum, Imms-Donnelly, and Schwab (Chapter 4) present a practitioner inquiry study of a student-centered, creativity- and inquiry-focused pedagogy offered through an intergenerational ESOL class at an urban faith-based community center. The authors describe the process of constructing a creative ESOL curriculum that supported the building of a collaborative classroom community.

Finally, Fine (Chapter 5) describes how a literacy clinic at an urban research university joined in a partnership with a local high school to conduct an after-school literacy program that promoted the literacy competencies of a primarily Haitian population while providing training for future reading specialists. Instructional programming delivered to the secondary school students is described along with activities used in training the university tutors.

Unique Populations

Those of us who attended the schools of the past century recall our teachers telling us that the United States was a great melting pot as all who came to the country worked together to become a unified one … a citizen of the United States of

America and hence, part and parcel of the American exceptionality. Here the myth was far more powerful than the truth, as we were always members of varied communities with our own heritages and customs as well as literacy practices both in formal education and after-school programs. In the experience of one of the authors of this text, during the elementary school years his colleagues went to what we knew as Greek school, Hebrew school, Chinese school, Catechism training, and Catholic Youth Organization activities, among others. Each supported the unique communities found within the school's catchment area. While the students in Miss Jameson's fifth-grade classroom did not understand the difference between the theory of the melting pot and the more realistic construct of society as a mosaic, we understood that our roots were rather different and that was cool.

Today, we as educators accept and relish in the beauty of what is the American mosaic. We have also come to understand that beyond the borders of the formal school there are numerous lifespan services and programs promoting literacies that serve the unique populations and communities that make up our mosaic. Section Two explores a number of programs serving different populations. The team of Harris, Diamond, Neill, McInnes, Brock, and Camaitoga (Chapter 6) present a critical participatory action research study in Fijian communities in which the team members developed culturally responsive and sustaining strategies that foster young children's literacy in both their heritage language and English through collaboration with learners, families, and the community. In Chapter 7, Hallman covers the experiences and activities undertaken by two future teachers enrolled in a community-based field experience as they were serving in an authentic literacy-focused tutoring program focused on homeless youth and families.

Then Wiseman, Cryer-Coupet, Atkinson, and Gibson (Chapter 8) discuss a family literacy program employing a trauma-informed approach to support fathers who are in rehabilitation for substance abuse disorder as they build relationships with their children. The fathers used the book discussions to share ways they hoped to read with their children and reflect on their own background experiences and their experiences with trauma. In Chapter 9, Sosnowski and Murillo introduce us to their participatory action research through a prison-based language and literacy program in which peer instructors explore practice and policies that further marginalize prison populations.

Finally, Delello, Consalvo, McWhorter, and Doepker (Chapter 10) present an exploratory case study undertaken at a senior living community with the purposes of describing older adults' literacy patterns, demonstrating how iPad technology can improve metaliteracy competencies in the population, and analyzing the benefits and barriers of using iPads to improve literacy skills.

Unique Settings and Contexts

Perhaps you have heard a speaker at a conference or colleague during a conversation in the hall say something to the extent that context is everything. While such a perspective is not a true universal, it does have implications for any discussion of community and the role literacy plays within it. The context can be defined by social or geopolitical boundaries that construct a setting or community. Those boundaries can be quite porous or rather impermeable, and such borders can change depending upon situation or passage of time.

In Section Three, Farris, Gardner, and Reed-Houck (Chapter 11) focus on the historical and current contexts as these factors impact literacy learners in the rural sections of the nation. Then they review several literacy programs that have been implemented within rural locales. Next, Ness (Chapter 12) explores a case study of a small-town public library's intergenerational literacy program that combines the activities of a monthly book club with the viewing of the motion picture that evolved from the chapter book of the month. The analysis examines the benefits received by a selected group of participants.

The intersection of nontraditional contexts and literacy practices follows with Lehman, Phillips, and Williams (Chapter 13) providing programming offered through an art museum that strives to build literacy competencies of students from the prekindergarten level through middle school (with an emphasis on ELL students). The process of delivering gallery lessons that promote each of the traditional language arts is integrated with elements of storytelling. Abas (Chapter 14) focuses on another museum program by presenting literacy practices and lessons such as storytelling and interactive theater used to develop competencies to intrepid exhibits and artifacts such that members of the community gain an understanding of the Holocaust and the past atrocities with the hopes of promoting a social transformation leading to a more compassionate and tolerant community. Finally, Nichols (Chapter 15) provides an extensive literature review with descriptions and evaluations of policies and programs so as to make the case that health services can be sponsors of literacy practices.

Identity Development and Empowerment

Empowerment theorists have long critiqued the influence of power and privilege on identity development and self-actualization (Bourdieu, 1979/1984; Freire, 1970/2018; Foucault, 2019). In their seminal works, these theorists leverage empowerment across three levels of identity construction that include individual, organizational or institutional, and community-based. Empowerment theory has been leveraged in classrooms to help struggling learners overcome negative self-efficacy as readers (Henry et al., 2012), in adult education programs to overcome the oppression of difficult life circumstances (Duckworth, 2013), and through technology-infused instructional models (e.g., Internet Reciprocal Teaching) to increase motivation and improve belief in one's own ability (Huang & Yang, 2015; see also Leu et al., 2008).

While empowerment theory and its influence on identity development is not a new construct, it has become uniquely relevant in an era of young, global influencers today (e.g., Greta Thunberg, 15-year-old Swedish activist on a crusade to fight climate change; *BBC News*, February 28, 2020). As King and colleagues note in their work, identity development is most influenced by ensuring authentic purposes for learning are linked to social action to best empower students to become agents of change within a variety of contexts.

Section Four opens with King, Hart, and Kozdras (Chapter 16) as they investigate the intersection of literacies that evolve within service learning as related to the development of adolescent identity. Emergent identities are viewed as resources and as embedded within service-learning projects they are treated as accomplishments. Castek and Jacobs in Chapter 17 provide coverage of research on volunteer/peer tutoring within adult education and community-based programs for adults. In reporting the research process as it spanned six states, the authors note that they encountered a number of tutors who began their participation as tutees. This factor lead to the foci of this chapter, the exploration of the role advancement from learner to tutor on the short- and the long-term impacts on both the programs and these individuals as well as the examination of both the personal and institutional relationships that were formed through the individuals' extended participation. Next in Chapter 18, Deetsch and Blake cover the Toledo Museum of Arts' pedagogical program for prekindergarten through eighth grade in which the curriculum centers on visual literacy in support of literacy instruction. The findings from three related investigations are reported as well.

Rolander and Watson (Chapter 19) investigate the transformative impacts an educational workforce development initiative has on learners and on their communities of residence and/or employment. The chapter covers how PluggedInVA has changed both employers' and instructors' perceptions of adult learners and their potential for transformation of self along with those individuals who are part of their lives. Finally, Bacon, Anders, Granados, and Murphy (Chapter 20) describe a community-based literacy initiative in which women holding GEDs tutored other women who were preparing to take the GED examination. Data drawn from the three projects were analyzed qualitatively with attention to the trends, issues, and impacts that evolved during the period of the investigation.

Partnership Programs

There are numerous organizations beyond the doors of the public and private school systems with their 8:00 am to 3:15 pm operations that promote literacy within the community. Examples of national organizations include Scouts BSA, the Girl Scouts of America, the Campfire Girls, 4-H clubs, Junior Achievement, Boys/ Girls Clubs, among others. At a more local level we find programming provided by museums, nature centers, forest preserves, parks and recreation services, aquariums, community centers, public libraries, etc. And clearly such programming goes beyond the basal reader to involve learners in authentic and contextualized literacy events. Section Five focuses on a number of programs and research endeavors serving as exemplars of the unique settings and contexts serving learners in varied communities.

Wickens, Werderich, and Walther (Chapter 21) argue that large national youth organizations integrate important life skills, including literacy, into activities and learnings associated within their varied projects such as rank achievement and merit badges. The role of literacy expectations has yet to be explored fully. Hence, the authors examine the literacy expectations (i.e., text complexity, text organization and features, and language use) within the handbooks issued by the Girl Scouts of America, Scouts BSA, and the 4-H to determine how these organizations explicitly or implicitly promote literate practices among the youth membership.

By employing social justice as theory, pedagogy, and process, Styslinger (Chapter 22) describes a summer literacy partnership undertaken by a pre-service English education program and a Department of Juvenile Justice serving incarcerated youth. Research is presented that focuses on teacher candidates' evolving understanding of literacy and its relationship to issues of culture and ability as promoted by the experience. Furthermore, discussion follows on the challenges encountered and the issues associated with project sustainability. Weaver, Murnen, Hartzog, and Bertelsen (Chapter 23) next focus on the development of a literacy program for a juvenile residential center and juvenile detention center by a group of university researchers, program administrators, and education majors serving as literacy mentors. The authors were particularly interested in the role that the collaboration between the stakeholders played in the planning and design of the structure of the program, guiding the approaches to instruction, and promoting reflective practice.

Next, Sableski, Pinnell, Driskell, Smith, and Franco (Chapter 24) examine the successes with programming designed to raise both literacy achievement and interest in STEM through an integrated curriculum offered through an after-school program housed in an urban elementary school. In Chapter 25, White and Puncochar discuss the impact of a long-term partnership between a rural university and a local housing development upon both the community and the school's teacher education program. In addition, the chapter next focuses upon how the interaction between the youth and pre-service teachers influenced their views on their evolution as educators. Finally, Lee, Picart, Schoonover, and Dufresne (Chapter 26) describe an interdisciplinary literacy project that promotes partnerships between a university and community-based organizations serving marginalized youth and immigrants so they develop literacy competencies. The curriculum supports writing, publishing, then dialoguing publicly through public readings. The Write, Engage, and Lead model leads the students to share with members of the community how others can advocate for underserved youth.

References

Bourdieu, P. (1979/1984). *Distinction: A social critique of the judgment of taste*. Routledge Kegan & Paul.

Duckworth, V. (2013). *Learning trajectories, violence and empowerment amongst adult basic skills learners*. Routledge. https://doi.org/10.4324/9780203383537

Foucault, M. (2019). *Power: The essential works of Michel Foucault 1954–1984*. Penguin UK.

Freire, P. (1970/2018). *Pedagogy of the oppressed*. Bloomsbury. https://doi.org/10.4324/9780429269400-8

Henry, L. A., Castek, J., Zawilinski, L., & O'Byrne, I. (2012). Using peer collaborations to support online reading, writing, and communication: An empowerment model for struggling readers. *Reading Writing Quarterly, 28*(3), 279–306. https://doi.org/10.1080/10573569.2012.676431

Huang, C. T., & Yang, S. C. (2015). Effects of online reciprocal teaching on reading strategies, comprehension, self-efficacy, and motivation. *Journal of Educational Computing Research, 52*(3), 381–407. https://doi.org/10.1177/0735633115571924

Hull, G. A., & Schultz, K. (Eds.). (2002). *School's out: Bridging out-of-school literacies with classroom practice* (Vol. 60). Teachers College Press. https://doi.org/10.1016/S0898-5898(03)00036-6

Leu, D. J., Coiro, J., Castek, J., Hartman, D. K., Henry, L. A., & Reinking, D. (2008). Research on instruction and assessment in the new literacies of online reading comprehension. *Comprehension Instruction: Research-based Best Practices, 2*, 321–346. https://doi.org/10.1598/0710.42

PART I

Language and Literacy Development

1

THE LANGUAGE AND LITERACY PRACTICES OF EMERGENT BILINGUALS IN A COMMUNITY-BASED WRITING PROGRAM

Stephanie Abraham, Kate E. Kedley, and Kate Seltzer

ROWAN UNIVERSITY

Using a translanguaging framework, we examined the language and literacy practices of racialized, emergent bilingual children in a bilingual (English/ Spanish), community-based writing program in urban Philadelphia. Located in South Philly's Italian Market, the program's target audience was emergent bilingual, Latinx children who were 7–17 years old. The center offered an afternoon academy program, week-day evening and Saturday morning workshops, and summer writing camps. When we began research at the center in 2015, we noted that despite its bilingual name, the center operated primarily in English. For instance, teachers and volunteers spoke overwhelmingly in English to the children, and the focal texts of lessons and the children's writing pieces were produced only in English. We were concerned about the apparent lack of bilingualism, and specifically the lack of active use of Spanish at the center. To address this, we approached the center's director about offering bilingual writing workshops on Saturdays where we would model a critical, translanguaging pedagogy. This chapter reports the findings from these workshops.

Making a Translanguaging Community Space

Specifically, we used a translanguaging framework to better understand and analyze the language and literacy practices of the emergent bilinguals in this study (García & Kleyn, 2016). We define translanguaging as both an ideological stance and a descriptive framework that accounts for the authentic linguistic practices of bi-/multilinguals. A translanguaging framework posits that people use a wide-ranging, complex, linguistic repertoire while speaking, writing, reading, and thinking. A translanguaging lens does not view languages as separate, societally defined "named languages" (Otheguy et al., 2015), such as English or Spanish, but instead considers languaging to be a set of practices deployed by people as they seek to meet the communicative needs of a given situation (Creese & Blackledge, 2015).

Furthermore, to prompt some change to what we perceived were monolingual language and literacy practices at this center, we embraced Li Wei's (2011) suggestion of intentionally creating a translanguaging space. Li Wei argued that a translanguaging space must be actively and intentionally made, a place where languages would not be bound, fixed, or co-existent with each other. Rather, in the translanguaging space, boundaries between languages dissolve and opportunities are opened for something new with and around language and literacy.

Finally, we embraced literacy as a dynamic, multimodal, social semiotic practice (Mills, 2015) that people do in their everyday lives. This expanded definition of literacy is meant to complicate, expand, and redefine literacy so that more ways of being literate are included, as we recognize that all people are literate in multidimensional ways (Dyson, 2016). Moreover, as we were positioned in a community-based space, we wanted to recognize and include the community literacy practices that intersected with the center. Those community-based literacy practices were rich and complex and evident in the stores, restaurants, art, and businesses surrounding the center. Throughout each workshop, we prompted the children to build upon these community literacy practices in their writing.

A Community-Engaged Methodology

We frame this study as an ethnographically grounded, community-engaged, case study (Dyson & Genishi, 2005; Kinloch et al., 2016). Data for this chapter were collected between September 2015 and May 2019 across four different workshops. We developed and facilitated each writing workshop around a specific topic that we chose given what we knew about the context and the participants. Each workshop lasted approximately eight weeks and met for two hours on consecutive Saturdays. The participants in each workshop ranged in number from five to more than 16 children, as well as in age, from 6 to 12 years old. Each child who participated was an emergent bilingual in English and Spanish with familial connections to Latin America, predominantly to Mexico, specifically to the states of Puebla and Tlaxcala; however, other transnational connections were evident, including familial connections to Honduras, El Salvador, and Colombia.

We focused on answering the question: How does a translanguaging pedagogy amplify and include the expansive linguistic repertoire of emergent bilingual children? The data sources included audio and video recordings of the workshops, students' written products, and participatory observations. We analyzed the data in two passes. First, we used ethnographic thick description (Geertz, 1973) in the form of a detailed, written narrative on each of the four workshops to display our overall findings. Second, we employed a critical discourse analysis (Rogers, 2011) of one salient child-created text from each of those workshops and included that analysis as part of the thick descriptions of each workshop.

In terms of our positionalities, we are all faculty in the same department and university. We identify as White Americans, non-immigrants, and are bilingual in English and Spanish, all having learned Spanish as adults. When we began this project, both the director and assistant director of the community center were White American women, one of whom did not speak Spanish; however, midway through the project both the director and assistant director moved to other jobs or left the center. Both of the newly hired directors were bilingual/bicultural immigrants, having family origins in Honduras and Colombia. We note this because we attribute some of the initial monolingual tendencies of the center to the racial and linguistic positions of the former directors; however, since the hiring of the new directors, there has been a shift to more of a translanguaging space throughout the center's practices.

Findings

We begin the findings with a brief ethnographic description of the community center. The initial participatory observations revealed a community space that was bilingual in name, but monolingual in practice. Furthermore, our interviews with the center director, teachers, and volunteers revealed that this space was shaped by traditional and positivist ideas of language and literacy. For instance, the teachers attempted to keep the use of Spanish and English separate, and at times took up deficit stances when evaluating both the children's and their own proficiencies in Spanish. For instance, some teachers expressed views of "semilingualism" (Escamilla, 2006) while others used the term "not fluent" to describe not only the language practices of the children but their own as well. One teacher described the children as "not speaking English nor Spanish very well," and several described their own Spanish as not being "good enough" to correct the children's "errors" in Spanish. These kinds of language and literacy ideologies are common, especially in educational spaces, where language ideologies tend to default to autonomous and monolingual stances (Rosa & Burdick, 2017).

To address this, we designed and offered several writing workshops that modeled a critical, translanguaging pedagogy (García et al., 2017). Since the fall of 2017, we have offered four workshops: Writing Bilingual Family Stories, Crossing Borders with Bilingual Poetry, Bilingual Superheroes, and Language Mapping My Community. In the following sections, we provide a summary and analysis of each of these workshops with sample student-created texts and recommendations for future practice.

Escribiendo Historias Bilingües Familiares/Writing Bilingual Family Stories

In this fall 2017 workshop, there were five participants, all boys who ranged from 9 to 11 years old. They were all emergent bilinguals in Spanish and English; four had familial connections to Mexico, and one was born in El Salvador. In the first workshop session, to model the writing of family stories, we told the children family stories from our backgrounds. We broadly defined a family story as any story that was passed down or told among family members, whether funny, sad, scary or even exaggerated and not completely true. We also read examples of published family stories, such as *Calling the Doves/El Canto de Las Palomas* by Juan Felipe Herrera (1995) and gave each child a family story interview protocol (in Spanish and English) to take home and use to interview their family members. In the subsequent workshop sessions, each child returned with their completed interview protocols, and we discussed the stories they heard and learned from their family members. Each child chose a story to draft into a narrative from beginning to end using a graphic organizer. The subsequent sessions followed a writer's workshop model of drafting, revising, and publishing. At the end of the workshop, each child created a final, illustrated version of their family story. Next, we will discuss one family story written by Daniel in more detail (Figure 1.1).

Transcript of Daniel's Family Story

Page 1: The Chicken Attack

Page 2: One day mi mama was little. She was visiting her abuela in Mexico because she lived there. Her abuela was making dinner. She making frijoles.

Page 3: Mama was done eating and she ask her abuela if she could go outside "Ok" she said "pero tienes cuidado" she said but mi mama didn't heard her.

Page 4: When she was outside there was a chicken "una gallena" she said. She try to pet the chicken. The chicken was big and fat. The chicken attack mi mama. She was poke 3 times but escape she ran to the door and lock it.

Each family story was varied in content. Two students wrote about immigrating to the United States, one wrote about his father's bicycle, and another detailed the stories told about the day of their birth. Daniel's story was notable because his narrative construed a transnational experience, without telling a traditional migration story. Instead of a "Coming to America" story, his narrative relayed a fond and funny story of his mother visiting her *abuela* in Mexico. They cooked and ate good food, and then his mother was attacked by a *gallina* [hen] when she was out in the yard.

Tales of human migration and immigration to the United States and other nations play an important part in conveying the difficult and complex experiences of immigrants. However, we want to point to the significance of Daniel conveying his translanguaging and transnational life through a comical story he titled "The Chicken Attack." First, his story shows the normalcy of transnational living,

FIGURE 1.1 Daniel's Family Story

crossing the US/Mexico border to visit his *abuela*, eating good food, and also being "attacked" by a hen. At the same time, his story also shows the translanguaging reality that runs through his life and that of his family, by employing words such as *mi mama, abuela, gallena,* and *frijoles* within a story told predominantly in English. Instead of viewing this story as some "Spanish" words in an "English" text, we see Daniel's work through a translanguaging lens. A translanguaging lens highlights the deployment of Daniel's full linguistic repertoire in a way of capturing this family story without suppressing any of its interrelated linguistic features.

Cruzando Fronteras con la Poesía Bilingüe/Crossing Borders with Bilingual Poetry

In the Spring 2018 Crossing Borders with Bilingual Poetry workshop, there were 16 participants on the roster, but due to somewhat irregular attendance, the workshop averaged about eight children per session. To model writing bilingual poetry, each Saturday session focused on a specific form of poetry. In the first session, we modeled bilingual, "I Am From/Soy de" poems, and each child wrote a "I Am From/Soy de" poem, filling in the sections of the format we provided them. In the subsequent sessions, we modeled and wrote bilingual found poems, bilingual shape poems, and parallel bilingual poems. Found poems are poems created from words or phrases "found" within other texts. To write found poems, the children were given copies of locally published bilingual magazines and newspapers and cut out words and phrases from them with scissors. Shape poems are written in the shape of an object, and typically the subject of the poem and the shape of the poem are related. Stephanie was unable to locate examples of bilingual shape poems, so she created some to share with the children as examples.

Finally, parallel poems are modeled after another poem, usually published, borrowing lines as frames to recreate another poem. For the parallel bilingual poems, we used published poems written by Jane Medina (1999) and Francisco Alarcón (1997) as models for the children to emulate. The following poems are examples of a bilingual shape poem of Philadelphia's Ben Franklin Bridge written by Edwin (see Figure 1.2), and a parallel poem written by Uriel (see Figure 1.3), modeled after Francisco Alarcón's (1997) bilingual poem, "Dew/El rocío."

In our ethnographic observations of the center, we again noted that some teachers and volunteers voiced monoglossic and "semilingual" views of their own language and literacy practices, as well as those of the children. Similarly, the children voiced deficit views of their language and literacy abilities, too. For example, sometimes the children protested, "But I can't write in Spanish!" or "I don't know how to spell that in Spanish!" However, we found that when they wrote bilingual poetry that was modeled after a bilingual example, it alleviated those anxieties and challenged many of these deficit positions. Instead, writing bilingual parallel poems and shape poems amplified their language and literacy abilities, demonstrating their linguistic virtuosity (García & Kleyn, 2016) in Spanish and English, as well as through other modalities. Specifically, as seen in Edwin's example, the children possessed a rich linguistic repertoire. They not only used creative bilingual writing in Spanish and English, but they also demonstrated their deep funds of knowledge about living in Philadelphia, including landmarks such as the Ben Franklin Bridge, the subway system, and the Italian Market in their narratives. In Edwin's shape poem, he communicated multimodally and bilingually to capture the significance of a local landmark, the aforementioned Ben Franklin Bridge, and demonstrated his funds of knowledge about Philadelphia and his linguistic

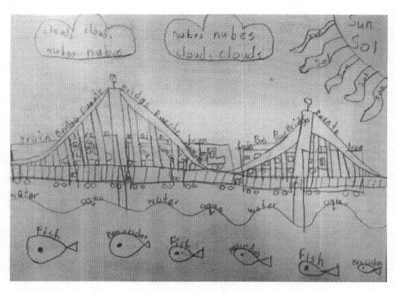

FIGURE 1.2   Edwin's Shape Poem of the Benjamin Franklin Bridge

FIGURE 1.3   Uriel's Bilingual Parallel Poem

virtuosity using a variety of modes. In Uriel's bilingual poem, he recognized complex poetic devices, including parallel lines and personification as used by Alarcón, and he appropriated those into his poem entitled "Wind/Viento."

Superhéroes Bilingües/Bilingual Superheroes

The third workshop session framed multilingualism as a superpower, and through this workshop we intended to undermine monolingual and "English Only" narratives that the children encountered in their daily lives that discouraged or ignored their bilingual language practices and identities. In this workshop, we prompted the children to think about how they used bilingualism in their everyday lives. In the first session, we showed the children a poster with a young character dressed as a superhero with a caption that explained "Being Bilingual is my Superpower." To further prompt the children's thinking about the advantages of bilingualism in their own lives, we gave each child a graphic organizer that mirrored the poster with sentence starters. Edwin, a ten-year-old, filled out his graphic organizer (see Figure 1.4) as follows:

Transcript of Graphic Organizer

> **I can …** *Speak English, Spanish, and Nahuatl. I can help everyone languages.*
> **I see … I hear …** *I see people speak English and Spanish.*

FIGURE 1.4 Edwin's Graphic Organizer

_____ is/are proud of my bilingualism because … My teacher are proud of me because I can help speak two languages to students.

I have seen people use their bilingualism to … I seen people use their languages to help student, other adult and teacher.

In the top left-hand bubble, Edwin identified the three languages he uses: English, Spanish, and Nahuatl, an Indigenous Mexican language. Edwin was one of several children whose families considered both Spanish and Nahuatl their home languages, although it was not part of the otherwise bilingual ecology of the writing center. In the third and fourth bubbles, Edwin highlights how his bilingualism helped people – from other students in his class to other adults and teachers he encounters in his daily life. This assumed role of bilingual "helper" was one that recurred in many of the children's work throughout the sessions of this particular superheroes workshop. What Edwin's graphic organizer demonstrates is that he was proud he could assist others and, perhaps, his bilingualism had been leveraged particularly in monolingual classrooms by teachers who themselves did not speak enough Spanish to assist their students (Abraham, 2012).

During a later session in the superheroes workshop, we used a picture book by Duncan Tonatiuh (2018) entitled *Undocumented: A Worker's Fight.* This text was meant to be a model for the children, as it offered an example of how to merge graphics with dialogue, inspired from the traditional Mixtec writing system. It also connected to the children's reality, which may have involved similar experiences or understandings of being undocumented in the United States. We covered the speech bubbles in order to hide the text and photocopied the panels and entire pages. We encouraged the children to practice writing dialogue or thoughts, inspired by the images on the page and their own imagination, and using their entire linguistic repertoire. Some children were familiar with the theme of the book, or what it is like being an undocumented immigrant in the United States, while others were not. In the drawings and samples we provided, the US Border Patrol and the local police were shown detaining and arresting immigrants.

In Marla's panel (see Figure 1.5), on the left-hand side of the image, is shown a man with brown skin wearing a baseball cap, holding his hands up in the air, a jug of milk and a shopping bag on the ground beside him indicating that he was walking home from the store when he was detained. Next to him is an empty thought balloon. Marla wrote inside the balloon, "What should I do?" On the right-hand side of the image, there is a police officer wearing blue, holding a handgun pointed at the man. Marla added a speech bubble and the police officer says, "Manos arriba! Hands up!" Marla also added a thought balloon from the police officer who is thinking, "Is he going to give himself up?"

Marla's dialogue countered narratives about the deportation of criminals, instead showing that people who aren't criminals, and may or may not even be

FIGURE 1.5 Marla's Panel

immigrants, are being targeted and deported. She also complicated the role of the police, representing both the man and the police officers as being unsure of what to do in the situation, noting that nothing had indicated that the man had committed a crime. Marla built from Tonatiuh's drawings and writing style to tell her version of this story, using both English and Spanish, she assigned a phrase in Spanish to the police officer. Using this text and providing them with the opportunity to represent their understanding of these stories using their translanguaging practices made space in the workshop for children to voice their unique positionalities as Latinx children of immigrants. It also provided them the opportunity to voice the characters from the book, complicating narratives about immigration that pervade the current social context.

Mapeando Los Idiomas de la Comunidad/Community Language Mapping

In this Spring 2019 workshop, the goal was for the children to document and "map" the languages of the local community where they lived and attended school, and of which the community center was located. Many of the children had participated in several of the previous workshops, and by this time we all knew each other well. During our first session, we prompted the children to draw a language map of their community. They were to note specifically the words they used to describe the various places they often visited, such as the Italian Market or a friend's house. In subsequent sessions, we focused specifically on how these spaces dictated different and unique kinds of language use. For instance, the children discussed how they used different languages to talk while on the playground as opposed to a classroom school setting, or how their language with their teacher is distinct from their language with a friend or a grandparent. The children noted important phrases while playing video games, including the specific words and phrases they used while playing Fortnite. Near the end of the workshop series, the children used iPods to document (with photos and videos) a walk around the community where the center was located. We asked the children to focus specifically on capturing language in use, such as signs in store windows or verbal exchanges in the market. Afterward, the children created a short film using the iMovie application on the iPod to represent the languages in the community. The next image (Figure 1.6) is a series of frames from Johnson's film of the Italian Market.

Johnson was somewhat unique in the program as he did not live in the neighborhood of the community center. His mother, who identified as Puerto Rican, brought him to this center and this workshop, specifically, to restore some of his Spanish knowledge. In Johnson's film, he captured two different examples of Spanish print. One example was a for-hire sign which advertised, "Se busca, bajista tecladista o ambos con experiencia en musica versatil." [We are looking for keyboarder or bassist or both with versatile music experience.] The other image was a concert poster, advertising the date for a popular band's concert in Camden, New Jersey. Johnson also filmed two examples of transactions in Spanish, one in a tortilleria and the other at a vegetable stand. In each of these, the vendor and buyers used predominantly Spanish, with some English to negotiate and complete the transaction. His short film, less than a minute, captured the translanguaging reality of the Italian Market, where people move in and out of spaces, deploying language as they see fit for the communicative event, whether buying tortillas or advertising attendance at a concert.

FIGURE 1.6   Johnson's Film

Discussion

Even though the program appeared to be monolingual from an outsider's perspective, the everyday languaging of the center was in reality bilingual. Translanguaging was the typical communicative practice for most of the children who attended the center. By tapping into this norm, rather than emulating a monolingual ideal, these workshops enabled the children to put their translanguaging and transnational lived experiences to use in meaningful bilingual literacy experiences.

Overall, our findings indicated that an out-of-school space promoted translanguaging opportunities due to the flexibility of choice in pedagogical practices and language use. This flexibility in pedagogical practice at the community center allowed us to be open to the translanguaging reality of the children. Each workshop highlighted a unique aspect of the translanguaging reality of the children and the community. One particular literacy experience, writing bilingual family stories, appeared to easily build a writing pedagogy that drew on the children's funds of knowledge and their translingual practices outside of the center. Also, offering models of bilingual writing and locally published bilingual texts relieved some of the social and linguistic stress around writing "correctly" in two languages, and provided creative and flexible options for children to demonstrate their linguistic repertoires. Similarly, the bilingual superheroes writing workshop provided the children with yet another way of representing their bilingual lived realities outside of traditional written literacy, which is often accompanied by monoglossic ideologies of standardization and correctness. This meant that the children in the workshop, many of whom were labeled "ELLs" or "struggling readers and writers" in their schools, expressed their ways of knowing using translingual, multimodal literacies. Finally, community language mapping heightened the linguistic awareness of the children. This included not only awareness of their own language practices, but also the linguistic practices of others.

In returning to our initial claims about how creating a translanguaging space is an important element in understanding acts of social justice, we present evidence that the reshaping of this discursive and physical space contributed to critical pedagogical practices for these emergent bilinguals. In terms of physicality, we noted the active presence of bilingual books, the specific reshaping of our language practices to demonstrate translanguaging, and the change in expectations of writing that focused and invited children's writing to demonstrate their translanguaging reality. For future implications, more research is needed in out-of-school and after school spaces, especially related to the language and literacy practices and pedagogies that are enacted and valued in those spaces. We recommend that pedagogies and practices be examined through a translanguaging lens; if researchers find that community spaces are also defaulting to language stances that value monolingualism and English-only practices, researchers should do more than simply document what exists and further act toward the exciting possibilities of creating translanguaging spaces.

References

Abraham, S. (2012). Critical biliteracy in the ESOL classroom: Bringing the outside in with dual language mentor texts. *TESOL: Bilingual Basics Newsletter.*

Alarcón, F. X. (1997). *Laughing tomatoes and other spring poems.* Children's Book Press.

Creese, A., & Blackledge, A. (2015). Translanguaging and identity in educational settings. *Annual Review of Applied Linguistics, 35,* 20–35. https://doi.org/10.1017/S0267190514000233

Dyson, A. H. (Ed.). (2016). *Child cultures, schooling, and literacy: Global perspectives on composing unique lives.* Routledge.

Dyson, A. H., & Genishi, C. (2005). *On the case* (Vol. 76). Teachers College Press.

Escamilla, K. (2006). Semilingualism applied to the literacy behaviors of Spanish-speaking merging bilinguals: Bi-illiteracy or emerging biliteracy? *Teachers College Record, 108*(11), 2329–2353.

García, O., Johnson, S. I., & Seltzer, K. (2017). *The translanguaging classroom: Leveraging student bilingualism for learning.* Caslon.

García, O., & Kleyn, T. (Eds.). (2016). *Translanguaging with multilingual students: Learning from classroom moments.* Routledge.

Geertz, C. (1973). *The interpretation of cultures: Selected essays.* Basic Books.

Herrera, J. F. (1995). *Calling the doves / El canto de las palomas.* Children's Book Press.

Kinloch, V., Larson, J., Orellana, M. F., & Lewis, C. (2016). Literacy, equity, and imagination: Researching with/in communities. *Literacy Research: Theory, Method, and Practice, 65*(1), 94–112. https://doi.org/10.1177/2381336916661541

Medina, J. (1999). *My name is Jorge on both sides of the river.* Wordsong.

Mills, K. A. (2015). *Literacy theories for the digital age: Social, critical, multimodal, spatial, material and sensory lenses.* Multilingual Matters.

Otheguy, R., García, O., & Reid, W. (2015). Clarifying translanguaging and deconstructing named languages: A perspective from linguistics. *Applied Linguistics Review, 6*(3), 281–307. https://doi.org/10.1515/applirev-2015-0014

Rogers, R. (2011). *An introduction to critical discourse analysis in education.* Routledge.

Rosa, J., & Burdick, C. (2017). Language ideologies. In O. Garcia, N. Flores, & M. Spotti (Eds.) *The Oxford handbook of language and society* (pp. 103–123). Oxford University Press.

Tonatiuh, D. (2018). *Undocumented: A worker's fight.* Abrams Books.

Wei, Li. (2011). Moment analysis and translanguaging space: Discursive construction of identities by multilingual Chinese youth in Britain. *Journal of Pragmatics, 43*(5), 1222–1235. https://doi.org/10.1016/j.pragma.2010.07.035

2

HERITAGE LANGUAGE AND LITERACY EDUCATION IN EAST ASIAN COMMUNITY-BASED HERITAGE LANGUAGE PROGRAMS

Kwangok Song

UNIVERSITY OF KANSAS

Introduction

Children growing up in families speaking languages other than English learn their heritage languages at home initially before they start learning English through schooling. Whether they can achieve language proficiency in their heritage language varies greatly depending on individuals and contexts. Maintaining a heritage language is essential for immigrants and their descendants to perpetuate intergenerational and familial communication and solidarity (Kim & Pyun, 2014). However, language deterioration or loss over time may occur because authentic opportunities for using heritage languages outside their homes and linguistic communities are quite limited (Valdés, 2014).

East Asian immigrant communities such as Chinese, Japanese, and Korean communities in the United States make concerted efforts to foster their descendants' heritage language maintenance and cultural competency by establishing nonprofit community-based language programs. These language programs borrow facilities from public schools, university classrooms, community centers, churches, or temples to offer language and literacy classes as well as extra-curricular activities (e.g., traditional dances, Taekwondo, calligraphy) as weekend or afterschool programs (Lee & Wright, 2014; Li & Wen, 2012; Peyton et al., 2001). Parents may actively participate as administrators, teachers, and volunteers to sustain and strengthen the programs (Shibata, 2000). The primary funding sources for heritage language schools mainly come from tuition and donations from local businesses. Additional funding is available from the sending countries' governments that have become interested in heritage language education for descendants of expatriates and nationals. As the number of heritage language schools in the United States has increased, associations for community-based heritage language schools have emerged to promote collaboration among heritage language schools. Associations offer professional development opportunities for teachers and administrators and speaking and writing contests for scholarship opportunities for K-12 students.

Although earlier studies discussed that community-based heritage language teachers developed the curriculum and created learning materials (Shibata, 2000; You & Liu, 2011), there have also been collective efforts to build a curriculum for heritage language learners. Sending countries' ministries of education have developed textbooks and learning materials (Lee & Wright, 2014). These teaching resources are distributed and adopted by many heritage language schools (Sun & Kwon, 2019). However, recognizing that curricularized language learning materials are not always developmentally appropriate, many teachers re-design the curriculum and obtain additional learning materials to meet the needs of their students (Lee & Bang, 2011).

Despite community-based heritage language programs' continued contribution to language diversity, the public awareness of these programs is still limited (Lee & Wright, 2014). Therefore, this chapter provides an overview of the history of East Asian community-based heritage language programs in the United States and the impact of these programs on immigrant descendants' and transnational students' learning of their heritage languages.

A Brief History of East Asian Community-Based Heritage Language Programs

East Asian community-based heritage language programs have long been serving immigrant descendants for their maintenance and development of heritage languages. The history of East Asian community language schools has intertwined with political and historical contexts of immigration of each ethnolinguistic group. The first Chinese school was founded in the late nineteenth century in San Francisco to provide education for Chinese immigrants and their descendants (Zhou & Kim, 2006). Since Chinese language schools were introduced in 1908 in New York and Chicago as a result of Chinese officials' diplomatic efforts, the number of Chinese schools continued to grow in large cities (Liu, 2010). After World War II, however, despite an increase in the Chinese population, the interest in learning Chinese somewhat decreased due to the growing aspiration to assimilate into American society. With the growth of Chinese-speaking immigrants as a result of the Immigration and Naturalization Act of 1965 that removed the restriction to immigration from non-Northern Europe, however, more Chinese language schools emerged to serve immigrant descendants from mainland China and Taiwan (McGinnis, 2005). As of 2020, approximately 500 schools are registered with the Chinese School Association in the United States (CSAUS), serving over 100,000 students (CSAUS, 2020).

The first Japanese school was also introduced in the late nineteenth century in Hawaii as a result of an attempt to support Japanese immigrants and their descendants (Chinen et al., 2013). Since then, additional Japanese schools were established in the cities on the west coast before World War II. These schools had to close during the war, but they resumed after the war to mainly serve immigrant descendants who were born in the United States and had limited experiences with Japanese outside their homes (Shimada, 1998). As the Japanese population with temporary status increased around the late 1970s, *hoshuukoo*, a new type of supplementary, private school, emerged to provide academic support in the Japanese language for school-aged children who would return to Japan after their families' residence in the United States ended (Doerr & Lee, 2012; Kataoka et al., 2008). The number of *hoshuukoo* reached a peak around the early 1990s, but has decreased since then. Because *hoshuukoo*'s goal was to educate the potential returnees to Japan, they used *Kokuko*, the Japanese language arts curriculum approved by the Japanese Ministry of Education, to provide support for academic literacy in Japanese. Although *hoshuukoo* is not initially intended to provide heritage language classes, *hoshuukoo* in some cities still serve immigrant descendants who learn Japanese as their heritage language (Tsukuda, 2013).

Finally, Korean heritage language schools bourgeoned around the 1970s as a phenomenon of the post Immigration and Naturalization Act of 1965 (Zhou & Kim, 2006). As the number of Korean immigrants increased dramatically, the number of Korean heritage language schools also proliferated in the last four decades (Lee & Shin, 2008). The student population of Korean heritage language schools has become diverse depending on families' immigration circumstances. As of 2020, there are approximately 1,000 Korean heritage language schools across the United States, according to the National Association for Korean Schools (NAKS, 2020).

Theoretical Perspectives

In understanding the role of community-based heritage language schools, three theoretical perspectives are relevant to this review. First, transnationalism explains sociocultural, political, and economic processes that take place across and beyond the borders of nations (Vertovec, 2001). In transnational practices, interconnections, and exchanges between sending and receiving countries are perpetuated while shaping and negotiating collective identities (Duff, 2015; Kearney, 1995). Maintaining a heritage language, therefore, can be deemed integral to transnational practices because it allows immigrants and transnationals to sustain ties with relatives and acquaintances in their parents' countries of origin and people in the same ethnolinguistic communities with themselves (Li, 2005; Shibata, 2000; You & Liu, 2011). Heritage language schools further facilitate transnational collaboration between immigrant communities in the United States and sending countries for immigrant descendants' and transnational students' heritage language learning.

The notion of *language socialization* is also helpful for understanding the role of heritage language schools. Language socialization explains individuals' acquisition of language practices through interactions with members of a speech community (Schieffelin & Ochs, 1986). Language socialization is related to literacy acquisition because literacy practices as social practices constitute the use of language in interactions with others with the mediation of written texts (Heath, 1983). Children become a legitimate member of society by acquiring specific ways to use language as they interact with other community members (Baquedano-López, 2003). Although children started to acquire ways to use language at home, they continue developing their use of language and literacy by participating in classroom practices (Kulick & Schieffelin, 2004). Whereas opportunities for immigrant and transnational descendants to interact with other people using their heritage languages are scarce outside their homes, heritage language schools could extend these opportunities for heritage language speakers to engage in language and literacy practices.

Finally, the sociocultural perspective of identity construction assumes that participation in literacy practices (re)shapes one's identities because individuals acquire ways to interact, communicate, and behave appropriately in different sociocultural contexts (Gee, 2015). Sociocultural and historical tools in literacy practices mediate individuals' identity development (Bartlett, 2007; Tappan, 2005). Identity construction is not always an effortless and straightforward process. Instead, individuals continuously negotiate their identities through their participation in literacy practices (Bakhtin, 1981; Penuel & Wertsch, 1995). Individuals may selectively adopt authoritative discourses as personally persuasive discourses or reject such discourses to justify their course of actions, to make sense of themselves, and to express themselves (Duff, 2015). The next sections address the ways community-based heritage language programs have impacted immigrant descendants and transnational students, as discussed in the current literature.

Summary of Empirical Findings

Inculcating and Reproducing Traditional Values

Community-based heritage language programs provide immigrant children with cross-cultural and multilingual experiences. As students participate in classroom literacy activities, they experience culturally and traditionally valued ways to communicate and interact with others (Irvine, 1998). Learning materials used in heritage language classrooms highlight traditional values deemed important to certain ethnolinguistic communities. It was highlighted that Chinese heritage language textbooks represented and reproduced cultural values such as perseverance, diligence, conformity, moderation, and altruism, those emphasized by the Confucius teaching (Curdt-Christiansen, 2008; Sun & Kwon, 2019).

Traditional values esteemed important in social interactions in certain ethnolinguistic communities are also reinforced in classroom interactions. For example, in Chinese heritage language classrooms, communication styles characterized by modesty and indirectness, as well as moral values deemed important by parents, were underscored in classroom interactions (He, 2001; Jia, 2006). He (2001) pointed out that the teacher of the focal classroom did not point out who made a mistake or who answered correctly. Instead of expressing disagreement with students, the teacher partially accepted students' incorrect responses while remaining ambiguous about her own perspective. Through circumlocutory interactions, students in this classroom learned to draw inferences in interactions with adults in their ethnolinguistic communities.

Likewise, in Korean heritage language classrooms, communication styles and manners considered essential for respectful communication are addressed. Particularly, teachers explicitly and implicitly teach honorifics systems in the Korean language, the systems to express respect and politeness in formal and informal communications (e.g., ages, people with authority). Honorific systems appear in specific nouns, pronouns, verbs, and lexical markers (Brown, 2011; Sohn, 1999). The appropriate use of honorifics to some degree is expected when children interact with adults. Although honorific systems are acquired as individuals participate in social practices, immigrant descendants may have limited opportunities to experience honorific systems. In Byon's (2003) study, heritage language teachers used honorifics when addressing the whole class to model how to use honorifics to some degree, although adults' use of honorifics in interactions with young children is not required. Teachers also provided the correct use of honorifics when they noticed children's incorrect use of honorifics. S. J. Kim (2017) also highlighted that the teacher overtly corrected four-year-old children's incorrect use of honorifics or lack of using honorifics while providing explicit instructions on how to use honorifics.

Culturally appropriate non-verbal behaviors are also promoted in heritage language classrooms. Examining teacher–student interactions in a Korean heritage language classroom, Lo (2004, 2009) noted that the teacher discussed what involved morally right behaviors in interactions with adults. Those behaviors included keeping well-mannered demeanors, suppressing one's emotions, and keeping one's thoughts to oneself when interacting with people with authority or adults. By examining interactions of pre-kindergarten children in a Korean heritage language classroom, J. Kim (2014) further demonstrated that maintaining group harmony highly valued in the Korean community was promoted as a form of interdependence and sharing. When internalized cultural values were emphasized in the classroom, the children displayed such values when resolving conflicts with each other.

Overall, the studies imply that literacy learning at heritage language schools involves not merely learning to read and write in a heritage language, but also learning how to communicate with others, how to behave appropriately, and how to use language in an acceptable way. By attending heritage language schools, therefore, children learn cultural values and communication styles while developing a sense of morality as expected in interactions with people in an ethnolinguistic community.

Immigrant Descendants' Construction of Ethnic Identity in Heritage Language Classrooms

Participating in literacy practices in heritage language schools can mediate immigrant descendants' emerging sense of self in association with their ethnolinguistic groups. In a study with Japanese-American adolescents in a Saturday Japanese school, Chinen and Tucker (2005) demonstrated that students who regularly attended the school and had higher language proficiency had a stronger sense of belongingness and attachment to the Japanese community than those who did not. Other studies discussed the complexities in heritage language learners' emerging ethnic identity and their motivation to learn their heritage languages. Interviewing Korean adolescents enrolled in a Korean heritage language school, You (2005) discussed that although some focal students expressed resistance to learning the Korean language and lack of confidence in their Korean language proficiency, they developed a desire to participate in the Korean community. Additionally, viewing their language proficiency as indispensable for their belongingness to the ethnic group, they expressed their willingness to develop their language proficiency in the future.

Likewise, in a study with Korean immigrant adolescents in a heritage language classroom, J.-I. Kim (2017) highlighted that participating in a heritage language classroom mediated the participating adolescents' identity construction. Although the focal students' use of Korean in their out-of-school activities varied, all students developed motivational reasons to learn Korean. Some students frequently used the Korean language to communicate with their parents at home and Korean-speaking peers at school, and they developed an idea that learning Korean was essential for Korean descendants. The other students who limitedly engaged in communicating in Korean expressed their desire to communicate better with their family members in the future.

Maguire and Curdt-Christiansen (2007) discussed that elementary children attending a heritage language school adopted ideological discourses from the heritage language school about the importance of learning heritage language despite their struggles with competing ideologies. Some students with limited experiences with the Chinese language did not see the value of developing their heritage language skills or attending the heritage language school. The others with more extensive experiences with their heritage language demonstrated a positive attitude that attending a Chinese language school was a venue for them to socialize with new friends. Additionally, they considered that learning Chinese and becoming knowledgeable about China was integral to their interaction with family members.

Overall, the studies demonstrate that routinized participation in the heritage language seems to contribute to immigrant adolescents' motivation to develop their heritage language proficiency and belongingness to their ethnolinguistic communities. Additionally, students attending heritage language schools develop an aspiration to improve their language proficiency and to gain legitimate membership in their ethnolinguistic communities.

Challenges in Heritage Language Schools

Although heritage language schools provide opportunities for immigrant descendants to engage in literacy practices in their heritage language outside their homes, several internal and external challenges do exist. First, culturally and developmentally appropriate learning materials are not always available (Lee & Bang, 2011). Despite textbooks designed for heritage language schools, these textbooks do not always provide resources to support heritage language learners (Chinen et al., 2013). Furthermore, the stories and other cultural materials to promote traditional values may cause estrangement because they do not reflect immigrant descendants' sociocultural experiences and because they contain vocabulary words and expressions that are rarely used in the present day.

Furthermore, professional development opportunities for heritage language school teachers are scarce. Many heritage language school teachers have inadequate professional training. Thus, they may possess an insufficient understanding of heritage language learners' unique characteristics and limited knowledge about literacy learning and effective instructional approaches (Lee & Bang, 2011). Although professional development programs have been developed and distributed by the sending countries' ministries of education and heritage language school associations in the United States, professional development opportunities are not always readily available for all teachers.

Conflicting ideologies on multilingualism in society seem to create additional challenges in encouraging immigrant descendants to understand the importance of learning the heritage language (Maguire & Curdt-Christiansen, 2007; You, 2005). Limited social recognition of community-based heritage language schools as legitimate educational institutions seems to make it even more difficult for immigrant descendants and transnational students to see the benefits of developing their heritage language proficiency (Lee & Wright, 2014). Although learning a heritage language can be promoted by parents and ethnolinguistic communities, the hegemony of English normalized in school and other social contexts can affect adolescents' resistance to heritage language education. Internalizing the monolingual English-only ideology permeated in society, immigrant descendants struggle with learning their heritage languages despite their desire to develop heritage language proficiency necessary for their membership to ethnolinguistic groups (J.-I. Kim, 2017).

Future Directions

Heritage language maintenance is indispensable for the vitality of marginalized ethnolinguistic communities because it allows family unity and solidarity with individuals from the same ethnolinguistic communities (Padilla & Borsato, 2010). Because international interconnectivity in various sociocultural contexts becomes prominent in the contemporary era, it is critical for immigrant descendants and transnational students to continue developing linguistic and cultural competence to participate in transnational activities. Despite several difficulties, East Asian community-based heritage language schools have played a critical role in immigrant descendants' and transnational students' language socialization and identity construction while providing opportunities to acquire and experience culturally appropriate ways to communicate and interact with their ethnolinguistic community members.

For sustaining linguistic diversity, heritage language schools may need collaborative and organized support not just from their ethnolinguistic communities but also from the broader society in which they are situated. Notably, it is necessary to acknowledge community-based heritage language schools as legitimate educational programs supplementary to public education and to recognize heritage language teachers' efforts and immigrant descendants' achievement in their heritage language learning (Lee & Wright, 2014). It is also critical to promote collaboration among community-based heritage language schools, the research community, and public education sectors. The collaboration between heritage language schools and public education sectors may create opportunities for K-12 students to build skillsets to understand and cooperate with various ethnolinguistic communities. The research community can expand our understanding of heritage language learners' unique characteristics as language learners and provide pedagogical implications for heritage language learning and teaching. Additionally, future research can comprehensively examine the impact of continued transnational mobility on community-based heritage language programs to obtain a better understanding of how these programs shape immigrant descendants' and transnational students' literacy experiences in communities.

References

Bakhtin, M. M. (1981). *The dialogic imagination: Four essays* (M. Holquist Ed., C. Emerson & M. Holquist, Trans.). University of Texas Press.

Baquedano-López, P. (2003). Language, literacy and community. In N. Hall, J. Larson, & J. Marsh (Eds.), *Handbook of early childhood literacy* (pp. 66–74). SAGE. https://doi.org/10.4135/9781848608207.n6

Bartlett, L. (2007). To seem and to feel: Situated identities and literacy practices. *Teachers College Record, 109*(1), 51–69.

Brown, L. (2011). Korean honorifics and 'revealed', 'ignored' and 'suppressed' aspects of Korean culture and politeness. In F. Bargiela-Chiappini, & D. Z. Kádár (Eds.),

Politeness across cultures (pp. 106–127). Palgrave McMillan. https://doi.org/10.1057/9780230305939_6

Byon, A. S. (2003). Language socialization and Korean as a heritage language: A study of Hawaiian classrooms. *Language, Culture and Curriculum, 16*(3), 269–283. https://doi.org/10.1080/07908310308666674

Chinen, K., Douglas, M. O., & Kataoka, H. C. (2013). Japanese heritage language schools in the United States. *Heritage Briefs Collection*. Retrieved from www.cal.org/heritage/pdfs/briefs/japanese-heritage-language-schools-in-the-united-states.pdf

Chinen, K., & Tucker, G. R. (2005). Heritage language development: Understanding the roles of ethnic identity and Saturday school participation. *Heritage Language Journal, 3*(1), 27–59.

Chinese School Association in the United States (CSAUS) (2020, March 10). *About CSAUS*. www.csaus.org/FHFRONT/csaus/about.jsp

Curdt-Christiansen, X. (2008). Reading the world through words: Cultural themes in heritage Chinese language textbooks. *Language and Education, 22*(2), 95–113. https://doi.org/10.2167/le721.0

Doerr, N. M., & Lee, K. (2012). "Drop-outs" or "heritage learners"? Competing mentalities of governmentality and invested meanings at a weekend Japanese language school in the USA. *Discourse: Studies in the Cultural Politics of Education, 33*(4), 561–573. https://doi.org/10.1080/01596306.2012.692962

Duff, P. (2015). Transnationalism, multilingualism, and identity. *Annual Review of Applied Linguistics, 35*, 57–80. https://doi.org/10.1017/S026719051400018X

Gee, J. P. (2015). *Social linguistics and literacies: Ideology in discourses*. Routledge. https://doi.org/10.4324/9781315722511

He, A. W. (2001). The language of ambiguity: Practices in Chinese heritage language classes. *Discourse Studies, 3*(1), 75–96. https://doi.org/10.1177/1461445601003001004

Heath, S. B. (1983). *Ways with words: Language, life, and work in communities and classrooms*. Cambridge University Press. https://doi.org/10.1017/CBO9780511841057

Irvine, J. (1998). Ideologies of honorific Language. In B. Schieffelin, K. Woolard, & P. Kroskrity (Eds.), *Language ideologies: Practice and theory* (pp. 51–67). Oxford University Press.

Jia, L. (2006). The invisible and the visible: Language socialization at the Chinese heritage language school (unpublished doctoral dissertation). The University of Texas at San Antonio, San Antonio, TX.

Kataoka, H. C., Koshiyama, Y., & Shibata, S. (2008). Japanese and English language ability of students at supplementary Japanese schools in the United States. In K. Kondo-Brown, & J. D. Brown (Eds.), *Teaching Chinese, Japanese, and Korean heritage language students: Curriculum needs, materials, and assessment* (pp. 47–76). Lawrence Erlbaum Associates. https://doi.org/10.4324/9781315087443-3

Kearney, M. (1995). The local and the global: The anthropology of globalism and transnationalism. *Annual Review of Anthropology, 24*, 547–565. https://doi.org/10.1146/annurev.an.24.100195.002555

Kim, C. E., & Pyun, D. O. (2014). Heritage language literacy maintenance: A study of Korean-American heritage learners. *Language, Culture & Curriculum, 27*(3), 294–315. https://doi.org/10.1080/07908318.2014.970192

Kim, J. (2014). "You don't need to be mean. We're friends, right?": Young Korean-American children's conflicts and references to friendship. *Journal of Early Childhood Research, 12*(3), 279–293. https://doi.org/10.1177/1476718X14538591

Kim, J.-I. (2017). Immigrant adolescents investing in Korean heritage language: Exploring motivation, identities, and capital. *Canadian Modern Language Review, 73*(2), 183–207. https://doi.org/10.3138/cmlr.3334

Kim, S. J. (2017). A situated perspective on bilingual development: Preschool Korean-English bilinguals' utilization of two languages and Korean honorifics. *International Journal of Bilingual Education and Bilingualism, 20*(1), 1–19. https://doi.org/10.1080/13670050.2015.1035228

Kulick, D., & Schieffelin, B. B. (2004). Language socialization. In A. Duranti (Ed.), *A companion to linguistic anthropology* (pp. 349–368). Blackwell. https://doi.org/10.1111/b.9781405144308.2005.00018.x

Lee, J. S., & Shin, S. J. (2008). Korean heritage language education in the United States: The current state, opportunities, and possibilities. *Heritage Language Journal, 6*(2), 153–172.

Lee, J. S., & Wright, W. (2014). The rediscovery of heritage and community language education in the United States. *Review of Research in Education, 38*, 137–165. https://doi.org/10.3102/0091732X13507546

Lee, S., & Bang, Y. (2011). Listening to teacher lore: The challenges and resources of Korean heritage language teachers. *Teaching and Teacher Education, 27*, 387–394. https://doi.org/10.1016/j.tate.2010.09.008

Li, G., & Wen, K. (2012). East Asian heritage language education for a plurilingual reality in the United States: Practices, potholes, and possibilities. *International Multilingual Research Journal, 9*, 274–290. https://doi.org/10.1080/19313152.2015.1086623

Li, M. (2005). The role of parents in Chinese heritage-language schools. *Bilingual Research Journal, 29*(1), 197–207. https://doi.org/10.1080/15235882.2005.10162831

Liu, N. (2010). Chinese heritage language schools in the United States. *Heritage Briefs Collection*. Retrieved from www.cal.org/heritage/pdfs/briefs/chinese-heritage-language-schools-in-the-us.pdf

Lo, A. (2004). Evidentiality and morality in a Korean heritage language school. *Pragmatics, 14*(2/3), 235–256. https://doi.org/10.1075/prag.14.2-3.08lo

Lo, A. (2009). Lessons about respect and affect in a Korean heritage language school. *Linguistics and Education: An International Research Journal, 20*(3), 217–234. https://doi.org/10.1016/j.linged.2009.07.002

Maguire, M. H. & Curdt-Christiansen, X. L. (2007). Multiple schools, languages, experiences and affiliations: Ideological becomings and positionings. *Heritage Language Journal, 5*(1), 50–78.

McGinnis, S. (2005). From mirror to compass: The Chinese heritage language education sector in the United States. In D.M. Brinton, O. Kagan, & S. Bauckus (Eds.), *Heritage language education: A new field emerging* (pp. 229–242). Routledge. https://doi.org/10.4324/9781315092997-17

The National Association for Korean Schools. (2020, March 10). *Introduction.* www.naks.org/jml/about-us-purpose

Padilla, A. M., & Borsato, G. N. (2010). Psychology. In J. A. Fishman, & O. García (Eds.), *Handbook of language & ethnic identity,* Vol. I (pp. 5–17). Oxford University Press.

Penuel, W., & Wertsch, J. V. (1995). Vygotsky and identity formation: A sociocultural approach. *Educational Psychologist, 30*(2), 83–92. https://doi.org/10.1207/s15326985ep3002_5

Peyton, J. K., Ranard, D. A., & McGinnis, S. (2001). *Heritage languages in America: Preserving a national resource.* Delta Systems Co.

Schieffelin, B. B., & Ochs, E. (1986). Language socialization. *Annual Review of Anthropology*, *15*, 163–191. https://doi.org/10.1146/annurev.an.15.100186.001115

Shibata, S. (2000). Opening a Japanese Saturday school in a small town in the United States: Community collaboration to teach Japanese as a heritage language. *Bilingual Research Journal*, *24*(4), 465–474. https://doi.org/10.1080/15235882.2000.10162778

Shimada, N. (1998). Wartime dissolution and revival of the Japanese language schools in Hawaii: Persistence of ethnic culture. *Journal of Asian American Studies*, *1*(2), 121–151. https://doi.org/10.1353/jaas.1998.0022

Sohn, H.-M. (1999). *The Korean language*. Cambridge University Press.

Sun, W., & Kwon, J. (2019). Representation of monoculturalism in Chinese and Korean heritage language textbooks for immigrant children. *Language, Culture and Curriculum*. https://doi.org/10.1080/07908318.2019.1642346

Tappan, M. B. (2005). Domination, subordination and the dialogical self: Identity development and the politics of "ideological becoming." *Culture & Psychology*, *11*(1), 47–75. https://doi.org/10.1177/1354067X05050743

Tsukuda, Y. (2013). Japanese American transnational families. In X. Zhao, & E. J. W. Park (Eds.), *Asian Americans: An encyclopedia of social, cultural, economic, and political history* (pp. 602–604). Greenwood.

Valdés, G. (2014). Heritage language students: Profiles and possibilities. In T. G. Wiley, J. K. Peyton, D. Christian, S. C. K. Moore, & N. Liu (Eds.), *Handbook of heritage, community and Native American languages in the United States: Research, policy, and educational practices* (pp. 27–35). Routledge.

Vertovec, S. (2001). Transnationalism and identity. *Journal of Ethnic and Migration Studies*, *27*(4), 573–582. https://doi.org/10.1080/13691830120090386

You, B. (2005). Children negotiating Korean American ethnic identity through their heritage language. *Bilingual Research Journal*, *29*(3), 711–721. https://doi.org/10.1080/15235882.2005.10162860

You, B., & Liu, N. (2011). Stakeholder views on the roles, challenges, and prospects of Korean and Chinese heritage language-community language schools in Phoenix: A comparative study. *Heritage Language Journal*, *8*(3), 67–92.

Zhou, M., & Kim, S. S. (2006). Community forces, social capital, and educational achievement: The case of supplementary education in the Chinese and Korean immigrant communities. *Harvard Educational Review*, *76*(1), 1–29. https://doi.org/10.17763/haer.76.1.u08t548554882477

3

BILINGUAL FAMILY LITERACY CHALLENGES

Matthew Knoester

RIPON COLLEGE

Introduction

Language and literacy learning continue to be important but mysterious and often counter-intuitive processes. This is perhaps especially true for second-language learning, and, given the centrality of these topics to multiple educational goals, they warrant continued research. There are many purposes offered for second language learning. The most common purpose, upon which educators and educational scholars primarily focus in the USA, is that of students learning English as a second language. As the dominant language, English is essential to success in school, as well as to many other parts of life in the USA, such as social relationships and economic opportunities (Baker & Wright, 2017).

Learning a second language for English-dominant learners, although less common, is also an interest of educators and educational scholars. According to the Center for Applied Linguistics (2018), approximately 91% of US high schools offer foreign language instruction, while approximately 58% of middle schools and 25% of elementary schools do so. More than 3/4ths of this foreign language instruction focuses on learning Spanish. A variety of purposes are offered as to why learning a foreign language is important or useful for English-dominant students in the USA. It is valued for increased economic and travel opportunities, for increased social opportunities with foreign language speakers in the USA, as well as increased vocabulary and language understanding of students' primary language, English, as patterns and similarities are noticed and a deeper understanding of grammar and English language usage might be reached (Baker & Wright, 2017; Cummins, 2001; Thomas & Collier, 2012).

Although instruction in a foreign language at the elementary level is relatively rare in the USA (second language learning in other countries is much more prevalent (Thomas & Collier, 2012, p. 1), powerful arguments have been made that the learning of a second language (L2) at the elementary level is an opportune time to develop the second language, including for students who are learning an L2 other than the dominant language in society. Recent research has demonstrated this to be the case (Baker & Wright, 2017; García, 2009; Thomas & Collier, 2012). For example, in their landmark longitudinal research studies, comparing various forms of bilingual education, such as English immersion for learners with a different L1, pull-out ESL models, one-way bilingual education, and two-way bilingual education, Thomas and Collier (2012) have demonstrated that two-way bilingual educational models have been most effective at teaching bilingualism and biliteracy to both dominant and minoritized language students alike. Thomas and Collier report, "dual language is the most powerful school reform model for high academic achievement that we have seen in all our 28 years of conducting longitudinal studies in our field" (p. 6). Perhaps most importantly, in their research they found:

> The bilingual classes reduced negative stereotypes, led to increased friendships among the two language groups, raised the status of the Spanish language to a level equal to that of English, affirmed the students' bilingual/ bicultural heritage, and led to increased academic achievement for both groups.
>
> *(p. 12)*

Despite these findings, the Center for Applied Linguistics (2019) estimates there are just 448 dual-immersion bilingual schools in the USA. The National Association for Bilingual Education reports that there are more than 2,000 dual-language programs, although many offer less than 50% of the minority language (Baker & Wright, 2017; Wilson, 2011).

The reasons for why there are not more two-way bilingual schools, despite strong research support, are many and complex. Part of the problem is logistical – there is already a shortage of qualified bilingual teachers even with small numbers of bilingual programs (Mitchell, 2019). But why is there not a more concerted effort to prepare bilingual teachers? Despite the estimated half of the world's population being multilingual (Thomas & Collier, 2012, p. 1), there has historically been a strong hesitance to develop speaking and literacy abilities in more than one language in the USA, and sometimes strong protest and political pressure to prevent such development (García & Sung, 2018). These pressures can be understood to coincide and operate in conjunction with one-language ideologies (Spolsky, 2004), as well as racism and white supremacy, a long history that is beyond the scope of this chapter, but is well documented (Kendi, 2016; Selden, 1999).

In this chapter, I focus on another reason bilingual education is sometimes not embraced: Many English-dominant parents assume that if their child learned

Spanish (or another language) in primary school, this would inhibit their learning to read and write in English (Dicker, 1993; Huddy & Sears, 1995). As noted above, the research does not reveal this to be true. However, as children in two-way bilingual Spanish/English schools focus on Spanish in the early grades (many such schools intentionally focus on Spanish with a ratio of 90:10 at the earliest grades; Beeman & Urow, 2013), English literacy learning comes second, after learning to speak and read in Spanish (or another L2). This can cause anxiety among English-dominant students and families.

I will focus here on the at-home learning of a second language by two young English-dominant children, both of whom were enrolled in a two-way bilingual Spanish/English school three years prior to this writing. This research is different from the other literacy studies I have conducted, in that the children under focus are my own two children. In 2016, my partner and I were fortunate to have the opportunity to send our two children to the neighborhood public two-way bilingual school in Milwaukee, just after moving to the city. Given the severe racial and economic segregation in Milwaukee, we strongly supported the idea of sending our (White) children to a school with a mix of approximately 60% Latinx, 25% Black, 11% White, and 3% Asian (Milwaukee Public Schools, 2020). The school further has an explicit mission of teaching for social justice and anti-racism, values that are deeply important to our family (Knoester, 2012a, 2012b; Peterson, 2007, 2017). We were new to the city at the time of our children's enrollment in the fall of 2016. At the time, my son, Nicolaus, was 8 years old, entering 3rd grade. My daughter, Jubilee, was 5 and entering kindergarten.

Both children struggled to understand, speak, read, and write in Spanish but incrementally improved over time. The younger child (age 8 at the time of this writing) also struggled to learn to read and write in English. The empirical research about two-way bilingual education should reassure such parents that children in these schools learn to speak and read and write in both English and in Spanish at grade-appropriate levels before they leave primary school, but it can take several years for these abilities to develop and the "waiting period" can become anxiety-producing, especially if parents know and see other children in monolingual English schools developing in reading and writing abilities well ahead of their children in the bilingual school. This chapter is, in part, my reflection on how our family dealt with these issues and attempted to support the literacy development of our children in both Spanish and English at home, even while the children focused on Spanish at school.

Background and Theoretical Framework

Prominent linguists have argued that learning to speak in one's first language (L1), barring severe disability, feels almost effortless and is more like an instinct than learned behavior (Pinker, 2007). Noam Chomsky (1988, p. 174; Knoester, 2003) described it as something that "happens to you," rather than something that takes a large amount of effort, although learning the many irregular grammatical rules in a language such as English may take considerable time and effort, despite children's early abilities to construct unique sentences in order to communicate, although imperfectly. However, learning to read and write in one's L1, as well as to both speak and read and write in one's second language (L2) takes substantially more time and effort. This is part of what is counter-intuitive about learning an L2. Individuals, including educators and educational scholars, may assume that the learning of an L2 can happen as easily and quickly as learning to speak in one's L1, but that is generally not the case.

A well-known theory that helps to describe the learning of both one's L1 and L2 comes from the work of Jim Cummins (1984, 2000, 2001). Cummins theorized two basic forms of language learning, one is represented by the acronym BICS (Basic Interpersonal Communication Skills), and, as the name implies, refers to initial verbal speaking and learning. The second, more difficult form of language understanding he describes as CALP (Cognitive Academic Language Proficiency), which is the form of language that becomes useful in school and in academic learning as children grow. Although not identical, I think of CALP as especially important to the ability to read and write ever increasingly sophisticated texts (Cummins, 1984; Rhodes, Ochoa, & Ortiz, 2005).

According to Cummins, when intensely learning a second language, students can become proficient in BICS within approximately 2–3 years; however, becoming proficient in CALP requires more time, approximately 5–7 years (Cummins, 1984). Further, Cummins argued that the learning of CALP in one's L2 is easier when a learner has already developed CALP in their L1. This is consistent with the more recent theory of translanguaging, which argues that bilingual individuals do not necessarily keep their L1 and L2 separate – they can and do use the skills and understandings from L1 in the use of their L2, and vice versa (García & Wei, 2014).

Placing language and literacy learning of one's L1 and L2 into these four categories (BICS of L1, CALP of L1, BICS of L2 and CALP of L2) is, of course, an oversimplification of highly complex processes that vary from person to person. There are far more ways to understand the development of language and literacy in two languages than four basic categories, which are also difficult to define. Gee (2015) has argued that literacy is always *situated* within particular discourses (communities of people who develop specialized language), even within one's L1 and L2, so learning a particular literacy in a particular discourse does not mean an individual has learned literacy that would apply to all discourses within that language (Knoester, 2009). Further, to make these issues even more complex, research on translanguaging (García & Wei, 2014), as mentioned above, has suggested that separating one's L1 and L2 as two completely separate sets of knowledge is also misleading, as individuals who are learning an L2 draw on their knowledge of their L1 in learning the L2, and that the lines between languages are quite blurry – as there are many similar cognates and overlaps among languages, especially languages such as English and Spanish, which have similar roots.

Nevertheless, for the purposes of this chapter, I will largely rely on Cummins's theory of BICS and CALP, as it has been quite useful in my understanding the language and literacy struggles and development of my own two children with quite different experiences in the same school. For example, I use Cummins's construct to make this point: An aspect about learning a second language that is quite counter-intuitive, but can be better understood with Cummins's theory, is that learning an L2 is not as straightforward as simply being immersed in that L2. Rather, learning both the BICS and CALP of an L2 is made easier with a strong foundation of BICS and CALP in one's L1. This theory is substantiated by the empirical work of Thomas and Collier (2012), which showed that Latinx students with Spanish as an L1 learned English (both BICS and CALP) as an L2 faster and more effectively if they had more years of schooling (learning CALP) in their L1, as compared with those students who were immersed in their L2 without first developing CALP in their L1. This became apparent to me as I observed the L1 and L2 (BICS and CALP) development of my own children.

Nicolaus and Jubilee

Our first child, Nicolaus, was born in Madison, WI in 2007, and our second child, Jubilee, was born in Evansville, IN, in 2011. As they grew and began to speak, my partner and I were most interested in teaching them to speak (and eventually to read) in English. It was a delight to hear them as they learned to speak in English. In fact, we have pages in our baby books of the funny and cute words that our children "mispronounced." For example, my daughter called toothpaste and toothbrush "poopase" and "poop brush" and called peanut butter "poop butter." We were too busy rolling on the floor laughing to correct her on those! Although even later into childhood, at ages 8 and 9, our children continued to have a hard time conjugating irregular verbs – "to bring" in the past tense is still "bringed" or "brang" rather than "brought" for my daughter, and the past tense of "to run" is still "runned," to name just a few grammatical mistakes that we continue to hear. Of course, many adults use phrases that are ungrammatical or playful, so these kinds of "errors" are normal and to be expected. Yet, observing my children learning to speak one language has demonstrated that learning English, their L1, has been plenty difficult on its own.

As a proficient Spanish speaker (although I began to learn Spanish late in life, in college classes followed by a semester abroad in Latin America, eventually becoming a teacher in a bilingual school), I did use Spanish in the home, including listening to large amounts of music in Spanish. However, because I was the only Spanish speaker in the family, speaking in Spanish among family members was infrequent. As suggested above, I thought at the time learning one language was "enough," and plenty difficult on its own, and I did not know at the time that they would have an opportunity to enter a bilingual school after a move to a different city. In terms of supporting English literacy for my children (and CALP in English), based on my research in this area, I knew that reading at home with children can have powerful effects on literacy development (Compton-Lilly, 2003, 2007; Knoester, 2009, 2010; Knoester & Plikuhn, 2015, 2016). I found in my research – corroborating that of many others – that there are powerful social aspects to reading, and that motivation to read often has a great deal to do with whether we could talk about the reading material with others. And, as admirers of Bowlby's Attachment Theory (Bowlby, 1988, 2005), my partner and I pursued the goal of building strong attachments with our children. Reading aloud along with children has been found to be strongly correlated with strong attachments (Bus, 2001; Bus & van Ijzendoorn, 1988), so reading aloud with our children has been a daily occurrence since they were born.

Both of our children also began attending (monolingual English) day care, at least part-time, starting at the age of 1. Nicolaus attended a day care that eventually included literacy aspects. For example, in his last year of daycare, when he was 4 years old, his teacher focused on a different letter each week. The students brought in "show-and-tell" items starting with that letter, there were many artworks created by students focusing on the letter of that week, etc. When my son started kindergarten at the age of 5 his teacher sent home a pre-primer book for him to either read or be read-to at home every day. I remember during the first week of kindergarten he read aloud to me a book with CVC words (consonant, vowel, consonant words), such as "sat" and "bat." It startled me. The school was a traditional monolingual English public elementary school and he thrived.

Three years later, our daughter also attended the same day care, but with different teachers, who did not give much attention to literacy development. It is also perhaps important to note that my daughter's birthday is July 1, so with school age cut-offs at September 1, she was among the youngest students in each of her classes. This contrasts with my son, whose birthday is in September, so he was always among the oldest in his classes. It became clear to us that this age difference in comparison to their peers sometimes led to what appeared to be delays in development, but were actually age-appropriate (NICHD, 2006).

Move to Milwaukee

In 2016 our family moved to another city. My partner desired to move to Milwaukee for a job opportunity there, and to be closer to her parents. The timing of the move made sense for several other reasons as well. Our daughter was "graduating" from her day care and our son had lost a good friendship and was indifferent to moving to a new school, just after 2nd grade. Emotionally, it felt like it would work for our kids. So, we moved to Milwaukee that summer to a house less than a mile from a two-way Spanish/English bilingual school, La Escuela Fratney, a school I read about many years prior and visited while in graduate school in Madison (Peterson, 2007). There was no guarantee that the school would accept our children, but I met with the principal and told her how much I knew about the school, had admired it for decades, and was a Spanish speaker and educator. She made an exception to allow our children to enter the school, despite not having attended a bilingual Spanish school previously. I promised the principal that I would work with our children on Spanish every day at home, a promise I have kept, although it has not always been easy.

As our family's resident expert at Spanish, comparatively speaking (and someone keenly interested in education), I took on the duty of helping the kids with speaking and reading in Spanish, along with continuing to read with the children in English. Of course, I saw their learning Spanish as a welcome opportunity to continue to practice/develop my own Spanish, as well as to create bilingual opportunities for the entire family. I began that summer by labeling many items in our house with Spanish words and speaking in Spanish as much as possible. That lasted throughout the summer. At the same time, our night-time routine included reading in Spanish every night, beginning with me reading to them in Spanish. We went shopping at local bookstores for all of the Spanish language children's books we could find.

Although in Evansville we focused on English, reading at night became a cherished bed-time routine throughout both of my children's lives almost from birth. After the Milwaukee move, and as both children began learning to read in both languages, the night-time reading routine became: (1) I read with Jubilee in English first while Nicolaus reads silently to himself in English. Jubilee first reads aloud to me, then I read aloud to her. (2) Jubilee reads to me and then I read to her (from the same book) in Spanish. (3) Jubilee can continue reading silently if she wishes, but I then start reading with Nicolaus in Spanish. First, he reads aloud to me in Spanish and then I read aloud to him in Spanish. Sometimes we switch every page.

I carefully chose books, along with the kids, that I thought they would be interested in, but were also an appropriate challenge. We already had favorite books in English. I began reading daily to my son and daughter in their infancy. However, when I challenged them to read aloud to me, starting at about age 5, we began with books that featured CVC words or were very predictable and familiar to them, such as *Bears on Wheels* (BR30L) and *Go, Dog, Go* (240L).

There are several ways in which I second-guess how I should have read aloud with my children. Should we have only read in Spanish (as the school focused on Spanish at a ratio of 90:10 in the earliest grades)? Should we have talked more about the books? Should we have avoided translations of the books? Should I have spoken more in Spanish (yes)? I believe the amount of Spanish learning that took place at home has meant not only that they have been perhaps more successful in their two-way bilingual school, but also that our family has been able to enjoy many bilingual experiences as a family in Milwaukee, as well as trips, such as to Mexico City. In Mexico our family was able to practice Spanish, enjoy time together, and our children could better understand the country in which many of their peers have roots and connections (my own ancestors are largely immigrants from the Netherlands, including my father, although, unfortunately, I did not learn the Dutch language or attend a school that offered a single course in Dutch, although I did overhear Dutch in my grandparents' house throughout my childhood).

The approach to literacy that I adopted at home could be characterized as "whole-language," In other words, I have read with both children using whole books (as opposed to worksheets or workbooks), which I have estimated to be on their reading level if I am asking them to read the book aloud to me, or above their reading level if I am reading the book aloud to them. The words in the books tell stories and are almost always accompanied by attractive illustrations. I realize that some educators and scholars argue that a better way to learn to read is by focusing on the phonemes and the phonics of reading, so children can see and better comprehend the complex rules of grammar, pronunciation, and spelling (Dehaene, 2009; Seidenberg, 2017). These educators and scholars are likely correct that understanding these patterns and rules are basic to reading; however, what they perhaps do not fully understand, or, at least I disagree with them on this, is that studying spelling, pronunciation, and grammatical rules is not a fun and endearing bed-time routine, leading to deeper attachments, day in and day out. If I taught my children to read intensely focusing on rules of grammar and spelling, I would expect much more resistance than I have ever faced with them by reading books of their choice (with gentle guidance regarding the appropriate reading level). By reading aloud with my children using attractive and compelling books – always with the element of choice on the part of my children about which book to read – I find almost no resistance (especially in English, although there is some resistance to Spanish at times), and, in fact, great enjoyment on their part and that of mine. This enjoyment has propelled us to reading literally thousands of books together over the past 12 years, a feat that I don't think would be possible if we were to study the tedious rules of English and Spanish spelling, pronunciation, and grammar.

Ongoing Questions

There are still substantial unanswered questions about the language and literacy learning of both of our kids, but for different reasons. The main challenge for Nicolaus seems to be that he can read Spanish phonetically, but he often does not understand the words that he is reading. However, because his BICS and CALP in English have been quite strong each step of the way, I feel that he has been able to better learn BICS and CALP in Spanish than if he had not developed solid reading skills or CALP in English. After conducting a running record with him in both Spanish and English, this intuition was confirmed. I found that he is reading substantially above grade level in English, and slightly below grade level in Spanish. I also know this in part because his writing in Spanish is decent, but still riddled with grammatical errors, while this is not the case in his English writing. He has said on multiple occasions that he feels he can express anything he wants to express using Spanish words, despite faulty grammar (particular difficulty with verb conjugations and misspelled words).

My daughter is a greater concern to me, for a variety of reasons. At the age of 8, based on running records she's completed with me recently, she is reading at the level "N" in English (equivalent to 530L–810L Lexile level) and the level "D" in Spanish (equivalent to 160L–310L Lexile level). So she is approximately on grade level in English and about two grade levels below her age/grade level in Spanish. Despite the fact that this chapter focuses on her at-home reading, I realize her reading ability involves a complex set of factors, and at-home reading is only one part of it (Meier & Knoester, 2017).

By design, La Escuela Fratney began teaching Jubilee both BICS and CALP almost entirely in Spanish, Jubilee's L2. This has been a challenge for her, and, understandably, she has at times resisted speaking and reading in Spanish at home, much more than did her older brother. Yet, I cannot blame the school. Of course, the primary focus of the school, as it should be, is to teach the most vulnerable students – native Spanish speakers – CALP in their L1, which then helps to facilitate learning CALP in their L2 (English). And research suggests that both native Spanish and native English speakers in the USA, where English is ubiquitous, learn BICS in English quite quickly and easily. At La Escuela Fratney, English is the *lingua franca* of the playground and social settings at school, part of the reason why the school chose to focus on Spanish at a 90:10 ratio in the early grades. However, for English-dominant students, such as my daughter, it does seem to be harder, or at least take more time, to learn CALP in an L2 if BICS in that same L2 is not yet firm, nor is CALP in her L1 well developed. So my observation is not that Fratney should change its approach, but it was important for me, as a parent, to realize that learning BICS and CALP in her L2, as well as CALP in her L1, would require a lot of time and patience (and faith) on our part, because learning CALP in her L1 was the last priority for the school, after teaching BICS and CALP in her L2. I imagine that she would struggle even more to read in both English and Spanish if she had not practiced reading in both languages at home on a daily basis.

As mentioned above, I sometimes question my own handling of this challenge in hindsight. There is not a lot of research literature available on parenting children enrolled in bilingual schools (Barbian, Gonzalez, & Mejía, 2017; Meshulam, 2019; Valdés, 1996). The extant literature almost always focuses on English language learners. Perhaps I should have begun reading to her in Spanish only, just as her school did. But reading and speaking in English was the "low-hanging fruit," so to speak, and felt almost effortless at home. In addition, I found that she did not want to practice Spanish at home. She wanted a respite, and given the ambitious goals of the school, and the initial stress of moving to a new school and city, I thought she could use one. Because speaking and reading in her L1 at home did not come with resistance at all, focusing on English literacy was easiest for us all.

The work of scholars such as Cummins, García, Baker and Wright, and Thomas and Collier, and other scholars of bilingual education demonstrate and remind us of the strong research support for two-way bilingual education. These schools offer crucial learning opportunities, not only in bilingualism and biliteracy, but in critical multicultural education and citizenship in a diverse democracy (Peterson, 2017). Further, La Escuela Fratney was intentionally designed to interrupt the severe racial segregation in Milwaukee (Peterson, 2007), intentionally serving both Spanish- and English-dominant students of all races. However, keeping a demographic balance has also been a struggle for the school, particularly with continuing to attract black English-dominant families (Meshulam & Apple, 2014).

This chapter has provided the opportunity to critically reflect upon and to analyze the experiences of two English-dominant children who have had different experiences in one two-way bilingual Spanish/English primary school. I have drawn on theory and empirical research to hypothesize about the various challenges these children have faced in their development of BICS and CALP in their LI and L2. More research is needed in these areas, but extant theory and research suggests that English-dominant parents or guardians who send their children to two-way bilingual schools may need a bit of extra patience and at-home reading support and practice as their children learn to read and write in two languages, often starting with their L2. However, research suggests that the benefits of bilingualism, biliteracy, and multicultural education far outweigh the additional efforts involved.

Acknowledgment

I would like to thank Assaf Meshulam, George Iber, Hervé Somé, Laurie Henry, and Norm Stahl for helpful comments on earlier drafts of this chapter.

References

Baker, C., & Wright, W. E. (2017). *Foundations of bilingual education and bilingualism* (6th ed.). Multilingual Matters. https://doi.org/10.1007/978-3-319-02258-1_2

Barbian, E., Gonzalez, G. C., & Mejía, P. (Eds.). (2017). *Rethinking bilingual education: Welcoming home languages in our classrooms.* Rethinking Schools.

Beeman, K., & Urow, C. (2013). *Teaching for biliteracy: Strengthening bridges between languages.* Carlson.

Bowlby, J. (1988). *A secure base: Parent–child attachment and healthy human development.* Basic Books.

Bowlby, J. (2005). *The making and breaking of affectional bonds.* Routledge.

Bus, A. G. (2001). Parent–child book reading through the lens of attachment theory. In L. Verhoeven & C. Snow (Eds.), *Literacy and motivation: Reading engagement in individuals and groups* (pp. 39–53). Lawrence Erlbaum Associates.

Bus, A. G., & van Ijzendoorn, M. H. (1988). Attachment and early reading: A longitudinal study. *Journal of Genetic Psychology, 149*, 199–210. https://doi.org/10.1080/00221325.1988.10532153

Center for Applied Linguistics. (2018). The national K-12 foreign language enrollment survey report. Retrieved from www.americancouncils.org/sites/default/files/FLE-report-June17.pdf

Center for Applied Linguistics. (2019). Databases and directories. Retrieved from www.cal.org/resource-center/databases-directories

Chomsky, N. (1988). *Language and problems of knowledge: The Managua lectures.* MIT Press.

Compton-Lilly, C. (2003). *Reading families: The literate lives of urban children.* Teachers College Press.

Compton-Lilly, C. (2007). *Re-reading families: The literate lives of urban children four years later.* Teachers College Press.

Cummins, J. (1984). *Bilingualism and special education: Issues in assessment and pedagogy.* Multilingual Matters.

Cummins, J. (2000). *Language, power and pedagogy: Bilingual children in the crossfire.* Multilingual Matters. https://doi.org/10.21832/9781853596773

Cummins, J. (2001). *Negotiating identities: Education for empowerment in a diverse society* (2nd ed.). California Association for Bilingual Education.

Dehaene, S. (2009). *Reading in the brain: The new science of how we read.* Penguin Books.

Dicker, S. J. (1993). The universal second language requirement: An inadequate substitute for bilingual education (A response to Aaron Wildavsky). *Journal of Policy Analysis and Management, 12*(4), 779–785. https://doi.org/10.2307/3325351

García, O. (2009). *Bilingual education in the 21st century: A global perspective.* Wiley-Blackwell.

Garcia, O., & Sung, K. K. (2018). Critically assessing the 1968 Bilingual Education Act at 50 years: Taming tongues and Latinx communities. *Bilingual Research Journal, 41*(4), 318–333. https://doi.org/10.1080/15235882.2018.1529642

García, O., & Wei, L. (2014). *Translanguaging: Language, bilingualism and education.* Palgrave Macmillan. https://doi.org/10.1057/9781137385765_4

Gee, J. P. (2015). *Social linguistics and literacies: Ideology in discourses* (5th ed.). Routledge. https://doi.org/10.4324/9781315722511

Huddy, L., & Sears, D. O. (1995). Opposition to bilingual education: Prejudice or the defense of realistic interests? *Social Psychology Quarterly, 58*(2), 133–143. https://doi.org/10.2307/2787151

Kendi, I. X. (2016). *Stamped from the beginning: The definitive history of racist ideas in America.* Nation Books.

Knoester, M. (2003). Education according to Chomsky. *Mind, Culture & Activity, 10*(3), 266–270. https://doi.org/10.1207/s15327884mca1003_10

Knoester, M. (2009). Inquiry into urban adolescent reading habits: Can Gee's theory of Discourses provide insight? *Journal of Adolescent & Adult Literacy, 52*(8), 676–685. https://doi.org/10.1598/JAAL.52.8.3

Knoester, M. (2010). Independent reading and the "social turn": How adolescent reading habits and motivation may be related to cultivating social relationships. *Networks, 12*(1), 1–13. https://doi.org/10.4148/2470-6353.1099

Knoester, M. (2012a). *Democratic education in practice: Inside the Mission Hill School.* Teachers College Press.

Knoester, M. (2012b). *International struggles for critical democratic education.* Peter Lang.

Knoester, M., & Plikuhn, M. (2015). Influence of siblings on out-of-school reading practices. *Journal of Research in Reading, 39*(4), 469–485. https://doi.org/10.1111/1467-9817.12059

Knoester, M., & Plikuhn, M. (2016). Inquiry into the independent reading development of first-generation college graduates with advanced degrees. *Journal of Literacy Research, 48*(1), 105–126. https://doi.org/10.1177/108629X16658739

Meier, D., & Knoester, M. (2017). *Beyond testing: Seven assessments for students and schools more effective than standardized tests.* Teachers College Press.

Meshulam, A. (2019). Cross-national comparison of parental choice of two-way bilingual education in the United States and Israel. *Comparative Education Review, 63*(2), 236–258. https://doi.org/10.1086/702539

Meshulam, A., & Apple, M. W. (2014). Interrupting the interruption: Neoliberalism and the challenges of an antiracist school. *British Journal of Sociology of Education, 35*(5), 650–669. https://doi.org/10.1080/01425692.2014.919847

Milwaukee Public Schools. (2020). District enrollment and demographics. Retrieved from https://mps.milwaukee.k12.wi.us/en/District/About-MPS/School-Board/Office-of-Accountability-Efficiency/Public-Items-Emjay/District-Enrollment.htm

Mitchell, C. (March 19, 2019). Bilingual teachers are in short supply. How can schools cultivate their own? *Education Week.* Retrieved from http://blogs.edweek.org/edweek/learning-the-language/2019/03/bilingual_teachers_shortage.html

NICHD Early Child Care Research Network. (2006). Age of entry to kindergarten and children's academic achievement and socioemotional development. *Early Education and Development, 18*(2), 337–368. https://doi.org/10.1080/10409280701283460

Peterson, B. (2007). La Escuela Fratney: A journey towards democracy. In A. Apple, & J. Beane (Eds.), *Democratic schools: Lessons in powerful education* (2nd ed.). Heinemann.

Peterson, B. (2017). La Escuela Fratney: Creating a bilingual school as a greenhouse of democracy. In E. Barbian, G. C. Gonzalez, & P. Mejía (Eds.), *Rethinking bilingual education: Welcoming home languages in our classrooms.* Rethinking Schools.

Pinker, S. (2007). *The language instinct: How the mind creates language.* Harper Perennial Modern Classics.

Rhodes, R. L., Ochoa, S. H., & Ortiz, S. O. (2005). *Assessing culturally and linguistically diverse students.* Guilford Press.

Seidenberg, M. (2017). *Language at the speed of sight: How we read, why so many can't and what can be done about it.* Basic Books.

Selden, S. (1999). *Inheriting shame: The story of eugenics and racism in America.* Teachers College Press.

Spolsky, B. (2004). *Language policy.* Cambridge University Press.

Thomas, W. P., & Collier, V. P. (2012). *Dual language education for a transformed world.* Fuente Press.

Valdés, G. (1996). *Con respeto: Bridging the distances between culturally diverse families and schools.* Teachers College Press.

Wilson, D. M. (2011). Dual language programs on the rise. *Harvard Education Letter, 27*(2), 1–2.

4

NURTURING MULTIPLE LITERACIES

The Role of Community and Creativity in an Intergenerational ESOL Class[*]

Lily Applebaum and Mara Imms-Donnelly

CABRINI CENTER

Emily Rose Schwab

UNIVERSITY OF PENNSYLVANIA

What does a learning community look like in a bilingual, mixed-level, inter-generational literacy classroom? How can adults and children learn together in the same environment? These questions and more emerged through our practice as educators in an adult English for Speakers of Other Languages (ESOL) program that expanded its offerings to include family literacy programming. Run through a faith-based community center – here called the Cabrini Center – in a northeastern United States city in a racially and ethnically diverse urban area, our work as ESOL educators was to be at once student-centered and responsive to larger communities' desires. Through our writing, we examine how we as educators worked to transfer and grow our values as a program through the new, intergenerational family ESOL class, ultimately reaching a group of students who were new to the center's ESOL programming and engaging new teaching approaches.

As a practitioner inquiry study (Cochran-Smith & Lytle, 2009), our research is a documentation of our experience bringing theory and practice together in a family literacy context. In this chapter, we begin with a history of the ESOL program, tracing the roots of our pedagogical commitments. We then describe how we re-evaluated and reshaped our pedagogy to fit the needs of the new ESOL class. Using data from class interactions, we analyze the reciprocal relationship between inviting student creativity and building community in family literacy contexts. We aim to be in conversation with other practitioners both at the

---

[*] All direct quotes found in the text have been translated from Spanish by the authors.

institutional and classroom level as well as researchers interested in responsive and student-centered teaching in adult and family literacy.

The Cabrini Center ESOL Program: A Brief History and Contextualization

The urban neighborhood where the Cabrini Center is situated contains an overlapping and complex web of communities that move through and shape the space. Historically, African American and Italian American communities called the neighborhood home, but throughout the past 40 years, immigrants and refugees representing a breadth of cultures, languages, and identities have put down roots, including significant numbers of people who identify as Indonesian, Vietnamese, Filipinx, Latinx, Sudanese, and Congolese (Campano, Ghiso, & Welch, 2016). A wide variety of community programming occurs within the space, some of it run by the Center itself (as is the case with the ESOL program), and some of it run by outside organizations and groups who use the space.

The Cabrini Center is located on a city block where it shares a campus with the larger St. Francis Cabrini church and affiliated Mission School. While the church and school have been present for many generations and have served as an anchor for the surrounding community, the Center was more recently established in 2013. Located within a former convent, the Center was founded with a new initiative to provide space for its many communities to have additional meeting room, engage in cross-cultural exchange, and further build community across faith, language, and cultural differences. One of the many projects that utilizes the Cabrini space and has shaped the history of Cabrini ESOL is the research practice partnership between the University of Pennsylvania and the larger St. Francis community. Through this partnership, established in 2010, researchers from Penn have worked with community members to identify the many ways they as racially and ethnically marginalized communities advocate for educational access. Part of this research has included co-constructing literacy learning opportunities with St. Francis community members as research inquiries.

While ESOL classes have been offered in the Cabrini community for decades by different community organizations, the most recent iteration of ESOL began in partnership with University of Pennsylvania (Penn). Initially begun in response to community members requesting English language classes, Penn practitioner-researchers taught a once-weekly intergenerational class serving Latinx families on Saturdays during Spanish language catechism. While this class met for several years, community members requested a shift to night classes for adult learners. Since 2014, volunteers from both Penn and Cabrini have run biweekly classes in the Center's basement. Over the years, Penn researchers worked with Cabrini staff to assume full responsibility for running the ESOL program to ensure long-term sustainability and responsiveness to students' needs. Each year of the program has involved consistent reflection between all teachers in service of being more responsive to students' interests and desires for learning.

Our flexibility and commitment to reflexivity has been a hallmark of our approach and is rooted in critical approaches to adult literacy pedagogy, which emphasize student-centered and culturally engaged approaches to teaching (Auerbach et al., 1996; Ramdeholl, 2011; Wong, 2006). Unlike ESOL classes taking an assimilationist approach that emphasize one proper way to teach and speak English, we attempt to teach English in a way that forwards communication and community. Our program also emphasizes the social dimensions of literacy, understanding that literacy is a social practice that extends beyond decoding the written word (Freebody & Luke, 1990; Street, 2005; The New London Group, 1996). We understand literacy and language learning to look different in different contexts and see that literacy and language are mobilized uniquely by each individual depending on their personal background and experiences. We take this theoretical approach into practice by starting from students' strengths and their initial inquiries that brought them to English class. Rather than using a predetermined curriculum or anchor textbook, we craft iterative curricula that attempt to encompass students' desires for learning. We also consciously look for funding that enables us to take this open-ended view, eschewing funding which would require large-scale testing and adherence to narrow definitions of success.

We as writers of this piece come to Cabrini through different channels and shape the narrative accordingly. Lily, whose primary job is in a community writing center outside of Cabrini, began volunteering at the Center in 2016 and continues to volunteer in the ESOL program. Mara joined Cabrini as an AmeriCorps VISTA-funded staff member in 2017, where she served for two years until 2019 as the ESOL coordinator and ran various arts-based programs at Cabrini. Emily was a Penn graduate research assistant and was brought to the work in 2014 as part of the larger Penn/Cabrini research partnership, eventually serving as a lead teacher for several years and collecting data for her dissertation on ESOL learning before leaving in 2018. As three people who identify as white, primarily English-speaking women living with documented status in the USA, a major aspect of our work as ESOL teachers attempting a progressive approach was to be reflexive about the limitations of our perspectives and the harmful ideologies we might perpetuate as beneficiaries of racist and anti-immigrant power structures that shape US society. Our inquiries as teachers are rooted in these concerns as well as those of our students.

Building a New Intergenerational Class

In the summer of 2018, a pastoral associate and leader in the Latinx community expressed the desire for Cabrini to provide an ESOL class that would coincide with Saturday morning bilingual catechism classes for children, called Catecismo, much like the Saturday intergenerational ESOL class that had been offered years before. In response, this intergenerational class for Catecismo parents was born, to be taught by Mara and Lily, who had collaborated before teaching in the adult ESOL program.

Neither Mara nor Lily had formal training in teaching ESOL but had spent several collective years teaching in the program and learning about ESOL pedagogy through practice and mentoring relationships, most directly with Emily. Through frequent planning meetings in our time teaching together, we all three discussed and sought to mobilize a pedagogy that saw students as experts on their own learning and that valued students' multiple literacies and language competencies. Both Mara and Lily were committed to extending these pedagogical values, assuming an inquiry stance with regard to their own teaching practice in forming an intergenerational ESOL class.

An extension of Mara and Lily's inquiry included a focus on creativity in their teaching. When they taught together in past adult ESOL classes, their planning often lead to creative, project-based curricula, drawing on Lily's experience teaching in a literary arts center and Mara's experience running youth arts-based programming. Mara and Lily conceptualized creative play and expression within the classroom as a way to level the playing field between parents and children, instructors and students, and learners' varying levels of familiarity with English. Confirmed by literature which spoke to the value of utilizing play, multimodality, and creative expression as a tool to rupture typical patterns of interactions and hierarchies that might be present in an ESOL classroom (Britsch, 2009; Smith, 2016), they decided to approach this new intergenerational class with the goal of deepening the role of creativity in order to create a playful, generative space where students could employ the creative skills already within them.

Because the class was a new program to the center, it initially received little funding. It largely relied on Lily's volunteered labor, Mara's compensated time as a VISTA-funded staff member, and the center's reserves of donated art and school supplies. By November 2018, the class had received a small grant with few outcome-based requirements, allowing Lily to be paid for her time. This was in contrast to many adult education programs, which, constrained by funding requirements, must comply with the neoliberal goal of preparing their students for the workforce (Abendroth, 2014). Instead of mediating instructor and student goals within imposed external standards, Lily and Mara worked within the more flexible framework of their own pedagogical approaches, the goals of their students, and the expectations of their community-based institution.

Methodology and Participants

Eager to document the class formation as a unique opportunity to transfer long-practiced pedagogical values into a new context, Lily and Mara decided to approach their first year of teaching the Creative Family ESOL class as a practitioner inquiry study (Cochran-Smith & Lytle, 2009). Instructors informed students that they were conducting an ethnographic study of the new class and a consent form was provided in English and explained in Spanish for students to sign if they chose to do so. All of the directly quoted data in this chapter were taken from students who gave their consent, although names are not included in this chapter to protect students' confidentiality. Data were collected during the first class year, from September 2018 to May 2019, and include student work, instructor reflections, student feedback, and classroom conversations that were recorded on whiteboards. Instructors reflected on how the day's lesson went after every class.

The class followed a model in which two instructors prepared lesson plans and facilitated most classroom activities with support from volunteers. The presence of volunteers was a strategy learned from the pre-existing ESOL classes, and students and children benefited from the extra support. Although no teachers or volunteers were required to speak Spanish, both instructors and all three volunteers spoke Spanish proficiently. Instructors encouraged volunteers to be active participants in the class, acting as supports for students and interjecting with clarifications and feedback during lessons.

In order to lower barriers to entry and learning for all students, the class followed a pay-as-you-wish model and provided supplies and snacks for students each week. The class had consistent attendance from week to week, likely due to the timing of the class which intentionally coincided with Catecismo for students' older children. The average weekly attendance was ten, and each adult, on average, brought one child to class. The students were primarily Spanish-speaking mothers and a few fathers who attended less frequently. Children of speaking age were bilingual in English and Spanish. Without formal testing to stratify English proficiency levels, the instructors informally identified almost all students as beginner to mid-beginner, although they did not separate proficiency levels during the class.

Constructing a Creative ESOL Curriculum

When asked at the midterm to answer the question: "Why do you come to English class?" student responses reflected concerns with family, social growth, and personal development: "Because I would like to learn to be able to converse with all types of cultures, and it's necessary to learn English here"; "I come to learn to be able to communicate with my daughter and to be able to make appointments with the doctor"; "For my own knowledge and to be able to help my children in their personal and academic development, and to not make mistakes filling out documents"; "I come to learn so that I can understand other people, to be able to understand my children"; "I come to class to be able to learn the language and therefore to teach it to my daughter with all the security that I am saying and pronouncing the words correctly."

Because the expected outcome of the ESOL classroom is, ultimately, learning English, it can be tempting to construct a curriculum that focuses on grammar only. The Center's ESOL classes have long resisted this model as part of rejecting the concept of ESOL solely being about language transference or workplace preparedness; as illustrated by student responses above, many ESOL students themselves don't subscribe to that narrative. We opted instead for content that hews closer to the conventional ELA classroom, where the learning of specific skills might be more incidental than direct. Students will likely walk away from class thinking "I learned about x" rather than "I learned how to x."

For example, students indicated that they wanted to learn how to ask for/read directions. To translate their goal into curriculum, we printed out maps of the neighborhood and asked students to draw their path to class, legitimizing non-language means of expression. We asked students to write a set of instructions for traveling to specific neighborhood landmarks, making them experts and shifting what is often a moment of vulnerability (being lost, asking for directions) to a moment of being in control (giving directions, telling their classmates about bus routes in the neighborhood). To practice cardinal directions/words for motion, we had the class shout instructions guiding a blindfolded instructor from the front of the classroom to the back, bringing in a sense of creativity, joy, and play with a silly activity. We played a version of Simon Says where all students stood up and moved in space according to a direction called out by instructors such as "left" or "behind you," which again brought a sense of play and also an activity parents and toddlers enjoyed doing together.

Community Building

The creativity, shifted expertise, and play involved in lessons like the directions unit example strengthened the overall class community. We argue that this sense of community was an essential tool for family literacy. When children and parents felt validated in all their various modes of thinking and expression within the ESOL classroom space, they took risks and formed family and community bonds. Below, we explore different aspects of the classroom community and its relationship to literacy learning.

Parent–Child Relationships as a Classroom Resource

In earlier ESOL classes at the center, making free childcare available increased accessibility. But for this new population of students, as confirmed by the midterm reflection cited above, students' goals for family literacy and goals for learning English were inextricable, and childcare needed to be less of a logistical burden to be solved by the institution, and instead, a classroom asset and resource we built together. Children ranged in age from infancy to early elementary, making a

FIGURE 4.1 Mother and Son Favorite Holiday Pictures
On the left, a mother's artwork illustrating a project about favorite holidays, worked side by side with her son's similar illustration from the same project on the right

rigid curriculum and learning goals for all ages nearly impossible given time and material constraints. We focused instead on making space for children's multiple literacies, with creative play toys and drawing supplies always available, and by allowing parents to enforce any rules for discipline or behavior. The result was that families maintained their sovereignty within the classroom space, and parents were free to leave their children to play independently or get them involved in class activities at a developmentally appropriate level.

In practice, sometimes parents and children sat side by side working on the same activity and used creativity as a bridge between generations/languages spoken, as in Figure 4.1, where a mother and son drew similar pictures in a creative activity. Students were asked to write a sentence about their favorite holiday of the year and how they celebrate, using a vocabulary list about holidays and celebrations. The visual similarities between the compositions and the shape of the Christmas tree show a shared visual dictionary and the differences between the drawings show the special, hybrid space somewhere between working collaboratively and working independently made possible by the classroom where parents and children work side by side.

In Figure 4.2, a son provided the illustration for his mother's vocabulary definition. In this example, students were asked to look up and define a new word they learned from a reading and write it in their own words. The son might not have been advanced enough to write the sentence definition of the word "looking," but he was able to use his creativity to convey meaning. In a case where a bilingual child might otherwise be taking the role as translator between parent and outside world, he is able to contribute equally to the making of meaning with his mother.

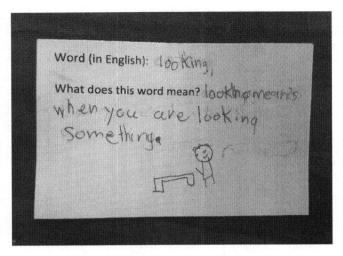

FIGURE 4.2 Student's Vocabulary Word Definition with Illustration

Challenging Classroom Hierarchies: Students as Resources for Each Other

It was essential to strive for shared power between students, volunteers and instructors to meet our students' goals for empowerment and family literacy, especially as white, native speakers of English who are not parents. One major strategy we employed was maintaining a room where students were a resource for one another.

One way that students became a resource for one another was in providing the communally shared snack. A few months into the year, students self-organized a system for sharing the work of bringing snacks to class. They did this on their own, many of them getting one another's contact information for the first time in order to organize, with one student taking charge to assign a snack calendar that was followed with precision. We did not intervene, despite the fact that the center would have provided snacks, instead recognizing that this was a defining moment for students feeling comfortable and taking ownership of the room. This was an essential moment where providing a snack shifted from an institutional structure applied to the class to a joyful and sometimes celebratory class community act, such as when students brought tamales on Día de la Candelaria so they could celebrate this meaningful holiday while in ESOL class.

Additionally, the site of many hierarchy-challenging interactions was the whiteboard, which was the most conventionally hierarchical space in our classroom. As often as possible, student voices guided our whiteboard writing, whether that was through brainstorming sessions where student answers were written on the board, through students themselves being the ones to write vocabulary or answers on the board, or through students correcting the instructors' Spanish at the board, emphasizing how Spanish is a second language for both Mara and Lily.

For example, the day before Easter break, we led students in a brainstorm, in Spanish, of ways they could practice their English over the break. Students shared suggestions with the whole class which instructors wrote on the board, such as "watch movies with subtitles in English, listen to music in English, practice at work, practice with your children." Another similar class brainstorm was for strategies for reading. Students gave suggestions for what to do when they don't understand something they're reading, or when their children don't understand something they're reading, such as (translated from Spanish), "ask someone, use Google translate, circle the words to return later, use context, look for cognates." In this way, students, instructors, *and* their children took turns being "experts" in reading and literacy and defined together what literacy in practice looks like for them.

Normalizing Vulnerability

The primary finding of this inquiry into our community building practices was simple but essential: time together in the classroom is the most necessary component. When that time was spent creatively engaged in play and expression, bonds formed quickly, and inhibitions lowered visibly as the first few months went on.

Particularly, the creative elements of the class helped to normalize expression and vulnerability, and thereby promote family literacy. Perhaps the best example comes from a unit on Yuyi Morales's picture book *Dreamers*. We chose this book, which features a migrant mother and her son using a library to harness their own story-telling capabilities, because it presented a story students could connect with as immigrants and as students engaged in defining their own literacy practices. As a pre-reading activity, students were asked to examine the book's illustrations and write one sentence describing a page of the story before ever reading it (see Figure 4.3). Students had to read the visual information on the page and practice the present progressive verb tense, asserting the validity of their own observations as much as the written information being studied on the page. Students wrote their sentences directly onto the whiteboard next to their image, so the overall effect was a class-created version of the story before reading the "real" written story.

Then, after listening to instructors read the book once while they followed along, students were invited to volunteer to read a page aloud to the class if they wanted to. With, at this point, a deep familiarity with the text, several adults volunteered. The most notable moment came when a child chose to volunteer to read a page. This child had spent most of the previous classes less engaged in structured class activities and instead drawing quietly with his younger cousin. During the *Dreamers* read-aloud activity, he unexpectedly volunteered, came to the front of the classroom, and when he read his page of the book all the students

She is walkin in the stree with her son.

She's looking up.

listening to the in his head

She is casing her shadow

They are catching the Library card

the dog is listening to voices in the in his head

FIGURE 4.3 Class-Created Version of Story

clapped and cheered. It was a victorious moment, a convergence of subject matter that dealt directly with family literacy from Morales's beautiful story, a legitimizing of art and creativity that came from spending an entire class year encouraging and legitimizing this student's visual literacy practice of drawing with his cousin during class, and a community built in the room over about seven months. In an environment where expression of all forms by all ages was encouraged, it is no wonder that this student, although shy and more comfortable in the visual realm, felt comfortable coming to the front of the room to read out loud.

Conclusion

Although we were largely satisfied with how the class went, moving forward, we want to note a few areas for continued evaluation and improvement. Our biggest inquiry concerns language. During the weeknight adult ESOL classes also held at the center, students come to class speaking a variety of languages; anyone is welcome to take the class, and a diverse range of people do. Because our class was held at the same time as Saturday morning Catecismo (Spanish Catechism classes) the vast majority of students were Spanish-speaking and parents of young children, except for one young, childless Vietnamese-speaking student who attended two classes before stopping attendance. Consequently, we grappled over the language of our instruction. Before the Vietnamese-speaking student stopped coming to class, we deferred to English instruction with individualized support in Spanish. After that student stopped coming, we switched to a bilingual instruction model, which was much better suited to the needs of the majority of the class. This highlighted an interesting tension regarding diversity and equity, raising many questions about the linguistic resources offered to students in the diverse Cabrini community. If this class was specifically geared toward Spanish-speaking students due to its timing, should we market the class for Spanish-speaking students only? If so, should there also be a class geared toward Vietnamese-speaking students, who also compose a large subset of the Cabrini community? Or should we continue to welcome students of all linguistic backgrounds to the class, knowing that, in a class of mostly Spanish-speaking students, they may feel alienated by our use of Spanish despite everyone's best efforts to make them feel welcome? In a community as large and diverse as Cabrini's, similar tensions often arise, and it merits further evaluation and conversation among the many subgroups of the Cabrini community.

Overall, in detailing the creation of a new Creative Family ESOL class within an already defined institutional structure, we hope to provide information helpful to both administrators and instructors of community-based ESOL programs and to researchers curious about adult and family literacy in community-based settings. To that end, we want to highlight the fact that the Creative Family ESOL class is situated within years of an ESOL program that sought to employ a student-centered, culturally responsive, strengths-based approach, and grounded itself in the idea of literacy as a social practice. Furthermore, the self-reflexivity built into the program, as well as strong mentorship relationships that transferred this pedagogical approach, were foundational to the Creative Family ESOL class described in this chapter. We were able to exercise a great deal of creativity when conceptualizing, planning, and teaching the class because of the responsiveness and flexibility already built into the ESOL program's structure. Furthermore, we find that qualitative, rather than quantitative, methods of evaluating the success of the course dovetailed nicely with our inquiry-based, student-centered, self-reflexive approach, allowing for conversation and, ultimately, relationship, among instructors, students, and volunteers, to guide adjustments we made to the class throughout its first two semesters.

Verbal expression is one of the dominant modes by which people interface with the world, and learning a new language is a uniquely vulnerable task. We sought to use community and creativity to build a space where this vulnerability was welcomed and celebrated. Our creative pedagogy didn't just provide space for people to learn English, it was a space open to social relationships and many different modes and practices of literacy. By posing literacy as a social practice (Freebody & Luke, 1990; Street, 2005; The New London Group, 1996), we were able to make the space for the varied practices that students brought to class with them, as well as the ones that were co-constructed in the social environment of the class itself. Students had many, valid options for self-expression in our ESOL classroom regardless of how advanced or beginner their English was, using creativity as a source for expression as they puzzled through improving their

English. This sense of play and safety worked to create a classroom that, instead of highlighting all the linguistic abilities students lacked, positioned the multitude of child and adult literacies as resources that students, and the classroom community as a whole, already possessed.

References

Abendroth, M. (2014). Adult education at risk: Fronts of resistance to neoliberalism. *Adult Education Research Conference*. https://newprairiepress.org/aerc/2014/papers/1

Auerbach, E. R., Barahona, B., Midy, J., Vaquerano, F., Zambrano, A., & Arnaud, J. (1996). *Adult ESL/literacy from the community to the community: A guidebook for participatory literacy training*. Lawrence Erlbaum Associates.

Britsch, S. B. (2012). ESOL educators and the experience of visual literacy. *TESOL Quarterly*, *43*(4), 710–721. https://doi.org/10.1002/j.1545–7249.2009.tb00197.x

Campano, G., Ghiso, M. P., & Welch, B. J. (2016). *Partnering with immigrant communities: Action through literacy*. Teachers College Press.

Cochran-Smith, M., & Lytle, S. (2009). *Inquiry as stance: Practitioner research for the next generation*. Teachers College Press.

Freebody, P., & Luke, A. (1990). Literacies programmes: Debates and demands in cultural contexts. *Prospect: An Australian Journal of TESOL*, *5*(3), 7–16. https://eprints.qut.edu.au/49099/

Ramdeholl, D. (2011). *Adult literacy in a new era: Reflections from the Open Book*. Paradigm.

Smith, A. S. (2016). Creative English: Balancing creative and functional language needs for adult refugees, asylum seekers and migrants. *Scenario*, *10*(1), 1–17. https://doi.org/10.33178/scenario

Street, B. V. (2005). Recent applications of new literacy studies in educational contexts. *Research in the Teaching of English*, *39*(1), 417–423. www.jstor.org/stable/40171646

The New London Group. (1996). A pedagogy of multiliteracies: Designing social futures. *Harvard Educational Review*, *66*(1), 60–93. https://doi.org/10.17763/haer.66.1.17370n67v22j160u

Wong, S. (2006). *Dialogic approaches to TESOL: Where the gingko tree grows*. Lawrence Erlbaum Associates.

5

A UNIVERSITY/SCHOOL PARTNERSHIP PRACTICUM WITH CULTURALLY DIVERSE STUDENTS AND TEACHERS

Joyce C. Fine

DEPARTMENT OF TEACHING AND LEARNING, FLORIDA INTERNATIONAL UNIVERSITY

A University/School Partnership Practicum with Culturally Diverse Students

As the result of the No Child Left Behind Act of 2001 (2002), the state of Florida designated a predominately Haitian high school in northeast Miami as an "F" school. The school was already a Title 1 school with 89% economically disadvantaged students and a minority rate of 99%. The threat of consequences to the school for that poor grade motivated the administration to reach out to the local, public, urban, minority-serving university, Florida International University (FIU), to see if there were any people or programs that might be able to work to improve the literacy of their students. That call was referred to me, the Master of Science, Reading/Literacy Education Program Director. I had been conducting a practicum focused on adolescent literacy at various locations including the Juvenile Detention Center, the Teen Court building, and another high school. I immediately said I would be delighted to work with the administration and the students in the school. We formed a partnership between the university and the school and have been working harmoniously ever since. This opportunity was a great match. The candidates in the Master of Science in Reading/Literacy Education, a K-12 program, would have a new, welcoming location for a practicum focused on adolescent literacy, and the school would have dedicated reading professionals to address their situation.

Design of the Program

The Master of Science in Reading/Literacy Education (MS) program at FIU is based on a sociocultural perspective which emphasizes social, cultural, and historical factors in the context of learning. Based on the writings of Bronfenbrenner (1979), Moll (1994), and Au (1997), students learn best when there is an understanding of the culture and "funds of knowledge" (Moll, 1994) that the students bring to their learning. Working with this school would help the predominantly Hispanic teachers, who were comfortable teaching in bilingual, English–Spanish, settings, stretch to learn about and work with students of the Haitian culture. This would give them the opportunity to explore culturally sustaining pedagogy (CSP; Alim & Paris, 2017), which seeks to foster linguistic, literate, and cultural pluralism rather than viewing the students as having deficits in their English Language Arts. This perspective of CSP builds on Ladson-Billings's (1995) theory of culturally relevant pedagogy, the master's students have studied in their earlier course work, which suggests that teachers include literature to motivate students of color to read and to learn (Olukolu, 2013). They would be able to appreciate the Haitian culture and community as well as to learn ways to communicate with and teach students who spoke Creole as their first language and yet are held accountable to meet the state standards that are based on the White, middle-class, dominant cultural and educational norms in order to graduate with a high school diploma.

The three-credit course, Practicum in Reading, focused on adolescent literacy, was a second practicum contributing knowledge toward the master's degree. The other practicum was focused on teaching reading at the elementary level and integrated diagnosis and remediation courses. This second practicum was designed as an afterschool literacy program. The high school tutoring program, named the Reading Scene, was initiated on Monday nights during the school year, with free tutoring from 5:00 to 7:00 p.m. and 40 minutes of graduate instruction by the professor after tutoring.

Because the high school students had been at school from early in the morning and were very hungry by 5:00 p.m., they were served pizza and drinks. Parents or guardians and students had signed consent forms in English, and translated in Spanish and Creole, before the students could participate in the sessions. The high school students were committed to learning and the master's candidates were dedicated to teaching their best lessons to improve students' reading and writing. High school students received extra credit attendance slips in the form of "pioneer bucks" that they gave to their Intensive Reading teachers to show they had participated. There has not been any funding involved, other than the university paying for the pizza and drinks.

The program was designed to give opportunities to differentiate lessons for students at different levels. The teacher candidates worked with 3–5 students for the first hour and a half and needed to adapt their lessons to be appropriate for their students' different abilities and needs. For the last half hour, communities of two teachers joined their groups together, forming multiple communities within the room. For the last half hour, there were different activities in each community involving interaction and performance between the students. When the practicum first began, the time was devoted to participation in games having to do with literacy, such as Scrabble© or Apples to Oranges©, other word games, or even Reader's Theatre. The goal was to motivate adolescent students (Wentzel & Wigfield, 2009) to see that literacy was entertaining, engaging, and enjoyable with friends. The thought was that if adolescents left with smiles on their faces after this type of socializing, they would be encouraged to return for more tutoring the next week. While this was productive, upon my further reflection and evaluation, I thought that the time could still be engaging and enjoyable, but it could also become more educational and empowering. By connecting to local, national, and worldwide current events, students were given a chance to develop another level of influence, the *exosystem*, which was deemed important for affecting student's development, according to Bronfenbrenner (1979). Starting last year, during the last half hour, students spent the time reading, discussing, and writing about the news. This gave students a chance to engage while learning about their world and to express their opinions. This connection to their literacy, especially reading and writing about the incidence of gun violence at a local high school, gave them a chance to express their emotions such as outrage and fears. They gained a voice on topics that low-achieving students do not often get to share during the regular school day. For adolescents, who are advancing toward voting age, this awareness of their world was an important reason to add this activity to the practicum.

This course was also designed as a service-learning course. Service-learning is based upon the work of Dewey (1916), who stated that true learning comes when students are actively involved in their own learning experiences and have mutual exchanges with people and the environment. Freire (1970) elaborated upon Dewey's ideas to emphasize the importance of reflection in service-learning. Service-learning in the context of this practicum is about providing a credit-earning educational experience for students to actively address the school's needs while reflecting on the teaching of reading to adolescents and to better understand the cultural, linguistic, and social environment. Service-learning courses have been created at the elementary, secondary, and higher educational levels. Kahne and Westheimer (1996) have studied concepts of citizenship in relation to service-learning. They describe three types of citizenship: (1) personally responsible, (2) participatory, and (3) justice-oriented citizenship. While they see these as distinct types, James and Iverson (2009) have studied citizenship in teacher education and found that there is a continuum and that pre-service teachers can move from being personally responsible (such as voting), to participatory (need to be part of something larger and taking action), to being change-oriented (hoping to make a difference). They preferred to think of justice-oriented citizenship as change-oriented citizenship because they felt that they could move students to be directed toward an awareness of social problems and developing critical consciousness.

Besides teaching the students at the high school, the MS teacher candidates also were required to teach an outside student, with parental consent, each of the lessons every week. The outside student needed to be an adolescent, age 10–18, who was reading below grade level. It was often someone from their home school or their own neighborhood who needed tutoring, which gave the teacher the chance to reflect on the needs of the students with different cultural backgrounds. Furthermore, this guaranteed that the MS teacher candidates taught each week's lesson twice and guaranteed that they had a complete set of data on a student for their end-of-course case study. The outside student gave the opportunity to double the magnitude of the outreach for the program. It also solved the problem of inconsistent attendance in the afterschool tutoring due to family or work-related obligations, which many of the Reading Scene students had, making it difficult for them to attend regularly.

Course Content

The course content was based on the idea that "effective instruction begins with assessment" (Cooter & Perkins, 2007), a data-driven instructional model. The students were first assessed using an interest inventory, an individual reading inventory, a phonics survey, if needed, and other instruments such as a morphological structure assessment and an attitude survey or anything else if necessary. This part of the tutoring session took place during the first hour and a half. The students were taught with lesson plans targeted to their needs and that were specifically designed to meet the indicators from the Florida Reading Endorsement and the Florida state standards for a Master of Science in Reading Education program. Each week the MS candidates planned, taught, and were given specific feedback on their assessment protocol reports and lesson plans. To meet the standards and Reading Endorsement indicators, there were readings from different resources and many strategies that involved active learning.

The strategies included Think-Alouds (to demonstrate the kind of thinking one needs to use to connect to text), Text Talk (to introduce vocabulary where they are first encountered and to emphasize context and connotation), Vocabulary Trees and Word Scrolls (to teach Greek and Latin prefixes as well as root words), Anticipation Guides and Possible Passages (to teach prediction and locating information to identify information in text and author's messages) and Tape, Mark, Reread and Reader's Theatre (to develop fluency). To teach the ability to identify information across multiple sources and to write information using claims and evidence, Reciprocal Mapping (Fine, 2004, 2005) was taught. This strategy uses graphic organizers to gather information and then requires the students to write using appropriate text structure to convey the ideas coherently. Each week the MS teacher candidates prepared lessons using these strategies, many of which are described in one of their textbooks, *What Teachers Can Do When Kids Can't Read* by Kathleen Beers (2003). The content for the lessons used a variety of both narrative and informational texts. Many of the strategies incorporated writing in some part because this helps to improve both writing and reading comprehension (Graham & Hebert, 2011). The MS teacher candidates were free to select children's literature that was of high interest based on the interest inventory they had conducted with the students. The selection of books and topics was chosen by the MS teacher candidates themselves.

Class Assignments with Differentiated Lesson Plans

Each week the MS teacher candidates wrote protocol reports on the assessments they had conducted and lesson plans that included the various above-mentioned strategies. They also explained how they were going to differentiate the lessons to meet the needs of the students in their small groups. All the assessment protocols, lesson plans, and reflections on what they thought they could have changed to improve the lessons were graded and returned with feedback. This was facilitated by doctoral students who participated in Tiered Cognitive Coaching (Fine et al., 2017) with the MS candidates. In Tiered Cognitive Coaching, the doctoral students discussed the lessons with the teachers, observed the lessons, discussed the outcomes with the teacher after he or she first self-appraised the lesson, and gave multiple suggestions after the tutoring to the teachers as to how they might address the students' needs. The teachers were able to decide how they might incorporate these suggestions in the next week's lessons.

Because the ability to differentiate the lessons was so important in the practicum, the students created a Community Profile Summary Analysis and Reflection Paper consisting of two charts. On the first chart, they listed each student with their respective achievement levels on the different assessments. They entered data on the second chart listing the lesson plans and how they differentiated the lessons to meet the needs of different students. They were expected to incorporate the feedback provided by the professor and the doctoral students, showing the progressive improvement in their ability to differentiate over the term.

Table 5.1 shows a sample from a students' data chart followed by Table 5.2, which shows a sample of the differentiation for the various lesson plans to meet the Reading Endorsement Competencies and Florida State Standards.

At the end of each term, the master's candidates demonstrate their ability to impact the reading achievement of the students in their community by recording their pre- and post-test scores on a university website established for accountability for state licensing of the program. This is also needed to meet a requirement from the state for candidates' graduation from the program. Some chose to document their inside and outside students' growth if the data were complete.

Latest Changes

After conducting the Reading Scene for several years, some changes were made. Because the tutoring sessions often included large numbers of high school students, there was a need to constrain the size of the program to make it more manageable. Because some students were unable to attend sessions regularly or were coming

TABLE 5.1 Student Data Chart

Assessment	Student 1's Name: Wesley P. Grade: 5th	Student 2's Name: Jason A. Grade: 12th
BRI – Oral Reading Comprehension performance levels	Wesley is able to read independently on the first-grade level, is instructional on the second- and third-grade level, and frustrated at the fourth-grade level.	For the oral reading comprehension levels, Jason is at the independent level on grade six, instructional for grades, 7, 8, and 9. Based on the results of the Basic Reading Inventory, Jason was frustrational on 10th grade.
BRI – Decoding (Qualitative Summary of Miscues)	In an analysis of Wesley's miscues, 80% had beginning and end graphic similarity. 0% of miscues had middle graphic similarity.	Based on the Qualitative Summary of Miscues, Jason relies heavily on beginning and end graphic (letter) cues for word identification and has less success in correcting unacceptable miscues.
BRI – Comprehension Monitoring (Qualitative Summary)	Wesley's performance on the comprehension questions shows strength in questions on the text's topic and making evaluations. However, Wesley shows the biggest area for growth in inference questions. Other areas for instruction are facts and vocabulary questions.	Jason's performance on the comprehension questions indicates a possible strength in answering topic and evaluation questions. Areas for growth include answering facts, inference and vocabulary-related questions.
BRI – Retelling	Wesley can retell stories in detail for early/middle first-grade texts. Beyond first-grade texts, Wesley has difficulty recalling key details.	Jason displayed an excellent ability to recall important facts and provide a general sense of sequence for the events of the text up until the passage for grade 8. After grade 8, his ability to retell what he had read in a way that made sense decreased.
Spelling Inventory	Wesley is working at the Middle Syllables and Affixes stage. He spelled 14 of 25 words correctly on the Elementary-Level Spelling Inventory.	Jason is at the within-word pattern stage and was only able to correctly spell 5 of the 20 words correctly. He will likely benefit from instruction that targets blends, complex consonants and various vowel teams.

BRI, Basic Reading Inventory.

late, the MS teacher candidates had to modify their lesson plans in the middle of the sessions. To address this, students were asked to commit to attending for the full two hours of tutoring regularly (as far as they could foresee their availability). The school invited 30 students from intensive reading classes. Of course, students and parents still needed to consent to their participation in the program.

TABLE 5.2 Differentiation of Lesson Plans

Research-based Strategy/Reading Endorsement Competency (REC) Indicator	Student 1 Name: Wesley P. Grade: 5th Instructional Reading level: 2nd and 3rd	Student 2 Name: Jason A. Grade: 12th Instructional Reading level: 7th, 8th, and 9th
Text Talk REC 5.3	To develop and demonstrate oral/aural language, the Text-Talk strategy was used with *Brave: Clara and the Shirtwaist Maker's Strike of 1909* by Michelle Markel. Students read the story and stopped periodically throughout to identify and define vocabulary words that were unknown or difficult to understand. Students defined each word, used them in a variety of contexts, and engaged in some word play activities that would be helpful for students to get an accurate representation of the word.	To develop and demonstrate oral/aural language, the Text-Talk strategy would be used with *Maya Lin: Artist-Architect of Light and Lines* by Jeanne Walker Harvey. This is a higher-level picture book about the woman who designed the Vietnam Veterans Memorial. This text is a picture book that could be used with upper-level students, including high schoolers.
Phonics REC 5.5 SAC 5.3	To develop phonics skills and word recognition, spelling pattern strategies were used with *Henry's Freedom Box: A True Story from the Underground Railroad* by Ellen Levine. Students identified spelling patterns in words throughout the book using the C, V, and *e* spelling pattern. Students created a running list of words and their codes to practice spelling.	To develop phonics skills and word recognition, spelling pattern strategies would be used with *Heroes of the Underground Railroad* by *Smithsonian Magazine*. The student would identify spelling patterns in words throughout the article using the C, V, and *e* spelling pattern. The article is an upper-level article the student would be interested in.

(continued)

TABLE 5.2 Cont.

Research-based Strategy/Reading Endorsement Competency (REC) Indicator	*Student 1 Name: Wesley P.* *Grade: 5th* *Instructional Reading level: 2nd and 3rd*	*Student 2* *Name: Jason A.* *Grade: 12th* *Instructional Reading level: 7th, 8th, and 9th*
Reader's Theatre REC 5.6	To develop reading fluency and reading endurance, the Reader's Theater strategy was used with *Leaving Home* by N. M. Ryan. Students took on character roles and practiced them on their own. After practice, students worked together to create a fluent and cohesive performance of their characters, read with fluency.	To develop reading fluency and reading endurance, the Reader's Theater strategy would be used with *The Fugitive Slave Act* by Anthony Burns. The student would take on a character's role and practice the lines to create a fluent performance. This text was selected because Jason has expressed interest in historical biographies.
Reciprocal Text Structure Mapping REC 5.15	To demonstrate intentional, explicit, systematic writing instruction as it relates to the ability to read written language, the Reciprocal Text Structure Mapping strategy was used with the text *Frogs at Risk* by ReadWorks.org. Students used the graphic organizer to identify important vocabulary words throughout the article, the text's structure, and signal words that helped them understand the text's structure. Students then created a cause-and-effect graphic organizer and identified two cause-and-effect relationships in the text. After, students created a short (3–4 sentence) summary of the text in their own words.	To demonstrate intentional, explicit, systematic writing instruction as it relates to the ability to read written language, the Reciprocal Text Structure Mapping strategy would be used with the text *Frogs at Risk* by ReadWorks.org. The student would create a cause-and-effect graphic organizer that demonstrated understanding that effects usually turn into causes of other situations. After, the student would create a one-paragraph summary of the text in his or her own words.

Other Changes as a Result of a State Problem-Solving Initiative

Other changes were made due to a legislative mandate. For many years, the MS teacher candidates based their instruction on the results of the assessments administered during the practicum. Recently, the State involved reading instructors in a problem-solving initiative as a result of changes in state regulations. These stated the following: 2017 Florida Statutes & Intervention s. 1004.04(2) F. S. Starting with Competency 2 of the Reading Endorsement Requirements:

- Teachers will scaffold student learning by applying the principles of research-based reading instruction and integrating the six components of reading.
- Teachers will engage in the systematic problem-solving process.
- Teachers will triangulate data from appropriate reading assessments to guide instruction.
- If done in Higher Ed classroom, teachers need to interpret and then *apply it in a practicum*, and work with teachers to triangulate data from other sources. Then use multisensory strategies to teach. Use 4-step problem-solving process. Get data from school district.

This initiative (Batsche, 2019) involves looking closely at students who have not made the kind of steady progress needed to achieve higher goals. There is a desire to make changes that will have better outcomes. There are critical components of the Multi-Tiered System involving leadership from the state down to the school level, communication, and collaboration between all the levels to build an infrastructure for educators to evaluate the data from multiple sources to make changes where needed. The acronym used is ICEL x RIOT. This means looking at Instruction (how the curriculum is taught), the Curriculum (what is taught), the Environment (where it is taught) and the Learner (who is taught). Then, considering a Review (of records and data), Interviews (with key stakeholders), Observations (of the students in real time, functional settings) and then Testing (using appropriately matched measurements). This problem-solving approach suggested that for the practicum at the high school, using just our assessments was not sufficient. With this mandate, the school agreed to share the data from students in our Reading Scene program. We were given the data from the school to use to help problem-solve the students' issues with learning. These data allowed us to evaluate how our program has added to students' achievement. In order to graduate from high school, students' total scale score had to be at least 350 on the 10th grade Florida Standardized Assessment (FSA). Table 5.3 gives a description of the students who were included in the case study.

Table 5.4 shows the breakout of the students' subscores by components on the FSA that was shared by the school. A comparison of the overall scores from October 2018 to March 2019 is shown in Table 5.5. Student's breakout subscores were not shared.

TABLE 5.3 Student Snapshots

Student Names*	Student Information
Jason August*	12th Grade, level 2 on FSA ELA, Haitian, attended the practicum 9 times out of 9
Andrea Gray*	11 Grade, level 2 on FSA ELA, Haitian, attended the practicum 8 times out of 9
Lucy Gaines*	11th Grade, level 2 on FSA ELA, Haitian, attended the practicum 5 times out of 9
Tania Parks*	11 Grade, level 1 on FSA ELA, Haitian, attended the practicum 9 times out of 9
Francine Perez*	11 Grade, level 2 on FSA ELA, Haitian, attended 7 times out of 9

*All student names are pseudonyms.

TABLE 5.4 Students' Scores on Florida Standard Assessment by Component

Student Names*	Key Ideas and Details	Craft and Structure	Integration of Knowledge and Ideas	Language and Editing	Text-Based Writing
Jason August*	6/14	10/16	3/11	6/12	4/10
Andrea Gray*	7/14	10/16	5/11	10/12	5/10
Lucy Gaines*	11/14	10/16	2/11	8/12	6/10
Tania Parks*	5/14	7/16	4/11	7/12	8/10
Francine Perez*	6/14	7/16	3/11	6/12	3/10

*All student names are pseudonyms.

TABLE 5.5 A Comparison of FSA Scores from October 2018 to March 2019

Student	FSA October 2018	FSA March 2019
Jason August*	319	329
Andrea Gray*	330	359**
Lucy Gaines*	325	361**
Tania Parks*	330	344
Francine Perez*	337	344

*All student names are pseudonyms.
**Scores over 350 = passing.

Student Scores on the FSA

A sample of student data shows the students' scores. They were assessed in the FSA in the multiple areas of Key Ideas and Details, Craft and Structure, Integration of Knowledge and Ideas, Language and Editing, and Text-Based Writing.

The overall scores on the FSA from October 2018 to March 2019, overlapping the tutoring, show that two students, Andrea and Lucy, made positive progress and passed the FSA and three students made questionable progress, meaning that they improved but are still at-risk and need to continue coming to the Reading Scene. Two of those students, Francine and Tania, still have time before they are in twelfth grade. Unfortunately, Jason was in twelfth grade and did not graduate.

In successive terms, different master's program candidates will continue tutoring in the Reading Scene and hope to successfully address the needs of students. They will select materials that are appropriate according to CSP and teach the high school students using strategies that allow the students to express their language, culture, and identities. The experience, hopefully, will not only improve the students' literacy and access to continued learning but will also increase the Master of Science in Reading/Literacy Education teacher candidates' level of expertise for instructing diverse students.

References

Alim, H. S., & Paris, D. (2017). What is culturally sustaining pedagogy and why does it matter? In H. S. Alim & D. Paris (Eds.), *Culturally sustaining pedagogies: Teaching and learning for justice in a changing world* (pp. 1–21). Teachers College Press.

Au, K. H. (1997). A sociocultural model of reading instruction: The Kamehameha Elementary Education Program. In S. A. Stahl & D. A. Hayes (Eds.), *Instructional models in reading* (pp. 181–202). Lawrence Erlbaum Associates.

Batsche, G. M. (2019, January 16–17). Problem solving cycle around early literacy data [Conference session]. Just Read Florida! Winter Literacy Institute. Orlando, FL, USA.

Beers, K. (2003). *What teachers can do when kids can't read.* Heinemann.

Bronfenbrenner, U. (1979). *The ecology of human development: Experiments by nature and design.* Harvard University Press.

Cooter, R. B., Jr. & Perkins, J. H. (2007). Looking to the future with *The Reading Teacher:* 900-year-old sheep and Papa na come! *The Reading Teacher, 61,* 4–7. https://doi.org/10.1598/RT.61.1.1

Dewey, J. (1916). *Democracy and education.* McMillan.

Freire, P. (1970). Cultural action and conscientization. *Harvard Educational Review, 40,* 452–477. https://doi.org/10.17763/haer.40.3.h76250x720j43175

Fine, J. C. (2004). Reciprocal mapping: Scaffolding students' literacy to higher levels. In A. Rodgers & E. M. Rodgers (Eds.), *Scaffolding literacy instruction: Strategies for K-4 classrooms* (pp. 88–104). Heinemann.

Fine, J. C. (2005). Reciprocal mapping: Scaffolding students' expository writing. *American Reading Forum Yearbook, 25,* 29–38. http://americanreadingforum/yearbook.

Fine, J. C., Lawrence, O., & Lawrence, A. (2017, December 6–9). An innovative design for peer mentoring: Tiered Cognitive Coaching [Paper presentation]. American Reading Forum Annual Conference, Sanibel, FL, USA.

Graham, S., & Hebert, M. (2011). Writing to reading: A meta-analysis of the impact of writing and writing instruction on reading. *Harvard Educational Review, 81*(4), 710–744. https://doi.org/10.17763/haer.81.4t2k0m13756113566

James, J. H., & Iverson, S. V. (2009). Striving for critical citizenship in a teacher education program: Problems and possibilities. *Michigan Journal of Community Service Learning, 16*(1), 1–33.

Kahne, J., & Westheimer, J. (1996). In the service of what? The politics of service learning. *Phi Delta Kappan, 77*(9), 593–599.

Ladson-Billings, G. (1995). Toward a theory of culturally relevant pedagogy. *American Educational Review, 84*(1), 465–491. https://doi.org/10.3102/00028312032003465

Moll, L. C. (1994). Literacy research in community and classrooms: A sociocultural approach. In R. B. Ruddell, M. R. Ruddell, & H. Singer (Eds.) *Theoretical models and processes of reading* (4th ed., pp. 179–207). International Reading Association.

No Child Left Behind Act of 2001. Pub. L. No. 107–110, 115 Stat.1425 (2002). www.ed.gov/policy/elsec/leg/esea02/107–110.pdf

Olukolu, R. M. (2013). The relationship of culturally responsive instruction and the reading comprehension and attitude of struggling adolescent readers [Doctoral dissertation, Florida International University]. Florida International Digital Commons. https://digitalcommons.fiu.edu/etd/910

Wentzel, K., & Wigfield, A. (Eds.). (2009). *Handbook of motivation at school.* Routledge. https://doi.org/10.4324/9780203879498

PART II
Unique Populations

6

FOSTERING YOUNG CHILDREN'S LITERACY IN HOME AND COMMUNITY SETTINGS

A Dialogic Approach to Developing Culturally Relevant and Sustaining Practices

Pauline Harris, Alexandra Diamond, Bec Neill, and Elspeth McInnes

UNIVERSITY OF SOUTH AUSTRALIA

Cynthia Brock

UNIVERSITY OF WYOMING

Ufemia Camaitoga

FIJI EARLY CHILDHOOD TEACHERS ASSOCIATION

Introduction

Focusing on culturally sustaining practices for fostering young children's literacy in their community settings, this chapter explores how a dialogic approach was used in Fiji communities to co-create multilingual books rendered in children's heritage languages and English – responding to communities' desires to have such books for developing children's literacy across these languages for cultural sustainability in their local and global worlds.

Whereas Fiji has three official languages – Bauan, Standard Hindi, and English – dialects proliferate, reflecting that, on a per-capita basis, the Pacific exhibits the world's highest linguistic diversity (Eberhard et al., 2019). As the language of Fiji's government, education, media, and communication, English is connected to school success, later life chances, and economic and social prosperity (Glasgow, 2010). However, the prominence of English has been seen to displace vernaculars preferred by many for teaching and learning success

(Herrman, 2007). Despite calls in the Pacific for multilingual literacy resources, such materials are scarce. The development of these resources – if they are to be culturally sustaining – necessitate community-based approaches that engage with community elders, leaders, families, and children in ways that build on community practices, languages, and cultures as they stand and as they evolve into the future, hence our study here to engage in developing such approaches in Fiji's community settings.

Setting the Scene

The study set out to address communities' desire to support their preschool-aged children's literacy and later transition to school, as confirmed with our research colleagues, partners, and communities in Fiji. The study was grounded in:

- Awareness that in Fiji, preschool education was not universally available and that most children spoke languages other than English at home, yet schooling is in English.
- Previous work in Fiji and the Pacific conducted by the research team's School of Education early childhood colleagues.
- The imperative from Pacific Education Ministers[1] for member nations to recommit to vernacular language education with appropriate policies and practices to support this priority.

Fifty-one children and their 44 families across three communities participated in the study. The communities had no access to early childhood services and pseudonymously were:

- *Duavata*, a small *iTaukei* village in a semi-rural locality, served by major roads and abundant in agricultural produce.
- *Dovubaravi*, a rural Indo-Fijian cane-farming and fishing community.
- *Wavu*, a culturally diverse urban community in Fiji's capital, with *iTaukei* Fijians and Indo-Fijians making up 52% and 48% of Wavu's population, respectively.

The study was undertaken as critical participatory action research with and by people in their settings to collaboratively build knowledge for understanding and transforming practice (Kemmis et al., 2014; Lincoln et al., 2018). Children, families, community elders, leaders and youth, and university researchers engaged as co-investigators.

---

[1] Islands Business (2012) www.islandsbusiness.com/2012, retrieved March 10, 2017.

Using Principles of Culturally Sustaining Pedagogy

Developing literacy strategies in communities was framed by principles of culturally sustaining pedagogy (CSP; McCarty & Lee, 2014), summarized in Table 6.1.

CSP builds on culturally relevant pedagogy (Ladson-Billings, 1995) that was developed to democratize children's formal education spaces and promote learning through: conveying high expectations for all children to succeed; valuing Indigenous knowledges and practices; foregrounding different cultural ways of knowing; fostering children's cultural identity and belonging; and ensuring educational experiences are responsive, relevant and authentic by building bridges between children's home/community and school experiences.

Grounded in the seminal work of scholars like Heath (1983) and Ladson-Billings (1995), CSP scholars attend to communities' practices and knowledge in ways that overtly resist cultural stereotypes. With a focus on pluralist outcomes rather than culturally dominant norms, CSP also extends the work of *resource* pedagogies arising from the funds of knowledge work of scholars such as Luis Moll and his colleagues (e.g., González et al., 2005; Moll & González, 1994) that seek to foster and build on students' and families' diverse funds of knowledge. Fiji's teachers, for example, use and value student-centered pedagogies, culturally inclusive pedagogies and seek to include more embodied ways of learning and knowing into their classrooms (Koya, 2015).

While various associated terms have arisen, such as culturally appropriate and culturally responsive practices, the term and praxis known as "culturally sustaining pedagogy" is explicitly underpinned by the core goal "to maintain heritage ways and to value cultural and linguistic sharing across difference, to sustain and support bi- and multilingualism and bi- and multiculturalism" (Paris, 2012, p. 95). CSP, therefore, explicitly and systematically supports the sustainability of linguistic and cultural dexterity and plurality by engaging with both traditional cultures, and cultures as they are lived and evolve through young people's experiences in contemporary times. As such, CSP was apt for our community project as both the project and CSP share an explicit focus on sustaining children's, families', and communities' cultural and linguistic worlds even as these worlds are evolving (Harris et al., 2020).

Understanding that social, cultural, historical, and linguistic contexts endow literacy practices with particular meanings, purposes and ways of being literate and doing literacy (Heath, 1983), we used a sociocultural literacy lens that afforded insight into the many guises literacy took in the children's lives. Such a lens aligned with Fiji's early childhood curriculum guidelines, *Na Noda Mataniciva*, which states that literacy involves "understanding and using the symbol systems of a culture – not just the alphabet and number systems, but also environmental and cultural signs and symbols" (Ministry of Education, National Heritage, Culture & Arts, 2009, p. 40).

TABLE 6.1 Co-Constructing CSP Literacy Pedagogy in Community Settings

Principle	Practices
Embrace community languages	Use **texts in community languages** to counter privileging of dominant languages over minoritized languages (Flores & García, 2013; Martínez-Roldán, 2015).
	• *We engaged with children, families and community members in co-creating books in children's words and languages; and used the languages communities wished to be included for cultural sustainability in their local and global worlds.*
Engage with community cultures	Focus on a community's **traditional languages and cultures in evolving ways** as lived by contemporary young people (Paris, 2012; Paris & Alim, 2014, 2017).
	• *The co-created books reflected traditional and contemporary aspects of children's lives, and were told through children's voices and experiences. We also engaged with children's siblings and a youth group in one of our communities.*
Understand community ways	Attend to **communities' practices and knowledges** in ways that do not essentialize culture and race (Paris, 2012; Paris & Alim, 2014, 2017).
	• *We tuned into communities' ways of knowing and doing through dialogic encounters; and used the artifacts and texts of children's, families, and communities' lives, and not those imported from outside sources that essentialize Indigenous Fijian and Indo-Fijian lives and experiences.*
Ensure community inclusion	Include **community elders and leaders** in maintaining and promoting knowledge of cultural histories, languages, and practices (Glasgow, 2010).
	• *We engaged with community leaders, elders, and mentors, as well as children's grandparents and extended families.*
Incorporate community modes	Use **community modes of textual expression**, e.g., visual, spoken, written, music, song, dance, multimodal texts (Kalantzsis & Cope, 2012).
	• *The books were co-created through spoken interactions, written words on paper and on screen, dramatic play, gesture, song, music, photos, children's drawing, and construction of props that supported story-telling and text development.*
Emphasize community relevance	Ensure **contextual relevance and responsiveness** of pedagogic practices.
	• *We actively, visibly listened to community's concerns and interests, around which strategies were collectively developed, and from which co-creating multilingual books emerged as an agreed priority.*
Connect with community identities	Promote **children's cultural identities, belonging and competence**.
	• *Children's co-created books represented their worlds and their place in their worlds, to themselves and others, showing that their lives matter.*

TABLE 6.1 Cont.

Principle	Practices
Mobilize community agency	Endow encounters with **participants' voices and ownership** that affords opportunity for participants to influence and transform their realities • *Children, families, and community leaders and members all engaged to shape the encounters, collectively develop strategies, and co-create the books.*
Enact ethics in communities	Infuse encounters with an **ethics of care and commitment** (Freire, 1983). • *Our interactions and actions were founded on an ethics of empathetic care and commitment that included Fijian values of patience, protection, reciprocity, and trust* (Rhodes, 2014; Tagicakiverata & Nilan, 2018).
Embed assessment in community contexts	**Document** children's learning and engagement through **culturally inclusive means**. • *We used a sociocultural framework of literacy to consider children's literacy competences in context and related to meaning, purpose, code, and critical thinking; and bench-marked children's literacy learning against Fiji's early childhood curriculum's literacy outcomes.*

Certainly, the children in our study were living rich, multimodal literacy lives, situated in their everyday realities. Their literacies involved engaging with: oral story-telling; religious and cultural texts and icons; music, dance and song; print; information, communication, and entertainment technologies; arts, crafts, and construction; making marks on paper, screen fabric, dirt, sand, cardboard, concrete, and other surfaces; reading and creating images of their worlds; dramatizing real or imagined stories; reading, recording, and talking about the environment; reading signs in the environment; reading and creating books and other kinds of texts. The project's written texts for children were texts rendered in children's vernaculars.

We incorporated children's and their respective communities' expression modes – such as visual, spoken, and written texts; texts of music, song, and dance; and texts combining several modes such as speech, image, and sound (Kalantzis & Cope, 2012) – recognizing and further fostering children as literate people who were developing literacy competencies related to: (1) interpreting and composing meaning; (2) purposefully producing and engaging with texts; (3) decoding and encoding texts; and (4) critically reflecting on texts (after Freebody & Luke, 2003).

In framing our study thus, we acknowledged the importance of multilingual texts for: validating and promoting multilingual literate identities that are shaped by how multilingual children understand literacy in relation to their multilingualism and multilingual literacy; affording opportunities for multilingual children's participation in literacy practices afforded by their respective linguistic communities (Barac et al., 2014, 2016; Hammer et al., 2014); and redressing hegemonic effects created by privileging dominant over minoritized languages (Flores & García, 2013; Martínez Roldán, 2015).

Strategies Developed with Communities

A core strategy used within and across all three communities was co-creating culturally relevant, multilingual books containing words and images in and about the children's worlds and languages. While this idea is not new in and of itself, how we *collectively* went about this work with children and their families and communities is significant for its culturally sustaining attributes.

The Dovubaravi example we describe below, with reference to Table 6.1's CSP principles and other incidents across the study, illustrates the community-wide development and implementation of this strategy. This example describes the co-creation of a set of family and community literacy resources, which was a trilingual picture book called "*Mandir*" ("The Temple"). "*Mandir*" is structured around routines of, and preschool children's engagement in, women's fortnightly Temple washing and prayers. To this example, we add insights from Duavata and Wavu communities. Throughout the account, we argue that the strategies we describe have their place in classrooms, providing means for teachers to work with children in ways that are inclusive and sustaining of children's cultures and communities.

Embracing Community Languages

Across all three communities, co-created texts used children's home languages and English. In Dovubaravi, through community and family dialogic encounters in the project's phase 1, we constructed shared meanings about words, protocols, and practices of Dovubaravi's family, spiritual, and linguistic lives, and appreciated the value accorded by the community to English, their vernacular (Fiji-Hindi) and heritage language (Tamil) for cultural and material sustainability in their children's local and global futures.

Literacy-support strategies responded to families' expressed linguistic aspirations for their children. Parents elicited wording from children to assemble the written text of "*Mandir*." Keshav's father, for example, showed him photos of the Temple washing day, asking: *Photo mei kaunchi hai? Battao* (What's in this photo? Tell me); *Kaunchi karte hai?* (What are you doing?); *Battao, photo mei kaunchi kare hai?* (Tell me, what's happening in this photo?). Keshav's transcribed audio-recorded answers, additionally translated into English and Tamil, became page texts. Page design of "*Mandir*" gave precedence to Fiji-Hindi and Tamil through text position and larger font size (see Figure 6.1).

Engaging with Community Cultures

Across all communities, book topics engaged with each community's cultures and were chosen by the children with their families. For example, in a Fijian Indian family in Wavu, the story of Rama and Sita from the Ramayana underpins the annual Diwali festival. In an *iTaukei* family in Wavu, children enacted a *meke*

Bhagwan hai.
Jaijai log hai.

Idu kadwale irkidu.
Edu alaram kadwale
erkarango.

This is God.
All these are gods.

FIGURE 6.1 A Page from the "Mandir" Book

(movements and rhyme) telling the story of *The Breadfruit Tree* – the book with this tale being shared by the children's grandmother, and breadfruit being a significant food source. In Duavata, Kuini lived with her parents, grandmother Meli, and her aunt, uncle, and cousins. Grandma Meli made *roti* (flat bread) for the family daily. Kuini chose to write her book about making *roti* with Grandma Meli.

In Dovubaravi, "*Mandir*" renders a view from Fiji's culturally and religiously diverse communities. It depicts Sangam (South Indian heritage) spiritual practices and artifacts as enacted/created in contemporary Dovubaravi, rather than practices essentialized as "Fiji-Indian." Hitherto, participating children's access to books was largely restricted to Disney stories (e.g., Snow White), which neither reflected their life-worlds nor afforded opportunities for their reading success. "*Mandir*," alongside ten other multilingual books (Harris et al., 2020), gave Dovubaravi's children novel access to books reflecting their life-worlds and families' aspirations for their futures.

Ensuring Community Inclusion

Co-creating "*Mandir*" involved children, parents, and elders participating in digital photography, eliciting children's narration of text wording from photos of their time at the Temple, and providing authentic translations from Fiji-Hindi to Tamil and English. Dialogic encounters occurred iteratively as together we created, translated, and edited the book's visual and written content.

Elders steered translations of children's spoken words into English, protecting the integrity of nuanced cultural meanings within children's narrations, and supporting Australian researchers' deeper understandings of these. For example, discussing meanings of "*Bhagwan hai. Jaijai log hai*" built understanding about integrative-pluralistic concepts of God(s) to render English translation as "This is God. All these are gods" (see Figure 6.1).

Temple elders conversed extensively with children and adults regarding their cultural histories, languages, practices, and beliefs, using the languages and photos in "*Mandir*" as open-ended resources. Engagement with elders was pivotal in Wavu, too, where children's family members and community leaders' contributions to book development included: acting as characters in book photographs; providing translations and explanations of particular artefacts and practices included in books; providing locations and props for stories; and making links between children's interests and practices and their wider community contexts. This inclusive engagement cut across age groups. For example, a unique feature of the work in Duavata was that members of the Methodist Youth Group chose to work closely with the project team.

Incorporate Community Modes

"*Mandir*" as a digital artifact, and its co-creation processes, engaged children, families, and the wider Temple community in multiple modes of text. Illustrations include prayer rituals and religious icons. Pages within "*Mandir*" capture preschool children's engagement in learning such symbolic and gesture-based texts, as they intensely attend to their elders' performance of prayer.

Dialogic encounters between researchers, child authors and women attending Temple washing day shaped the design of "*Mandir*." Early encounters included researchers' play-based interactions with children, and preparing and sharing *prashad* (food offerings) with children and women. Such immersion in multimodal practices helped researchers see layered and multiliterate modes critical to devising culturally relevant literacy activities for children. For example, participating in Temple activities attuned us to the importance and meanings of colors, icons, and numbers within Dovubaravi's Sangam practices. We digitally rendered simple line drawings from photos of Temple icons and symbols to produce coloring-in activities, with introductory bilingual text and unrendered images to evoke the Temple's recent repainting.

Emphasize Community Relevance

During dialogic encounters, parents emphasized preparing children for school success; specifically speaking, reading and writing in English, often by asking children to produce formulaic English. Our project sought pathways for families' extended, culturally relevant, knowledge of literacy-support strategies.

Researchers initially suggested parents "read the book" to support children's literacy learning. Parents and mentors looked doubtful, some telling us they did not know what to do. Dialogic encounters established the Fiji-Hindi word for "read" also means "teach"; their understanding being that parents were to "teach" the book to children. Consequently, our colleague, Mere Krishna, an early childhood educator fluent in Fiji-Hindi, visited Dovubaravi to share and talk about books with children. Observing her, one of our Dovubravi mentors, said, "I can do that!," likening the process to adults "talking nicely" to young children. The mentor modeled this book-sharing technique with mothers and grandmothers, who employed their existing cultural practices of talking with children in respectful, enjoyable ways as a "teaching"/literacy-support strategy when sharing books with children.

Community relevance also was highly prized in Wavu and Duavata. As a diverse community, Wavu residents identified strongly with their communities of origin, often located many kilometers away from the capital, which they had come to for work and education opportunities. Children's stories were a reflection of their experiences, possessions, cultural perspectives, and aspirations which in turn were embedded in the lives of their families and community.

Connect with Community Identities

In Dovubaravi, photos and text in "*Mandir*" illustrate children's identity, belonging, and competence as members of Dovubaravi's Sangam Hindu community and their social peer group. Developing culturally relevant literacy strategies with children, parents, and community mentors strengthened their literate identities.

"*Mandir*" strengthened literate identities in Dovubaravi as adults with limited read–write literacy, as well as children, used photos to boost their literate engagement with the text. Co-participants' delight in Vivan's demonstration of competence, the mentor naming Vivan as a "smart boy" and her evident pride in her newly discovered "reading with children" skills (see Figure 6.1) reveal enhanced individual and communal literate identities.

In all three communities, children's pride in their growing literate identities that were embedded in their cultural identities was palpable. Children were excited to recognize themselves and family members in their books and were enthusiastic in sharing their books with other families taking part in the project. In Duavata, when the family of one child, Peni, went to a different village to visit his grandparents, Peni chose to take his book to share with his grandparents.

Mobilize Community Agency

Revised ethics protocols not only increased children's access to books, but also built community leaders' and parents' capacity for agency on behalf of themselves and their children. Elders and families questioned initial authorship attributions, use of pseudonyms for children, and Australian individual-privacy concerns. They proposed children's and community interests were better served when children were, with family consent, authentically named as authors. The final round of ethics protocol negotiations accorded children's right to be identified as book authors.

Understand Community Ways

Entering, and learning to be and become within Dovubaravi, necessarily required Australian researchers to critically reflect on their personal responses to the community's contexts and circumstances. By exploring connections and commonalities between their own lived experiences and Dovubaravi ways, and looking at community strengths, they avoided essentializing Dovubaravi's social and economic circumstances.

Dovubaravi children typically live in extended family compounds, frequently moving between houses and kin-carers, and sharing resources. This community strength, along with amendments to ethics protocols previously discussed, allowed for relational planning of book distribution, maximizing book titles available to each child.

Enact Ethics in Communities

Enacting an ethics of care and commitment to communities' interests was paramount across all three communities during the three-year research project. Families and children were able to choose whether to participate in the research and whether to remain connected over time. Those who participated over the period welcomed researchers into their homes and gave time to the processes of developing and sharing the books with their children and discussing how the children had engaged with the books. Researchers took care to avoid disrupting families at meal times so they felt no obligation to provide food and to ensure that the research did not disrupt family routines. Researchers also ensured that meetings of participants included refreshments for adults and children to share.

Key to ethical engagement was researchers' adherence to cultural protocols. For example, in Duavata, we carefully followed the guidelines and suggestions of the respected community mentor who ensured we were given permission to work in Duavata by the *iTaukei* Chief prior to visiting the community. As the study unfolded, the researcher and the community mentor continued to check in with the Chief to make sure that he was comfortable with the manner in which the work was progressing.

In Dovubaravi and Wavu, enacting an ethics of care and commitment to children, families, and community entailed researchers listening respectfully during dialogic encounters, honoring and engaging with each community's spiritual and social practices, and attending to children's interests and their family's aspirations for them. Such actions generated community trust. This facilitated involvement of the wider Dovubaravi populace, so that by our project's end, the eleventh and final co-created book *Gaon Mei Saal Ke Karikaram* ("A Year in Our Community") included celebrations more central to Dovubaravi's Christian and North Indian heritage families and common seasonal activities such as cane-cutting and catching *netli* (whitebait). In Wavu, *iTaukei* families and Indo-Fijian families developed a shared commitment to their young children's literacy development, transcending their cultural and language differences in a plan to begin their own local preschool.

Making research outputs such as children's books widely available within communities was not without ethical challenges, including dilemmas arising from differing Fijian and Australian protocols and cultural meanings ascribed to assent and consent, intellectual property, and privacy across the community. Both *iTaukei* and Indo-Fijian cultural protocols premised relational-embodied forms of consent (equivalent to assent but not qualifying as consent in Australian legal and ethical protocols). At times, our co-researchers and stakeholders were bemused, frustrated, and dismissive of the individualistic documentary evidence required by Australian legal and ethical defaults, which ignored families' oral assents and their understanding of original written consents. Families were patient as we renegotiated consent changes within our university's protocols to better reflect local relational permissions (Rhodes, 2014; Tagicakiverata & Nilan, 2018), and increase children's access to photographic and written portrayals of themselves and their worlds, authentic home and English language texts, and experiences of literacy success.

Embed Assessment in Community Contexts

Na Noda Manaticiva, Fiji's curriculum document for kindergarten education, recognizes parents and families as children's first teachers (Ministry of Education, National Heritage, Culture & Arts, 2009). As children experience their family's social and cultural practices, they learn the many ways of communicating that create diverse pathways to becoming literate adults. Sharing "*Mandir*" with young children provides many opportunities for children to demonstrate their communicative competencies, as detailed in Figure 6.2 and detailed below.

Impact and Evaluation of this Work

This study enacted principles of culturally sustaining pedagogy to work with communities to develop strategies for fostering their children's literacy in their heritage languages and English. These principles, summarized in Table 6.1 and detailed through the examples we have shared here, provided the means by which the participating children and their families and communities now have access to multilingual books. These books were created with children in and about their life worlds, using their heritage languages and English. This work aligned with Fiji's early childhood guidelines to ensure relevance and authenticity and was further informed by multilingual literacy knowledge and strategies that are known to foster children's literacy.

The children's co-created multilingual books, and the processes by which they were developed with children, provided a culturally sustaining alternative to imported, monolingual literacy products that had prevailed in Fiji. The participating communities have taken steps to sustain and expand the study's work into the future for and with their families:

- Duavata established a community library for accessing culturally sustaining books written by the children; and a play group, securing culturally sustaining resources through Duavata's leader and Catholic Women's League. The play group leader applied to Australia Pacific Technical College, Suva, to become a certified early childhood educator.
- Wavu established a preschool in a building the local Methodist church offered for free, while seeking official status and government funding support.
- Dovubaravi Temple has inaugurated its own Facebook page, drawing on digital literacies developed during the project. Posts include children's *tirrakuttu* (Sangam sacred drama) performance in Tamil.

Through enacting principles of culturally sustaining pedagogy, communities now view their languages with renewed power, affirming their individual and collective cultural identities, with renewed impetus as well as means to sustain these identities. As Dovubaravi elders expressed, "Before this Project, we were just fishermen and farmers; Now, we are somebody." Participants attributed these changes to valuing and documenting heritage languages in the books created with children – voicing their family and community lives through embracing their languages.

The study benchmarked 51 children's preschool literacy outcomes against Fiji's preschool literacy outcomes documented in *Na Noda Mataniciva* (Ministry of Education, National Heritage, Culture & Arts, 2009), using observational data of children's engagement, as illustrated in Figure 6.2. This benchmarking revealed that, across the study, children's multilingual literacy developed to a standard not only concomitant with, but indeed exceeding Early Childhood Education curriculum guidelines.

In consequence of the collective work with and in each community, and as illustrated in Figure 6.2 and evidenced in our previous Temple book example, participating children engaged and developed as readers and writers who, after Freebody and Luke (2003):

We photographed four-year-old Neharika and Warsha as they participated in the Temple washing afternoon. Later we visited them with a laptop and directly typed their narratives next to specific photos on PowerPoint slides for the 'Mandir' book. Months later we visited Neharika's and Warsha's home to deliver 'Mandir' to them. Mothers and siblings/ cousins gathered in the living room to hear the DVB mentor read it aloud. At one page, depicting a woman pounding garlic, the mentor read aloud: "*Lesun koote*" ('She is pounding garlic'). Vivan (aged 38 months, seated on the mentor's lap, emphatically responded: "*Hanh*" ('Yes'). The mentor turned to a page depicting a woman hanging up washed clothes with the text: '*Kapda jurawe*' ('She is drying the clothes'). Before the mentor had time to read it, Vivan interjected: "*Kapda jurawe*". The mentor responded "Oh!", looking at Vivan with raised eyebrows and a smile. As captured in the video still below, everyone laughed, Neharika clapped and Vivan smiled broadly. The mentor, smiling widely, told Vivan: "Smart boy". From here-on Vivan and his older siblings/ cousins attempted to join in as the mentor read aloud.

Later still, Neharika's 22-month-old sister (Nishika), interacted with her aunt Sapna using '*Mandir*'.

Nishika: (pointing to a boy in an illustration) *Ee kaun hai?* ('Who is this here?')

Sapna: *Hum nai jaanta.* ('I don't know.')

Nishika: (pointing to Neharika in the illustration) *Neharika puja kare.* ('Neharika is praying.').

Sapna: *Ee kaunchi hai, babba?* (What is that, darling?)

The next page is that of Figure 4.

Nishika: *Puja hai.* ('It is prayer.')

Sapna: *Baghwan ke kaise puja karajai?* ('How do you pray to god?')

Nishika: (puts her own joined hands up to her forehead.)

Benchmarking against *Na Noda Matanciva's* 'Language, literacy and communication' outcomes:

- Neharika and Warsha's participation in the inscription of their own words, and their later participation in joining the DVB mentor in reading the text aloud, demonstrated their **recognition that print could convey meanings** and that they had begun to see culturally relevant **purposes for writing materials** (NNM p. 41 and 44).

- In pre-empting the DVB mentor's reading aloud from '*Mandir*', Vivan **used illustration to interpret written text** in his home language (NNM p. 44).

- Nishika's used simple vocabulary in three-word sentences in her home language (Fiji-Hindi) to describe and ask about the book's illustrations demonstrate that she meets NNM's aspirations for 36-month-olds' **listening and communicating**, including **taking turns in conversations, responding to age-appropriate stories by asking and answering questions and making comments** when the story is familiar within her life-world. Nishika responded contingently when her aunt asked her questions about what she could see and about how to pray. By bringing her joined hands to her forehead, Nishika expressed her understanding about prayer within her home culture through gesture, one of **many ways to communicate ideas**. At only 22 months-of-age, Nishika was demonstrably well on her way to becoming an **effective communicator in her first language** and was developing culturally sustaining **foundations for literacy**.

FIGURE 6.2 A Literacy Learning Story of Neharika and Warsha from Dovubaravi

- Made and talked about meaning, supported by dialogue with children in which adults noticed, observed, prompted, scaffolded, and responded to children's thinking and development of their ideas for their books, and their interpretation and discussion of their own and other children's completed books.
- Created and used texts for real-life purposes, informed by knowing what texts and genres were germane to children's lives, and the functions these texts served for children and their families.
- Critically reflected on texts, in which children made life-to-text and text-to-life connections; expressed opinions; developed and projected their perspectives and experiences; reflected on their lives; and made connections to new learning.

- Cracked the codes of texts and transferred codes into texts, supported by the development of children's personalized word banks, dictionaries, and alphabet charts, song charts and books, and labeled scrapbooks of images and artifacts in children's lives, which accompanied the co-creation of books.

The collective action of fostering children's literacy across the community through a culturally sustaining pedagogic approach built sustainable pathways to children's ongoing literacy learning and engagement, while opening doors with families and communities to ways of supporting their children's multilingual literacy. Here in our account lie key strategies for teachers to do likewise in classrooms through enacting principles of culturally sustaining pedagogy, such as we have modeled in this chapter.

Acknowledgments and Disclaimer

This paper reports a study by Pauline Harris, Anne Glover, Elspeth McInnes, Alexandra Diamond, Jenni Carter, Bec Neill, and Cynthia Brock, funded by the Australian Government Department for Foreign Affairs and Trading through the Category 1 Australian AID Development Research Awards Scheme under an award titled "Developing a community approach to supporting literacy for preschoolers in Fiji." The views expressed in this publication are those of the authors and not necessarily those of the Commonwealth of Australia. The Commonwealth of Australia accepts no responsibility for loss, damage or injury resulting from reliance on any of the information or views contained in this publication.

References

Barac, R., Bialystok, E., Castro, D. C., & Sanchez, M. (2014). The cognitive development of young dual language learners: A critical review. *Early Childhood Research Quarterly, 29*(4), 699–714. https://dx.doi.org/10.1016%2Fj.ecresq.2014.02.003

Barac, R., Moreno, S., & Bialystok, E. (2016). Behavioral and electrophysiological differences in executive control between monolingual and bilingual children. *Child Development, 87*(4), 1277–1290. https://doi.org/10.1111/cdev.12538

Eberhard, D. M., Simons, G. F., & Fennig, C. D. (Eds.). 2019. *Ethnologue: Languages of the world* (22nd ed.). SIL International. www.ethnologue.com

Flores, N., & García, O. (2013). Linguistic third spaces in education: Teachers' translanguaging across the bilingual continuum. In D. Little, C. Leung, & P. van Avermaet (Eds.), *Managing diversity in education: Key issues and some responses* (pp. 243–256). Multilingual Matters. https://doi.org/10.21832/9781783090815-016

Freebody, P., & Luke, A. (2003). Literacy as engaging with new forms of life: The "Four Roles Model." In G. Bull & M. Anstey (Eds.), *The literacy lexicon* (2nd ed.). Pearson Education.

Freire, P. (1983). *Pedagogy of the oppressed.* Continuum.

Glasgow, A. (2010). Measures to reserve Indigenous language and culture in the Reo Kuki Airani (Cook Islands Māori Language): Early-childhood education models. *AlterNative: An International Journal of Indigenous Peoples, 6*(2), 122–133. https://doi.org/10.1177/117718011000600204

González, N., Moll, L., & Amanti, C. (2005). *Funds of knowledge: Theorizing practices in households, communities, and classrooms.* Lawrence Erlbaum Associates. https://doi.org/10.4324/9781410613462

Hammer, C. S., Hoff, E., Uchikoshi, Y., Gillanders, C., Castro, D. C., & Sandilos, L. E. (2014). The language and literacy development of young dual language learners: A critical review. *Early Childhood Research Quarterly, 29*(4), 715–733. https://doi.org/10.1016/j.ecresq.2014.05.008

Harris, P., Brock, C., McInnes, E., Neill, B., Diamond, A., Carter, J., Giannakis, E., with Camaitoga, U., & Krishna, M. (2020). *Children's multilingual literacy – Fostering childhood literacy in home and community settings.* Springer. https://doi.org/10.1080/02568543.2019.1692105

Herrman, U. (2007). Access to language: A question of equity for all children. In P. Puamau & F. Pene (Eds.), *The basics of learning: Literacy and numeracy in the Pacific* (pp. 32–43). Pacific Education.

Heath, S. B. (1983). *Ways with words.* Cambridge University Press. https://doi.org/10.1017/CBO9780511841057

Kalantzis, M., & Cope, B. (2012). New learning: A charter for change in education. *Critical Studies in Education, 53*(1), 83–94. https://doi.org/10.1080/17508487.2012.635669

Kemmis, S., McTaggart, R., & Nixon, R. (2014). *The action research planner: Doing critical participatory action research.* Springer. https://doi.org/10.1007/978-981-4560-67-2

Koya, C. 2015. Pedagogical practices in Fiji schools. In E. Hau-Fai Law & U. Miura (Eds.), *Transforming teaching and learning in Asia and the Pacific: Case studies from seven countries,* 2243. UNESCO. https://unesdoc.unesco.org/ark:/48223/pf0000232909

Ladson-Billings, G. (1995). Toward a theory of culturally relevant pedagogy. *American Educational Research Journal, 32*(3), 465–491. https://doi.org/10.3102/00028312032003465

Lincoln, Y. S., Lynham, S. A., & Guba, E. G. (2018). Paradigmatic controversies, contradictions, and emerging confluences, revisited. In N. K. Denzin & Y. S. Lincoln (Eds.), *The Sage handbook of qualitative research* (5th ed., pp. 97–150). SAGE.

Martínez Roldán, C. M. (2015). Translanguaging practices as mobilization of linguistic resources in a Spanish/English bilingual after-school program: An analysis of contradictions. *International Multilingual Research Journal, 9*(1), 43–58. https://doi.org/10.1080/19313152.2014.982442

McCarty, T., & Lee, T. (2014). Critical culturally sustaining/revitalizing pedagogy and Indigenous education sovereignty. *Harvard Educational Review, 84*(1), 101–124. https://doi.org/10.17763/haer.84.1.q83746nl5pj34216

Ministry of Education, National Heritage, Culture & Arts. (2009). *Na Noda Mataniciva: ECE curriculum guidelines for the Fiji Islands.* Republic of the Fiji Islands.

Moll, L. C., & González, N. (1994). Lessons from research with language-minority children. *Journal of Reading Behavior, 26*(4), 439–456. https://doi.org/10.1080/10862969409547862

Paris, D. (2012). Culturally sustaining pedagogy: A needed change in stance, terminology, and practice. *Educational Researcher, 41*(3), 93–97. https://doi.org/10.3102/0013189X12441244

Paris, D., & Alim, S. (2014). What are we seeking to sustain through culturally sustaining pedagogy? A loving critique forward. *Harvard Education Review, 81*(1), 85–100. https://doi.org/10.17763/haer.84.1.982l873k2ht16m77

Paris, D., & Alim, S. (Eds.). (2017). *Culturally sustaining pedagogies: Teaching and learning for justice in a changing world.* Teachers College Press.

Rhodes, D. (2014). *Capacity across cultures: Global lessons from Pacific experiences.* Inkshed Press.

Tagicakiverata, I. W., & Nilan, P. (2018). *Veivosaki-yaga*: A culturally appropriate Indigenous research method in Fiji. *International Journal of Qualitative Studies in Education, 31*(6), 545–556. https://doi.org/10.1080/09518398.2017.1422293

7

LITERACY LEARNING IN "UNOFFICIAL" SPACES

Prospective Teachers' Tutoring Initiative for Homeless Youth

Heidi L. Hallman

UNIVERSITY OF KANSAS

This chapter explores how prospective teachers learned to teach literacy within a community-based field experience, a component of a content area methods course within a teacher education program. The teacher education program at Green State University (GSU), a public university in the Midwest (all names of people and places are pseudonyms), is an undergraduate teacher education program that includes coursework in education and experiences in schools. At GSU, prospective teachers' work within Family Partnership, a community organization that serves homeless families, was a field experience embedded within an English language arts content area methods course. This field experience was premised on the idea that prospective teachers' work tutoring youth in spaces outside of the formal space of the school English language arts classroom might foster a deeper understanding of what it means to be a teacher of literacy.

Prospective Teachers' Work with Homeless Youth

The Family Partnership model can be contrasted with a "shelter model" of assisting homeless individuals and families, as the program is founded on an integrated approach to addressing issues of homelessness. The organization works with a small group of families over the course of a period of three to four months with the intention of fostering families' independence. In the community of Cedar Creek, Family Partnership is one of several programs that serve homeless individuals. GSU's partnership with Family Partnership was purposeful, as the directors at Family Partnership sought connections with GSU, intending to initiate an after-school initiative for the youth who were part of the Family Partnership program.

An emphasis on this demographic of students, students who are homeless, acknowledges that the education of this population has been represented in limited ways in the research literature. It is now estimated that approximately 36,900 unaccompanied youth or minors in the United States are homeless for six months or longer (National Alliance to End Homelessness, 2017). The National Alliance to End Homelessness recognizes this number is likely inaccurate, as youth are a particularly difficult population to account for as they often reside in different places than homeless adults reside. This number also does not include homeless families, of which youth comprise a significant proportion. Chronically homeless families represent 2% of the homeless population (approximately 13,105 people). Most typically, the homeless youth population has been represented as residing in the inner city with single-parent (female)-headed families.

Homelessness is a complex concept, and the definitions of who is homeless and the question of how many in the United States are homeless, especially homeless children, has been the subject of debate (James & Lopez, 2003; Miller, 2011). Three elements that separately or in combination characterize homelessness include "the transience or instability of *place*, the instability or absence of connections to *family*, and the instability of *housing*" (Burt et al., 2001, p. 2). Some scholars (e.g., Karabanow, 2004) have claimed that the oft-used definition of homelessness is actually a catchword that focuses attention on only one aspect of an individual's plight: lack of residence. A broader definition of homelessness would include, for example, those doubled-up with friends or family.

The concept of transience, associated with homelessness, has also been a part of the literature on homelessness (McAllister et al., 2010). For those who teach and work in schools, the by-product of transience is school mobility. Students whose families experience homelessness often attend multiple schools in the course of one school year. The high amount of school mobility can be disruptive to students' educational trajectories. School-based social work professionals are often the personnel tasked to provide interventions for youth who experience homelessness (Canfield, 2015). This chapter extends the focus to classroom teachers of these youth.

Since 2014, the national trend for numbers of homeless individuals and families has continued to decline (National Alliance to End Homelessness, 2017). Yet, many people experiencing homelessness experience "unsheltered" homelessness, meaning that they are in a place unfit for human habitation, such as living on the street or in a car. The "face" of homelessness also continues to change; it is now estimated that 14 out of every 10,000 people are "rural" or "suburban" homeless, as compared to 29 out of every 10,000 people who are "urban" homeless (National Alliance to End Homelessness, 2017). Cedar Creek, a community of approximately 90,000 people, is classified as a suburban community, and the suburban nature of the community, as well as the presence of Green State University, challenges the idea that homeless individuals and families can exist in such communities. It perhaps makes it more imperative that prospective teachers enrolled at

Green State University become aware of and acquainted with the diversity within their local community.

Critical Conceptions of Literacy

The field of literacy studies has undergone great shifts in recent decades (Alvermann & McLean, 2007; Gee, 2000; Gutiérrez, 2008). Responding to these shifts has led scholars in the field in new directions, and one such direction has been the movement away from a conception of a singular, school-based literacy to a recognition of literacy as *multiple* (New London Group, 1996), suggesting that "modes of representation [are] much broader than language alone … [and that they are situated within] increasing local diversity and global connectedness" (Cope & Kalantzis, 2000, pp. 5–6). The term *multiliteracies* stresses the importance of context and the role it plays in acknowledging the legitimacy of multiple literacy practices. "School-based" literacy, then, has become just one way to understand students' literate competencies within the boundaries of school.

Literacy research that has embraced a concept of *multiliteracies* has been thought of by some (e.g., Cherland & Harper, 2007) as advocacy research specifically directed at redesigning the future for and with those students who are labeled "at risk." The goal of redesigning these students' futures becomes a form of social action, a term that is synonymous with working toward change, whether this change be pursued in classrooms or schools (Alvermann, 2009; Heffernan & Lewison, 2005), in community centers or arenas (Sanders-Bustle & Lalik, 2017), in families (Compton-Lilly, 2016; Rogers, 2003), or in individuals themselves (Jones, 2006). Furthermore, scholarship embracing a *youth lens* (Lesko & Talburt, 2012; Petrone et al., 2014) has aimed to bridge research and conversations about youth with conversations about youths' literacy learning. A youth lens also promotes a shift toward recognizing multiple literacies in students' lives and invites the students, themselves, to question and challenge curriculum. Petrone et al. (2014) argue that the "action" that students take from such a stance must begin with not only questioning curriculum but also with an inherent questioning of identity.[1]

Studies specifically focused on the link between literacy and adolescents' identities in out-of-school spaces have greatly increased educators' understanding of their students as literate individuals (Hull & Schultz, 2002). Yet, understanding this in-school/out-of-school "divide" and what bearings this "divide" has on the literacy learning of youth is essential to prospective teachers' growth as educators. Because we know that prospective teachers are still socialized into a traditional, teacher-centered model of instruction (Cuban, 1993; Portes & Smagorinsky,

---

[1] The term *identity* as used in this chapter emphasizes that one's position within society is constituted both by inhabiting a position of agent and subject. Identities always move between these two positions and are variable, multivocal, and interactive, as opposed to coherent and static (Holland et al., 1998).

2010), comprised, in part, of "a conception in which a teacher stands before students who face forward in seats and who are supposedly poised to listen and learn" (Portes & Smagorinsky, 2010, p. 236), prospective teachers need multiple experiences in diverse settings to contemplate the roles of teacher and learner, as well as understand the interaction between instruction and learning.

The Community-Based Field Experience: Context and Method

The chapter focuses on assisting prospective teachers in viewing literacy more broadly than a set of decontextualized skills; it also focuses on providing literacy experiences to youth labeled "at-risk" of school failure, particularly homeless youth. Alongside acknowledging the demographics of the students depicted, the chapter places value on learning to teach in settings outside the traditional class-room and school space. Field experiences in teacher education have long been viewed as a pivotal feature of teacher education programs because prospective teachers enter such programs with strong beliefs and values about teaching and learning (Darling-Hammond, 2006); experiences in field sites have the poten-tial to mitigate these beliefs. Community-based field experiences, in contrast to "traditional" field experiences in classrooms, encourage beginning teachers to contextualize students' lives as part of the fabric of the larger community, and emphasize that familiarity with students' communities is important to the work of teaching.

At the start of the experience at Family Partnership, I, as their instructor, hoped that prospective teachers would be better able to view the students with whom they worked as individuals who used literacy in a variety of ways outside of the classroom. Framing community-based field experiences as spaces that foster the recognition of literacy as a social practice (Coffey, 2010; Gee, 2000; Hallman, 2012; Hallman & Burdick, 2015) allows for the possibility that prospective teachers will question the roles that teachers and students play in the teaching act.

This contemplation of the roles of "teacher" and "learner," and the repositioning of "expert" in the teaching of literacy, was another goal that I had for pro-spective teachers when they began the experience. Oakes et al. (2006) assert that community-based field placements possess the potential for teachers to draw on local knowledge that extends outside of the school. The notion of "expert," then, becomes not only a role for teacher or teacher educator, but rather a role that can be assumed by others in the community. Because many prospective teachers who took part in the experience were previously unaware of any students who were homeless in the schools they had attended, homelessness remained an often "invis-ible" aspect of students' lives in the classroom (see Barton, 1998).

Now, this chapter turns to a focus on prospective teachers' work in the Family Partnership tutoring experience. The tutoring experience aimed to promote lit-eracy in the after-school hours with youth who were part of the Family Partnership program. Prospective teachers could choose to complete literacy-related homework with the youth or design literacy-related activities. Prospective teachers spent approximately one hour with the youth each week; prospective teachers from GSU were at the Family Partnership day center Monday, Tuesday, and Thursday afternoons.

In the remainder of the chapter, the experiences of two particular prospective teachers are discussed. These two teachers were those who maintained a relationship with the Family Partnership tutoring initiative that extended beyond the required semester-long experience. Many prospective teachers had fulfilled the community-based field experience requirement of completing 20 hours of tutoring homeless youth and concluded their experience at the end of the academic semester; in fact, this was the norm, across the eight years. However, there were some prospective teachers who went above and beyond the expectations for participating in the community-based experience, and it is critical that we learn from these individuals in order to encourage other beginning teachers to consider their stance and commitment. Bryce and Ming, featured next, were two of these teachers.

Bryce Adam

Bryce Adam, a white student in his early 20s, attended a predominantly African American high school in the state's metropolitan center. Because of this experience, Bryce frequently discussed his comfort with working with students from diverse backgrounds. Unlike his peers, Bryce understood that Family Partnership, as a non-profit organization, did not have unlimited funds to supplement the programs they had in place. Instead, Bryce was fully aware that the organization relied heavily on volunteers. Throughout the semester, Bryce affiliated with the concept of "volunteer" and was one of the few in his cohort to join Family Partnership families during their dinner hour at a local congregation several times during the semester.

Bryce's adoption of the volunteer role opened doors for expanding his relationship with the youth at Family Partnership. Instead of working only on homework and academic tasks, Bryce was most proud of the relationship he developed over the semester with one nine-year-old, Dominic. Dominic had a love for fishing and would often relate stories of fishing with family and friends to Bryce. Because this was such a topic of interest to Dominic, Bryce encouraged him to draw pictures of himself fishing. After Dominic completed one of the pictures, he gave it to Bryce.

After this, drawing became something that Bryce and Dominic did together in their hours at Family Partnership. One day, Bryce taught Dominic how to do "perspective drawing." Dominic was very excited about learning this new technique and went on to create several perspective drawings. After completing the drawings, Bryce encouraged Dominic to write down the stories that he had already shared with Bryce about particular fishing experiences. As the weeks went by, Dominic and Bryce compiled several stories and drawings.

Dominic, who was in the Family Partnership program with his family members that included his mother, father, and two sisters, discussed how the abrupt change in his life, due to homelessness, had impacted the things he loved to do, including fishing. Before entering the Family Partnership program, Dominic and his father resided in another metropolitan area of the state, Barton, three hours south of Cedar Creek. Dominic confided in Bryce that all the familiarity of living in the city of Barton was now gone.

With his peers in the methods class, Bryce commented that sharing this experience of drawing and writing with nine-year-old Dominic helped Dominic "open up to him [Bryce] and create a more personal relationship" with an adult/teacher. Bryce told his peers that when Dominic described his whole life changing as a result of leaving Barton and entering Family Partnership in Cedar Creek, he began to really understand what homelessness meant to Dominic. Bryce said,

> Dominic's description of leaving behind everything familiar to him really struck me. I learned that, at 9 years old, Dominic had lots of ties to Barton and the schools he had attended there. Now, he was not only homeless, but living in a brand-new community. It really struck me.

Bryce also began to view himself beyond the role of "volunteer" and in the role of "teacher."

Despite having this success with Dominic, Bryce noted that there were also, at times, difficult aspects of working with the children at Family Partnership. The following excerpt is from Bryce's tutoring journal, an ongoing assignment for his content-area methods course:

> The shear resistance I got from a couple of the children reinforced my apprehensions about certain behaviors that aren't always the easiest to assuage and alleviate. Namely, it is the apathy and refusal to perform that shakes me ... I will not make them [the kids] fearful with empty discipline threats, so at least working with them becomes less tense, in that regard, and allows for reciprocity.

In the out-of-school environment of the Family Partnership, Bryce noted that he saw apathy and disengagement in ways that he thought were similar to what one might sometimes witness within a traditional classroom. However, his deep relationship and empathy for Dominic's life situation gave Bryce a new perspective. He said, "I get the apathy a little bit more now. I've heard the defeat in some of the kids' voices and I get it. They're struggling with big issues in life at a young age."

Sometimes the prospective teachers encountered youth who resisted their efforts to engage them in reading and writing. In the after-school hours at Family Partnership, there were times when youth would claim that they were done with the school day and ready to take a break. In these cases, prospective teachers wondered what it might take to change students' attitudes, some which may have been ingrained for many years, and, as prospective teachers guessed, exacerbated by homelessness. At the same time, prospective teachers often understood the youths' position of wanting to take a break in the after-school hours.

These paradoxes – of wanting to encourage authentic literacy learning in the "unofficial" space in which they worked while recognizing that youth didn't always wish to engage in these practices – were what spurred the most learning for prospective teachers. Above, Bryce's commentary about the difficulty in working with youth who were apathetic urged other prospective teachers to recognize the positive work they do with students while grappling with the work that remains troubling or raises questions. Bryce specifically points out that working with apathetic students was challenging. Alongside these challenges, Bryce was able to share the tremendously positive experience he had with Dominic and how he understood apathy differently as a result of really getting to know who Dominic was as a person.

Upon sharing this with his peers in the content-area methods class, Bryce's peers were able to present possible options for working with students who might be apathetic or disengaged in both the classroom and the after-school space. Through this collaboration, prospective teachers began to consider the power of gaining multiple perspectives of working with youth. Multiple perspectives became a door to new possibilities for practice.

Later in the semester, when Bryce talked about another student, Michael, who he had previously characterized as an apathetic student to a group of peers in the content-area methods class, Bryce was able to think about how Michael had become more open to reading over time. Bryce wrote in his field experience journal:

> I thought giving Michael a choice of what to read would not work at all. But, he did then show me a graphic novel that he was willing to read with me. He had the book already – and possibly had already read it once – but started telling me about the characters. I was able to use this and eventually found that there was an entire series … *Big Nate*, the series is called. It's by author Lincoln Peirce (2010–2016). It became ok not to work on Michael's assigned reading for school. Honestly, he didn't really ever tell me if he was completing that or not. But, he always gave me the *Big Nate* update. The *Big Nate* experience is what we shared and I became ok with that and less of a person who felt I had to gauge whether or not he was doing his homework.

Through this experience, Bryce began to think about what he and Michael could accomplish around literacy learning, as opposed to only focusing on what Michael wasn't accomplishing. Bryce took the initiative to assist Michael in selecting a book that was of interest to him and then worked with Michael to continue the relationship with this book series. Bryce continued to work with youth at

Family Partnership into the next semester and summer. Oftentimes Bryce's work extended into informal activities with the youth, such as walking to the park or playing basketball. Bryce noted that he felt as though he understood more about youths' motivations for reading and writing as a result of knowing them outside of school.

With the experience that Bryce had working with youth on reading and writing activities, he learned about some of the trajectories that families took once they left Family Partnership. Because Bryce became a somewhat regular fixture at Family Partnership for almost a year, he learned that Dominic and his family had moved on to a permanent living situation in Cedar Creek once Dominic's father became employed. Bryce mentioned how, even after Dominic moved on, he would occasionally see Dominic at the basketball courts downtown. Bryce relayed to me that seeing this path that Dominic's life had taken over a year gave him a fuller portrait of the lives of students, especially those like Dominic, who experience homelessness for a period of time.

Ming Nguyen

Ming Nguyen, a student in her early 20s, was one of two non-white students in her cohort of English Language Arts education majors. Unlike many of the students enrolled in the teacher preparation program at Green State University, Ming, a self-identified Chinese-American student, lived with her extended family in a community 40 miles from the university. This community, a suburb of Marshall City, afforded more diversity as well as more employment opportunities for members of Ming's family. Most days, Ming took the university bus back and forth from Marshall City to Cedar Creek.

In the experience at Family Partnership, Ming saw how situating students' reading interests and abilities was not a simple split between in-school and out-of-school arenas. Throughout two semesters of tutoring at Family Partnership, Ming spent a great deal of time reading with middle-school students. One particular student, Penny, a 13-year-old middle-school student, liked to read aloud to Ming. Ming would interact with Penny during the reading, usually in the form of asking questions and asking for clarifications. Penny was particularly fond of vampire books, and she and Ming read aloud Kimberly Pauley's (2009) *Sucks to Be Me: The All-True Confessions of Mina Hamilton, Teen Vampire (maybe)* over the course of several tutoring sessions. Ming, at first, viewed the book as pure pleasure reading for Penny, yet came to reflect on how her view of Penny's reading changed as she spent more time reading with Penny. Below is an excerpt from Ming's journal that she wrote for her methods class:

> Penny loves reading vampire books, and I thought this was fine but saw it as outside of school reading. I thought that reading aloud a book like this was really only good for her fluency with reading. As we got more into the

book, though, I could see how Penny was really imagining things about the story-world presented in the book. The book was a creative place for her mind, not just a fun book. This is what English teachers want books to do for kids, and I am not so judgmental of these types of books anymore.

Ming was able to move from an either/or conception of knowledge to a both/also view of the benefits of young adult books – particularly "vampire books." Instead of dichotomizing reading choices into out-of-school and in-school books, Ming saw the literacy learning space she created with Penny as a place where knowledge could reside in new ways. This space became a hybrid space of both school-based knowledge and out-of-school based knowledge, and this shift in how the space was considered allowed Ming to see the benefits that Penny's reading choices gave to her.

The community-based field experience allowed Ming to discover new conceptions of teaching, conceptions that assist those early in their careers to focus not just on teaching but on students' learning. For Ming, Penny's learning began to take precedence over Ming's "teaching," and Ming could really see how Penny was growing as a literacy learner as a result of the experience. Gutiérrez et al. (1997) recognize that in this focus on learning, teaching becomes "consciously local, contingent, situated, and strategic" (p. 372).

Despite her success with Penny, Ming sometimes seemed perplexed by the book choices that she saw students making outside of school. As a student who had loved the reading choices presented to her in school, Ming wondered why more students had trouble finding books that interested them. In her mind, adolescents would be well-served if they replicated the school environment in their out-of-school lives. To Ming, such a replication looked like a seamless pathway to success.

However, when asking Penny why she preferred the books she did, Ming learned some important lessons about adolescents' agency and life outside of school. Penny responded to Ming's query by stating the power of student choice, replying that, "my interest in reading vampire books matches who I am. It's not that I don't like what we read in school, but I feel like choosing books that I'm interested in reading makes me a more interesting person." Ming shared this response with other prospective teachers, and they agreed that adolescents typically valued the agency they had in becoming an individual. Ming reflected on the perhaps stifling nature that schools might create for some students and began to see the value in Penny's reading choices.

Ming completed her required semester at Family Partnership but then extended her commitment to the organization throughout the following spring semester. Over the course of this next semester, Ming collected unwanted books from thrift stores, libraries, and garage sales in an effort to build a modest young adult/children's library at the Family Partnership Day Center. While Ming continued to work with students at Family Partnership, she also saw her role as one that sustained the work being done there. The contributions Ming made to the Day Center library were utilized by prospective teachers in future cohorts.

Due to her prolonged experience at the Family Partnership Day Center, Ming got to see youth utilize the books she had contributed to the center. She told me,

> the first time I saw kids take a book from the shelf and put it in their back-pack, I thought that what I had done was really meaningful as these kids have very few possessions. They are homeless and are sleeping in churches that volunteer to host them each week. Each week, they eat and sleep in a different "home." When I saw kids make the Day Center and the books part of their home, it really made me happy.

Ming's recognition of the transience in the students' lives provided her with a new-found meaning to the work she was doing.

Learning from Bryce and Ming

Work in community-based field sites encourages beginning teachers to think about and enact new relationships between teacher and student. Some scholars, including Howey and Zimpher (2006), have written about alternative conceptualizations of the work of teachers. They write about "boundary spanners," or those individuals who "[blur] the lines of responsibility between traditionally assumed by those in universities, schools, and school districts" (p. 5), as those teachers who seek to challenge the roles that they are socialized into, and instead renegotiate those roles.

Bryce and Ming became, throughout their experience at Family Partnership, "boundary spanners," as they took it upon themselves to enact agency with the students with whom they worked. This allowed them to be responsive and create possibilities for literacy learning for the students they engaged and helped them grow and develop. Literacy learning became located within the student rather than located within a pre-determined curriculum or set of activities; it was apparent that the community-based space, without a defined curriculum, almost encouraged Bryce and Ming to see a new starting point – the students them-selves – for literacy learning.

As prospective teachers, Bryce and Ming also questioned and compared the work they undertook in the community-based setting to the work they under-took in the traditional classroom space. Both prospective teachers featured in this chapter were able to work toward a more expansive and creative vision for the role of "teacher," encompassing aspects of volunteer, tutor, mentor, and teacher. They were able, also, to incorporate the real circumstance of the students' homelessness into the deliberations they had about what was best for the students. Because the work of "teaching" still stands as a binary to mentoring/tutoring for many pro-spective teachers, it was significant to see how these two teachers' conception of the role of "teacher" evolved. In many ways, a strict adherence to a presumed teacher role is not surprising, as it has been shown that beginning teachers' adherence to an "apprenticeship of observation" (Lortie, 1975) is one of the salient themes that runs throughout research on field experiences in teacher education (see Zeichner, 2010).

Many teacher educators (Cochran-Smith, 1995; Gay, 2003) have asserted that what is needed in teacher education programs is space and opportunity for prospective teachers to undertake work in contexts that can broaden their belief systems and construct more sophisticated understandings of students as learners. As Bryce and Ming illustrate, literacy learning in community-based field sites, such as Family Partnership, has the potential to be this opportunity. As the field of teacher education reiterates a commitment to prepare teachers to teach diverse groups of students, it is important that this move beyond rhetoric and into the spatial and temporal contexts in which we live.

References

Alvermann, D. (2009). Sociocultural constructions of adolescence and young people's literacies. In L. Christenbury, R. Bomer, & P. Smagorinsky (Eds.), *Handbook of adolescent literacy research* (pp. 14–28). Guilford.

Alvermann, D. E., & McLean, C. (2007). The nature of literacies. In Rush, L., Eakle, J., & Berger, A. (Eds.), *Secondary school literacy: What research reveals for classroom practice* (pp. 1–20). National Council of Teachers of English.

Barton, A. C. (1998). Teaching science with homeless children: Pedagogy, representation, and identity. *Journal of Research in Science Teaching, 35*(4), 379–394. https://doi.org/10.1002/(SICI)1098–2736(199804)35:4<379::AID-TEA8>3.0.CO;2-N

Burt, M., Laudan, Y. A., & Lee, E. with Valente, J. (2001). *Helping America's homeless: Emergency shelter or affordable housing?* Urban Institute Press.

Canfield, J. (2015). *School-based practice with children and youth experiencing homelessness.* Oxford University Press. https://doi.org/10.1093/acprof:oso/9780190213053.001.0001

Cherland, M. R., & Harper, H. (2007). *Advocacy research in literacy education: Seeking higher ground.* Lawrence Erlbaum Associates.

Cochran-Smith, M. (1995). Color blindness and basket making are not the answers: Confronting the dilemmas of race, culture, and language diversity in teacher education. *American Educational Research Journal, 32,* 493–522. https://doi.org/10.2307/1163321

Coffey, H. (2010). "*They* taught *me*": The benefits of early community-based field experiences in teacher education. *Teaching and Teacher Education, 26,* 335–342. https://doi.org/10.1016/j.tate.2009.09.014

Compton-Lilly, C. (2016). *Reading students' lives: Literacy learning across time.* Routledge. https://doi.org/10.4324/9781315641201

Cope, B., & Kalantzis, M. (2000). Introduction: Multiliteracies: The beginnings of an idea. In Cope, B. & Kalantzis, M. (Eds.), *Multiliteracies: Literacy learning and the design of social futures* (pp. 3–8). Routledge.

Cuban, L. (1993). *How teachers taught: Constancy and change in American classrooms, 1890–1990.* Teachers College.

Darling-Hammond, L. (2006). *Powerful teacher education.* Jossey-Bass.

Gay, G. (Ed.). (2003). *Becoming multicultural educators: Personal journeys toward professional agency.* Jossey-Bass.

Gee, J. P. (2000). The new literacy studies: From "socially situated" to the work of the social. In Barton, D., Hamilton, M., & Ivanic, R. (Eds.), *Situated literacies: Reading and writing in context.* Routledge.

Gutiérrez, K. (2008). Developing sociocultural literacy in the third space. *Reading Research Quarterly, 43*(2), 148–164. https://doi.org/10.1598/RRQ.43.2.3

Gutiérrez, K., Baquedano-López, P., & Turner, M. (1997). Putting the language back into language arts: When the radical middle meets the third space. *Language Arts, 74*(5), 368–378. www.jstor.org/stable/41482886

Hallman, H. L. (2012). Community-based field experiences in teacher education: Possibilities for a pedagogical third space. *Teaching Education, 23*(3), 241–263. https://doi.org/10.1080/10476210.2011.641528

Hallman, H. L., & Burdick, M. N. (2015). *Community fieldwork in teacher education: Theory and practice.* Routledge. https://doi.org/10.4324/9781315795065

Heffernan, L., & Lewison, M. (2005). "What's lunch got to do with it?" Critical literacy and the discourse of the lunchroom. *Language Arts, 83*(2), pp. 107–118. www.jstor.org/stable/41962088

Holland, D., Lachicotte, W. S., Skinner, D., & Cain, C. (1998). *Identity and agency in cultural worlds.* Harvard University Press.

Howey, K., & Zimpher, N. (Eds.). (2006). *Boundary spanners.* American Association of State Colleges and Universities.

Hull, G., & Schultz, K. (2002). *School's out! Bridging out-of-school literacies with classroom practice.* Teachers College Press.

James, B. W., & Lopez, P. D. (2003). Transporting homeless students to increase stability: A case study of two Texas districts. *Journal of Negro Education, 72*(1), 126–140. Retrieved from www2.lib.ku.edu/login?url=https://search.proquest.com/docview/222069502?accountid=14556 https://doi.org/10.2307/3211296

Jones, S. (2006). *Girls, social class, and literacy: What teachers can do to make a difference.* Heinemann.

Karabanow, J. (2004). *Being young and homeless: Understanding how youth enter and exit street life.* Peter Lang.

Lesko, N., & Talburt, S. (2012). *Keywords in youth studies: Tracing affects, movements, knowledges.* Routledge. https://doi.org/10.4324/9780203805909

Lortie, D. (1975). *Schoolteacher: A sociological study.* University of Chicago Press.

McAllister, W., Kuang, L., & Lennon, M. C. (2010). Typologizing temporality: Time-aggregated and time-patterned approaches to conceptualizing homelessness. *Social Science Review, 82*(2), 225–255. https://doi.org/10.1086/654827

Miller, P. M. (2011). A critical analysis of the research on student homelessness. *Review of Educational Research, 81*(3), 308–337. https://doi.org/10.3102/0034654311415120

National Alliance to End Homelessness. (2017). Retrieved July 20, 2019 from www.endhomelessness.org/

New London Group. (1996). A pedagogy of multiliteracies. *Harvard Educational Review, 66,* 60–92. https://doi.org/10.17763/haer.66.1.17370n67v22j160u

Oakes, J., Franke, M. L., Hunter Quartz, K., & Rogers, J. (2006). Research for high quality urban teaching: Defining it, developing it, assessing it. *Journal of Teacher Education, 53*(3), 228–235. https://doi.org/10.1177/0022487102053003006

Peirce, L. (2010–2016). *Big Nate* series. HarperCollins.

Petrone, R., Sarigianides, S. T., & Lewis, M. A. (2014). The youth lens: Analyzing adolescence/ts in literary texts. *Journal of Literacy Research, 46*(4), 506–533 https://doi.org/10.177/1086296X15568926

Pauley, K. (2009). *Sucks to Be Me: The all-true confessions of a Mina Hamilton, Teen Vampire (maybe).* Mirrorstone.

Portes, P. R., & Smagorinsky, P. (2010). Static structures, changing demographics: Educating teachers for shifting populations in stable schools. *English Education, 42*(3), 236–247. Retrieved February 5, 2020, from www.jstor.org/stable/40607989

Rogers, R. (2003). *A critical discourse analysis of family literacy practices: Power in and out of print.* Lawrence Erlbaum Associates. https://doi.org/10.4324/9781410607690

Sanders-Bustle, L., & Lalik, R. (2017). Writings on the wall: Nurturing critical literacy through a Community-based Design Project. *Journal of Adolescent & Adult Literacy, 61*(1), 65–73. https://doi.org/10.1002/jaal.641

Zeichner, K. (2010). Rethinking the connections between campus courses and field experiences in college- and University-based teacher education. *Journal of Teacher Education, 61*(1–2), 89–99. https://doi.org/10.1177/0022487109347671

8

FAMILY LITERACY THROUGH SEPARATION AND TRAUMA

Integrated Perspectives for Fathers*

Angela M. Wiseman, Qiana R. Cryer-Coupet, and Ashley A. Atkinson

NORTH CAROLINA STATE UNIVERSITY

Stephen M. Gibson

VIRGINIA COMMONWEALTH UNIVERSITY

Introduction

As you enter the conference room, seven fathers are sitting around a large wooden table, holding their own copies of the picture book, *A Chair for My Mother* (Williams, 1982), and taking turns to read aloud. The group of men gathered here are diverse; they range in age from 26 to 48, some are high school graduates and others have completed four-year degrees. They represent three countries and at least three distinct first languages. Despite these differences they share an integral identity, they are fathers who are recovering from substance use disorders at a residential treatment facility. They are separated from their children and have decided to participate in a family literacy program to improve or establish communication with their children.

A Chair for My Mother tells the story of a little girl living with her mother and grandmother. The family's house burns down in a fire and the community bands together to help them. They all work together to save money to buy a comfortable chair for the mother. After reading, Stephen leads the fathers in a discussion by asking open-ended questions such as, "Do you feel hopeful about this family's future? Why or why not?" The fathers' discussion initially focuses on the characters'

---

* This chapter discusses a program for fathers separated from their children due to addiction, incarceration, and/or homelessness. It provides insight into the ways in which family literacy happens beyond the traditional boundaries of "home."

loss and familial strength. They connect the story to their experiences as parents and consider how they might read this text with their children. Many of the fathers notice the absence of a father or father figure in the story. Allan expresses his frustration in being separated from his children and explains that he is excluded from decisions with his children, stating, "... if you can't contribute financially, they don't want you to contribute emotionally at all." From the ensuing discussion, we learn some of the fathers' parenting challenges while they are separated from their children, and we decide that our next session will focus on communication techniques with the guardians of their children.

We present this vignette to describe a program that uses a trauma-informed approach to support families who are separated from each other, particularly while in a residential drug rehabilitation program. This program emanates from our experiences across literacy education, social work, and educational psychology. We partner with Louise, a community member who works at the facility and is intimately involved in the details of the individual fathers' experiences. In this chapter, we present findings from family literacy sessions and describe how our integrated, community-based approach has been used to support the development of families. The research questions guiding our study are:

- How do fathers respond to children's literature and make sense of their experiences parenting from afar in a trauma-informed family literacy program?
- How can a trauma-informed family literacy program support fathers who are separated from their children?

Theoretical Perspectives and Related Research

A sociocultural perspective has informed our understanding of families, recognizing that social institutions, cultural contexts, and power relations affect human experiences and that it is crucial to create responsive programs for families and communities (Chao & Mantero, 2014; González et al., 2006). Researchers using a sociocultural framework have provided important contributions to family literacy; such as documenting the complexities of literacy practices in the home (Mui & Anderson, 2008; Perry & Moses, 2011), recognizing participants' social and cultural ways of knowing (Compton-Lilly et al., 2012), and emphasizing the importance of teachers recognizing diverse literacy practices (Souto-Manning & Rabadi-Raol, 2018).

The National Child Traumatic Stress Network (NCTSN) defines family traumas as

> ... frightening, often life-threatening, or violent events that can happen to any or all members of a family ... [that] can cause traumatic stress responses in

family members with consequences that ripple through family relationships and impede optimal family functioning.

(NCTSN, n.d.)

Families who have experienced such trauma have unique needs occurring from their conditions prior to separation, the absence of family members, as well as the transition back to reunification (Suchman, 2016). The relationships that children have with their parents are important to their own development, and separation can cause physical and mental health issues, as well as behavioral difficulties that affect all aspects of their lives (Anderson et al., 2015). Although often overlooked, interactions between fathers and children are significant to all aspects of family well-being (Cryer-Coupet et al., 2020; McLeod et al., 2019). The implications for educational contexts are numerous; many students in classrooms are immeasurably affected in ways that affect their participation, engagement, and peer interactions (Jennings & Siegel, 2019).

There are different goals for family literacy programs. Some family literacy programs have focused on improving the literacy skills of parents and children alike (Wasik & Van Horn, 2012), but our purpose for creating this program was to provide parenting support through literature and literacy. All of the fathers in the program had young children and came to the meetings wanting to develop their own parenting abilities, particularly since they were separated from their children. We built our understanding of family literacy as the way that caregivers, parents, children, and extended family members use literacy at home, in their community, and in other contexts where they interact and engage with each other (Crawford & Zygouris-Coe, 2006). While there is sparse research on family literacy from a trauma-informed perspective, research demonstrates how responsive literacy practices can support families as they build relationships with children (MacGillivray et al., 2016; Muth, 2011, 2016). In addition, cultivating positive relationships between fathers and their children can be mutually beneficial for everyone involved (Brookes & Baile, 2011; Hansen, 2018) and reading together can be one way to foster positive interactions. Therefore, we approached the sessions with the idea that our interdisciplinary approach that included literacy, social work, and psychology would support the fathers as they considered their needs as parents.

Reading and responding to literature has been identified as a powerful method for addressing critical social and emotional issues for children and adults (Dutro, 2019; Wiseman & Jones, 2018). While shared book reading can support children's language and vocabulary development (Barnes et al., 2017), responding to literature can also support conversations about sensitive topics and difficult emotions (Wiseman, 2012; Wiseman et al., 2019). It is important to note that the benefits of shared reading can support parents as well as children, positively affecting adults both emotionally and cognitively (Anderson et al., 2010). Opportunities to discuss literature that focus on the most fundamental emotions and experiences of life can encourage adults to examine their own feelings, consider their own childhood worlds, and imagine future possibilities (Maine & Waller, 2011).

Research Methods

This qualitative study is part of an ongoing project. For several years, the authors have been collaborating with a community partner at Healthy Transformations Rehabilitation Facility (HTRF, a pseudonym) and several community organizations that work with families who are separated due to parental substance misuse and incarceration. Angela has been working with Louise (pseudonym), the community partner, for six years; Ashley has supported this research for the past three years. Qiana has been engaged in qualitative and participatory research with fathers at HTRF for three years. In this section, we describe the context and participants and explicate our methods of data collection and analysis.

Context and Participants

The research site HRTF is at a private not-for-profit organization that offers recovery-oriented services to both homeless and underserved people who are experiencing substance use disorders. The site provides overnight emergency facilities, non-medical detoxification, outpatient services, and a recovery program. HTRF has separate campuses for men and women with various activities including visitation hours, family days, and regular educational sessions. A majority of participants have been incarcerated; however, participation at this facility is not mandated by the court system and is voluntary. The fathers in this study ranged from 26 to 48 years old. Some fathers were high school graduates and others had completed four-year degrees. They were racially and linguistically diverse as well, representing three countries and at least three distinct first languages. The participating fathers had children between 10 months and 17 years of age, but the majority of children were elementary school age. We surveyed the fathers prior to implementing the program, and they reported that they were concerned about mending relationships with their children, being present during visits, and addressing financial concerns related to parenting.

We are an interdisciplinary team of four members who facilitate this family literacy program. Angela is a literacy education associate professor who focuses on children's literature and responding to picture books. Ashley is a doctoral student in literacy interested in children's literature and reader response. Qiana is an assistant professor in social work whose research focuses on father involvement in fragile families. Stephen is a graduate student in educational psychology interested in father's socialization practices and children's educational outcomes.

Description of Family Literacy Program

Book club sessions consist of six two-hour sessions where the fathers read picture books and then participate in discussions. Our focus is not a skills-oriented approach; rather, we are influenced by a sociocultural lens to consider how literature discussions can foster important conversations and teachable moments around parenting. During each session, book discussions are open-ended; we encourage parents to respond to literature in ways that are relevant to them. Our sessions follow a pattern. We begin by reading a book together and then use discussion to encourage personal connections to the text. Then, we talk about how the fathers might read the text with their children. Finally, we present information about parenting that is relevant to their situation and follow up with an activity that encourages reflection, such as journaling or sketching.

Collaboratively, we have engaged in research and/or implemented cycles of book clubs over the past four years; for this paper, we focus on one group of fathers who participated during a six-week period. In addition to discussing how to read and talk about the books with their children, we also created opportunities for addressing the social and emotional issues as parents who are experiencing trauma make sense of their experiences (MacGillivray et al., 2016).

Data Collection and Analysis

We consider literacy as a "diverse set of contextualized practices" (Perry, 2012, p. 62) that are connected to the fathers' background knowledge and experiences. The book discussions are an opportunity for open-ended responses where fathers can discuss concerns, explore feelings, and share emotions. Qualitative techniques of participant-observation and descriptive analysis were used to document reading sessions (Creswell & Poth, 2018). Data were generated from fieldnotes and audiotaped discussions and all sessions were transcribed.

In order to analyze data, we engaged in the process of thematic analysis (Saldaña, 2015). To begin, Angela, Ashley, and Qiana collaboratively reviewed one transcript, creating codes and then noted how the codes were connected to larger themes that were defined by our research questions. We engaged in the process of defining and refining codes and findings by reading through the transcripts together, discussing our analysis, and rereading data multiple times to clarify our codes.

Findings

Our findings consist of two main themes. The first theme was how the fathers responded to literature which included comments that were related to the texts that we were reading, ways to read with children, and sharing background experiences. We found that the participants' responses to literature opened up opportunities to reflect on their roles as fathers. Second, we found that trauma was a significant theme; traumatic experiences were shared and the facilitators used a trauma-informed approach in the lessons. The theme of trauma included approaches such as creating a safe space for response, considering recovery, and parenting while separated from their children.

Responding to Literature

The purpose of reading picture books was multifaceted; most of the fathers have young children and our goal was to encourage them to read with their child. Also, picture books can address important themes and can be read from cover to cover in one session. The fathers responded by analyzing the personalities of the characters, sharing their reactions to stories, and relating stories to their own life. Their responses to literature were focused on relationships with their children and their own recovery process.

Across all the sessions, the fathers related personally to the picture books. For example, the book *In My Family/En Mi Familia* (Garza, 1996) the author tells her own experiences as a child growing up on the Mexico–Texas border through descriptive stories and vivid illustrations. Garza's images of cooking, eating, and celebrating with family encouraged the fathers to think about their own family. For instance, Aiden offered this response:

> The page where they were making the empanadas reminds me of my family around Thanksgiving and Christmas time. When everyone's in the kitchen and helping out and the kids are doing their own thing, and steal the food without being seen, or feeding it to the cat like she was doing over here … I did this a lot when I was a kid, because no one in my family is an addict. So, with my son, and me not being present is like me reading this to him, it puts it in his mind to wonder, where is this at in my life right now. So, those are questions I'm sure I'll be asked …

Aiden initially reflected on how he related to the story and moved to his relationship with his son. Imagining his own family experience caused him to wonder about his son's perceptions.

Analyzing characters in the story was a recurring focus. As they discussed the tragedy of the fire which burned the house of the family in *A Chair for My Mother* (Williams, 1982), the fathers reflected on their own family experiences and how the mother, daughter, and grandmother supported each other. One father noted the importance of their relationship, saying, "Something happened that was bad and they still was [sic] together. You know, they still had each other."

The fathers shared that they were skeptical at first about reading picture books, wondering if the stories would truly engage them. Jamal shared that when Louise first told him that the sessions would use picture books, he,

... didn't know what to expect, but now after we did read them and share about them, it kinda makes you relate more to your children, that's pretty good. And then you can relate to the fathers in the room, as well. You take something from the book, and hopefully use it in your parenting.

It was common for fathers to identify with characters or themes in stories and imagine how they would read with their children. For instance, the mother in *A Chair for My Mother* reminded Aiden of his own mother:

I can relate to, when they're running, when they see the fire. Look, you see the woman holding the shoes in her hand. My mom was like a fashionista so she would not have like, she would have done the same thing. She would not have ran in her shoes. She would have put them in her hand instead of throwing them away.

Allan also reflected on how he enjoyed not only reading the picture books but also the process of engaging in discussion. He shared his excitement with us by saying "I really can't wait to apply a lot of this stuff. It makes me feel better. Just being able to talk about these kid books. I really like it a lot." In addition, Aiden confirmed that it was important to have a space to share and discuss together, saying:

... I just listen to everyone and talk to everyone, I don't know everything, and I can take advice. And I can get responses, on my own judgment as a parent, to see how I'm doing ... And I don't ... so I don't know everything, and that's okay.

Our analysis showed that the fathers used the texts as a springboard for thinking about their own experiences and imagining interactions with their children — even if they were not seeing them regularly. While we tried to schedule a family day with the children, the fathers were unable to secure the date with their children and their caregivers. However, the fathers did report that the books helped them imagine conversations they would have when they were together again.

Trauma

Trauma was a significant theme and included affirmative responses, creating a safe space, reflecting on recovery, and sharing feelings about parenting from afar. Our trauma-informed and recovery-focused approach entailed creating sessions around the expressed needs of the fathers. Sessions were designed based on the idea that being responsive in research requires learning from all our participants, community partner, and interdisciplinary research team. It was important to us that the fathers were able to trust each other and share their experiences with each other. In past sessions, parents have shared that focusing on their parenting was a missing part of their recovery – something they needed in the process of transitioning back to their children's lives.

The process of building trust was important and our relationship with the community partner Louise who worked with HTRF allowed us to establish trust with the fathers. Louise's relationships with fathers was an impetus for them to participate and a bridge for developing connections with us. This was evident to us in many ways, including one father that told us he came to the class "just to support" Louise and felt he benefitted, so he was "glad he did [participate in the program]."

The fathers expressed that they needed a space to address their experiences as parents. Some of the fathers had not told their children why they were absent and wondered how to build relationships with them and explain their situation, particularly if their children were very young. For instance, Aiden expressed concerns about how he might explain his separation with this three-year-old, wondering how, "... it puts it in his mind to wonder, where is this at in my life right now?" and describing his absence as "... like the elephant in the room." Comments such as Aiden's provided us with opportunities to give parenting support that was relevant to their experiences. In this case, Qiana responded to his concerns, saying, "... being present in the here and now, what will Jai remember from that moment, sitting down and reading this book with you and how it made me feel in that moment."

An important aspect of our trauma-informed approach was for both the researchers and participants to openly share our own experiences during the book discussion. Our research team and community partner shared about their families, parenting issues, and other interests as well as stories of family trauma and parental addiction in order to help facilitate relationship building. One example of this was evident when Stephen and several of the fathers brought up how they played football in college. This connection facilitated a conversation both on allowing their own sons to play the sport and also how they can support their children in sports from afar as a co-parent. One of the fathers expressed remorse at missing some of his child's games, and Stephen could empathize with the importance of sports, family, and mentorship.

Affirming fathers' perspectives and ideas was central to our trauma-informed approach, but the fathers also were supportive of each other during the sessions. The fathers often encouraged each other as they expressed their concerns and questions about their children. In the exchange below, Allan is expressing his struggles with separation from his children, particularly due to the strained relationship with their mother.

Allan: That's the thing; I am being held hostage.
Aiden: And you'll do anything that she's, wherever she'll go, you'll meet her right there.

Allan: I'm being held hostage.
Aiden: I know you are.
Allan: On every single decision I've made, it's finally come to bite me in the ass.
Aiden: Well, you may have to just eat it for a little while, man.

This response shows support and understanding and affirms Allan's experiences and feelings. In this exchange, Aiden affirms Allan's feelings by both repeating and agreeing with him. He challenges him to "eat it for a little while," knowing that he might need to make amends to work with his child's mother.

Our findings reveal that trauma was an important aspect of this program. The fathers expressed trauma and also created a supportive environment for sharing trauma in various ways, particularly by affirming each other's experiences. As researchers, we incorporated a trauma-informed approach by using their responses to guide our book selection and discussions.

Discussion/Implications

Family literacy entails various goals with multiple outcomes. Traditional approaches to family literacy focus on increasing literacy skills for families and their children, with the end goal of increasing reading and writing with children and adults. We acknowledge the importance of this approach; however, we posit that a trauma-informed approach is also important. The end goal of a trauma-informed program is to provide socio-emotional support for parents and children using literacy; in our case, using literature discussions. An analysis of the program revealed the importance of trauma-informed components in building relationships, making intentional connections to the fathers' lives, and in the role of affirmation. In addition, the fathers responded to the trauma-informed approach and felt that the time spent in these sessions was valuable to them and worthy of their time.

Our family literacy program was strengthened by an interdisciplinary approach. Angela and Ashley have facilitated book discussions, mostly with children and in classroom settings, where difficult topics have emerged and topics of trauma have been shared (Wissman & Wiseman, 2011). Qiana and Stephen, with backgrounds in social work and educational psychology, provided foundational experiences for a trauma-informed approach. Our community partner Louise was essential to establishing trust and ensuring that our program was responsive and relevant. In our study, responding to picture books was a significant way of addressing social and emotional topics in ways that recognized the needs for fathers who were in recovery and separated from their children. Not only did the picture book evoke deep connections between their lives and the stories, it also encouraged them to read to their children if they could or consider how they might read to their children when they are reunited.

From this collaborative project and our understanding of families and children in various contexts, we conclude that more work needs to be done to consider the role of trauma in family literacy program development. Trauma can manifest itself in many ways and emanates from varied experiences such as poverty, racism, separation, and homelessness. While many other macro-level issues need to be addressed to appropriately support families, we advocate for interdisciplinary trauma-informed approaches to family literacy programming when the need exists.

References

Anderson, J., Anderson, A., Friedrich, N., & Kim, J. E. (2010). Taking stock of family literacy: Some contemporary perspectives. *Journal of Early Childhood Literacy, 10*(1), 33–53. https://doi.org/10.1177/1468798409357387

Anderson, E. M., Blitz, L. V., & Saastamoinen, M. (2015). Exploring a school–university model for professional development with classroom staff: Teaching trauma-informed approaches. *School Community Journal, 25*(2), 113–134. Retrieved from www.schoolcommunitynetwork.org/SCJ.aspx

Barnes, E. M., Dickinson, D. K., & Grifenhagen, J. F. (2017). The role of teachers' comments during book reading in children's vocabulary growth. *The Journal of Educational Research, 110*(5), 515–527. https://doi.org/10.1080/00220671.2015.1134422

Brookes, L. & Baille, D. (2011). Parents in prison: Justice literacy and public policy. *Reclaiming Children and Youth, 20*, 31–35. Retrieved from https://reclaimingjournal.com/

Chao, X. & Mantero, M. (2014). Church-based ESL adult programs: Social mediators for empowering family literacy, ecology of communities. *Journal of Literacy Research, 1*, 90–114. https://doi.org/10.1177/1086296x14524588

Compton-Lilly, C., Rogers, R., & Lewis, T. Y. (2012). Analyzing epistemological considerations related to diversity: An integrative critical literature review of family literacy scholarship. *Reading Research Quarterly, 47*(1), 33–60. https://doi.org/10.1002/rrq.009

Crawford, P. A., & Zygouris-Coe, V. (2006). All in the family: Connecting home and school with family literacy. *Early Childhood Education Journal, 33*(4), 261–267. https://doi.org/10.1007/s10643-005-0047-x

Creswell, J. W., & Poth, C. N. (2018). *Qualitative inquiry and research design: Choosing among five approaches*. SAGE. Retrieved from www.sage.com

Cryer-Coupet, Q. R., Dorsey, M. S., Lemmons, B. P., & Hope, E. C. (2020). Examining multiple dimensions of father involvement as predictors of risk-taking intentions among black adolescent females. *Children and Youth Services Review, 108*, 104604. https://doi.org/10.1016/j.childyouth.2019.104604

Dutro, E. (2019). *The Vulnerable Heart of Literacy: Centering Trauma as Powerful Pedagogy*. Teachers College Press. Retrieved from www.tcpress.com

Garza, C. L. (1996). *In my family, En mi familia*. Children's Book Press.

González, N., Moll, L. C., & Amanti, C. (Eds.). (2006). *Funds of knowledge: Theorizing practices in households, communities, and classrooms*. Routledge. https://doi.org/10.4324/9781410613462

Hansen, G. V. (2018). Does fatherhood training in prison improve fathering skills and reduce family challenges? *Child Care in Practice, 24*(2), 198–211. https://doi.org/10.1080/13575279.2017.1420036

Jennings, P. A., & Siegel, D. J. (2019). *The trauma-sensitive classroom: Building resilience with compassionate teaching.* W. W. Norton & Company. Retrieved from wwnorton.com

MacGillivray, L., Curwen, M. S., & Ardell, A. (2016). "No matter how you word it, it's for me" Mandated writing practices in a homeless shelter for mothers in recovery. *Journal of Literacy Research, 48*(2), 192–220. https://doi.org/10.1177/1086296x16662174

Maine, F., & Waller, A. (2011). Swallows and amazons forever: How adults and children engage in reading a classic text. *Children's Literature in Education, 42*(4), 354. https://doi.org/10.1007/s10583-011-9139-y

McLeod, B. A., Johnson Jr, W. E., Cryer-Coupet, Q. R., & Mincy, R. B. (2019). Examining the longitudinal effects of paternal incarceration and coparenting relationships on sons' educational outcomes: A mediation analysis. *Children and Youth Services Review, 100,* 362–375. https://doi.org/10.1016/j.childyouth.2019.03.010

Mui, S., & Anderson, J. (2008). At home with the Johars: Another look at family literacy. *The Reading Teacher, 62*(3), 234–243. https://doi.org/10.1598/rt.62.3.5

Muth, W. (2011). Murals as text: A social–cultural perspective on family literacy events in US prisons. *Ethnography and Education, 6*(3), 245–263. https://doi.org/10.1080/17457823.2011.610576

Muth, W. (2016). "A big circle of unity": Incarcerated fathers being-in-text. *Journal of Literacy Research, 48*(3), 317–345. https://doi.org/10.1177/1086296x16661609

National Child Traumatic Stress Network (NCTSN). (n.d.). Trauma types. Retrieved August 14, 2019, from www.nctsn.org/what-is-child-trauma/trauma-types.

Perry, K. H. (2012). What is literacy? – A critical overview of sociocultural perspectives. *Journal of Language and Literacy Education, 8*(1), 50–71. Retrieved from http://jolle.coe.uga.edu/wp-content/uploads/2012/06/What-is-Literacy_KPerry.pdf

Perry, K., & Moses, A. (2011). Television, language, and literacy practices in Sudanese refugee families: "I learned how to spell English on Channel 18." *Research in the Teaching of English, 45*(3), 278–307. Retrieved from https://ncte.org/resources/journals/research-in-the-teaching-of-english/

Saldaña, J. (2015). *The coding manual for qualitative researchers.* SAGE. Retrieved from www.sage.com

Souto-Manning, M., & Rabadi-Raol, A. (2018). (Re)Centering quality in early childhood education: Toward intersectional justice for minoritized children. *Review of Research in Education, 42*(1), 203–225. https://doi.org/10.3102/0091732x18759550

Suchman, N. E. (2016). Mothering from the inside out: A mentalization-based therapy for mothers in treatment for drug addiction. *International Journal of Birth and Parent Education, 3*(4), 19–24. https://doi.org/10.1017/s0954579417000220

Wasik, B. H., & Van Horn, B. (2012). The role of family literacy in society. In Wasik, B. H. (Ed.), *Handbook of family literacy* (pp. 3–18). Routledge. https://doi.org/10.4324/9780203841495.ch1

Williams, V. B. (1982). *A chair for my mother.* MacRae.

Wiseman, A. M. (2012). Summer's end and sad goodbyes: Children's picture books about death and dying. *Children's Literature in Education, 41*(1), 1–14. https://doi.org/10.1007/s10583-012-9174-3

Wiseman, A. M., & Jones, J. S. (2018). Examining depictions of bullying in children's picturebooks: A content analysis from 1997 to 2017. *Journal of Research in Childhood Education, 32*(2), 190–201.

Wiseman, A. M., Atkinson, A. A., & Vehabovic, N. (2019). "Mom, when are you coming home?": Family literacy for parents who are addicted, incarcerated, and/or homeless. *Language Arts*, *97*(1), 36–41. Retrieved from https://ncte.org/resources/journals/language-arts/

Wissman, K. & Wiseman A. M. (2011). "That's my worst nightmare": Poetry and trauma in the middle school classroom. *Pedagogies: An International Journal*, *6*(3), 234–249. https://doi.org/10.1080/1554480X.2011.579051

9

INCARCERATED LANGUAGES AND LITERACIES

Attempting Liberatory Language and Literacy Pedagogies in a Prison Setting

Jim Sosnowski

UNIVERSITY OF ILLINOIS AT URBANA-CHAMPAIGN

Luz Murillo

TEXAS STATE UNIVERSITY

Introduction

In recent years there has been growing social and political interest in reducing prison populations (Council of Economic Advisors, 2016), a response to the fact that the USA leads the world in incarceration rates, incarcerating individuals at nearly four times the international average, and mostly impacting African American and Latinx populations (Pfaff, 2017). In addition to reconsidering sentencing and release policies (Fandos, 2018), adult language and literacy education is being positioned as a response to mass incarceration, following historical trends in the USA in which adult language and literacy education has been mobilized in response to societal crises, real or perceived (Brandt, 2004).

The reinstitution of Pell Grants for incarcerated individuals in 2016 as part of a three-year pilot program (Kreighbaum, 2020) and the introduction of new legislation in 2019, which would assure that incarcerated individuals continued to be eligible for Pell Grants (Davis, 2019; Kreighbaum, 2020), is evidence of the increased bipartisan support favoring the expansion of educational programming in prisons (Davis, 2019; Fain, 2020). Davis, a policy researcher with the RAND Corporation, explains that education is seen as "another lever that policymakers can use" (2019, p. 12) to reduce recidivism and lower prison populations. Reports such as the often cited meta-analysis conducted by the RAND Corporation which concluded that individuals who participated in correctional education were 43% less likely to recidivate (Bozick et al., 2018) provide some of the strongest support for utilizing education as a means of alleviating rates of incarceration.

These arguments are further buttressed by neoliberal capitalist discourses equating reduced recidivism with economic cost saving, as correctional education is believed to contribute to creating "productive citizens." Spangenberg (2004), President and Founder of the Council for Advancement of Adult Literacy, articulates this argument in stating:

> Educators must get their messages across to the public: rehabilitation will improve certain societal problems; education is a cost-saving measure that ultimately reduces recidivism; and because inmates will eventually rejoin society, it is in everyone's best interest to enable them to lead productive lives.
>
> *(p. 10)*

This chapter does not seek to engage these claims concerning recidivism, as other scholars have already done (Butts & Schiraldi, 2018; Maltz, 2001), but instead critically questions how programs like Language Partners (LP), the focus of this study, can contribute to perpetuating deficit perspectives of already marginalized individuals. Through focusing on LP, a peer-taught, prison-based language and literacy program situated in a state-run medium-security prison, we explore how monoglossic language ideologies and the positioning of language as a reified object (García & Torres-Guevara, 2009; Pennycook, 2010) shaped the teaching policies and practices in LP and the instructors' perspectives of the students. Additionally, we discuss efforts to challenge these ideologies through engaging in participatory action research with the peer-instructors, demonstrating both the potential and the challenges which can emerge.

A Brief History of Language Partners (LP)

LP is part of a larger college-in-prison program offered by a large, public, land-grant, research university. Ramon, an incarcerated individual involved in the college-in-prison program, proposed LP after observing how the absence of English language and literacy courses in the prison further minoritized some men because they did not have the linguistic practices necessary to navigate that environment. A unique aspect of his proposal involved the training of incarcerated men to be peer-instructors, providing an opportunity to build skills and experiences while also recognizing the situated knowledge peer-instructors held of the prison.

Since 2010, LP has had six cohorts, each serving 10–12 students, predominantly from Mexico. During each 18-month cohort, the peer instructors (incarcerated men) were responsible for planning and conducting three-hour classes each Tuesday and Thursday night based on the textbook *Focus on Grammar* (Schoenberg & Maurer, 2006). University-affiliated volunteers provided teaching feedback, teaching materials, and planned workshops and for-credit courses which served as professional development and training. Jim, a graduate student who has been involved since LP's inception, and Luz, a professor, who offered a for-credit course, fit into this final category.

Growing Concerns

Through for-credit courses and from reflecting on their own language learning experiences, the peer-instructors came to better understand how language and literacy education has been utilized to minoritize students in the USA (McCarty et al., 2015; Pac, 2012), resulting in a debate questioning what LP was actually accomplishing. The following quotes from two peer-instructors encapsulate this debate.

> Language Partners is so important because it doesn't only help the students to navigate the prison environment, but it will also help them when they are released. Eventually the students will be deported back to Mexico. They will be able to find better jobs in restaurants or hotels because they will be able to speak English.
>
> *(Michael, Peer-instructor)*

> Since the start of the Language Partners program, the pedagogical approach to teaching in the classroom has been "full-immersion," an approach that requires the use of English-only in the classroom … I have come to question the exclusionary manner and nature of such pedagogy and the way in which the student–instructor relationship suffers by creating oppressed–oppressor roles in the classroom.
>
> *(Orlando, Peer-instructor)*

This debate, questioning whether LP represented a liberatory space or one which contributed to further minoritizing the students, provided the motivation for this study.

Constructing Knowledge through Participatory Action Research

Data Collection and Analysis

The work of resolving this debate began with a for-credit course, *Funds of Knowledge for Teaching and Learning*, offered by Luz during the fall of 2016. This course was designed to engage the peer-instructors in critically examining their beliefs about language and literacy in part through composing educational auto-biographies and conducting case studies focused on the language and literacy practices and beliefs of another individual in the prison. Following this course, over an 18-month period, the peer-instructors and Jim partnered to conduct an in-depth study of LP, during which the research team documented the policies and practices that characterized LP through approximately 75 hours of ethnographic observations of the LP classroom (Frank, 1999). Informed by these observations, a smaller team conducted in-depth semi-structured interviews with former and current LP students, peer-instructors, and volunteers. Additionally, throughout the study we collected artifacts pertinent to LP.

Data analysis was conducted using the constant comparative method (Lincoln & Guba, 1985). The research team met monthly in the prison to analyze the data and ask the question "What are we learning about LP?," using a list of characteristics formed between Jim and the LP peer-instructors at the outset of the study as start codes. Additionally, outside of the prison, Jim utilized ATLAS.ti 8 to further analyze the data.

Participatory Action Research (PAR)

This study was informed by PAR, an epistemology that assumes knowledge is rooted in social relations and most powerful when produced collaboratively through action (Fine et al., 2004, p. 95). Cammarota and Romero (2009) argue the purpose of PAR is to "… [initiate] critical changes that produce greater social justice" (p. 54) through involving community members in the research process, instead of only valuing the knowledge of outside "objective experts," who have traditionally entered communities of color, conducted research, and returned to their academic institutions with few resulting benefits for the community from which data was extracted (Torres & Reyes, 2011). To the extent possible in the prison, the peer-instructors participated as co-researchers, shaping the course of this research.

Monoglossic Language Ideologies

Through this study, it became evident that LP's policies and teaching practices were premised on monoglossic language ideologies and the positioning of language as a reified object. García and Torres-Guevara (2009) describe monoglossic language ideologies as seeing "language as an autonomous skill that functions independently from the context in which it is used" (p. 192). Routinely, LP lessons reflected a "curricularization of language" in which language was approached as an autonomous object that could be dissected into discrete components and taught outside of a social context (Valdés, 2019).

A lesson focusing on constructing Wh- questions provides an example of the enactment of the curricularization of language in LP. During this lesson, Antonio, a peer-instructor, helped students produce the formula, Wh word + Do/ Does + subject/pronoun + verb, a pattern which was then presented on the top of a worksheet (Figure 9.1). Students then worked to complete the worksheet, inserting words into the grammatical pattern. The activity concluded with

Instructions: Use Wh-, do/does, sub. /pronoun, verb, ?, and anything else to complete the questions in the chart.

WH	Do/does	Sub/pronoun	Verb	? / anything else
Where		Joe-Joe		
	do		play	
		he		?
How		it		
Why				apples?
		Tonio		
			work	
	does			
				?

FIGURE 9.1   Classroom Handout Utilized in a Lesson Focused on Teaching Wh–Question Formation

Writing checklist
1. Are all the words spelled correctly?
2. Is the first word in every sentence and personal names capitalized?
3. Does every sentence end with correct punctuation?
4. Do your subjects and verbs agree?

FIGURE 9.2   Writing Checklist

the students asking each other the questions they had written, such as "Why do you like apples?" and "When does the bus leave?" Throughout, language was not situated within any particular social context and did not align with the students' daily experiences.

Similarly, during journaling activities, when students were encouraged to incorporate their thoughts and experiences, the focus remained on mechanics and dissecting language into discrete components. Following a journal assignment, another peer-instructor, Joseph, presented a "checklist" (Figure 9.2) and explained, "You could check your own writing without the help of a [peer-instructor]." While this checklist helped draw students' attention to issues of punctuation, capitalization, and grammar, noticeably absent was a focus on meaning. Similar to the previous example, language was understood to be a set of linguistic codes and rules and learning a language was a matter of assembling these codes appropriately.

Student interviews also revealed how the *Focus on Grammar* (FOG) textbook reinforced monoglossic language ideologies. Diego and Jorge identified the grammatical charts in FOG as one of the most useful tools for learning English.

Similarly, Gilberto explained that FOG was helpful because he could follow the pattern which helped him know what he needed to do. Ruffo suggested that FOG was like having another teacher, explaining that he especially liked activities which required him to unscramble sentences and use grammatical charts. To the students, the textbook presented an idealized "standard" and set of rules toward which they were supposed to strive.

These and numerous other examples demonstrate how language and literacy was not conceptualized as "a series of social practices and actions that are embedded in a web of social relations" (García & Leiva, 2014, p. 201), but instead became a reified object which was dissected and taught as an autonomous system. LP's teaching was consistent with "bottom-up decoding" that Gee (2015) claims is often associated with literacy teaching. Instead of learning through living the meaning of the language, instruction was isolated from the lives of the students (Vasquez, 2015).

Challenging Language Ideologies

Language ideologies shape how a person views language and its use in society, but in many cases individuals are only partially aware of their ideologies (Kroskrity, 2006). Participating as co-researchers provided a means for the peer-instructors to begin to critically examine the language ideologies which shaped their understanding of the classroom and students.

During an interview, Raul, an LP student, admitted that he often did not complete the homework because he did not have time. Instead, he created thank you, birthday, and greeting cards (Figure 9.3), which he traded with other incarcerated men for commissary items. Unlike many of the men in the prison, he did not have family supporting him financially, and trading these cards allowed him to supplement the $10 per month state stipend given to all incarcerated individuals to purchase hygiene products and other necessities not provided by the state. Additionally, Raul explained how these cards also supported his language learning. Most of his cards were written in English and while he initially needed to ask people to provide the necessary language such as "I love you" or "I miss you," over time he developed the linguistic practices necessary to create a variety of types of cards.

Raul added that he often replaced homework assignments by writing more in his journal assignments because he liked writing more than the fill-in-the-blank style homework. He explained that when he started writing, "a lot of things come to mind, and I put them in my journal and write a lot." Journals provided a means of going beyond learning isolated grammatical concepts, allowing him to communicate his thoughts and feelings about topics such as immigration, past memories, and future dreams. Janks (2010) emphasizes how important it is for teachers to provide opportunities for students to share ideas in their writing, and for teachers to resist the urge to focus solely on mechanics. Although the focus in class often

FIGURE 9.3 Sample Greeting Card Produced by an LP Student

turned to mechanics, journals represented an opportunity for students to write their stories and share who they were in an environment that often silenced them and where sharing personal feelings was not common.

Raul was not the only student to share ideas like these. Others also explained the various situated ways in which they were utilizing and building their language practices to accomplish their needs in the prison (Hernandez-Zamora, 2010). Hearing how the students were learning and utilizing their literacy practices outside the classroom impacted how the peer-instructors viewed their teaching and the students. In describing this changing perspective of the students, Bryan, a peer-instructor, wrote (Dean et al., 2018):

> Our perspectives came from the same school of thought that to this day is telling kids nationwide that they have to sit in a class and be open receptacles. They come from the perspective that the teacher is the holder of knowledge and therefor the student has nothing to offer. They came from being

mostly educated using the banking method throughout my life and being comfortable with the familiarity and thus applying it. As much as it pains me to admit this, I approached our students from a deficit perspective and participating in this study allowed for me to acknowledge that.

The peer-instructors also began questioning how the approaches they used in the classroom contributed to maintaining deficit perspectives of the students. In particular, some instructors began to question the use of the BEST Literacy test for language proficiency (Center for Applied Linguistics, 2017). As an assessment tool commonly utilized in community college adult education settings; the test results from previous cohorts went unquestioned. However, some problematic scores indicated that students had a lower English proficiency at the conclusion of the program than when they began LP. While in the past, teachers pointed toward a lack of motivation in the students, some now began to question the validity of this test for the LP setting. Notes from an LP planning meeting stated, "There was a strong feeling that the BEST test did not do justice to the ways in which the students had improved (confidence and facility in communicating). Something else is desired test wise." Instead of questioning students' commitment to learning to explain the perceived decrease in proficiency, the instructors began questioning if the problem was not with the student but with the test and practices in the classroom, which failed to recognize the contextualized ways in which students were practicing language and literacy.

Toward a Heteroglossic Classroom

As the peer-instructors became more aware of how monoglossic ideologies shaped their deficit perspectives of the students, they began to question how to change the LP classroom to better recognize their students' agency and their abilities to utilize their linguistic funds of knowledge (Smith, 2001) to improve their situations. One example of this was evident in a lesson facilitated by Orlando, a peer-instructor. In a previous class, Joseph provided a portion of an essay detailing a former LP student's immigration from Mexico. Recognizing the students' interest in the story, Orlando provided the rest of the story to the students in the subsequent class and then, based on a students' suggestion, the class proceeded to turn this story into mini-plays. Throughout this activity, the students, who all reported crossing into the USA as undocumented immigrants, pulled from their own personal stories as they negotiated which details to include in their dialogue and how to best convey their ideas linguistically. The original essay contained few direct quotations, so Orlando encouraged the students to imagine what each character would say.

The final products were multilingual scripts which moved between languages as the characters negotiated the different interactions (Figure 9.4). When asked why they had chosen to include Spanish, one student explained he needed to use both Spanish and English because some of the ideas did not make sense in both languages. This student recognized that language was not a simple code that could mechanically be translated between English and Spanish. Mignolo (2012) describes this idea through the concept of *bilanguaging*, an understanding of language that goes "beyond sound, syntax and lexicon, and beyond the need of having two languages" (p. 264). The students understood that the same ideas and feelings could not be conveyed through a single set of linguistic practices and their choice to translanguage (García & Leiva, 2014) was a challenge to monoglossic ideologies which defined LP.

Additionally, shifting away from a monoglossic and reified understanding of language included instances of integrating more relevant topics into the curriculum, using the LP space to facilitate discussions and action in response to challenges the students were facing. These instances included lessons focused on exploring possible responses to the high cost of telephone calls and the loss of one of the only two Spanish TV channels offered in the prison. Through translanguaging, students were invited to share their experiences and knowledge of the prison as they considered potential responses to these situations and how to build the language practices that would be necessary. Instead of a curricularized approach to teaching, a problem-posing curriculum (Auerbach & Burgess, 1985) provided the opportunity for students to be producers of knowledge and through working with the peer-instructors were socialized into language practices (Hernandez-Zamora, 2010) that they could utilize to advocate for themselves in the prison. These instances were based more on an understanding of language as a set of situated practices embedded within the prison context (García & Torres-Guevara, 2009).

Room for Improvement

While the LP peer-instructors moved toward a more situated approach to language and literacy teaching, there were still cases when they struggled to envision language teaching beyond the monoglossic ideologies which shaped LP. In addition to continuing to base the curriculum on the FOG textbook, there were other instances when peer-instructors continued to focus on discrete linguistic features. During two interviews, students commented that teaching the alphabet "would help with spelling and writing" and "[the peer-instructors] should teach the alphabet because most of [the students] can't say it completely." Based on these comments, Anastacio designed an alphabet lesson for the next LP cohort. Providing feedback on the lesson, an LP volunteer wrote, "… they focused on creating a song using the alphabet. I noticed that there was plenty of repetition of the letters and the students certainly found the activity interesting (this repetition and focus on task represents excellent pedagogy)." Auerbach and Burgess (1985), in a critique of adult language teaching materials, draw attention to how materials often lead to students being "portrayed as incompetent and addressed

Scene 2

Group 1

Felipe's job in Rodales. Mal Paso Chiapas, Felipe's friends Pascasio and Romulo, Felipe's boss Tiofilo. Fellipe and friends talk about irse pal norte.

Felipe: Hey guys, I have something to say.

Pascasio: What's up Chaparro? Si el jefe te ve te va a regañar.

Felipe: You know what/ Ya estoy cansado de todo esta Miecceeercoles. I work so hard every day and the money no me alcansa. Ustedes saben que tengo two children and with the money que gano no me alcansa para nada.

Romulo: That's true Chaparrin. Pero que quiere decir?

Felipe: Que me voy pa norte.

Tiofilo: Hey ustedes do you come here to work not to talk! Ponganse a trabajar because this is what I pay you for.

Pascasio: yes, Chaparrin es lo que te iba a proponer often work, dices that there the people gana lo doble que uno gana aqui, ademas there we can conoci a lot of ladies.

Romulo: No, do not listen to him Chaparrin. Think, of your family. A lot of people die when they intentan crusar lo frontera.

Pascasio: yes
Romulo, but we will find the easy way to cross the frontera, you know what? I know someone who cross a lot of people every Saturday.

Felipe: En serio guey?

Romulo: Yo sigo diciendo que es a bad idea.

Felipe: I know Romulo, but tu sabes that this job is not suficiente.

Romulo: I know but here you are with your family and there you do not know a ninguno and you will be alone.

Pascasio: Yo guey si el desidio irse para el norte, dejalo. I am willing to go with him. There we'll have a better life.

Felipe: Solo voy a ir to work hard to send money to my family. That's the only thing I will do.

FIGURE 9.4 Immigration Play Written by LP Students

like children" (p. 486). In LP, a continued understanding of language and literacy learning focused on the acquisition of discrete linguistic items contributed to the infantilization of the adult learners.

Also problematic was a perspective that student's full linguistic repertoires were only useful for moving students toward English proficiency. Following a workshop offered by a university professor focusing on how a bilingual teaching approach could be implemented in LP, the peer-instructors decided to utilize Spanish in the classroom, but cautioned that "it [Spanish] shouldn't be used just to have an escape." Pablo elaborated that "the focus in the classroom should be on the L2 as much as possible," adding that the Spanish could be used when they reach an impasse but that he didn't think it should be a teaching tool. This decision to only incorporate Spanish as a tool for building English fluency reflects Lin's (2013) criticism of TESOL pedagogies which have worked to maintain "classroom monolingualism, or 'bilingualism through parallel monolingualism'" (p. 521). While recognizing Spanish as a pedagogical tool represented a significant shift in policy, Spanish was still only a means for moving toward English proficiency, contributing to messages which positioned English monolingualism as the goal to which to strive, mirroring messages communicated in US schools and society (Rosa, 2016).

Conclusion

Education within prisons is often supported by claims of increased educational and employment opportunities for individuals after their incarceration. However, critical scholars have questioned similar claims regarding education more generally, arguing that schools serve to reinscribe values and beliefs found in society and contribute to the maintenance of societal structures and hierarchies instead of reimagining them (Bourdieu & Passeron, 1977; Levinson & Holland, 1996). Considering the growing importance being placed on education within carceral contexts (Kreighbaum, 2020; Wilson et al., 2019), it is necessary to question what is being accomplished in these educational spaces.

A curricularized approach to language and literacy education contributed to shaping which forms of language and literacy mattered and were valued in the classroom. Luke (2004) argues that literacy scholars need to question "which kinds of textual practice count, for whom, where, and in what contexts" (p. 333). Building on Luke's argument, it is also important to consider how the policies and practices employed in a classroom contribute to conceptions of what counts and for whom. In LP, monoglossic language ideologies shaped a curricularized approach to language and literacy education, which in turn positioned the ways in which students were learning and engaging with language and literacy practices on a daily basis as irrelevant to the students' progress as learners of additional language and literacy practices.

In fact, the curricularized approach to language and literacy education not only contributed to further minoritizing the students but the peer-instructors as well. While it is often argued that a key advantage of adult language and literacy learners is the wealth of knowledge and life experiences that the students bring with them to the classroom (Noriega, 2013), the curricularized approach in LP made it difficult for the students and peer-instructors to draw on their life experiences and knowledge of the prison. While the peer-instructor model was premised on a belief that individuals who were also incarcerated would be better able to develop contextualized learning that was relevant to the students' lives, that very knowledge was pushed out of the classroom in place of teaching discrete and decontextualized linguistic features. Instead of being a mechanism for empowerment, language and literacy instruction remained an avenue with which to maintain and recreate social and linguistic hierarchies (Gramsci, 1971).

However, when language and literacy was understood as social practices, opportunities arose for both peer-instructors and students to build on their situated knowledge of their life experiences and the prison in particular. In these instances, both inside and outside of the classroom, students were socialized into new language practices through interacting with more experienced users (Hernandez-Zamora, 2010; Moll, 2014) allowing them to build on their already existing language and literacy practices, and also to provide opportunities to use these developing literacy practices in response to challenges they experienced in the prison.

PAR provided the opportunity for the peer-instructors to critically examine the policies and practices which characterized LP. The peer-instructors began to transform their thinking about the nature of language and literacy, moving from an understanding of literacy "as a set of skills thought to be universal and applicable anywhere" (Barton, 2007, p. 197) toward an understanding that "people acquire language and literacy by being informally socialized into the practices and values of contexts in which they are immersed" (Auerbach, 2005, p. 365). Through PAR, the peer-instructors began to reimagine what mattered and to whom concerning language and literacy education in the prison and started the process of questioning the language ideologies which had shaped their approach to teaching.

Choices regarding language and literacy teaching policies and practices are not simply a question of identifying best practices but are by nature political (García, 2019). Ignoring this political nature and failing to consider how pedagogical choices can replicate oppressive systems allows similar dynamics to be recreated in so called transformative spaces. Approaching language and literacy education as a social act and not a discretely bounded enumerable object provides the opportunity for students and instructors to bring their understandings and situated knowledges to their learning and teaching.

References

Auerbach, E. (2005). Connecting the local and global: A pedagogy of not-literacy. In J. Anderson, M. Kendrick, T. Rogers, & S. Smythe (Eds.), *Portraits of literacy across families, communities, and schools: Intersections and tensions* (pp. 363–379). Lawrence Erlbaum Associates. https://doi.org/10.4324/9781410612830

Auerbach, E., & Burgess, D. (1985). The hidden curriculum of survival ESL. *TESOL Quarterly, 19*(3), 475–495. https://doi.org/10.2307/3586274

Barton, D. (2007). Adults and world literacy. In *Literacy: An introduction to the ecology of written language* (pp. 186–204). Blackwell.

Bourdieu, P., & Passeron, J.-C. (1977). *Reproduction in education, society and culture.* SAGE.

Bozick, R., Steele, J., Davis, L., & Turner, S. (2018). Does providing inmates with education improve postrelease outcomes? A meta-analysis of correctional education programs in the United States. *Journal of Experimental Criminology, 14*(3), 389–428. https://doi.org/10.1007/s11292-018-9334-6

Brandt, D. (2004). Drafting U.S. literacy. *Encyclopedia of Educational Reform and Dissent, 66*(5), 485–502. https://doi.org/10.4135/9781412957403.n296

Butts, J., & Schiraldi, V. (2018). Recidivism reconsidered: Preserving the community justice mission of community corrections. *Papers from the Executive Session on Community Corrections.*

Cammarota, J., & Romero, A. (2009). A social justice epistemology and pedagogy for Latina/o students: Transforming public education with participatory action research. *New Directions for Youth Development, 123*(Fall), 53–65. https://doi.org/10.1002/yd

Center for Applied Linguistics. (2017). BEST literacy. Retrieved from www.cal.org/aea/bl/

Council of Economic Advisors. (2016). Economic perspectives on incarceration and the criminal justice system. Retrieved from https://doi.org/10.1525/fsr.2016.28.5.361

Davis, L. (2019). *Higher education programs in prison: What we know now and what we should focus on going forward.* RAND Corporation. https://doi.org/10.7249/pe342

Dean, B., Esparza, A., Mendoza, P., & Rodriguez, F. (2018, November). The power and limits of PAR: Exploring a prison-based ESL program. Paper presented at the Annual Meeting of the Literacy Research Association, Palm Springs.

Fain, P. (2020, May 22). Study on prison-based college program. *Inside Higher Ed.* Retrieved from www.insidehighered.com/quicktakes/2019/05/22/study-prison-based-college-program

Fandos, N. (2018, December 18). Senate passes bipartisan criminal justice bill. *New York Times.* www.nytimes.com/2018/12/18/us/politics/senate-criminal-justice-bill.html

Fine, M., Torre, M., Boudin, K., Bowen, I., Clark, J., & Hylton, D. (2004). Participatory action research: From within and beyond prison bars. In L. Weis & M. Fine (Eds.), *Working method: Research and social justice* (pp. 95–119). Routledge.

Frank, C. (1999). *Ethnographic eyes: A teacher's guide to classroom observation.* Heinemann.

García, O. (2019). The curvas of translanguaging. *Translation and Translanguaging in Multilingual Contexts, 5*(1), 86–93. https://doi.org/10.1075/ttmc.00026.gar

García, O., & Leiva, C. (2014). Theorizing and enacting translanguaging for social justice. In A. Blackledge & A. Creese (Eds.), *Heteroglossia as practice and pedagogy* (pp. 199–216). Springer. https://doi.org/10.1007/978-94-007-7856-6_1

García, O., & Torres-Guevara, R. (2009). Monoglossic ideologies and language policies in the education of U.S. Latinas/os. In J. Enrique, G. Murillo, S. Villenas, R. Galván, J. S. Muñoz, C. Martínez, & M. Machado-Casas (Eds.), *Handbook of Latinos and education: Theory, research, and practice* (pp. 192–193). Routledge.

Gee, J. (2015). *Literacy and education.* Routledge.

Gramsci, A. (1971). *Selections from the prison notebooks.* International Press.

Hernandez-Zamora, G. (2010). *Decolonizing literacy: Mexican lives in the era of global capitalism.* Multilingual Matters.

Janks, H. (2010). *Literacy and power.* Routledge.

Kreighbaum, A. (2020, April 22). The case for Pell in prisons: Broad coalition puts focus on lifting ban on student aid in prisons. *Insider Higher Ed.* www.insidehighered.com/news/2019/04/22/broad-coalition-puts-focus-lifting-ban-student-aid-prisons

Kroskrity, P. (2006). Language ideologies. In A. Duranti (Ed.), *A companion to linguistic anthropology* (pp. 496–517). Blackwell.

Levinson, B., & Holland, D. (1996). The cultural production of the educated person: An introduction. In B. Levinson, D. Foley, & D. Holland (Eds.), *The cultural production of the educated person: Critical ethnographies of schooling and local practice.* State University of New York Press.

Lin, A. (2013). Toward paradigmatic change in TESOL methodologies: Building plurilingual pedagogies from the ground up. *TESOL Quarterly, 47*(3), 521–545. https://doi.org/10.1002/tesq.113

Lincoln, Y., & Guba, E. (1985). *Naturalistic inquiry.* SAGE.

Luke, A. (2004). On the material consequences of literacy. *Language and Education, 18*(4), 331–335. https://doi.org/10.1080/09500780408666886

Maltz, M. (2001). *Recidivism* (2nd ed.). Academic Press.

McCarty, T., Nicholas, S., & Wyman, L. (2015). 50(0) years out and counting: Native American language education and the four Rs. *International Multilingual Research Journal, 9*(4), 227–252. https://doi.org/10.1080/19313152.2015.1091267

Mignolo, W. (2012). *Local histories/global designs: Coloniality, subaltern knowledges, and border thinking.* Princeton University Press.

Moll, L. (2014). *L.S. Vygotsky and education.* Routledge. https://doi.org/10.1017/CBO9781139878357.001

Noriega, D. (2013, December 11). Why no literacy programs for 30 million in U.S.? Remapping Debate. Retrieved from www.remappingdebate.org/sites/default/files/Why%20no%20literacy%20programs%20for%2030%20million%20in%20U.S.%3F.pdf

Pac, T. (2012). The English-only movement in the US and the world in the twenty-first century. *Perspectives on Global Development & Technology, 11*(1), 192–210. https://doi.org/10.1163/156914912X620833

Pennycook, A. (2010). *Language as a local practice.* Routledge.

Pfaff, J. (2017). *Locked in: The true causes of mass incarceration and how to achieve real reform.* Basic Books.

Rosa, J. (2016). Racializing language, regimenting Latinas/os: Chronotope, social tense, and American raciolinguistic futures. *Language and Communication, 46,* 106–117. https://doi.org/10.1016/j.langcom.2015.10.007

Schoenberg, I., & Maurer, J. (2006). *Focus on grammar: An integrated skills approach.* Pearson Education ESL.

Smith, P. (2001). Community language resources in dual language schooling. *Bilingual Research Journal, 25*(3), 375–404. https://doi.org/10.1080/15235882.2001.10162799

Spangenberg, G. (2004). *Current issues in correctional education: A compilation & discussion.* Council for Advancement of Adult Literacy.

Torres, M., & Reyes, L. (Eds.). (2011). *Research as praxis: Democratizing education epistemologies* (4th ed.). Peter Lang.

Valdés, G. (2019). Curricularizing language: Implications for heritage language instruction. In M. Fairclough & S. Beaudrie (Eds.), *Innovative strategies for heritage language teaching: A practical guide for the classroom* (pp. 255–270). Georgetown University Press.

Vasquez, J. (2015). Disciplined preferences: Explaining the (re)production of Latino endogamy. *Social Problems, 62*(3), 455–475. https://doi.org/10.1093/socpro/spv011

Wilson, M., Cooper, D., & Alamuddin, R. (2019). *Unbarring access: A landscape review of postsecondary education in prison and its pedagogical supports.* Ithaka S+R. https://doi.org/10.18665/sr.311499

10

SPONSORING OLDER ADULTS' IMPROVEMENT OF METALITERACY USING IPADS

*Julie A. Delello, Annamary L. Consalvo,
Rochell R. McWhorter, and Gina Doepker*

THE UNIVERSITY OF TEXAS AT TYLER

America is graying at an unprecedented rate as the population of adults 65 and older continues to increase (Vespa et al., 2018). In fact, by the year 2030, there will be a demographic shift for the United States, as one in every five Americans will be of retirement age. Baby Boomers (born between 1946 and 1964) will be more numerous than the number of children alive (US Census Bureau, 2018) and while they generally do use digital tools on a regular basis, according to O'Keefe (2014), there is a marked within-group competence difference between younger and older Boomers, with the younger Boomers using these tools more frequently. The oldest Boomers in 2020 are 74–75 years old; in 2030, they will be in their mid-eighties. While currently a much smaller percentage of the overall population, the numbers of *pre*-Baby Boomers, or Silent Generation, is significant and represents those born from around 1920 (centenarians) to 1940 or so (in their eighties) (Mather et al., 2015, p. 3). Representing the majority of the participants in this study, this group's familiarity and competence with current digital technology is patchy at best.

As life expectancies continue to rise, improving technology literacies may help older adults participate more fully in modern society, which today includes identifying, accessing, and understanding online resources. For example, competently using online banking, accessing medical services and records, and renewing prescriptions require people to navigate finance and health resources through the use of digital tools. Research suggests that as older adults become more experienced using the Internet, playing online games, and reading text online, they demonstrate a greater neural circuitry, improved cognitive skills, and reduced memory loss that was not apparent when reading paper text-based pages (Small et al., 2009). Yet, only 4% of adults over age 65 have read an online book (eBook)

(Perrin, 2018). The question becomes, are we, as a society, underestimating the opportunity that engaging with online text has for older adults in terms of the strengthening and updating of their literacy skills?

This chapter describes an exploratory case study conducted at a senior living center in the Southwestern United States with adults who were age 65 and older. The aims of this chapter are to (a) demonstrate how iPad technology can improve metaliteracy in older adults; (b) describe literacy patterns in older adults across gender, age, and education; and (c) analyze the benefits and barriers to using mobile technologies such as iPads to improve literacy skills.

Review of Relevant Literature

Older adults "grew up in a time when technology meant a wall telephone, a radio and a TV set with three channels. Today they're in the midst of a monumental transition" (Allis, 2017, para. 1) as society wants devices that can do more things better, faster, and easier. Literacies of all kinds are ever-changing. Since the dawn of the digital age, those changes have been and continue to rapidly increase. The truth is that if individuals do not have the access to acquiring up-to-date literacies, including those associated with technologies, they may be left behind. As Kularski and Moller (2012) reflected, "Those who lack the knowledge or resources to access information technology fall further behind than those who find it to be not only a ubiquitous element but an integral component of their social functioning" (p. 2). Thus, it makes sense to provide older adults with opportunities for both systematic and individualized opportunities for updating their literacies, and specifically, their digital literacies. Ignoring seniors' lack of knowledge only strengthens the digital divide.

Digital Divide

Digital technologies are ubiquitous. Due to an increase in the number of mobile devices and access to the Internet, more than half of those over 65 are connected to the Internet and 40% own a smartphone (Anderson & Perrin, 2017). However, there is a notable digital divide and for some, even a digital exclusion, as many senior citizens have little to no access to technology (Delello & McWhorter, 2015). For example, only 30% of those from the Silent Generation (age 74 and over) have a smartphone (Jiang, 2018) and for those seniors with less education, the divide is even greater (Anderson & Perrin, 2017), which may translate to a lower quality of life. Chen and Chan (2013) reported that older adults may not utilize technology due to a lack of knowledge and training, the perceived need for it, and the overall costs involved with it. Although the main determinant of digital exclusion is age, individuals who are less affluent may also be physically and/or psychologically disconnected from technology (Nimrod, 2018). According to The Chartered Institute of Taxation (2012), other significant factors may also contribute to digital exclusion such as disability, learning difficulties, ethnic origin, culture, location, and/or language barriers.

For some older adults, there is even a fear of technology or "technophobia" correlated with age, health, or a lack of experience (Delello & McWhorter, 2015), defined as: "technophobia represents a negative psychological reaction toward technology, which can arise in varying forms and intensity" (Sinkovics et al., 2002, p. 478). Nimrod's (2018) research found that for many seniors, technophobia may be an unjustified fear, affecting up to 30% of the population. And for the "gray-divide" (Friemel, 2016, p. 313), this fear may be more closely related to age as younger generations have had more exposure to technology than older adults. Thus, those less likely to use technology have either a lower perception toward technology use, or a sense of diminished autonomy. In addition, such techno-phobia may reduce the amount of time older adults use technology for reading (Hou et al., 2017). Conversely, studies have shown that older adults experiencing less technophobia have greater digital literacy skills (Nimrod, 2018) and greater self-efficacy (Prior et al., 2016). However, there is still "an ever-increasing gulf between the haves and the have-nots, not only in terms of access but in levels of digital literacy" (The Chartered Institute of Taxation, 2012, p. 5).

Gerontechnology and the iPad

Gerontechnology is a growing interdisciplinary field "in which technology is directed toward the aspirations and opportunities for the older persons [that] aims at good health, full social participation and independent living up to a higher age" (Geron Technology, 2019, para. 1).

The iPad is one digital tool that can help to slow the ever-widening digital divide for older adults. Due to its graphical interface, portability, and capability for users to choose and use larger icons for easier viewing, the iPad is user-friendly and allows "the user to experience full color images, videos, online books, music, social networking platforms, and inspiring applications available for download" (Delello & McWhorter, 2015, p. 7). At this point, there is limited research regarding the effects of iPads on seniors' well-being and because "greater numbers of people are living longer; we must consider how mobile technology such as the iPad may be used to improve their quality of life" (p. 7). The good news in all of this is that the next generation of seniors will not have to experience the same degree of frustration, fear, and insecurity that current seniors may feel regarding technology because the new generation already has the basic digital literacy functions well within their metaliteracies wheelhouse. Of course, even newer tools will demand that people continue to upgrade their literacies. Until then, it behooves society to make an organized and concerted effort to provide current seniors with devices and learning opportunities to enhance their lives through confident and compe-tent use of technologies.

Conceptual Framework

Whether and how people acquire particular literacies, including digital, has a great deal to do with whether and how they are taught, the access they have, and the practices of communities in which they are situated (Barton et al., 2000). In other words, their encounters with sponsors of literacy (Brandt, 2001) are important. Literacy is a moving target as what sufficed in 1960, 1980, 1990, or even later is no longer sufficient due to both the technological advances in the tools that are widely available and the expectations of culture in which we live. The guiding framework for this study is one of metaliteracy, a reboot of information literacy, which "provides an overarching and unifying framework that builds on the core information literacy competencies while addressing the revolutionary changes in how learners communicate, create, and distribute information in participatory environments" (Jacobson & Mackey, 2013, p. 84). That a person possesses information literacy, or the ability, according to the American Librarians Association (2006), to recognize when information is needed and have the ability to locate, evaluate, and use effectively the needed information is critical to personal and social well-being. If a person does not possess the ability to access and then to use necessary information, it can be said that their information literacy is suffering. Thus, the metaliterate individual is one that attends, competently and in an individualized manner, to the communication, creation, and distribution of their own information. Not everyone exhibits digital competency, however, and according to a recent Pew study of digital readiness (Horrigan, 2016), those considered less eager or prepared to embrace digital tools are consistently age 50 and above. Because neither digital literacy nor information literacy is enough on its own, the research team sought to support the metaliteracies of the participants in this study.

Method

Design

The design for this research was an exploratory mixed-methods case study conducted at a senior living center. Mixed-methods case study research combines quantitative and qualitative methods for data collection, integration of data, and analysis (Creswell, 2015) to yield "a more complete understanding through the integration of qualitative and quantitative research" (Guetterman & Fetters, 2018, p. 900). According to Patton (2015), mixed-methods yield both "statistics and stories" (p. 15) which, at the simplest level, may ask a set of fixed-choice questions along with open-ended ones. This research explored whether and how the learning experiences provided to a small group of senior citizens impacted their abilities to incorporate more robust digital literacies into their personal repertoires.

Context, Site, Participants

Conducted at a private senior living center in the south-central USA, this study was undertaken as a single case in a real-world setting (McWhorter & Ellinger, 2018). Five researchers travelled weekly to the retirement center and held technology training sessions on various topics related to the iPad technology. Those participants who did not already have an iPad were loaned university-purchased iPads for the duration of an eight-week period. During the training period, the researchers delivered beginner- to intermediate-level training to the participants starting with the basics of operating an iPad, the safety and care of the iPad, and advanced to more complex lessons such as connecting to the Internet, taking photos, using social media platforms, videoconferencing, and electronic book (eBook) lending through free apps such as Overdrive and Kindle.

Because the retirement center had Wi-Fi Internet connectivity, participants practiced their skills on the iPad while being taught by one faculty member who projected skills lessons onto a large video screen, while other researchers reinforced the skill through hands-on practice with four or five participants at each table. In addition, each participant was loaned a binder that had step-by-step directions for the participants to use both during the session and between trainings for additional practice. Also, at the end of each training session, the residents were given one or more homework assignments to reinforce skills between sessions.

Participants

The participants ($N = 31$) in this study were residents at a senior retirement center. On the pre-experience survey, the participants self-reported as male ($n = 10$; 32.3%), female ($n = 21$; 67.7%), and noted that their generation was either the "Silent Generation" (born between 1925 and 1945, $n = 28$; 94%), or the Baby Boom Generation (born between 1946 and 1964; $n = 3$; 6%). All participants identified their ethnicity as Caucasian ($n = 31$). Fourteen (46.7%) of the participants reported they were currently married, 13 (43.3%) were widowed, and three ($n = 10$%) reported as single. The educational level of the participants reflected "completed between 9th and 12th grade" ($n = 4$; 12.9%); "completed some college" ($n = 16$; 51.6%); "graduated from college with a 4-year degree" ($n = 7$; 22.6%), and "completed graduate school (Masters or Doctorate)" ($n = 4$; 12.9%).

Data Sources and Collection

The primary data sources for this study include a pre-experience survey, attendance records, and a post-experience survey. The initial data were gathered through pre-experience surveys consisting of the Institutional Review

Board-required consent plus 13 items that contained both quantitative demographic information and multiple-choice questions. Following the six-week training, a summative evaluation was conducted through a post-experience survey containing both quantitative demographic information and an open-ended response question to elucidate what the numbers meant but also to generate additional findings.

Data Analysis

Data analysis was conducted in three phases. First, one of the research team members generated survey reports for both the pre- and the post-experience surveys from which any identifying information had been redacted. Descriptive techniques were used to report the open-ended responses, frequencies were included of closed-ended items such as the participants' demographics, social media use, their use of technology, training requests, and their current access to technology. Then, through an iterative process, the research team examined each of the reports, noting their first impressions connected to data snippets drawing upon the informal observations that each had noted for themselves. In the second phase, the team collected these open codes and compiled them into possible thematic groups, meeting to amend, approve, move, or discard codes and categories. In the third phase, the team built thematic categories that were talked through to the point of consensus.

The trustworthiness of the data was heightened through several recognized qualitative strategies. Triangulation and reliability were enhanced by the use of several sources of data, as well as by multiple investigators who each observed as well as interpreted the data (Merriam & Tisdell, 2016). In addition, spanning six weeks of regular weekly sessions, prolonged engagement (Lincoln et al., 1985) was achieved, while working with and observing the participants over multiple sessions.

Pre-Experience Survey Results

A pre-experience survey and consent for the study was completed by all 31 participants. The 13-question survey included demographic information (e.g., gender, age, ethnicity, level of education), use of technology, access to information (e.g., newspaper, television), social media use, training requests, and the need for a library card.

Technology Use

The pre-experience survey reflected that all the participants reported owning a cell phone (61.3%) or smartphone (41.9%), 13 (41.9%) a laptop; 18 (58.1%) an iPad; 11 (35.5%) a desktop computer; while eight (25.8%) possessed a Kindle or Nook e-reader. Almost all (*n* = 30, 96.8%) of the participants had a television in their residence and 18 (58.1%) owned a DVD or VHS player. In addition, all (100%) had access to a single shared computer at the residential facility. When asked how familiar the participants were with an iPad, only one (3.2%) reported they were very familiar, 14 (45.2%) somewhat familiar, six (19.4%) somewhat unfamiliar, and ten (32.2%) were not familiar with iPads. These results suggest that the mobile technology that most participants used regularly were their cell phones or smartphones with laptops, e-readers, and iPads following. Of non-mobile technology, television ownership was widespread, and less so, desktop computer ownership. The relative lack of familiarity with iPads owned by participants suggests limited familiarity with their smartphones as well.

Access to Information

Whether and how people access information and how widely they are able to look for and find it, speaks to their levels of information literacy (American Library Association, 2006). The participants in the study reported their primary sources of their information in the following order: television (67.7%), Internet (58.1%), newspapers, magazines, and/or books (54.8%). With widely available Internet having been around since the mid-1990s, computers may have been familiar to the participants long before they more recently determined that they needed the support of a senior-focused residence. Whether meaning to or not, the digital readiness of participants to always upgrade their skills may have been lacking for any number of reasons, including absence of perceived need, or even of technophobia.

Social Media Use

Participants reported their social media use prior to iPad training. Almost half (51.6%) of the participants described Facebook use; 11 (35.5%) utilized YouTube, six (19.4%) had used Pinterest, three (9.7%) stated using LinkedIn, and three (9.7%) had used Instagram. No participants reported having used Twitter. As a way to stay in touch with family and friends on a casual basis and considering the widespread use of Facebook, it is not surprising that some reported, in conversation with the researchers, that family members had helped them to set up their Facebook accounts. Although YouTube is mentioned, the participants reported, also in conversation, that they *consumed* content available on YouTube rather than *creating* it on the platform. In addition to currently created content, YouTube hosts episodes of discontinued television shows, as well as a great many how-to videos, suggesting that the use of YouTube was part of their information literacy competency.

iPad Training Requests

Before iPad training, the participants were asked about their technology interests for training. The most frequent requests were for taking and sharing pictures (80.6%), using the Internet (77.4%), using video conferencing (61.3%), social networking (51.6%), receiving emails (61.3%), checking out and reading books (45.2%), and watching movies or reading the news online (45.2%). The pre-survey results suggest that participants had an awareness that iPad use presented them with a powerful tool that may have held affordances that they were not yet able to access, but desired to. These results seem to uphold O'Hanlon et al.'s (2010) findings that refuted the idea that older adults were disinterested in attaining technological knowledge. Albeit a self-selected group and not a cross-section of the general population of older adults, these participants did show interest in improving their lives through the literate use of technology in both meaningful and self-directed ways, echoing Barton et al.'s (2000) notions of literacy – and technological literacy, as well as situated practices. When participants were asked whether they had a card to the local public library, nine (29%) stated yes and 22 (71%) reported no.

When a more secure living situation is needed, older adults sometimes relocate to be near relatives, as was shared by participants with the researchers during the training sessions. Some participants shared that they moved to the senior housing because of failing health. Some gave up their cars; others were unfamiliar, still, with the locale. Thus, while the residence facility had a van and scheduled weekly trips for errands, the leisurely browsing through a library was likely not part of the itinerary. That e-books could be available for borrowing through the library held appeal. The city librarian facilitated a training session in which she helped the residents both to obtain library cards and to learn to use the OverDrive app, thus mediating the participants' use of public library services via community outreach. This service helped participants browse, select, and borrow books of their choice, thus serving as an example of digital technology providing access where before access was limited or non-existent.

Post-Experience Survey Results

A total of 17 participants completed the post-survey. Of these – all Caucasian – seven were male, and 11 were female. Sixteen (94%, 6 male/10 female) were born in the Silent Generation and one male (6%) was a Baby Boomer.

Acquisition of Literacy Skills

On the post-experience surveys, ten (58.8%) of the participants described their iPad skills as great; four (23.5%) reported average; and three (18%) reported still having some difficulty. In addition, as a result of the training, 12 (71%) were able to set up their own email accounts. Participants described using email daily (40%), several times per week (27%), or occasionally (27%). Only one (6%) participant reported not using email. Eight (47%) participants played games on their iPad as a result of the training. Of the whole group, 43% reported playing games daily, and 14% reported doing so several times per week. When participants were asked if they had taken pictures with their iPad and how many since the training, ten (24%) reported they had taken more than 10 images; five (29%) reported between 6 and 10; five (29%) reported 1–5; and three (18%) had not taken any pictures.

After the training, the participants also reported using the Internet to search for information. Five (29%) reported daily use; four (23.5%) noted weekly use; four (23.5%) stated occasionally searching; and four (23.5%) did not use the Internet for searches. Of those that searched the Internet, seven (28%) looked for events taking place within the community; seven (28%) searched for hobby-related interests; seven (28%) searched for basic information or used an online dictionary; and four (16%) stated other (e.g., phone numbers, online shopping, medical information).

When participants were asked about reading electronic print books (eBooks) on their iPad, two (12%) read daily, two (12%) read several times per week, three (17%) read occasionally, but ten (59%) noted they did not read eBooks. When asked which of the following did the participants use more, audio or eBooks, seven (87%) reported using eBooks over audio books (13%). For those that read eBooks, participants reported using Kindle on Amazon (71%), or using the Overdrive app through the public library (29%). Several reported purchasing reading materials: eBooks (50%), newspaper subscriptions (12.5%), magazine subscriptions (25%), and other reading materials on their iPads (12.5%).

These results indicate that many participants were better able to use the iPad and its affordances than they were before the training. Given that the iPad mimics an iPhone – except larger, greater visibility, and easier to manipulate – some participants may be better able to more competently use their iPhones after practicing the functions on the iPad. Taken together, the participants in this study demonstrated their metaliterate awareness (Jacobson & Mackey, 2013) of the need for managing their literacy growth and welcomed the researchers as sponsors (Brandt, 2001).

Overall Training Experience

The final open-ended question of the post-test asked the participants for additional comments regarding their experience with the iPad intervention. The three themes that participants raised were, first, a sense of continued digital illiteracy; second, a need for additional training; and third, gratitude for the opportunity to have had individualized instruction.

Technological Illiteracy

Many of the participants discovered that they lacked general technological knowledge:

- "I was surprised by some of the things I did not know";
- "The variety of the uses of the iPad that I was unaware [of]";
- "How little I know";
- "I do not own an iPad. It was very interesting to learn how to use one"; and
- "I learned I had way too many pages open and was not aware of it; it made my iPad work faster when I cleared them out."

Additional Training

Participants (71%) also expressed enthusiasm for learning and stated they would like to continue training on the following topics:

- Instagram
- Texting
- Searching for items such as U247 submarines
- Additional photography skills
- Using the Library card on the Internet
- Facebook

Gratefulness

Almost all the participants noted they were appreciative of the iPad intervention sessions. For example, one participant stated, "I have so much to learn and enjoy – especially foreign languages … thank you for this new experience." Others wrote sentiments such as, "Excellent [training]" while another remarked, "thank you for the library card" and "I would like to thank all the instructors who were so willing to help each one of us …"

It is clear from the variety of comments concerning the difficulties faced during the training that this was, very likely, not an easy experience for the seniors. To confront one's lack of understanding, awareness, or even ability can be sobering if not discouraging. Yet, again, most of the post-experience respondents indicated commitment to improving their metaliteracy at the same time that they acknowledged a continued need for technological sponsorship in their learning.

Barriers to Using iPads to Improve Digital Literacy

There were several barriers reported by participants in the use of iPads including those of health, age, and memory, access, and the devices. Reporting barriers related to health issues, one participant stated, "Thank you for introducing me to the iPad. I enjoyed each class; however, I did miss several classes (doctor's appointments, etc.)." Participants noted that age and memory were factors as stated in the following sentiments: "I was disappointed that I was not able to learn the iPad. Since I have gotten old, my mind doesn't pick up on things the way it once did," and "The lessons were presented well. I was the problem." Another barrier was the lack of reliable, high-speed Internet access. One participant noted that Wi-Fi was not available in his or her apartment: "I had no Internet in my apartment and missed being able to read as you described." Another expressed frustration at the Wi-Fi not working at the meeting location during some of the training sessions: "Wish the Wi-Fi had worked; classes would have been great and less confusing." In terms of the perceived disadvantages of using iPads, one participant wrote, "I was not as impressed with the iPad as I had assumed … I use a [F]ire [T]ablet which is useful and less expensive." Furthermore, this participant wanted additional training on devices "other than the iPad." Health limitations can be discouraging, and not having access to high-speed Internet or reliable Wi-Fi are real barriers to participation. Like any other utility, its erratic distribution is an equity issue. Lastly, the critical awareness of options that the Fire Tablet owner voiced reflects a growing metaliteracy, part of which is the ability to critically evaluate the use of one's resources because there exist many devices, all of which require technology know-how and resources.

iPad Technology Facilitated a Sense of Community

Participants reported experiences which point to their use of iPads having facilitated a sense of community. The majority of participants described connecting with family members (31%), friends outside the residence (20%), friends within the residence (17%), news (14%), students and faculty at the university (6%), businesses and organizations in the community (9%), and other connections (3%). The one participant who noted having made other connections stated he had made contacts: "Overseas in Holland, Wales, Canada, Thailand, etc."

Limitations

Several limitations to this study were noted, all of which likely influenced the results. First, the Wi-Fi Internet connection was the most frequent barrier for several residents who had difficulty connecting throughout the training sessions, hampering their overall experience with the iPad, and a likely explanation why many of the participants did not persist through all sessions. Second, several participants had medical appointments during the training sessions that took them away; thus, only 17 of the residents completed the training and post-survey. Third, the small number of the participants cannot be generalized for a wider demographic. Fourth, the study's participants were not representative of a wide range of people in their age group as they were all white and none were living in poverty.

Discussion and Conclusion

The American Library Association (2019) defined digital literacy as the capability to use digital devices "to find, evaluate, create, and communicate information, requiring both cognitive and technical skills" (para. 1). Initially, over 50% of the original 31 participants reported that they were unfamiliar with using an iPad; however, at the conclusion of this study, over 80% (82%) of the 17 who remained noted that their iPad skills were "Great" or "Average" with only three participants reporting still having difficulty. The participants also reported an increased sense of community, likely from the various training activities. Some of these activities included using the iPad to take selfies and sharing those online, sharing pictures between participants and family members through email and social media, and utilizing video conferencing and email to connect with others in the center and beyond.

The Pew Research Center reported that only 4% of adults 65 or older read books in digital formats (Perrin, 2018). With training, library cards, and access to the local online library, 41% of our participants noted having read at least one eBook. It appeared that the majority of the participants needed more time to process the information necessary to master the skills needed to navigate the device, the app, and the selection and check-out process for borrowing eBooks from the library. One prevalent misconception is that older adults may not be interested in using technology (see O'Hanlon et al., 2010). However, the majority of the participants (71%) in the study were clearly interested in upgrading their digital competencies and, thus, their metaliteracy skills. While it is possible that the participants may have experienced some degree of technophobia, it was not apparent to any of the researchers.

Future research points to more individualized technology training with seniors. Even though the study was designed to have groups of three or four learners to each instructor, for many participants it was not intensive enough. As well, tailoring training to each individual's specific interests could help bolster older adults' confidence, motivation, and self-efficacy that could impact their future learning of digital tools. Overall, the findings in this study indicate that for older adults, access, training, and an increased connection to community through digital inclusion may in fact help to close the digital divide.

References

Allis, S. (2017, December 15). For elderly, wired world holds terror or delight. *Boston Globe* . www.theglobeandmail.com/technology/for-elderly-wired-world-holds-terror-delight/article1366595/

American Library Association. (2006). Presidential committee on information literacy: Final report. Retrieved from www.ala.org/acrl/publications/whitepapers/presidential

American Library Association. (2019). Digital literacy. Retrieved from https://literacy.ala.org/digital-literacy/

Anderson, M., & Perrin, A. (2017). Technology use among seniors. Pew Research Center. www.pewinternet.org/2017/05/17/technology-use-among-seniors/

Barton, D., Hamilton, M., & Ivanic, R. (2000). *Situated literacies: Reading and writing in context.* Taylor & Francis.

Brandt, D. (2001). *Literacy in American lives.* Cambridge University Press.

The Chartered Institute of Taxation. (2012). Digital exclusion. Retrieved from www.litrg. org.uk/sites/default/files/digital_exclusion_-_litrg_report.pdf

Chen, K., & Chan, A. H. (2013). Use or non-use of gerontechnology – A qualitative study. *International Journal of Environmental Research and Public Health, 10*(10), 4645–4666. https://doi.org/10.3390/ijerph10104645

Creswell, J. W. (2015). Revisiting mixed methods and advancing scientific practices. In Hesse-Biber, S., & Johnson, R. B. (Eds.), *The Oxford handbook of multimethod and mixed methods research inquiry* (pp. 57–71). Oxford University Press. https://doi.org/10.1093/oxfordhb/9780199933624.013.39

Delello, J., & McWhorter, R. (2015). Reducing the digital divide: Connecting older adults to iPad technology. *Journal of Applied Gerontology, 36*(1), 3–28. https://doi.org/10.1177%2F0733464815589985

Friemel, T. N. (2016). The digital divide has grown old: Determinants of a digital divide among seniors. *New Media & Society, 18*, 313–331. https://doi.org/10.1177%2F1461444814538648

Geron Technology. (2019). What is gerontechnology? Retrieved from http://gerontechnologie.nl/what-is-gerontechnology/

Guetterman, T. C., & Fetters, M. D. (2018). Two methodological approaches to the integration of mixed methods and case study designs: A systematic review. *American Behavioral Scientist, 62*(7), 900–918. https://doi.org/10.1177%2F0002764218772641

Horrigan, J. B. (2016, September). Digital readiness gaps. Pew Research Center. www.pewinternet.org/2016/09/20/digital-readiness-gaps

Hou, J., Wu, Y., & Harrell, E. (2017). Reading on paper and screen among senior adults: Cognitive map and technophobia. *Frontiers in Psychology, 8*(2225), 54–63. https://doi.org/10.3389/fpsyg.2017.02225

Jacobson, T. E., & Mackey, T. P. (2013). Proposing a metaliteracy model to redefine information literacy. *Communications in Information Literacy, 7*(2), 84–91. www.comminfolit.org/index.php?journal=cil&page=article&op=view&path%5B%5D=v7i2p84 https://doi.org/10.15760/comminfolit.2013.7.2.138

Jiang, J. (2018). Millennials stand out for their technology use, but older generations also embrace digital life. Pew Research Center. www.pewresearch.org/fact-tank/2018/05/02/millennials-stand-out-for-their-technology-use-but-older-generations-also-embrace-digital-life/

Kularski, C. M., & Moller, S. (2012). The digital divide as a continuation of traditional systems of inequality. *Business.* www.semanticscholar.org/paper/The-Digital-Divide-as-a-Continuation-of-Traditional-Kularski/bc47c52d12fbe8dfbdaf6fb47488c74dca4 5ac63

Lincoln, Y. S., Guba, E. G., & Pilotta, J. J. (1985). Naturalistic inquiry. *International Journal of Intercultural Relations, 9*(4), 351–450. https://doi.org/10.1016/0147-1767(85)90062-8

Mather, M., Jacobsen, L. A., & Pollard, K. M. (2015). Aging in the United States. *Population Bulletin, 70*(2), 1–19. www.prb.org/wp-content/uploads/2016/01/aging-us-population-bulletin-1.pdf

McWhorter, R. R., & Ellinger, A. D. (2018). Qualitative case study research: An initial primer. In Wang, V. X., & Reio Jr., T. G. (Eds.), *Handbook of research on innovative techniques, trends, and analysis for optimized research methods* (pp. 185–201). IGI Global. http://doi:10.4018/978-1-5225-5164-5.ch012

Merriam, S. B., & Tisdell, E. J. (2016). *Qualitative research: A guide to design and implementation* (4th ed.). John Wiley & Sons.

Nimrod, G. (2018) Technophobia among older Internet users. *Educational Gerontology*, *44*(2–3), 148–162. https://doi.org/10.1080/03601277.2018.1428145

O'Hanlon, A. Bond, R., Knapp, B., & Carragher, L. (2010). The nestling project: Attitudes toward technology and associations with health, relationships, and quality of life. *Gerontechnology*, *9*(2), 236. https://doi.org/10.4017/gt.2010.09.02.271.00

O'Keefe, R. J. (2014). Baby Boomers and digital literacy: Their access to, and uses of, digital devices and digital media [unpublished doctoral dissertation]. Pepperdine University. https://pepperdine.contentdm.oclc.org/digital/collection/p15093coll2/id/510

Patton, M. Q. (2015). *Qualitative research & evaluation methods*. SAGE.

Perrin, A. (2018). Nearly one-in-five Americans now listen to audiobooks. Pew Research Center. www.pewresearch.org/fact-tank/2018/03/08/nearly-one-in-five-americans-now-listen-to-audiobooks/

Prior, D. D., Mazanov, J., Meacheam, D., Heaslip, G., & Hanson, J. (2016). Attitude, digital literacy and self efficacy: Flow-on effects for online learning behavior. *The Internet and Higher Education*, *29*, 91–97. https://doi.org/10.1016/j.iheduc.2016.01.001.

Sinkovics, R. R., Stuttinger, B., Schlegelmilch, B. B., & Ram, S. (2002). Reluctance to use technology-related products: Development of a technophobia scale. *Thunderbird International Business Review*, *44*, 477–494. https://doi.org/10.1002/tie.10033

Small, G., Moody, T., Siddarth, P., & Bookheimer, S. (2009). Your brain on Google: Patterns of cerebral activation during internet searching. *The American Journal of Geriatric Psychiatry*, *17*(2), 116–126. https://doi.org/10.1097/JGP.0b013e3181953a02

US Census Bureau. (2018). *Older people projected to outnumber children for first time in U.S. history*. Retrieved from www.census.gov/newsroom/press-releases/2018/cb18-41-population-projections.html

Vespa, J., Armstrong, D. A., & Medina, L. (2018). *Demographic turning points for the United States: Population projections for 2020 to 2060*. United States Census Bureau. www.census.gov/library/publications/2020/demo/p25-1144.html

PART III

Unique Settings and Contexts

11

COMMUNITY-BASED PROGRAMS IN RURAL SETTINGS

Pamela J. Farris and Mary E. Gardner

NORTHERN ILLINOIS UNIVERSITY

Teri Reed-Houck

OREGON ELEMENTARY SCHOOL

Community-Based Programs in Rural Settings

This chapter outlines the challenges of reading instruction in rural communities. Starting with a historical perspective and moving to current issues and problems, sections included are the need for community-based support for teachers, at-risk students, and parents with emphasis on the support of school and community. The chapter will explore the support roles played by faith-based and service organizations in programming that meets the needs of these populations. It will examine programs aimed to promote and support early literacy, summer reading loss, and increased access to books in general. Concerns of rural areas such as limited library access, small schools, and pockets of low-income housing are addressed.

Historical and Philosophical Background

Some of the greatest intellectuals in America, such as Thomas Jefferson and Ralph Waldo Emerson, wrote of the importance of a strong and healthy rural society. They believed that only in the countryside would life take on the best qualities so that humankind would flourish, unlike in the noise, filth, and commotion of cities (Shi, 1985).

One-room schools for grades 1–8 were commonplace in small communities, particularly in the Midwest and West. Textbooks such as *The New England Primer* and Noah Webster's *The New England Spelling Book*, commonly referred to as the "blue-backed speller," and later the McGuffey Readers graded readers would be passed down from sibling to sibling and neighbor to neighbor. The school library usually consisted of a bookshelf of well-worn books that had been read and reread several times by students.

The promotion of reading in small communities of the 1800s and 1900s was largely left to the teacher. Rural school board members consisted of prominent citizens in the community, and often those with large families, insisted on hiring quality teachers who could teach their own children how to read and write as well as do math. In some communities, the trustee of a township in a county was responsible for the hiring and firing of teachers. By the time large-scale school consolidation began in rural areas in the late 1950s and 1960s, reading instruction had generally moved to basal readers published by such education publishers as Macmillan, McGraw-Hill, and Scott Foresman, which had the popular Dick and Jane basal reader series. Rural public libraries were generally in the county seat with a few having outreach to smaller surrounding communities via library bookmobiles. Poorer counties required users then (and still now) to pay a fee for library use.

In the mid-1800s, Frances Parker took up the call for rural education, starting his teaching career at age 16 in a village school in New Hampshire. Desiring to learn new methods of pedagogy, he traveled to Europe to examine theories put forth by Jean-Jacques Rousseau, Friedrich Frobel, Johann Heinrich Pestalozzi, and Johann Friedrich Herbart to include in the normal school he headed in Ohio after the Civil War. Upon his return, Parker became superintendent of Quincy Schools in Quincy, Massachusetts, where he developed his ideas into the Quincy Method, a progressive approach to instruction (Farris & Riemann, 2014). John Dewey would deem Parker as the founder of the progressive education movement (Farris & Werderich, 2019).

The McGuffey Readers of the mid 1800s were popular in rural areas. Collecting stories, parables, and poetry from a wide variety of authors, William Holmes McGuffey believed a structured, graded set of readers would enhance the teaching of reading. Having a combination of repetition of letters, sentence length, and vocabulary, it offered a graded series. Due to loose copyright laws of the day, selections of literature from all over the world were included from such authors as William Shakespeare and Henry Ward Beecher. Handwriting lessons were also part of the McGuffey Readers (Farris & Werderich, 2019).

Farm life benefitted children's learning as they gained first-hand knowledge of science and applied math skills to daily tasks such as building chicken houses or measuring feed mixtures for cattle, according to Parker. Asserting that students benefit most from reading what interests them which in turn activates prior background knowledge, Parker supported balanced instruction – phonics, word families, onsets and rimes – for word recognition. The integration of the language arts – reading, writing, listening, and speaking – was advocated by Parker, as was process writing as a methodology. Writing across the curriculum on topics of their own interest and enjoyment would help to develop writing skills. Thus, writing should be natural and authentic based on the student's own experiences (Farris & Werderich, 2019).

President Theodore Roosevelt believed rural America was the "backbone of our nation's efficiency" (The Report of the Commission on Country Life, 1909, p. 41) but that rural life risked being left behind in the modern America emerging in the first decade of the twentieth century. Roosevelt created the Commission on Country Life. Headed by Liberty Hyde Bailey of Cornell University in upstate New York, both Bailey and Roosevelt regarded rural citizens as the "balance force" of American society. They viewed the growing migration from rural areas to the cities as putting society at risk by creating an imbalance. Flight by young rural citizens to urban areas highlighted modern amenities of electricity, indoor plumbing, telephones, and highways. The Commission suggested rural free mail delivery, an agricultural extension program, improvement of rural roads, and reform of rural schools.

Bailey urged rural schools to adopt progressive education advocated by Parker and John Dewey, centering around the study of nature. Bailey was convinced that if rural students could appreciate the beauty and wonder offered by the countryside, they would not be lured to big cities as adults. Thus, students would remain in rural areas and the "balance force" would continue to keep society stabilized. Due to the small size of rural schools, merging of schools into a central school was advocated but was fought by most rural communities and remains a volatile issue in rural communities today.

It took World War I for the nation to realize how dramatically different educational opportunities were for rural versus urban students. Many recruits from rural areas could not read or write, with some signing their names with a witness and a marking of X on a line. Scientific advancements in other areas such as indoor plumbing and electric lights led to a push for literacy to be taught to all students no matter where they lived.

School consolidation in the 1950s and 1960s particularly impacted rural schools. It wasn't unusual for three or four neighboring school districts to merge together to create a large, centrally located high school which offered greater selection of courses. While the old former grade 1–12 schools still contained the elementary students, those in grades 7 through 12 were bused to the often newly built high school.

This period coincided with the push toward phonics. Many farmers liked the idea of breaking down words into simple sounds and compared it to tasks farming required. By the 1980s, the push was toward whole language and the reading of vast quantities of quality children's and young adult literature which rural children generally lacked the access to reading as newly published works were generally not available to rural children.

During the later twentieth century, writer and farmer Wendell Berry of Kentucky emerged as an advocate for a rural lifestyle. If rural dwellers are to have thriving communities, then, according to Berry, the equilibrium with nature must be re-established and sustainable agriculture must be embraced. People must care for and respect one another and cherish the land upon which they reside. They must also care more closely for the ways they know one another, the rituals of their daily lives, and their knowledge of the local environment (Berry, 1990).

As presently constituted, rural education fails to meet this standard, according to Berry. In his view, rural citizens are taught to be producers and consumers. Instead they should be taught that the measure of production must be how well it can be sustained over time. Sustainable production is necessary for establishing and nurturing the real community – the common cultural ground – of rural communities. If this does not occur, the American national economy will continue to destroy rural society and the natural environment (Berry, 1978).

Research by Susan Neuman and Jillian J. Knapczyk (2018) pointed out that providing access to resources in literacy deserts by reaching families and encouraging adult support may be an important enabler toward encouraging parental engagement as well as children's reading and writing development. Because there is often limited or no access to libraries in rural areas, this chapter points out ways to fill the literacy needs of rural children.

Low-Income Housing in Rural Communities and Reading Access

Rural communities are often characterized by pockets of various kinds of low-income housing. Generally, the population in these areas is largely made up of families with children. Educators and community leaders know that these children are likely to have problems being successful at school. Efforts to provide support are certainly made by school programs and personnel, but there is often a need for additional support outside of school (Adelman & Taylor, 2008). Community and faith-based support can often be found in many different formats. The following example is one program that illustrates the levels of support that might be needed.

One particular community in rural northern Illinois had a mobile home park with over 200 homes. Many families with children lived there. Teachers in the local school district had long been aware that these students often experience learning difficulties. One teacher began discussions with colleagues as well as the pastor and members of her local church geared toward helping the children.

After many meetings with the park's owners and financial considerations by the church trustees, a plan emerged. Eventually it was suggested that the church rent a mobile home and try programming on site. The park owners were surprised at the proposal but understood the benefits for the children. From the beginning, the park owners established that the program would not have to pay rent for a small mobile home but only pay the standard monthly lot rental fee.

Initially, programming was planned for three morning sessions during the summer for younger children and an afternoon program for older ones with lunch for all served in between. Quickly it was evident that this schedule did not meet the needs of the participants as most slept late. The schedule was adjusted to lunch served first with programming following. Lessons learned about the culture of the mobile home park were key to the response of the volunteers.

Food security issues arose as those children who came for lunch had not eaten any breakfast. Some indicated that they were not certain that there would be food for an evening meal. Even though educators were involved in all phases of the program, the idea that those who receive free or reduced lunch during the school year might also need support in the summer was another lesson learned. After that initial first year, volunteers worked with the Northern Illinois Food Bank. Nutritious, free lunches were delivered to the site.

As word spread about the program, community support came in many forms. Some people donated money to help pay for rent and utilities. Local contractors donated services for plumbing, heating, flooring, and other improvements. Eventually, central air was installed with the help of many individuals. Neighbors at the mobile home park continue to mow the lawn and help put garbage out. Volunteers of all ages come from the community at large, including from several churches. The greater community understands the needs of these children and their families and are willing to support the efforts.

Knowing the risk of summer reading loss for these children (Allington & McGill-Franzen, 2013), summer programming has focused on activities and experiences of high interest to the children. Literacy is a big part with books provided on site as well as given to participants to take home to read and share with others.

Organizers know that these children are not as likely to have additional experiences that support literacy learning and build background knowledge as well as vocabulary, such as traveling and visiting museums or zoos (Murnane et al., 2012). Art, math, science, and social studies topics have been explored along with some local field trips. The school district has supported the program by providing school bus transportation for field trips. A trip to a local farm is a favorite destination.

Another asset in rural areas is the University of Illinois Home Extension Service. Their staff have come to the mobile home park and provided education in nutrition, working with the children in planting a salsa garden, along with science and art activities. A ripple from these activities has been that some families have planted small gardens on their own lots.

During the school year the program meets after school two days per week. Volunteers meet the children as the school bus drops them off in the mobile home park. During good weather, they play on the park's playground (which was refurbished by a local Boy Scout for his Eagle Scout project) for a few minutes. When they go into the mobile home, a substantial snack is provided such as macaroni and cheese or peanut butter and jelly sandwiches, then participants are split up by grade level. Volunteers give homework help or do reading and math activities.

Social skills are woven into all aspects of the program. Respect for each other and volunteers has been a cornerstone, although not always evident. During the school year, the children share something about their day as they get ready for snack. All year long they write and sign thank you notes and send get well or sympathy cards as appropriate. Manners and healthy habits with snacks and meals are emphasized. The children help plan for and serve at a volunteer thank you in May.

Communication with classroom teachers and the school has been a key part of the program. Teachers know about the program and can make contacts with volunteers if there are concerns or requests. Needs are anticipated when possible. Before school begins in the fall, supplies are gathered (many are donated, some are purchased) and children and their parents bring their school supply list and gather what is required. At times, school library fines have been covered by program funds so that a student can continue to check out books from the school library. During winter months, volunteers make sure all students have necessary winter gear such as hats, gloves, coats, and boots.

Originally, discussions about the mobile home park program involved ideas for parent education. While several things have been tried, participation has not been strong. However, the program has built relationships with families and is known as a resource. The manager gives information about programming to new families when they move into the park. One parent and her children have been involved since the program began. That parent now volunteers in a leadership role, and her now high school-level children volunteer in the program to earn service hours for their schools.

Little Free Libraries in Rural Communities

The program described above provides access to books in several ways as organizers know that access to books is a key factor in literacy development. Access can be an obstacle for low-income children, but adding books to home libraries greatly impacts these children (Evans et al., 2010). Public libraries in rural communities are funded by local taxes. For many, as the tax base has eroded, difficult decisions are being made to reduce hours, limit materials purchases, or to cut staff. Some small communities lack public libraries either because one was never established or the library has closed due to lack of funding. Some communities base the funding for libraries on the number of books, DVDs, etc. checked out by members of the communities. Other issues for library access include the area the public library serves. For instance, some areas of low-income housing may be out of the library district which means that residents are unable to obtain a free library card and have to pay high fees for use of the library in addition to finding transportation to the facility.

The primary goal is not only access to books but to promote an interest in reading. Having one's own library of books in the home helps children think of themselves as readers (Neumann & Knapczyk, 2018). One way to provide books is to provide small, readily accessible libraries within a community.

Teachers and community members in many rural communities have strategically placed Little Free Libraries around parks and neighborhoods and by schools, stores, gas stations, and churches. Begun as a way to honor a former teacher who died, there are currently over 80,000 Little Free Libraries registered worldwide as the program celebrates its tenth year. The principle of Little Free Libraries is "Take a book, leave a book."

In many instances, local service organizations such as the Lions Club and Rotary International often provide funds for building the Little Free Libraries or their members build the libraries for the communities. Then the service organizations in subsequent years donate funds for the purchase of books for inclusion in the libraries, which volunteers stock. Books for the Little Free Libraries come from donations, book sales by area libraries and garage sales, or bought online from Thriftbooks at thriftbooks.com. Other sources are book round-ups by service organizations or holiday book drives by Barnes and Noble stores. These small libraries take many forms and sizes. Some are hand-built and some repurpose furniture, old mailboxes or newspaper vending machines. They are often creative works of art. All have the theme "take a book, leave a book" so reading is promoted.

In one school district, reading teachers have worked to provide the structure, gather books, and place Little Free Libraries in the two communities that make up the district. Each community has one in a high-usage park, plus one inside each of the two local food pantries. Additionally, there is one at a mobile home park. These teachers accept the responsibility of keeping the libraries stocked with books year-round.

In a neighboring school district, Little Free Libraries have been placed on the school grounds in front of the elementary school with different-level reading books in each library. This helps meet the needs of all K-6 students. They hope to expand to meet the reading needs of middle and high school students. The goal is to have three to four libraries with several choices for students because they lack access to the school library, and there is no public library in one of the communities.

Promoting the Little Free Libraries varies from notes sent home with students, to having a "Bike to the Library" with parents, teachers, volunteers, and children biking around town to two or three different Little Free Libraries with teachers and volunteers doing book talks about a few of the books at each location. Notes on community bulletin boards at local churches, gas stations, and restaurants also promote the libraries and need for book donations.

Designing Effective Summer Reading Programs

Most teachers are familiar with the phenomenon of students returning to school in the fall having lost significant amounts of reading skill. The loss of reading skill from May through August, known as *summer slide*, is a source of frustration for teachers and students alike. Summer reading loss is especially common for at-risk learners. Research suggests at-risk children, when compared to their peers from middle-income homes, arrive at school with less-developed vocabularies, weaker conceptual knowledge, and fewer enriching experiences that form a foundation for strong school achievement (Stanovich, 1986). Although some may arrive underprepared for school success, at-risk students achieve at rates commensurate with their more fortunate peers during the school year, and with supplemental services often even achieve gains toward closing the achievement gap between the groups (Bracey, 2006).

At-risk children are less likely to participate in educational summer experiences common to middle-income children, such as camps, vacations, museum visits, and reading. Attempts to encourage children from low socioeconomic status (SES) homes to use the public libraries tend to be unsuccessful for a number of reasons: lack of transportation, reliance on over-extended families to take children to the library, or being ineligible for a free library card (Jensen, 2009). In addition, when self-selecting books, at-risk readers often choose books at their frustration reading level and later abandon them because of difficulty. Lack of appropriate books in the home is another challenge for children in low-SES families. Middle-income children, on the other hand, continue to participate in educational opportunities over the summer, and as a result, tend to retain or even increase their academic skills due to these experiences. These conditions lead to an increasing achievement gap between middle-income and low-SES students, which in turn contributes to greater need for costly intervention services during the school year.

Summer slide is a well-documented effect in Oregon School District (OES). OES Title I teachers looked each year for creative, effective, and economically sustainable programs to help at-risk students retain their school-year achievement over the summer. Previous attempts to engage students in reading activities, such as opening the school library over the summer, supplying calendars with daily literacy suggestions, and sending home used books with students at the end of the school year had resulted in minimal participation and poor maintenance of skills. One third grade teacher began to track her students' spring-to-fall reading levels and was dismayed to learn that 70% of her at-risk readers had dropped by at least one reading level. With the documentation of skills loss creating an urgent need, Title I teachers read the available research for guidance in devising an effective summer reading program.

White and Kim (2008) matched at-risk third to fifth grade students to books at their reading level. Students received a book in the mail weekly, and requested parents listen to students read briefly. Fall assessments revealed students who read experienced stable reading levels or growth in their reading skill throughout the summer.

Summer reading loss prevention was targeted in the study of Allington and McGill-Franzen (2010) in which at-risk children were allowed to self-select

TABLE 11.1 Annual Comparison of Reading Levels Maintained/Increased (Success Rates)

Year	2012	2013	2014	2015	2016	2017	2018
Grade	Control – no intervention						
1			66%	80%	53%	87%	64%
2			67%	46%	36%	63%	54%
3	30%	83%	100%	81%	77%	82%	94%
4			90%	89%	93%	93%	80%
5				100%	100%	100%	89%

12 books to keep and read over the summer. After three consecutive summers of participation, a significant reduction in summer reading skill loss was noted. Although successful and economical, a drawback of this study is the length of time necessary for effects to be demonstrated.

With the guidance supplied by the above studies, teachers obtained administrative support to supply at-risk third graders with eight free, self-selected books that would be mailed to their homes over the summer. Eighteen students were selected based on them meeting at least three of the following criteria: achievement in the bottom 25th percentile in reading, participation in a literacy intervention, free or reduced lunch status, and home support for learning. Teachers helped students select books at their instructional levels from the Scholastic FACE catalog, a source for low-cost books to be distributed to children. Students' reading levels were recorded in May, and again in August. Following participation in the 2012 summer reading program, 83% of the students maintained their reading level, and in fact, 50% of participants gained at least one full reading level. Teachers and students alike were thrilled!

Due to the success of the summer reading pilot, additional grade levels were added to the project with encouraging results. Table 11.1 illustrates the success rates for maintaining or increasing student reading levels.

Procedures and Costs Associated with the Summer Reading Project

Oregon's summer reading program costs approximately $60 per student, including books, envelopes, and postage. In March, students are nominated by their classroom teachers and must meet at least three of four criteria (participation in a reading intervention that year, lower guided reading level, free/reduced lunch status, and home support for learning). In April, parents are sent a letter explaining the program and the need for continued reading practice over the summer. Once parents have agreed their child can participate, teachers help students select eight

TABLE 11.2 Summer Books Distribution Timeline

Date	Task
April 8	20 students per grade level identified as possible participants.
April 15	Parent invitation letter sent home.
April 22	15 students selected to participate (first come, first served). Acceptance letter sent home.
April 25–29	Students select books from FACE catalogue with grade level teacher-supervisor. Books are selected based on (1) current reading level and (2) interest. Submit spring reading levels to Title 1 Coordinator for spring-to-fall data comparison.
Week of May 1	Student address labels printed in office, eight per student.
May 6–17	1. Cross-reference books as they arrive against list of students' titles.
	2. Substitute and reorder any books that are out of stock.
	3. Prepare small notes of encouragement to be added to each book for packaging (e.g., "I think you will really like this one").
	4. Organize 8 books for each student, easier to harder, alternate fiction/nonfiction if applicable.
	5. Stuff 8 manila envelopes per student with books, notes.
	6. Apply address labels to envelopes.
	7. Place envelopes in boxes labeled "week 1," etc. for mailing.
June 3	Office secretaries mail books in box labeled "week 1."
Each of next 7 Mondays	Office secretaries mail books in box labeled "week 2," "week 3," etc.
August 19–23	Receiving classroom teachers conduct running records on all first–fourth grade students.
	Data sheets are completed and given to Title 1 Coordinator. Title 1 teachers generate a report based on spring-to-fall reading level comparison. Report is shared with teachers, administrators and School Board.
September	Students who exceed their spring reading level (demonstrated reading growth over the summer) receive a $10 voucher to be used at the fall book fair.
	Students who maintained their spring reading level are invited to a pizza party hosted by Title 1 teachers.

books from the Scholastic FACE catalog at their independent or instructional reading levels. When the books are received at school, teachers put the books into envelopes, which are mailed throughout the summer one per week (see Table 11.2).

Student reading levels are recorded in May and are compared with their August reading levels once school begins in the fall. Classroom teachers and Title I staff assess students, collect, and organize the data. The Title I Coordinator collects all data and summarizes it in a report to the School Board.

The summer reading program time commitment by teachers is significant: grade-level teams must meet and determine potential participants. One grade-level representative teacher will need a day to meet with students to select books and half a day to organize, stuff, and address envelopes. Office staff take the boxes to the post office, who will bill the school for the postage. Title I teachers need release time to help assess, collect data, and write the summary report. It is estimated classroom teachers will devote 20 hours to the effort, with the Title I Coordinator requiring about 40 hours. The program is a significant investment in time and expense, but the retention of skills has been worth the effort.

Throughout the years of conducting the summer reading program, we learned some noteworthy lessons. Home support for reading is essential to the success of the program, especially in the younger grades. Early readers need parents to listen to and encourage their efforts. The need for parent involvement appears to lessen as students grow into more capable, independent readers in the later grades. We learned Kindergarten students are unable to maintain their early reading skills, and as a result, we dropped this grade from the program. Students with Individualized Education Programs for a Learning Disability are not helped by the summer reading program, as practice alone appears not to be sufficient to maintain their skills. We've come to realize that student self-selection of books is key, as personal choice and interest in the books is essential for engagement and follow-through with independent reading. It is also necessary to mail books one per week to the home, rather than giving the students all eight books to take home at the end of the school year. Students become excited each week as the book packet arrives and enthusiasm for reading can be maintained.

Attempts to have students respond to books in writing have met with minimal participation. OES teachers have tried a number of ways to entice student response: stamped postcards with space to write to their teachers, journals to return in the fall, and a Facebook page to correspond with teachers about the books. Unfortunately, each attempt was met with limited success. Although teachers would love to have students respond in writing to books, we've determined that these tasks may be perceived as too "schooly" by students and are avoided. It is evident the books are being read and enjoyed, however. Teachers have encountered students over the summer who report their excitement at receiving the books and fall data on reading skills retention are encouraging. Most significantly, participating students return to school enthused about learning and happy to know their skills have been maintained, or improved, over the long break.

Summary

The challenges of meeting the literacy needs of rural children and teenagers are ongoing, but they can be met when creative ideas are engaged. Lack of funding and/or lack of public libraries hinder reading development. Library access, book access, and summer programming to help prevent summer reading loss require community support outside of the school that meets the particular needs of rural communities. Providing literacy access to children who live in mobile home parks via special volunteer efforts; Little Free Libraries at gas stations or near the post office; or a mailed book program can make up for living in rural literacy deserts.

References

Adelman, H., & Taylor, L. (2008). *Rebuilding for learning: Addressing barriers to learning and Teaching and re-engaging students.* Scholastic.

Allington, R.L. & McGill-Franzen, A. (2010). Addressing summer reading setback among economically disadvantaged elementary students. *Reading Psychology, 31,* 411–427. https://doi.org/10.1080/02702711.2010.505165

Allington, R., & McGill-Franzen, A. (2013). *Summer reading: Closing the rich/poor reading achievement gap.* Teachers College Press.

Berry, W. (1978). *The unsettling of America: Culture and agriculture.* Avon.

Berry, W. (1990). *What are people for?* North Point Press.

Bracey, G. (2006). *Reading educational research: How to avoid getting statistically snookered.* Heinemann.

Evans, M., Kelley, J. Sikorac, J., & Treimand, D. (2010). Family scholarly culture and educational success: Books and schooling in 27 nations. *Research in Social Stratification and Mobility, 28*(2), 171–197. https://doi.org/10.1016/j.rssm.2010.01.002

Farris, P. J., & Rieman, P. (2014). *Teaching, bearing the torch: Introduction to education foundation.* 3rd ed. Waveland.

Farris, P. J., & Werderich, D. E. (2019). *Language arts: Process, product, and assessment in diverse classrooms.* 6th ed. Waveland.

Jensen, E. (2009). *Teaching with poverty in mind: What being poor does to kids' brains and what schools can do about it.* ASCD.

Murnane, R., Sawhill, I., & Snow, C. (2012). Literacy challenges for the twenty-first century: Introducing the issue. *The Future of Children, 22*(2), 3–15. https://doi.org/10.1353/foc.2012.0013

Neuman, S., & Knapcyzk, J. J. (April 30, 2018). Reaching families where they are: Examining an innovative book distribution program. *Urban Education,* https://doi.org/10.1177/0042085918770722.

Report of the Commission on Country Life (1909). Sturgis and Walton.

Shi, D. (1985). *The simple life: Plain living and high thinking in American culture.* Oxford University Press.

Stanovich, K. (1986). Matthew effects in reading: Some consequences of individual differences in the acquisition of reading. *Reading Research Quarterly, 21,* 360–408. https://doi.org/10.1598/RRQ.21.4.1

White, T., & Kim, J. (2008). Teacher and parent scaffolding of voluntary summer reading. *The Reading Teacher, 62,* 116–125. https://doi.org/10.1598/RT.62.2.3

12

LITERACY AT THE PUBLIC LIBRARY

An Intergenerational Book Club

Molly K. Ness

FORDHAM UNIVERSITY

For many towns, villages, and cities, the public library is the epicenter of the community. As children's book author Neil Gaiman explains, the public library is a "community space … a place of safety, a haven from the world." As such, public libraries often serve as the heart of community-based literacy, and thus, must evolve to meet the ever-changing needs of the community. According to an annual survey of Institute and Museum of Library Services, nearly 311 million Americans who lived within a public library service area visited public libraries over 1.35 billion times in 2016. With an increase in use and patronage, public libraries strive to offer additional current, relevant, and engaging programs; 113 million people attended 5.2 million programs in 2016.

This chapter explores a newly created public library program that epitomizes community-based literacy. Situated in a public library in a small town in the Northeast, Books in Motion invites residents to a monthly book club and viewing of the book's film adaptation. To understand the impact of the low-cost program, I follow five sets of participants and their responses to Books in Motion. This low-cost, engaging program serves as a model of an intergenerational literacy program that offers many benefits to participants and the community.

An Overview of Books in Motion

Books in Motion is a public library book club which invites young readers and community members to read a preselected children's chapter book, provides participants with free copies of the book, and culminates in a family film night. During the film night, participants view the book's film adaptation in the town's public library. Books in Motion is the brainchild of the children's librarian, who previously was an elementary school teacher. With the town's per-capita income of $23,146, the librarian became concerned that children from low-income homes lacked access to books; she subsequently created Books in Motion in an effort "to get books into the hands of kids who otherwise might not have them."

Books in Motion is a monthly program. The children's librarians at the public library select a chapter book to read and discuss. Several criteria guide public librarians in their book selection: the selected book must (a) appeal to readers of various ages, (b) present opportunities for meaningful conversation around themes, characters or events, and (c) have a film translation. These films are both classics, such as the 1962 film adaptation of *To Kill a Mockingbird*, and current, such as the 2006 production of Carl Hiassen's *Hoot* (see Table 12.1 for a partial list, and Appendix 12.1 for the entire list).

Local businesses sponsor the program and provide participants with free paperback copies of each book. Over the course of the month, participants share the book in a variety of ways, including reading aloud, reading silently, and listening to audio books. Books in Motion culminates with a family film night, in which participants view the film adaptation on a weekend evening in the public library. Before the showing of the movie, librarians lead brief book club discussions. After the movie, participants discuss similarities and differences between the book and the film and evaluate which version they prefer.

Typically, 50 participants attend the family film nights. Only two months after its creation, the film night overflowed to standing room only capacity. Although

TABLE 12.1 Partial List of Books Covered by Books in Motion

Title	Author
The Lion, the Witch, and the Wardrobe	C.S. Lewis
The Princess Bride	William Goldman
Ella Enchanted	Gail Carson Levine
Holes	Louis Sachar
Charlotte's Web	E.B. White
The Black Stallion	Walter Farley
Howl's Moving Castle	Diana Wynne Jones
The Bridge to Terabithia	Katherine Patterson
Tuck Everlasting	Natalie Babbitt
Charlie and the Chocolate Factory	Roald Dahl
Because of Winn-Dixie	Kate DiCamillo
Freaky Friday	Mary Rogers
My Friend Flicka	Mary O'Hara
How to Eat Fried Worms	Thomas Rockwell

initially geared toward the families of young children, access to the program is widespread; participants include teachers, school media specialists, members of the public library's board of directors, public librarians, and local school administrators. Community members of all ages are invited, regardless of whether they have children. Participants do not need to be library members, do not need to register to attend, and can attend as many or as few events as they choose. In designing the program, Cindy aimed

> to create a program that was highly motivational but did not exclude participants who could not commit every month. There is a solid group of families who are there month after month, but there are also new faces each month.

Flyers and advertisements for Books in Motion regularly appear in the town's grocery and convenience stores, laundromats, doctor's offices, school bulletin boards, and local newspapers.

Books in Motion as a Model of Intergenerational Literacy

At the heart of Books in Motion is the understanding that literacy today is no longer confined to the institution of school, but that the institutions outside of school, including family and community, significantly impact a child's construction of literacy (Street, 1993). With the inclusion of a wide variety of community participants, Books in Motion exemplifies *intergenerational literacy* (Gadsden, 2000). In its broad focus, intergenerational literacy explores how relationships between children, parents, families, and community members impact literacy beliefs and practices. Intergenerational literacy includes "the processes of learning and teaching, the engagement of children by their parents, and family members, and teaching in the acts of reading, writing, and problem solving; and the inculcation of values and practices that sustain such engagement" (Gasdsen, 2000).

Books in Motion differs from many intergenerational literacy programs in that it was conceptualized solely to increase literacy opportunities within the community, not to train or teach caregivers how to incorporate literacy into parenting; participants in Books in Motion were not told how to approach their book reading. Thus, Books in Motion does not operate under the deficit model or the notion that the goal of intergenerational programs is to encourage desirable literacy practices in low-income or minority families who otherwise may not create space for literacy practices in their homes (Gadsden, 2000). In fact, Books in Motion was constructed under the belief that parents across diverse cultural and ethnic groups already engage in literacy activities with their children (Auerbach, 1989).

Who Benefits from Intergenerational Literacy?

The benefits of community literacy programs are well documented (Anderson & Morrison, 2007; Daisey, 1991; Elish-Piper, 1996; Shanahan et al., 1995). Padak and Rasinski reported that multiple groups of participants, including children, parents, families as units, and the larger society, all benefit from community literacy programs (Padak & Rasinski, 2003). Children are perhaps the most obvious group to reap the benefits of family literacy programs. These academic, personal, and social benefits are widespread and far-reaching; in a review of 53 studies, Hendersen (1988) found unequivocal evidence of positive student achievement linked to parent involvement. Adults also benefit from participation in community literacy programs. Philliber, Spillman, and King (1996) found that adults gained an average of 1.15 grade equivalents on the Test for Adult Basic Education as a result of year-long participation in a family literacy program. Schools may also benefit from community literacy programs; in studying a literacy project involving parents and young children, Cairney and Munsie (1995) found that, as a result of the program, parents became more involved in school activities, classroom work, and decision making within the school community. As McNicol and Dalton (2002) revealed, community literacy projects benefit public libraries by recognizing the roles that libraries have in promoting literacy and by providing a higher profile through increased publicity. Finally, Edwards and Turner (2009) suggested a high likelihood that family literacy programs support young children's reading comprehension.

An Inside Look at Books in Motion

As a frequent visitor to the small town in the Northeast that houses Books in Motion, I am a frequent patron of the public library. In my work as a university professor focusing on childhood education and literacy, I was attracted to Books in Motion because of its efforts to bridge the gap between school and home literacies. Upon learning about Books in Motion, I believed it to be a motivating and innovative community literacy program, one that could easily be replicated in other communities at minimal cost. To examine how various community members benefited from their participation in Books in Motion, I began a year-long case study with five different groups of Books in Motion participants. I wondered how participants of all ages would evaluate their participation in Books in Motion and how the program influenced literacy within individuals, families, and the community.

My work was informed by two paradigms: (1) literacy as a social practice (Clay, 1993) and (2) the social–contextual perspective (Auberbach, 1989; Heath, 1983; Hiebert, 1991). From the literacy as a social practice perspective, literacy entails complex social processes that vary according to context. As Fagan (1995) explained, "Literacy cannot be described outside of social networks and the

TABLE 12.2 Books in Motion Participants

Family	Members and Ages
Powell	Lisa (age 39), Ed (age 42), son Ted (age 9.5), son Toby (age 5.5)
Flanagan	Hannah (age 39), her fifth-grade son Billy (age 10), and Hannah's mother Rose (age 75)
Pierce	Mother Tess (age 43) and son Matthew (age 9)
Greene	Mother Mary (age 39), Caleb (age 7.5), and Jake (age 5)
Washburn	Public school teacher (age 53)

relationships that exist among their members." The social–contextual perspective highlights that literacy is practiced for social purposes in social contexts. Through this socio-contextual approach, the personal and family strengths and needs are seen as valuable assets that provide a framework for the family literacy program (Elish-Piper, 1996; Freire, 1970). As such, a community literacy program builds upon the preexisting literacy patterns within families and the larger community (Morrow et al., 1995).

A Year-Long Case Study

In order to understand the impact of Books in Motion as a community literacy project, I applied a case study approach in which I followed five groups of participants over the course of one year (see Table 12.2). As the principal investigator, I used purposeful sampling to include participants of various ages. Nearly 99% of the town's population is white; all participants in this study identified themselves as white. Over the course of the year, I collected written surveys from participants and conducted both small-group and individual interviews. I also attended four two-hour Books in Motion family film nights and subsequent discussions, taking detailed field notes and keeping a reflective journal. Interviews occurred in person, over the phone, and via email communication.

Participant Group #1: Building Community Relationships through Literacy

Self-described as a "very reading-oriented family," the Powells joined Books in Motion as "a way to stay involved in library programs, get exposure to books we may not have already read, and be a part of community-oriented nights out." As relative newcomers to the area, the Powells valued Books in Motion for easing their transition into the community and introducing them to other families. Furthermore, the Powells found that Books in Motion encouraged their older son to become an independent reader. Lastly, Lisa Powell appreciated the collaboration between the library and local businesses, citing Books in Motion as "good community morale."

Participant Group #2: Enhancing Preexisting Literacy Practices

The only group in the study to span three generations, the Flanagans were drawn to Books in Motion because of "the free books and the chance to see a movie on a big screen with other families at the end of the month." All three family members described themselves as "avid readers." Thus, for the Flanagans, Books in Motion strengthened the literacy practices that already existed within the family by providing a collaborative format. Hannah also attributed Books in Motion with creating fruitful discussions between the generations of her family. Prior to the film night of *To Kill a Mockingbird*, she explained,

> Reading this particular book together created juicy opportunities to talk about values like honesty, courage, tolerance, and respect with my son. I actually gained a new appreciation for this book, which until Books in Motion, I had viewed as a book for adults.

Participant Group #3: Supporting Reading and Writing Development

The Pierce family joined Books in Motion because Matthew heard several of his classmates talking about the program and subsequently begged his mother to attend. Tess reported that, prior to Books in Motion, it was "a constant struggle" to engage Matthew in reading, most likely because of his low reading level. Tess very much believed that her son's "explosion of storytelling and writing" came as a result of their participation, explaining, "Matthew's enjoyment and interest in reading independently has strengthened. Books in Motion has influenced his reading and writing progress."

Participant Group #4: Introducing New Genres to Young Readers

Although Books in Motion did not alter the frequency of reading in the Greene household, it changed the nature of the books they read together, as chapter books were added to their reading repertoire. Second-grader Caleb explained, "Before, chapter books were just for school. Now my mom reads a chapter before bed and even more on snow days." The Greenes also appreciated the social aspect of Books in Motion, referring to the film night as "fun for everyone." To further celebrate the social aspect of Books in Motion, the Greenes frequently got together with other participants for pizza at the conclusion of the monthly film nights. Over the two years of participating, Mary Greene has become a vocal advocate of Books in Motion:

> Not only do you get a free book, you get a chance to read together. On top of that, you get a chance to see the movie and find out what was different from the movie and the book. It's a great program that gets families to the library in a fun way for everyone involved.

Participant #5: Creating School and Community Connections

The final participant was Henry Washburn, who served both as a member of the public library's Board of Directors and as a fifth-grade teacher at the local elementary school. Henry's involvement in Books in Motion stemmed from his goals "to (1) expose my students to good literature and (2) introduce my students to the wonders of all public libraries in general." Tapping into the students' motivation to read books associated with the monthly film nights, Henry used the library's selection as a daily shared reading activity. For approximately 20 minutes each day, Henry read aloud from the book while students followed along in their individual copies. He also encouraged students to continue independently reading the books at home and through repeated readings to build fluency, and explained the following:

> The bulk of our classroom participation came when students made posters and storybooks illustrating the book using their imaginations and creativity … and would then loan them to the library for display purposes, encouraging students to visit the library to see their handiwork.

The Benefits of Books in Motion

Books in Motion is a promising intergenerational literacy project, which created successful avenues for literacy interactions within the community. Participants were overwhelmingly positive about their experiences with the program and would encourage other community members to participate. Most immediately, Books in Motion increased community literacy interactions – both inside and outside of their homes. Although all participants self-reported independent reading prior to Books in Motion, they all largely read in isolation with little interaction with their fellow readers. Participants valued how Books in Motion paved the way for parents, children, teachers, and librarians to discuss their reactions to books and their film adaptations in a communal forum. A mother explained how Books in Motion built bridges that previously were absent:

Books in Motion was one of my first experiences in which literacy was shared. It wasn't me reading the book alone; I read each month knowing that I'd come together with fellow readers of all ages in hopes of connecting and sharing our experience with the book.

Although Lisa Powell had participated in book clubs before, she had never done so with a group of readers of diverse ages, noting,

Previously my book clubs were all women of similar ages and life experiences, so often our text selections and our reactions to the books were limited by that homogeneity. Never before had I discussed books with readers ranging from age 6 to age 75!

Not only did Books in Motion increase literacy interactions within households, but the program also facilitated relationships between teachers, families, and the community, as explained by Lisa Powell:

Books in Motion is a way to stay connected. Through reading, I stay connected with my family. My children stay connected to their classmates at school, as they discuss their reading. My entire family has stayed connected with the community as we meet monthly to discuss the books and watch the films.

Furthermore, the program facilitated relationships between families at home and their teachers at school. Hannah Flanagan noted that her son's classroom teacher notified families of upcoming Books in Motion titles and film nights in weekly newsletters. She also recalled seeing her son's teacher attend at least two film nights. Similarly, classroom teacher Henry pointed to Books in Motion as a "concrete way for students and families to see powerful connections to the public library":

Books in Motion created a space for my students to see everyone in the community – teachers, parents, siblings, classmates, grandparents, librarians, community leaders – as readers. It was empowering for my students to be a part of this engaged community of readers.

Thus, the Books in Motion program helped participants modify and re-envision their understandings of reading and literacy. Furthermore, reading became a community event; reading was transformed from a solitary event to a collaborative forum within participants' homes and the larger community.

Additionally, Books in Motion motivated participants in innovative ways. Because of the unique forum of reading a book and watching the film adaptation, participants reported new enthusiasm for reading. A grandmother reported,

"Books in Motion has inspired us to read books out loud to each other – whether by the fire, before bed, or in the car – which really adds a different element to a story." Additionally, Hannah Flanagan reported that discussions emerged naturally as "having both modalities makes for interesting discussions comparing the book and the movie." The incentive of watching the film adaptation motivated reluctant readers to finish books. Furthermore, the social element of Books in Motion inspired families to keep reading. Parents reported that their children were eager to read in order to participate in film nights, knowing that their friends and classmates would be in attendance. As Tess Pierce explained,

> Books in Motion can be very social. The children at school keep each other up to date as to which chapter they're currently reading, what parts of the story they like and dislike. They also plan their nights out, who they'll see, who they'll ride with, where they'll meet up for pizza after the movie.

Mary Greene explained how Books in Motion benefited her second-grade son:

> My oldest son has benefited from Books in Motion the most of all. He is not a strong reader but since a lot of his classmates participate in the program, he *wants* to finish the books. He can't wait to get to school and talk about what he had read and what happens next. He could have cared less to read a chapter book before we started, but now we have a list of chapter books he wants to read.

Finally, classroom teacher Henry noted that his students came to the classroom more motivated to read particular books, knowing they were a part of Books in Motion. It seems that the library program increased participants' desire to begin reading the monthly text selection, provided concrete incentives to finish books, and promoted interaction between readers of various ages.

Additionally, Books in Motion offered community members access to a variety of literacy resources. Participants also appreciated the new resources introduced through Books in Motion, including unfamiliar titles, individual text copies, and new ways to access the public library. One parent attributed a plethora of untapped chapter books to Books in Motion, explaining, "We've read books through the program that we either hadn't heard of – like *Howl's Moving Castle* – or hadn't thought to read yet – like *To Kill a Mockingbird.*" Fifth-grade teacher Henry noted that Books in Motion put individual copies of books into the hands of all of his students. Because Books in Motion supplied participants with free individual copies, students were able to have their own copies for in-class shared reading and out-of-school independent reading.

For other participants, Books in Motion provided them with new ways to access their community's public library. More specifically, the program also encouraged participants to use their public library with increased frequency and renewed interest. Several of the families, including the Pierces and Flanagans, had been avid participants in early childhood story hours and had missed these opportunities as their children outgrew programs. One mother explained, "At most libraries, story hours are for young children and book clubs are for grownups. I appreciate there being something for this school-aged group." One participant explained, "Books in Motion got us connected to the library and all it has to offer." As such, Books in Motion transformed the public library into a community meeting spot.

Future Directions and Concluding Thoughts

Books in Motion created a valuable community literacy experience in which parents, children, teachers, and librarians learned from each other and grew as readers in a motivating forum. Books in Motion thrives as a community literacy program that meets the needs of a variety of participants, as confirmed by previous research on the benefits of intergenerational literacy programs (Anderson & Morrison, 2007; Cairney & Munsie, 1995; Daisey, 1991; Elish-Piper, 1996; Philliber et al., 1996; Shanahan et al., 1995). In particular, this library-based program seems to benefit its children, parents, family units, and other community members (Padak & Rasinski, 2003). It is also possible that their participation in Books in Motion may lead parents to become more involved in school activities and their children's classroom work. Finally, the public library has most certainly attained a higher public profile and increased publicity in its efforts to promote literacy (McNicol & Dalton, 2002).

Although these participants were overwhelmingly positive about their experiences with Books in Motion, this trend may not be true for all participants of similar intergenerational community literacy projects. It would be prudent to seek out participants who made conscious decisions to end their participation with such projects in order to understand any possible feelings of exclusion, intimidation, disinterest, or dissatisfaction. These critical voices might be useful in shaping similar projects that are even more diverse and more inclusive.

Books in Motion appears to have helped participants understand that "literacy entails a broader web of social relationships than between child and teacher or principal" (Fagan, 1995). In encouraging participants to share books through collaborative conversations and monthly meetings, Books in Motion exemplifies that "literacy does not and cannot occur in isolation. It is always part of social relationships" (Fagan, 1995). Participants have begun to understand that reading can support both "social as well as personal activities" (Behrman, 2002).

The Future of Books in Motion

Nearly seven years after its creation, Books in Motion continues to thrive and impress even its original creators. Each month has brought a new surprise, with adults outnumbering children for *To Kill a Mockingbird*, a surge of older children for *Hoot*, and minimal participation for more current movies, such as *The Diary of the Wimpy Kid*, which children had recently seen in theaters. The children's librarian has also reached out to local schools through school newsletters and emails to encourage teacher and administrator involvement.

The success of Books in Motion has led the public library to start a teenage version, replicating the program for adolescent readers in the community; rather than a film night housed at the public library, participants in Books in Motion for Teens now travel together by bus to a local movie theater.

Although research by the National Endowment for the Arts (2007) points out the decline in reading habits of young people, reading continues in engaging and creative formats through programs like Books in Motion. As communities and public libraries seek to influence children's reading today, Books in Motion exemplifies how community members can benefit from a low-cost community literacy program. In creating Books in Motion, the public library simply provided space, resources, and opportunities rather than any sort of instruction about how participants should approach literacy. An easily reproducible model for communities across the nation, Books in Motion has transformed reading into an act of community engagement.

References

Anderson, J., & Morrison, F. (2007). A great program ... for me as a gramma: Caregivers evaluate a family literacy initiative. *Canadian Journal of Education, 30*(1), 68–89. https://doi.org/10.2307/20466626

Auerbach, E. (1989). Towards a social–contextual approach to family literacy. *Harvard Educational Review, 59*, 165–181. https://doi.org/10.1080/10862969509547903

Behrman, E. (2002). Community-based literacy learning. *Reading: Literacy and Language, 36*(1), 26–32. https://doi.org/10.1111/1467–9345.00181

Cairney, T., & Munsie, L. (1995). Parent participation in literacy learning. *The Reading Teacher, 48*(5), 392–403.

Clay, M. (1993). Always a learner: A fable. *Reading Today, 3*(10), 3–11.

Daisey, P. (1991). Intergenerational literacy programs: Rationale, description, and effectiveness. *Journal of Clinical Child Psychology, 20*(1), 11–18. https://doi.org/10.1207/s15374424jccp2001_3

Edwards, P., & Turner, J. (2009). Family literacy and reading comprehension. In S. Israel, & G. Duffy (Eds.), *Handbook of research on reading comprehension* (pp. 364–382). Routledge.

Elish-Piper, L. (1996). Literacy and their lives: Four low-income families enrolled in a summer family literacy program. *Journal of Adolescent and Adult Literacy, 40*(4), 256–268.

Fagan, W. (1995). Social relationships of literacy. *The Reading Teacher, 49*(3), 260–262.

Freire, P. (1970). *Pedagogy of the oppressed*. Seabury Press. https://doi.org/10.4324/9780429269400-8

Gadsden, V. (2000). Intergenerational literacy within families. In M. Kamil, P. D. Pearson, E. B. Moje, & P. P. Afflerbach (Eds.), *Handbook of reading research: Vol 3* (pp. 871–888). Lawrence Erlbaum Associates.

Heath, S. B. (1983). *Ways with words.* Cambridge University Press. http://dx.doi.org/10.1017/CBO9780511841057

Hendersen, A. (1988). Parents are a school's best friend. *Phi Delta Kappan, 70*(2), 148–153.

Hiebert, E. (1991). *Literacy for a diverse society: Perspectives, practices, and policies.* Teachers College Press.

McNicol, S., & Dalton, P. (2002). The best way is always through the children: The impact of family reading. *Journal of Adolescent and Adult Literacy, 46*(3), 246–253.

Morrow, L., Tracey, D., & Maxwell, C. (1995). *A survey of family literacy in the United States.* International Reading Association.

National Endowment for the Arts. (2007). *To read or not to read: A question of national consequence.* Retrieved from www.nea.gov/research/ToRead.pdf

Padak, N., & Rasinski, T. (2003). *Family literacy: Who benefits?* Kent State University, Ohio Literacy Resource Center.

Philliber, W., Spillman, R., & King, R. (1996). Consequences of family literacy for adults and children. *Journal of Adolescent and Adult Literacy, 39*(7), 558–565.

Shanahan, T., Mulhern, M., & Rodriguez-Brown, F. (1995). Project FLAME: Lessons learned from a family literacy program for linguistic minority families. *The Reading Teacher, 48*(7), 586–593.

Street, B. (1993). *Cross cultural approaches to literacy.* Cambridge University Press.

Children's Works Cited

Babbitt, N. (1975). *Tuck everlasting.* Farrar, Straus, & Giroux.

Dahl, R. (1967). *Charlie and the chocolate factory.* Knopf.

DiCamillo, K. (2000). *Because of Winn-Dixie.* Candlewick.

Farley, W. (1941). *The black stallion.* Yearling.

Goldman, W. (1973). *The princess bride.* Harcourt Brace.

Hiassen, C. (2004). *Hoot.* Random House.

Jones, D. W. (1986). *Howl's moving castle.* Greenwillow Books.

Lee, H. (1960). *To kill a mockingbird.* Lippincott.

Levine, G. C. (1998). *Ella enchanted.* HarperCollins Children's Books.

Lewis, C. S. (1950). *The lion, the witch, and the wardrobe.* The Macmillan Company.

O'Hara, M. (1941). *My friend Flicka.* J.B. Lippincott.

Patterson, K. (1977). *Bridge to Terabithia.* HarperCollins.

Rogers, M. (1972). *Freaky Friday.* HarperCollins.

Rockwell, T. (1973). *How to eat fried worms.* F. Watts.

Sachar, L. (2000). *Holes.* Random House.

White, E. B. (1952). *Charlotte's web.* Harper & Row.

Appendix 12.1: List of Books Used by Books in Motion

Title	Author	Movie
The Lion, the Witch, and the Wardrobe	C.S. Lewis	*The Chronicles of Narnia: The Lion, the Witch and the Wardrobe (2005)*
The Princess Bride	William Goldman	*The Princess Bride (1987)*

Appendix 12.1 Cont.

Title	Author	Movie
Hoot	Carl Hiassen	*Hoot (2006)*
Ella Enchanted	Gail Carson Levine	*Ella Enchanted (2004)*
To Kill a Mockingbird	Harper Lee	*To Kill a Mockingbird (1962)*
The Bad Beginning: A Series of Unfortunate Events	Lemony Snickett	*Lemony Snicket's A Series of Unfortunate Events (2004)*
Harry Potter and the Sorcerer's Stone	J.K. Rowling	*Harry Potter and the Sorcerer's Stone (2001)*
Charlotte's Web	E.B. White	*Charlotte's Web (2006)*
The Black Stallion	Walter Farley	*The Black Stallion (1979)*
The Bridge to Terabithia	Katherine Paterson	*Bridge to Terabithia (2007)*
Howl's Moving Castle	Diana Wynne Jones	*Howl's Moving Castle (2004)*
Charlie and the Chocolate Factory	Roald Dahl	*Willy Wonka and the Chocolate Factory (1971)*
Tuck Everlasting	Natalie Babbitt	*Tuck Everlasting (2002)*
Because of Winn-Dixie	Kate DiCamillo	*Because of Winn-Dixie (2005)*
The Secret Garden	Frances Hodgson Burnett	*The Secret Garden (1993)*
Freaky Friday	Mary Rogers	*Freaky Friday (2003)*
Prince Caspian	C.S. Lewis	*The Chronicles of Narnia: Prince Caspian (2008)*
My Friend Flicka	Mary O'Hara	*My Friend Flicka (1943)*
Stuart Little	E.B. White	*Stuart Little (1999)*
Nim's Island	Wendy Orr	*Nim's Island (2008)*
The Wonderful Wizard of Oz	Frank Baum	*The Wizard of Oz (1939)*
A Christmas Carol	Charles Dickens	*A Christmas Carol (2009)*
The Borrowers	Mary Norton	*The Borrowers (1997)*
The Thief Lord	Cornelia Funke	*The Thief Lord (2006)*
Babe the Gallant Pig	Dick King-Smith	*Babe (1995)*
Escape to Witch Mountain	Alexander Keys	*Escape to Witch Mountain (1975)*
Chitty Chitty Bang Bang	Ian Fleming	*Chitty Chitty Bang Bang (1968)*
The Incredible Journey	Sheila Burnford	*The Incredible Journey (1963)*
The Guardians of Ga'Hoole	Kathryn Lasky	*Legend of the Guardians: The Owls of Ga'Hoole (2010)*
Hotel for Dogs	Lois Duncan	*Hotel for Dogs (2009)*
The Water Horse	Dick King-Smith	*The Water Horse: Legend of the Deep (2007)*
Mary Poppins	P.L. Travers	*Mary Poppins (1964)*

(continued)

Appendix 12.1 Cont.

Title	Author	Movie
The Railway Children	E. Nesbit	The Railway Children (1970)
101 Dalmatians	Dodie Smith	101 Dalmatians (1996)
James and the Giant Peach	Roald Dahl	James and the Giant Peach (1996)
Treasure Island	Robert Louis Stevenson	Treasure Island (1950)
How to Eat Fried Worms	Thomas Rockwell	How to Eat Fried Worms (2006)
Holes	Louis Sachar	Holes (2003)

13

BEYOND VISUAL LITERACY

Listening, Speaking, Reading, and Writing in the Art Museum

Meredith Lehman

MILDRED LANE KEMPER ART MUSEUM, WASHINGTON UNIVERSITY IN ST. LOUIS

Sabrina Mooroogen Phillips

ART INSTITUTE OF CHICAGO, SCHOOL OF THE ART INSTITUTE OF CHICAGO

Ray Williams

BLANTON MUSEUM OF ART, UNIVERSITY OF TEXAS AT AUSTIN

A Picture Is Worth a Thousand Words

If your memories of field trips to an art museum are filled with unruly kids being shepherded by chaperones to keep up with a very informative, fast-talking "tour guide," you should know that times have changed! Museum-based educators today are expected to be familiar with child development and curricular standards at all grade levels; we offer carefully designed experiences with works of art (and the museum environment itself) that support core competencies. Looking at art with others motivates interpretive conversations and creative responses, both written and visual. Literacy skills and Social Emotional Learning (SEL) can be integrated quite naturally into the goals of a museum visit, as this chapter based on initiatives at the University of Texas will show.

Whether we are decoding a text or an image, meaning making is based on noticing details; and persuasive interpretive theories must be grounded in evidence that others can also see. Because most works of art were inspired by human experience, we often find that our own life experiences prepare us with skills (our understanding of facial expression, body language, or dialect, for example) relevant to the interpretive encounter. We have ideas to share, perhaps based on our own reactions or memories, and we are eager to hear from others with different ideas and experiences. We find a communal pleasure in developing one or more viable theories of meaning. Although both written and visual expressions can stimulate such conversations, considering works of art may offer more immediate rewards: they stay still, available all at once for the group to consider diverse areas of interest, eventually rewarding the accrual of observation with flashes of insight.

The Blanton Museum of Art in Austin, Texas has a strong commitment to serving a diverse range of communities and schools, providing customized gallery lessons for some 14,000 school visitors annually. Approximately 60% of these visitors come from low-resource (Title I) schools and receive free admission and subsidized transportation to the museum; approximately 28% speak a language other than English at home; 30% of school visitors come for a three-visit sequence, complemented by pre- and post-visit lesson plans for classroom use.

Over the past few years, museum educators at the Blanton have developed a series of gallery activities and experiences that, considered as a whole, constitute robust support for students developing literacy skills at key developmental moments. For students in pre-K through first grade, our focus is on introducing the joys of reading books and looking at pictures. Upper elementary students are able to participate in a three-visit sequence designed to support specific literacy skills being taught in school. Middle school students have an opportunity to meet an author and/or illustrator and learn more about creative processes. The Museum's focus on literacy has resulted in new partnerships with local school systems, including professional development workshops and collaborative curriculum development.

The Joys of Reading in Early Childhood

Tales and Trails [Cuentos y Caminos] supports both verbal and visual literacy development in early childhood, pairing the more familiar joys of reading a good story with looking at related works of art during what may be a first visit to a museum. The Blanton provides carefully selected books to be read and discussed in the classroom before the museum visit.[1] Two books for each grade level (pre-K, kindergarten, and first grade) are chosen for the quality of their illustrations; their reference to creative processes; and their link to SEL competencies around self-awareness, social awareness, and relationship skills.

Pre-visit lesson plans accompanying the book introduce students to themes that will be explored in the galleries through discussion questions, an activity, and a preview of the museum visit. The classroom lesson prepares students for the gallery experience by providing an opportunity to practice visual literacy skills in the classroom and framing expectations about the museum visit. Teachers appreciate that the pre-visit lesson plan corresponds to TEKS (Texas Essential Knowledge and Skills) and TEA (Texas Education Agency) Guidelines Alignment and that core learning goals are embedded in the museum experience. After the

---

[1] See Table 13.1 for a comprehensive list of books and related artworks from the Blanton's collection.

museum visit, additional readings and activities are provided in both English and Spanish, in hopes of extending the learning at home.

The 45-minute museum visit puts into practice the connections between visual literacy and verbal literacy through object-based learning. By noticing details and making meaning based on their observations and different perspectives, students develop visual literacy habits that are translatable outside of the museum context. According to Lopatovska (2016), the close looking and interpretation skills needed to "read" images broaden student vocabulary and improve verbal skills, including oral, reading, and writing literacy (Stewig, 1994), self-expression (Flynt & Brozo, 2010), foreign language proficiency (Tomaseviae-Daneeviae, 1999), and multiliteracy skills (New London Group, 1994). The benefits of establishing strong visual literacy in early childhood is essential for later success in understanding, interpreting, and communicating information about texts in its varied forms.[2]

At the museum, volunteer gallery teachers choose 4–6 works of art that relate thematically or stylistically to the book. Rather than re-read the entire text, gallery teachers have the book on-hand as a reference, introducing a relevant work of art and inviting students to share details from the book that resonate for them. For example, groups who have selected *Verdi* (Janell Cannon, 1997), a story about the eponymous yellow snake who is scared to grow up and become green, students might start at Thomas Glassford's 30-foot hanging sculpture, *Siphonophora* (2016). Sitting or lying underneath the monumental work, students are invited to be curious about what habitat or creature the sculpture represents. Is this an environment that Verdi would like to live in? Noticing the scale of the artwork, students might wonder whether this object was always this size, or if it grew and changed over time. At other works of art, students will continue to explore the theme of change and how it relates to identity, self-expression, and the creative process. Are there times they have experienced change like Verdi, and what emotions did they feel during that transition? Throughout the *Verdi* gallery experience, students practice social awareness, noticing differences and similarities between themselves, classmates, and figures represented in artwork; and self-awareness, relating their feelings and thoughts to behavior.

For classes that have selected *The Most Magnificent Thing* (Ashley Spires, 2014), a story about a young girl whose idea to construct an extraordinary object leads to frustration over the creative process, students might first look at Joan Mitchell's *Rock Bottom* (1960–1961). At this painting, a drama-based strategy asks students to reflect on how artists express emotions through color, line, and form, and how we also convey and identify emotions through non-verbal cues including body language and facial expression. Working with a partner, one student chooses an emotion that they see in the work of art and, without speaking, uses their body to communicate this to the other person, who then tries to guess the emotion before

---

[2] Visual literacy asks students to move beyond description of an artwork to develop higher-order learning skills like critical thinking. See Williams (2007).

switching roles. As a group, students reflect on what strategies the young girl in the book uses to manage her stress and to find creative solutions for realizing her work of art, as well as what strategies they use to overcome challenges. Bringing in students' lived experiences and prior knowledge to construct meaning deepens literacy learning and the joy of reading through personal and cultural connections (Rosenblatt, 1938, 1978). Following this, students delve into the creative process. At Louise Nevelson's *Dawn's Presence – Two Columns* (1969–1975), for example, groups imagine the steps the artist took to create their artwork, considering materials, experimentation, and construction. In small groups, they work together to create their own magnificent artwork using found materials. Guided reflection prompts (see Figure 13.1) ask students to share what problems they encountered, what solutions they generated, and what emotions came up while collaborating on a group project. The empathetic imagination is sparked as students discuss how they can help each other when they recognize someone is struggling. Students think about the feelings of frustration and the joys of inventing with the artwork *Dawn's Presence-Two Columns* by Louise Nevelson.

The *Tales & Trails [Cuentos y Caminos]* program expands art-related vocabulary and develops communication strategies for self-expression and social awareness in its integration of Social and Emotional Learning. Extending student engagement with a book in an art museum deepens reading comprehension, offering a new space to respond to the text and make connections through multiple modalities. In addition to close looking and interpretation, hands-on, process-based art activities promote early childhood literacy through creative response. These different modes

FIGURE 13.1 A Museum Experience with the Book *The Most Magnificent Thing* by Ashley Spires

of expression – visual, kinesthetic, and verbal – support literacy and impact future writing, reading, speaking, and listening skills, while also accommodating diverse learning styles and abilities.

Reading Between the Lines

Between the Lines consists of a sequence of three 60-minute museum visits designed to support literacy skills in students grades 3–8. In each gallery lesson, students are asked to speak, listen, read, and write. Students are introduced to basic principles of visual literacy, looking closely at works of art and working together toward satisfying interpretations grounded in visual evidence.[3] These interpretive conversations are structured to invite each of the dozen or so members of the group to participate actively in considering one work of art for 15–20 minutes. The facilitator may begin by asking for a one-word response to the work of art, repeating each individual's word, making it clear that all contributions will be respected. Questions are invited – *"what do you notice, or wonder about?"* – and explored by the group, with the facilitator paraphrasing, noting connections, and generally supporting the generation of multiple theories of meaning. Consensus is not necessarily the goal; active participation in the process of looking and thinking together is valued in itself. We consider how our reactions and ideas are informed by our own experiences, as well as choices that the artist (or author) made in creating the work. Although visual learners may have a special opportunity to shine in these object-based discussions, every participant can share in the pleasure of noticing details, articulating a response, posing a question, and exploring interpretive possibilities with peers. These pleasures, these skills, are directly relevant to the analysis and understanding of literary texts.

While interpretive conversations in pursuit of meaning are central to each museum visit, these exercises in looking, speaking, and listening are punctuated by activities that involve reading and writing. Activities are scaffolded to accommodate different learners' needs, with an emphasis on supporting dual-language learners. For an example of adjusting the complexity for diverse developmental stages, let's consider several approaches to working with images that represent a story: (1) The gallery teacher might *tell the story* aloud, then ask students to list several moments in the narrative that could be illustrated, then invite drawings with captions – or ask teams to recreate the composition with their bodies in a frozen tableau, as well as what came before and after the moment depicted in the work of art; (2) The teacher passes out bare-bones versions of the plot, and invites students

---

[3]   For those who may be unfamiliar with facilitating interpretive conversations about visual art, one useful approach may be found in the work developed by Philip Yenawine based in Abigail Housen's research on aesthetic development. Information about how to use Visual Thinking Strategies (VTS) to motivate looking and stimulate interpretive theories grounded in visual evidence may be found online or in Yenawine's *Visual Thinking Strategies: Using Art to Deepen Learning Across School Disciplines* (2013).

TABLE 13.1 List of Books and Related Artworks Used in the Blanton's "Tales and Trails" Program

Book	Blanton Artworks	Teaching Questions
The Most Magnificent Thing Ashley Spires (2014)	Louise Nevelson Dawn, ***Presence – Two Columns***, 1969–1975, Painted wood Joan Mitchell, ***Rock Bottom***, 1960–1961, Oil on canvas	How did she start her project? What happened when it didn't turn out the way she imagined? Has a friend ever helped you when you were feeling mad or sad? How? This sculpture took six years to complete. Why do you think it took the artist that long? What takes you a long time? [Nevelson] What do you do when you feel sad or angry? How might those emotions look if you painted them? [Mitchell]
What To Do With a Box Jane Yolen & Chris Sheban (2016)	Sonya Clark, ***Madam C.J. Walker***, 2008, combs Donald Moffett, ***Lot 102807X (Yellow)***, 2007, acrylic polyvinyl acetate on linen and wall, with rayon and steel zipper	What color is the box? How does the way the box looks change the way you use it? If you were making a portrait of somebody, what objects would you use, and who would you portray? [Clark] What does the shape of the construction remind you of? [Moffett]
Verdi Janelle Cannon (1997)	Thomas Glassford, ***Siphonophora***, 2016, white cement, polyurethane and steel rods Jules Buck Jones, ***Atlantic vs Pacific***, 2005–2006, ink on two sheets of paper	What is the difference between Verdi and the green snakes? Why is Verdi afraid of changing/growing up? If this was a creature, what would it look like alive? [Glassford] Do you relate to the fish in some way? [Jones]
Stellaluna Janell Cannon (1993)	Luca Cambiaso, ***Esther and Ahaseurus***, circa 1569, 16th century, oil on canvas Anselm Kiefer, ***Sternenfall [Falling Stars]***, 1998, mixed media on canvas	What does it feel like when you're lost? What did Stellaluna learn from her time with the birds? Esther and King Ahaseurus loved one another even though they were different. How is this similar to Stellaluna? [Cambiaso] Have you ever looked at the stars in the night sky? Where were you? What did you see? [Kiefer]

TABLE 13.1 Cont.

Book	Blanton Artworks	Teaching Questions
Journey Aaron Becker (2014)	Teresita Fernandez, **Stacked Waters**, 2009, cast acrylic	How did the main character in the book deal with feeling sad, lonely, or bored? What are some things you can do to help someone else when you notice they are feeling that way? How is the artist helping people step into another world? What would they call this installation, if they could give it a name? [Fernandez]
Quest Aaron Becker (2014)	Edgar Negret, **El Puente**, 1972, aluminum, paint Regina Bogat, **Cord Painting 14**, 1977, Acrylic with nylon and satin cords on canvas	What kind of world do the two main characters explore? Why do you think the king was captured? How do the shapes connect in this work of art? Where might this bridge take you? [Negret] What colors in this work of art stick out to you? Can you find your color in this work? [Bogat]

to embellish the text with description, dialogue, and motivation based on the related image and their own imaginations; (3) The source text (often mythological or biblical) is cut up and parts distributed to students who are asked to re-sequence the excerpts before reading the story aloud; and (4) A dramatic script based on the original source material is provided to students, who read through the assigned parts in preparation for a reader's theater presentation.

Other museum-based activities that foster literacy invite students to: engage in descriptive or reflective writing; collaborate on a group poem; complete a dialogue bubble for a character in a work of art; or redact a museum label (or related poem) to get at the essence of a work of art. Reading and annotating the museum's floor plan based on exploratory prompts is an empowering introductory activity for some groups. Because SEL content is integral to our work, students may be invited to look around and "Find a work of art that has something to say about courage (or family, joy, creativity, anger, etc.)" prior to sharing their choices and ideas verbally. Although the possibilities seem endless, the common elements are looking closely, responding with (or to) words, finding connections, and making meaning.

As the gallery lessons are not scripted, facilitators draw on a wide range of key images and activities to design experiences that develop literacy skills. Perhaps a brief outline of a three-visit sequence for fifth- and sixth-graders will be useful as a model for others who want to pursue this use of the art museum. The *first visit* might begin with students making nametags and writing a fun fact about themselves to share in an introduction (15 minutes). An initial object-based conversation might include hearing one word from each student that describes their first reaction to the work of art, encourage the group to notice significant details, and invite questions. Students might be asked to read a brief quote from the artist or from the curator's explanatory label to fuel further discussion (15 minutes). Continuing the exploration of relating images to texts, a second work of art might be used to develop a "word inventory." Individuals make a list of words that come to them, as they silently examine the image; then the facilitator records a list of responses on a large easel pad. Finally, they categorize the words as Feeling, Describing, Analyzing, action words to get a sense of the many ways we might respond to a work of art *or use as a starting point for writing* (15 minutes). The first visit might culminate in a MadLibs-inspired activity in which groups of three or four students generate word inventories for different works of art, then apply their choices to fill in blanks in a related script before sharing verbally with the other groups (15 minutes).

A *second visit* could focus on portraiture/characters, drawing on student knowledge of facial expression and body language, noticing details of setting and costume that help define a sense of character, and reading biographical information about known sitters. The session might begin with close looking at a conventional European portrait, encouraging students to note details of physiognomy, costume, and setting; and then to make inferences about the sitter's character and social role. The facilitator will include information about what defines a portrait, and why portraiture was second only to history painting in the traditional hierarchy of genres defined by European academies of art (15 minutes). Next, students are invited to select a nearby portrait and, recalling the prior visit, generate a word inventory to describe the sitter. Drawing on their own word bank, the curator's explanatory label, and their imagination, students then craft a "Six Word Biography" for the individual they are contemplating (20 minutes, including shared looking/reading responses). At the Blanton we move on to more contemporary portraits of known historical figures, including the prominent entrepreneur and philanthropist Madam C. J. Walker, actress and artist Farrah Fawcett, and member of Congress Barbara Jordan. Students are divided into three groups. In each group, individuals will choose to read a 150-word biography of either the sitter or the artist – underlining one "revealing or important" line in each paragraph, then circling a key word in each selected line, and finally sharing their "essential" word to characterize the person they have been reading about. Finally, small groups introduce their chosen works of art and share basic information about artists and sitters synthesized from their reading, looking, and discussion (25 minutes).

The *third visit* in this Between the Lines series would focus on narrative paintings, the highest in the hierarchy of genres introduced in the previous visit. These paintings typically integrate several figures into a complex composition to present a didactic message or to display knowledge of classical mythology or the Bible. During the introductory conversation, based on considering Claude Vignon's *David with the Head of Goliath*, students make inferences and develop questions based on the imagery, before listening to a retelling of the biblical story. We consider the many moments in this story that the artist might have selected, and wonder about Vignon's decision to emphasize David's psychological experience (20 minutes). Next, three groups move to narrative paintings and are given a reader's theater script to rehearse. Reader's theater motivates repeated readings in order to develop expression and rhythm; frequent choral responses support less fluent readers in participating. At the Blanton, students would perform these scripts in front of Scorza's *Orpheus Charming the Beasts*, Cambiaso's *Esther and Ahasuerus* (Figure 13.2) and Ricci's *Return of the Prodigal Son* (25 minutes). Finally, students are invited to sketch out a composition that depicts another scene in one of the four stories introduced in the session and add a descriptive caption (15 minutes).

FIGURE 13.2   Luca Cambiaso, circa 1569, "Esther and Ahasuerus"[a]
[a] Oil on Canvas, 98.4 cm × 88.5 cm (38 3/4 in. × 34 13/16 in.), Blanton Museum of Art, The University of Texas at Austin, The Suida-Manning Collection.

The Art of the Book

The underworld; a futuristic high rise; the belly of the deep sea: all are worlds imagined by middle school students inspired by an author/illustrator team's creative process and their experience of the Blanton Museum's collections. *Art of the Book*, an annual event developed in collaboration with Austin's independent bookstore, BookPeople, introduces students to nationally recognized authors and artists – and positions the museum as a source for creativity.

In our first meeting with the bookstore's representative, we talked about what partnering could look like and our shared values and interests. Delving deeply into favorite picture books, we considered Aaron Becker's *Journey* (2014) and the way it wordlessly moves the reader through imagined worlds and adventures. We explored the varied relationships between image and text found in other recent children's fiction and the creative work behind such products. Making the creative process more visible through the voices of professional author-illustrators could have a profound impact on young readers. How were authors thinking about the visual as they wrote and planned? What sources were illustrators using as inspiration? How might a museum experience lead to new stories and images? How are new ideas developed and presented to others?

In January 2019, BookPeople and the Blanton brought together the creative team of M.T. Anderson and Eugene Yelchin and 200 middle school students from various campuses around central Texas. They discussed the creation of their latest book, *The Assassination of Brangwain Spurge* (2018), which alternates chapters of text with chapters of complex images that further this fantastical narrative of goblins and elves. What follows is a description of the event to provide a useful model for community collaborations in an art museum for middle school students.

The event started early in the morning, with enthusiastic students filing into the Blanton's auditorium, unsure of what this new museum experience would bring. The author and illustrator began their presentation by recounting the decision to work separately at first, allowing for the illustrations and narrative to take a life of their own, creating a fascinating component of interpretation and uncertainty with the images and text. The humor of the creators' work was infectious as students became intrigued by this duo whose creative process was so adventurous and rooted in discovery and exploration of their own and collective creativity.

With this spirit in mind, the creators joined us in the museum to explore artworks that similarly tell a narrative, but also leave space for imagination to flourish. Some students engaged with the seventeenth-century painting of *Orpheus Charming the Beasts* (Figure 13.3) some saw *Dawn's Presence*, a towering sculpture of found materials by Louise Nevelson, and others saw Thomas Glassford's *Siphonophora*, a giant sculpture reminiscent of a sea creature. Students were led through a process of guided looking to explore the works from multiple angles and perspectives, investigating the narratives and characters that might live within

FIGURE 13.3   Sinibaldo Scorza, circa 1615, "Orpheus Charming the Beasts"[a]
[a] Oil on canvas, 65.5 cm × 100.2 cm (25 13/16 in. × 39 7/16 in.), Blanton Museum of Art, The University of Texas at Austin, The Suida-Manning Collection.

them. As students started to imagine worlds that these artworks inspired, they were encouraged to discuss their settings in small groups. At this stage of the gallery experience, students were invited to create costumes with only newspaper and tape for a character from their world.

Students were engrossed in discussion, challenging each other to generate ideas and problem solve. The book creators, Anderson and Yelchin, were on hand, encouraging and pushing the creativity, their presence underscoring literacy connections and the creative process. As students discussed their creations, they began to see themselves as makers of characters, worlds, and language. For middle school students, where personalities are constantly rehearsed and revised, seeing themselves and each other as directors, leaders, and negotiators builds literacy within their developmental moment.

As the experience drew to a close, we reflected with the teachers and students on some of the literacy skills that were practiced throughout this world-building exercise inspired from the fantastic world of *Brangwain Spurge*. In this case, art worked much in the same way as a mentor text, where inspiration was generated and could be returned to again and again to reference as their collaborative stories took shape. It is within this collaboration that students were able to show their understanding of a creative process and to use each other in a similar way to Anderson and Yelchin as partners in adventurous exploration. Teachers noticed their students explaining to each other elements of the costume, and why, for example, a huge tentacle needed to be built into a headdress. This reasoning through demonstration and discussion is a key literacy component that supports written and oral expression. Beyond the costume-building activity, the presence of the authors and their active participation in the galleries demonstrated to students and teachers the correlations between the artistic process and close looking at works of art in a museum.

Art, Literacy, Social and Emotional Learning

The development of a meaningful literacy program in an art museum must be done in collaboration with community partners, including the students who participate in and enrich our educational programs. While we cannot follow individual students over time or have access to test scores that might demonstrate a specific impact on students, we can reflect on our teaching and student engagement after a gallery lesson. As practice, we debrief with docents and reflect in writing on student engagement. In the galleries, we observe enthusiastic participation in reading, interpretation, and creative response. We also work closely with teachers to refine and revise the curriculum. Teacher surveys are sent out after class visits with targeted questions that assess the relevance of a gallery experience and that give feedback on what worked well and what could be improved. Teachers have indicated surprise at some students' willingness to contribute ideas or to write a paragraph, suggesting that visual stimulation can support learners who thrive in multimodal contexts. Annual professional development workshops with the school district's literacy specialists also provide an important opportunity for the museum to ensure that our curriculum supports what is taking place in schools. We understand that, like our teaching, our curriculum must be flexible and responsive to the changing needs of students.

Building literacy skills within a museum setting might seem unexpected at first, but our work shows that the galleries can be the site for originality and creativity beyond the classroom walls. The works of art not only spark inspiration, but also confirm and validate complex social and cognitive developmental moments. By incorporating opportunities for students to listen, read, write, and speak in its gallery lessons, the art museum utilizes multi-modal entry points that align with school district objectives and initiatives. Moving beyond a museum's traditional close looking and interpretive strategies, Blanton educators have explored how process-based art-making and writing activities promote literacy through creative response. The many modes of expression – visual, kinesthetic, and verbal – support fundamental skills, while also responding to the needs of students with diverse learning styles and abilities. The immediacy and accessibility of a work of art provides all viewers with an equal entry point for individual and group discovery. Art can transcend cognitive and social barriers and provide space for open interpretation, inviting exploration in a safe space. Progressive museum educators can be strong partners to our colleagues in schools, as we support and augment formal curricular efforts in the realm of social emotional learning and literacy.

Acknowledgment

We would like to acknowledge the inspiration and curricular contributions of our former colleague, Andrea Saenz Williams, who is now the director of education and civic engagement at the di Rosa Art Center for Contemporary Art.

References

Anderson, M.T., & Yelchin, E. (2018). *The assassination of Brangwain Spurge*. Candlewick Press.

Becker, A. (2014). *Journey*. Walker Books.

Becker, A. (2014). *Quest*. Walker Books.

Cannon, J. (1993). *Stellaluna*. Harcourt.

Cannon, J. (1997). *Verdi*. Harcourt Brace.

Flynt, E. S., & Brozo, W. (2010). Visual literacy and the content classroom: A question of now, not when. *The Reading Teacher, 63*(6), 526–528. https://doi.org/10.1598/RT.63.6.11

Lopatovska, I. (2016). Engaging young children in visual literacy instruction. *Proceedings of the Association for Information Science and Technology, 53*(1), 1–5. https://doi.org/10.1002/pra2.2016.14505301101

New London Group. (1996). A pedagogy of multiliteracies: Designing social futures. *Harvard Educational Review, 66*(1), 60–92. https://doi.org/10.17763/haer.66.1.17370n67v22j160u

Rosenblatt, L. M. (1938). *Literature as exploration*. Appleton-Century.

Rosenblatt, L. M. (1978). *The reader, the text, the poem: The transactional theory of the literary work*. Southern Illinois University Press.

Spires, A. (2014). *The most magnificent thing*. Kids Can Press.

Stewig, J. W. (1994). First graders talk about paintings. *Journal of Educational Research, 87*(5), 309–316. https://doi.org/10.1080/00220671.1994.9941259

Tomaseviae-Daneeviae, M. (1999, September 21–26). Do you "speak" the visual language? *Cultures and Transitions*. International Society for Education through Art (InSEA), Brisbane, Australia.

Williams, T. L. (2007). "Reading" the painting: Exploring visual literacy in the primary grades. *The Reading Teacher, 60*(7), 636–642. https://doi.org/10.1598/RT.60.7.4

Yenawine, P. (2013). *Visual thinking strategies: Using art to deepen learning across school disciplines*. Harvard Education Press.

Yolen, J., & Sheban, C. (2016). *What to do with a box*. Creative Editions.

14

DOING PEDAGOGIC WORK TO ILLUMINATE THE WORLD

Participatory Literacy in a Community Museum

Suriati Abas

HOBART AND WILLIAM SMITH COLLEGES

Introduction

Museums play a significant role in cultivating out-of-school literacy as they showcase objects, spaces, and concepts considered by many people to be most valued (Barbara, 1998). While commonly described as discrete skill sets for reading and writing, literacy here is taken as a social practice, inferred from events mediated by texts (Barton, 2007). Hence, to engage in conversations centering on literacy within school and in out-of-school contexts means opening up conversations for understanding particular events, practices, activities, ideologies, and/or identities that shape the contributions afforded by agents in society who act as "sponsors" of literacy, supporting, teaching, or suppressing literacy learning for economic or political gain (Brandt, 2001, p. 166). Thus, aside from valuing artifacts as objects of historical preservation, museums additionally function as institutions for promoting social transformation through texts and/or images that are often displayed as exhibits. Historically, museums have been regarded as spaces of social and political power (Marstine, 2006). The CANDLES Holocaust museum is an exemplar of an institution invested in cultivating compassionate values by disseminating messages of healing and forgiveness.

Located in Terre Haute, Indiana, the CANDLES Holocaust museum was chosen as the subject of investigation due to its unique existence. Abbreviated as CANDLES, an acronym for "Children of Auschwitz Nazi Deadly Lab Experiments Survivors," this museum is the only non-profit organization in the world dedicated to the memory of Mengele twins involved in the medical experimentation at Auschwitz, Germany. It constructs learning beyond knowing historical facts; it offers a broad view of learning focusing on "creat[ing] an empowered community of critical thinkers who will illuminate the world with hope, healing, respect, and responsibility" (CANDLES Holocaust Museum and Education Center, 2019). Despite being in a small rural Midwestern city, this informative six-exhibit-area museum draws visitors both locally and internationally. The exhibits and panels, comprising snippets of images and texts, provide informative messages that are concomitantly educational. Following other literacy researchers, I share the perspective that texts are not neutral but designed and produced for particular ideological purposes, specific audiences, and involve power relations (e.g., Collins & Blot, 2003; Gee, 1996; Lemke, 1995; Street, 1984). Thinking along the Freirean tradition (Freire, 1970), becoming literate also means being able to link the act of naming and renaming the world for the purpose of enacting a change or transforming society. On that note, the study sought to respond to the following questions: (1) What literacy practices exist in the CANDLES museum that render it as a pedagogue? (2) How does the CANDLES museum use the works of literacy to engage the community and the world at large?

To discuss the ongoing literacy practices and vibrancy of literacy in out-of-school contexts such as this small, non-profit organization, some background knowledge about the museum is essential. In the next section, I offer brief information on the CANDLES museum to set the context for the study.

Brief Background of CANDLES Museum and the Holocaust

The CANDLES Holocaust Museum, founded in 1995 by Eva Mozes Kor, centers on her experiences as a Holocaust survivor. "Holocaust" is a Greek word, meaning "sacrifice by fire." The Holocaust, which occurred between 1933 and 1945, was a state-sponsored persecution and murder involving six million Jews under the Nazi regimes. The Nazis, who ruled Germany in January 1933, believed that Germans were "racially superior" and that the Jews, deemed "inferior," were posed as an alien threat to the Germans.

As a child, Eva and her twin sister, Miriam Mozes Zieger, was one of the 3000 subjects for Nazi doctor Josef Mengele's experimentations on twin children at Auschwitz, Germany. Mengele injected chemicals into different parts of the twins' bodies, including the eyes to try to change the eye color, performed sex change operations, sewed twins together to create conjoined twins, and even performed removal of organs and limbs. Many of these twins were as young as five years old; they were murdered at the end of the experiments, but Eva and Miriam were among the survivors. Moving forward from their tormented pasts, Eva, who emerged as the most active Holocaust survivor in the world, set up the CANDLES museum to encourage peace and kindness.

Literacy Practices, Critical Literacy, and Literacy Across the Community

Central to CANDLES museum is the focus on narratives of the holocaust. Within this six-exhibit-area, multiple literacy practices were continuously being produced and reproduced. Literacy practices, understood as the ways in which people use written languages in everyday lives, is not limited to observable behaviors but include values, attitudes, feelings, and social relationships (Street, 1993, p. 12). Simply put, they are "what people do with literacy" (Barton et al., 2000, p. 7) and how they are connected with one another. It is this intricate yet interesting connection that calls for an understanding of how literacy is distributed across the community to make the world a safe place. As Barton and Hamilton (1998) note, "literacy practices are more usefully understood as existing in the relations between people, within groups and communities, rather than as a set of properties residing in individuals" (p. 7). Additionally, given that museums make ideological uses and implications of texts apparent (Simpson, 1998; Vicenti Carpio, 2006), it is apt to examine the CANDLES museum from the perspective of critical literacy. The term "critical literacy," first coined by social critical theorists, was used to describe unequal power relationships and injustices in society. Through critical literacy, readers/viewers are given the opportunity to question, explore, or challenge the power relationships that exist between authors/creators and readers/viewers. CANDLES mission of developing critical thinkers who can make a change to the world largely aligns with the notions of critical literacy. Hence, I employed critical literacy to engage more deeply with critical analysis of the literacy practices, exhibits, and artifacts at the museum. My analysis was guided by the following questions:

- Who is in the text/picture/situation? Who is missing?
- Whose voices are represented? Whose voices are marginalized or discounted?
- What are the intentions of the author?
- What does the author want the reader/viewer to think?
- What would an alternative text/picture/situation say?
- How can the reader/viewer use this information to promote equity?

A consolidation of these responses was used to understand how the small, non-profit, community-serving museum promotes literacy across the community. By informally assuming a position as a pedagogue, CANDLES museum provided access for understanding the atrocities that occurred during the Holocaust.

Walking as a Mode of Inquiry

To understand how the museum has served as a pedagogue, I employed the methodology of walking interview, "framed by a 'place' that can be walked" (Evans &

Jones, 2011, p. 849). Using walking as a mode of inquiry, scholars have investigated sensory, material, and ephemeral intensities beyond the logics of representation (Springgay & Truman, 2017; Vannini, 2015). While walking, I employed ethnographic tools and qualitative methods. Hence, the data collected over three visits to the museum included (a) observational field notes taken on my cell phone and 5–10 minutes video-recording of activities occurring inside the museum, (b) artifacts, (c) promotional fliers, and (d) social media postings. Analysis of the data was conducted in four different phases. Firstly, the data were reviewed through "data walking" (Eakle, 2007), or a process where each of the different types of data were examined and sorted according to relevance and clarity of information. I inserted bracketed notes and highlighted keywords that communicate notions of critical literacy. (Examples: problem-posing, critical thinking, and self-reflection). Based on these notes and keywords, I developed questions and revisited the museum for clarification. From the data walks and returned visits, I created preliminary open data codes using tables and visual maps. Finally, I identified commonly occurring themes and created subthemes. In the section below, I present the overarching theme that characterizes CANDLES museum as a pedagogue.

Advocating Participatory Literacy

Much like schools, there are printed texts at museums. Presented as labels on panels, artifacts, subtexts, and captions below visuals, as Eakle and Chavez (2003) claim, museum walls can take on the appearance of school textbooks. In fact, those at CANDLES museum were not merely texts to be read, but also texts that strongly encourage participation. As a pedagogue, the museum has been advocating participatory literacy through multiple forms of literacy practices, such as storytelling and questioning the norms, to promote social transformation. In participatory literacy, learners, which in this context are the museum viewers or visitors, are at the heart of the learning (Fingeret & Jurmo, 1989). Key to this approach, which originated from Brazilian educator Paulo Freire, is the idea of providing solutions to social problems that impact daily lives. Similarly referred to as the Freirean Approach to language literacy education, the two features of participatory literacy that contribute to CANDLES museum's character are: dialogue and problem-posing. The dialogue component involves two-way communication between Eva and/or museum exhibits and visitors of the museum. Problem-posing, however, exists in the form of making visible real-life problems, discussing the causes and consequences, and proposing simple actions that lead to a resolution. At the museum, the ongoing literacy practices and static exhibits draw on multiple modes of representations (audio, video, visuals, and written texts) to convey messages of peace, forgiveness, and healing. In the following section, I offer an instance of how the museum leverages storytelling and its small-scale exhibits to promote literacy across community and the world at large.

Storytelling, generally understood as "a story told in a natural manner" (Peck, 1989), includes a traditional, literary oral tradition or narrative based on one's personal experiences. Recognized as the oldest form of education (Hamilton & Weiss, 2005), stories have been told for decades as a way of disseminating their cultural beliefs, traditions, and history to future generations. In Eva's storytelling session, she revealed the traumatizing experiences of being in the Nazi camp at the age of ten. Her voice represented one out of the many sufferings among the twins who were detained. Under the guise of Josef Mengele's medical "research" program, 3000 twins were taken away as unwilling experimentation subjects and exposed to disease, disfigurement, torture, and illness through inhumane actions. As according to Eva:

> We were given short haircuts. Our dresses were returned with a huge red cross on the back, and we were tattooed by heating a needle over the flame of a lamp. And when the needle got hot, they dipped it into ink, and they burned into my left arm, dot by dot, the capital letter A-7063. Miriam became capital A-7064. Auschwitz was the only Nazi camp that tattooed its inmates. My husband is a survivor of four years in Buchenwald. He does not have a tattoo. Once we were processed, we were taken to our barrack. Crude and filthy modular horse barns. There were no windows. We were given bunk beds on the bottom that were covered with a thin straw mattress. And we finally thought, after four days in the cattle car, that we could stretch out and maybe sleep.
>
> *(Excerpt #1: Eva Kor's talk; December 8, 2018)*

FIGURE 14.1 Chronological Timeline of the Holocaust (Photographer: Author, December 2018)

FIGURE 14.2   Exhibit Area Explaining the Groups of People Targeted by the Nazis (Photographer: Author, December 2018)

Eva's vivid descriptions of Auschwitz were complemented by static exhibits that surrounded the CANDLES museum. Each of the panels by the walls had visuals that helped viewers make connections with Eva's story. For instance, walking down the hallway, you will find a chronology timeline giving an overview of the unprecedented genocide perpetrated by Nazi Germany (see Figure 14.1).

In another exhibit area, a concise explanation was given on the groups of people targeted by the Nazis (see Figure 14.2). The brief, simple, and accessible language on each of the panels contributed to developing literacy across the community. The panels reinforced the stories that were told by Eva.

Among all, what made Eva's story most compelling was the takeaways or "life lesson" that she said could be drawn under the Nazi regime. Through her personal experiences, she connected with the community of visitors more broadly by transforming the horrifying experiences that she had undergone into optimistic ways of viewing the world:

> **Life lesson Number One**. Never ever give up on yourself, or on your dreams. If you give up, nothing will happen. And as I look at many of your young faces, I realize I remember growing up is very hard. And it's very hard even if you live in the United States, and even if you have loving parents. And what a thought that is. That every child in the world would be born to loving parents ... **Life lesson Number Two** deals with prejudice. One of the reasons that Adolf Hitler and the Nazis rose to power, it was a

bad economy. And once Hitler convinced his fellow Germans to vote for him – and he had only 1/3 of the vote, but somehow, he became chancellor of Germany. Instead of taking care of the economic problems, he decided it would be a lot faster to blame it on somebody, and Jews were always a good group of people to blame it on. And many of the Germans accepted the fact, because for centuries – generations – Jews were always used as the scapegoats for all the problems in the world. And they are used again. Few years ago, I got on Twitter a piece of information that Angela Merkel asked many Jews in Germany – as Rosh Hashanah and the high holy days are approaching – not to go to the synagogue, because they might be firebombed, and they cannot protect them all. So in 70 years, I don't see how much has changed. And in many countries in Europe that is a problem. Prejudice – I call prejudice a cancer of the human soul. It destroys the people who practice it, and it destroys everything in its sight. But that's what Hitler used. And prejudice, as we look around in the world today, is rampant … **Life lesson Number Three.** I forgave the Nazis. I forgave everybody. And if anybody would have asked me 22 years ago today if I forgave the Nazis, I would've told you, please find a really good psychiatrist. I had no intention of forgiving anybody. I was angry with the world, and I hated everybody. And I can tell you people have difficulty today to really believe that …

(Excerpt#2: Eva Kor's talk; December 8, 2018)

Integrating "life lessons" in her storytelling creates opportunities for learning about the consequences of choices, the importance of never giving up, the dangers of prejudice, and the need for genocide prevention today. As Sobol et al. (2004) claim, "storytelling is a medium of connectivity and of community" (p. 3). Connectivity in Eva's story is seen through simple daily examples that she cited to illuminate what was/is going on, in today's families, the community, and in other countries. While Eva's story serves the community, it also reaches out to all visitors through participatory literacy that takes the form of encouraging visitors to articulate what they could do to make the world a better place (see Figure 14.3). Hung on the branches of a paper-made tree mounted onto a wall, some of the responses and messages that reiterated Eva's life lessons were messages of forgiveness, kindness, and social acceptance, thus raising public awareness on the importance of living together harmoniously to prevent atrocities of the past from recurring.

Engaging the Community and the World

As sponsors of literacy, the educational work at the museum draws from the physical presence of Eva and her storytelling sessions, but most often it occurs without face-to-face interactions; the community's literacy was additionally shaped by

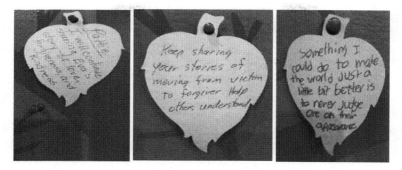

FIGURE 14.3 Messages Voluntarily Written by Visitors of the Museum to Illuminate the World (Photographer: Author, December 2018)

artifacts placed at visibly strategic locations such as the hallways and the main exhibit areas. An example of a poster that attempts to reinforce Eva's message of peacefulness from the storytelling session includes the following message:

> So I call forgiveness a seed for peace. If any of you are angry, all you will really need is a piece of paper and a pen, and start writing a letter to the person, or persons, who hurt you. At the end, you must write the words, "I forgive you," and you must mean them. And if it is not going to make you, I believe you will feel liberated, elated. I would describe the experience like Maria in "The Sound of Music," being at the top of the hill, and fresh air breezing all around her. And if it works for you, I hope you pass it on to other people who need it, because I need everybody to help me sow those seeds for peace.
>
> *(Excerpt#3: Eva Kor's talk; December 8, 2018)*

By the hallway, there was also a laminated, computer-printed poster inviting museum visitors to send messages of peace. On the poster, the following words were accompanied by a single flower, made up of red and green hearts, to symbolize peace:

> Eva says that, "Forgiveness is (line 1)
> the seed for peace."
> What do you think is the "seed for peace"? (line 3)
> Create a peace flower and write your own
> Ideas for spreading peace on the petals. (line 5)
> Feel free to plant your flower in our garden
> Or take home with you as a reminder of (line 7)
> Eva's words and what you can do to help
> spread peace. (line 9)

As can be seen from the first line, Eva's voice is clearly represented. This simple poster serves as a follow-up activity, encouraging viewers to engage in the enactment of social change. Through the question, "What do you think is the "seed for peace'" (line 3)?, the poster sets the stage for viewers to articulate their thoughts on what peace personally means to them. By extending invitations to create a "peace flower," visitors were drawn to think deeper on how they could use visual representations to spread messages of peace. The imaginary peace flower calls for envisioning a future that is free from prejudices and social injustices harkening back from the genocidal Holocaust. A sturdy, single-stalk red flower, comprising a universally recognized peace symbol, surrounded by hearts and green, heart-shaped leaves printed on the poster were used to illustrate an example of how a peace flower might look. The poster calls for further actions by voluntarily asking viewers (using the words "feel free") to place the "flower" at the museum's garden or their home to help them recall that it is their responsibility to disseminate messages of peace to everyone.

On another poster, only Eva's words were quoted (see Figure 14.4). In this quote, she aims to promote social transformation through daily dealings. This includes greeting someone, putting on a smile, sending praises, looking after the environment, and demonstrating good behaviors, such as valuing one another by being kind and caring.

> "Each day, do something to make this world better. Say hello, smile, give a compliment, pick up trash, help a neighbor, be kind and caring."
>
> -EVA KOR

FIGURE 14.4 A Quote from Eva's Words Encouraging Viewers to Engage in Simple Actions That Promote Social Change

CANDLES museum creates opportunities for visitors to obtain factual and historical information on the Holocaust. The authenticity of this information was enhanced through personal narratives told by Eva, the Holocaust survivor. The narratives bridge the past to the present through three key takeaways which Eva called "life lessons" for moving forward (see Excerpt #2). Using the artifacts and exhibits, the museum invites visitors to envision for their future by asking them to articulate what they plan on doing to make the world a better place.

Research Direction, Pedagogical Implications and Suggestions for Classroom Teaching

The methodology of walking interviews has been helpful for examining how a non-profit organization such as CANDLES museum acts as a sponsor of literacy. Specifically, through participatory literacy, the museum has been disseminating messages of forgiveness and healing drawn from personal narratives of a Holocaust survivor, Eva Kor, who has recently passed away. Works of literacy, such as storytelling sessions, posters, and artifacts have been used to promote social action. By displaying posters that encourage participation, the museum is engaging the community through simple everyday activities, thus connecting the local to the global, creating awareness on what needs to be done to make the world a better place. Future research might examine such practices in similar spaces to understand the impact of a community-serving pedagogue across larger communities.

Given its small size, CANDLES museum is ideal for school trips to introduce K-12 children to the topic of the Holocaust. With the rich amount of information presented in a concise and accessible language, elementary school teachers may want to consider developing a language arts lesson and expanding it across disciplines. Table 14.1 shows an example of a simple lesson outline on the holocaust, using children's literature that can be adapted across grade levels.

A sketch of how this small, non-profit museum utilizes works of literacy such as storytelling and displays of exhibits to engage the community and the world at large is shown in Figure 14.5. To engage the community further, the museum establishes partnerships with schools and universities and expands its mission and vision through multiple social media channels (see Facebook page: CANDLES Holocaust Museum and Education Center, Twitter handle: @candlesmuseum and website: CANDLES Holocaust Museum and Education Center). In this aspect, social media tools provide alternative means for knowing more about the holocaust. As Abas (2019) notes, the digital platforms can be taken as a continuity to real life where they can transcend across physical–digital spaces to reach out to a wider audience.

TABLE 14.1 Literacy Practices Used in Response to Children's Literature

Activities	Instructional procedures
Pre-reading	• Draw three columns on a butcher paper and label them as "What We Know," "What We Want to Know," and "What We Have Learned." • Ask the children if they know anything about the Holocaust. • List their responses on a butcher paper. • Ask the children what they would like to know about Holocaust. • List their responses on the same butcher paper. • Get them to look at the illustrations on the cover page of the book. • Elicit responses on what they think the book is all about, based on the title and illustration
Reading	• Read segments of the story aloud or, have a copy for each child to read independently during class time
Post-reading	• Ask the children what they have learned from the story. • List their responses on a butcher paper. • On another day, bring the children for a school trip to CANDLES museum. If this is not possible, get them to visit the website at https://candlesholocaustmuseum.org/25th-candles-home.html • During the tour or online tour, instruct the children to take note of the following: timeline of events leading to the Holocaust, Eva Kor's story, life lessons gained from Eva's stories, and other historical information related to the Holocaust. • For more ideas, visit the collection of teaching resources on Scholastic website at: www.scholastic.com/teachers/collections/teaching-content/holocaust-collection-teaching-resources/

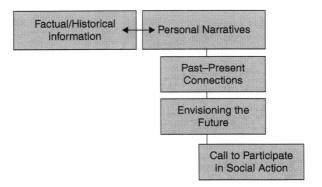

FIGURE 14.5 How Works of Literacy Have Been Used at CANDLES Museum

References

Abas, S. (2019). Repatriating desaparecidos across spaces. In P. Damiana, R. Ryan, & W. Julie (Eds.), *Negotiating place and space in digital literacies: Research and Practice* (pp. 261–276). Information Age.

Barbara, K. (1998). *Destination culture: Tourism, museums, and heritage.* University of California Press.

Barton, D. (2007). *Literacy.* Blackwell.

Barton, D., & Hamilton, M. (1998). *Local literacies: Reading and writing in one community.* Routledge.

Barton, D., Hamilton, M., & Ivanic, R. (Eds.). (2000). *Situated literacies: Reading and writing in context.* Routledge.

Brandt, D. (2001). *Literacy in American lives.* Cambridge University Press. https://doi.org/10.1017/CBO9780511810237

CANDLES Holocaust Museum and Education Center (2019). *CANDLES Holocaust Museum and Education Center.* Retrieved from https://candlesholocaustmuseum.org/

Collins, J., & Blot, R. K. (2003). *Literacy and literacies: Text, power and identity.* Cambridge University Press. https://doi.org/10.1017/CBO9780511486661

Eakle, A. J. (2007). Literacy spaces of a Christian faith-based school. *Reading Research Quarterly, 42,* 472–510. https://doi.org/10.1598/RRQ.42.4.3

Eakle, A. J. & Chavez, R. A. (2003). Critical museum literacy in Mexico. Paper presented at annual meeting of the National Reading Conference, Scottsdale, Arizona.

Evans, J., & Jones, P. (2011). The walking interview: Methodology, mobility and place. *Applied Geography, 31*(2), 849–858. https://doi.org/10.1016/j.apgeog.2010.09.005

Fingeret, A., & Jurmo, P. (Eds.). (1989). *New directions for continuing education: Participatory literacy education.* Jossey-Bass. https://doi.org/10.1002/ace.36719894202

Freire, P. (1970). *Cultural action for freedom.* Harvard Educational Review and Center for the Study of Development and Social Change.

Gee, J. P. (1996). *Social linguistics and literacies: Ideology in discourses.* Taylor & Francis.

Hamilton, M., & Weiss, M. (2005). *Children tell stories: Teaching and using storytelling in the classroom* (2nd ed.). Richard C. Owen.

Lemke, J. (1995). *Textual politics: Discourse and social dynamics.* Taylor & Francis. https://doi.org/10.4324/9780203975473

Marstine, J. (Ed.). (2006). *New museum theory and practice: An introduction.* Blackwell. https://doi.org/10.1002/9780470776230

Peck, J. (1989). Using storytelling to promote language and literacy development. *The Reading Teacher, 43*(2), 138–141.

Simpson, M. G. (1998) *Making representations. Museums in the Post-colonial era.* Routledge.

Sobol, J., Qentile, J., & Sunwolf (2004). Storytelling, self, society. *Storytelling, Self, Society: An Interdisciplinary Journal of Storytelling Studies, 1*(1), 1–7. https://doi.org/10.1080/15505340409490254

Springgay, S., & Truman, S. E. (2017). *Walking methodologies in a more-than-human world: WalkingLab.* Routledge.

Street, B. (1984). *Literacy in theory and practice.* Cambridge University Press.

Street, B. (1993). *Cross-cultural approaches to literacy.* Cambridge University Press.

Vannini, P. (2015). *Non-representational methodologies.* Routledge. https://doi.org/10.4324/9781315883540

Vicenti Carpio, M. (2006). (Un)disturbing exhibitions: Indigenous historical memory at the National Museum of the American Indian. Special Issue: National Museum of the American Indian. *American Indian Quarterly*, *30*, 4. https://doi.org/10.1353/aiq.2006.001

15

HEALTH SERVICES IN THE LITERACY LANDSCAPE

Sue Nichols

UNIVERSITY OF SOUTH AUSTRALIA

Introduction

Health services are increasingly getting involved in the promotion and delivery of literacy programs and in designing and implementing forms of literacy assessment, for both children and adults. Health services can be considered sponsors of literacy in the sense that they "enable, support, teach, model ... recruit [and] regulate" literacy participation and learning (Brandt, 1998, p. 166). How they do so is the focus of this chapter, which takes the form of a literature overview. Drawing on descriptions and evaluations of programs and policies, the chapter surveys a range of ways in which literacy sponsorship by health services operates.

Defining Terms

In this chapter, a distinction is made between literacy in general and a subfield referred to as health literacy or HL. This distinction relates to the roles of health services as, on the one hand, promoting literacy development as part of a holistic approach to infant and child health and, on the other, being concerned with how health consumers navigate the health information landscape. A holistic view of child health incorporates language and literacy as one domain within development overall (Puchner, 1995). The first part of this chapter will examine the role of health services in this level of literacy promotion and support.

Health literacy is a specialized domain, reflective of the specific communication and comprehension demands made when individuals are searching for and using health information (Nutbeam, 2000). Research in this area has tended to focus on adults or older children. The second part of the chapter will review

HL studies, with a focus on how services have responded to literacy challenges experienced by health consumers.

Many of the studies described in this chapter report on intervention programs. A distinction commonly made is between universal and targeted interventions. However, a more fine-tuned understanding is needed in relation to distinguishing programs that target *regions* based on the demographic profile of the community and those that target *individuals*, often referred for services (Smith, 2019). Many of the programs delivered by health services are regionally targeted, that is, they are located in neighborhoods that serve low-income communities; however, they aim to reach all parents in these communities through such strategies as routine child health checks. We will return to this issue in the concluding discussion.

Early Literacy Promotion by Health Services

Programs of early intervention into infant and child literacy have a decades-long history (Snow et al., 2000). The involvement of health services in this domain is in part a response to arguments for a more holistic or ecological approach to support child development (Vimpani, 2003). It has also received a boost from popularizations of neuroscience, which have emphasized the role of early experiences in brain development (Einboden et al., 2013). Contributing to this direction has also been a shift to measurement, data collection, and aggregated population profiles in the early childhood area (Peers, 2011), an approach with which those trained in health disciplines are familiar.

In the United States, the American Academy of Pediatrics (AAP) has been particularly active in advocating for early literacy to be an integral aspect of primary health care. The Academy's Council on Community Pediatrics has released a statement on poverty and child health which argued that reading readiness should be viewed as one of the protective factors that can help to ameliorate the impacts of socio-economic disadvantage (AAP Council on Community Pediatrics, 2016). This rationale reflects the longstanding influence of the inoculation hypothesis on support for early learning interventions more generally (Palmer, 1983). A vaccine metaphor is often used when a primary health care model is adopted for early literacy promotion. In a published interview, a key advocate stated:

> … children who do poorly in school and continue to do poorly in school tend to have more difficulty in learning to read and don't develop as much skill in reading and are at higher risk for not graduating high school … all children have to see us for vaccines and if they don't, they are not allowed to enter school.
>
> *(Mendelsohn in Nichols et al., 2012, p. 88)*

This language can be off-putting to literacy practitioners and researchers coming from a sociocultural perspective; however, its utility in translating literacy knowledge for use by a professional health community must be acknowledged. I will return to this point in the concluding discussion.

One of the longest-standing and widespread programs delivering early literacy intervention through health services is *Reach Out and Read* (ROR; Needleman & Silverstein, 2004; Rikin et al., 2015). This program utilizes volunteers reading to children in waiting rooms, in combination with advice from the pediatrician, to encourage parents, particularly in low-income areas, to read regularly to babies and young children. This program has achieved considerable scale since it was first initiated in 1989 in the United States. Within three decades it was being offered in more than 5000 sites nationally and has served as a model for similar programs in Australia and the United Kingdom (Cates et al., 2016).

In seeking to establish the effectiveness of ROR, health researchers have developed the Child-Centered Literacy Orientation (CCLO) instrument (High et al., 2000). Caregivers are given a score for CCLO based on an aggregate of three factors: whether reading to the child is one of the parent's three favorite activities; whether it is one of the child's three favorite activities; and the number of children's books in the house (High et al., 1999, 2000). A large-sale study was conducted across 19 sites in the USA, including nine hospitals, seven community health clinics and two private practices, all located in low socio-economic areas (Needleman et al., 2005). On the basis of comparison between an intervention cohort of 730 parents and a non-participating group of 917 parents, the study found that ROR was associated with increases in the frequency with which parents read to children and the identification of book-sharing as a favorite activity. These changes were seen across the cohort with the exception of white parents with higher education levels.

Home visiting by a nurse or community health practitioner is another avenue through which literacy promotion can take place (Hall & Jones, 2016). Health visits are generally scheduled in the first months following birth and include routine health checks and monitoring of mother and child. When literacy promotion is involved, this often takes the form of book gifting with encouragement to read to the baby (Moore & Wade, 2003). Information about language development may also be given (Hewer & Whyatt, 2006).

Many health services have produced resources in the form of leaflets, pamphlets, websites, and videos. Often, early literacy promotion is treated as one of the topics in a broader suite of advice provided to parents, particularly of infants. An example reported in the literature is the "Parenting Easy Guides" produced by the Child Youth and Women's Health Service (CYWHS) in South Australia (Nichols et al., 2009). Sets of these guides are displayed in hard copy form in doctors' waiting rooms and are downloadable from the CYWHS website. An example is titled "Why stories are important" and argues for the importance of sharing books for children's emotional growth, bonding with carers, and self-esteem. This health service has also produced a bright and sturdy board book, *Right from the Start … Loving Reading With Your Baby*, which integrates advice to parents on how to read to their babies (Linke, 2006).

Supporting Language Development

While book reading has been the most common focus of literacy interventions delivered through primary health care, language development has often been mentioned as a positive correlation with shared book interactions. More recently, language has been identified as the primary focus of interventions by health services, particularly those dealing with parents of newborns and infants. The term "language nutrition" has been taken up as an umbrella term for the quality and quantity of talk that surrounds children (Bang et al., 2020) as well as for programs that seek to intervene in children's language environment to promote language development (Zauche et al., 2017). This metaphor makes an analogy between a healthy diet for physical growth and enriched talk for linguistic growth.

Talk With Me Baby (TWMB), originating in the state of Georgia, USA, is an example of a program that draws on the concept of language nutrition to engage health practitioners in supporting parents to become "conversational partners with their babies and children" (Mahoney et al., 2017, p. 48). Nurses are trained to coach parents in fostering language interaction as an integral part of everyday care. To assist parents in adopting this practice, TWMB has created resources including a smartphone app, videos, and linguistically rich books (Zauche et al., 2017). Evidence for change in the home language environment is not yet available; however, health practitioners' understanding of how to explain language development to parents has increased with targeted training (Mahoney et al., 2017).

Commercial Services Piggybacking on Health

Making links between the values of health and educational success is not only the province of official health providers, such as doctors, clinics and hospitals. Commercial entities are also active in the marketing of health services, which are claimed to assist with developing children's learning in general and literacy in particular. Maternity sample bags are commonly distributed to women who are expecting or who have given birth to a baby. Analyzing the contents of one set of sample bags, Nichols et al. (2009) found that messages about school readiness, linked to literacy skills such as alphabet recognition, were woven through the materials provided to new mothers while in hospital or undergoing postnatal health checks. These messages were particularly evident in advertisements for toys claimed to deliver educational benefits. Through these messages, the parent's role in supporting children's healthy development is implied to require not only participation in practices such as reading to children but also willingness to invest in educational toys and devices.

Health Literacy

Health literacy (HL) is an umbrella term covering a number of practices and competencies. One accepted model comprises three domains: functional HL, communicative HL, and critical HL (Nutbeam, 2000). *Functional* HL, as with functional literacy more generally, involves the ability to comprehend information in print and oral language forms, at a level sufficient for functioning as an informed health consumer. *Communicative* HL, sometimes referred to as interactive HL, refers to effective participation in interactions with health services and information providers, for instance by volunteering relevant information and asking questions. *Critical* HL refers to the ability to analyze and evaluate health information, in order to determine whether it is trustworthy and liable to improve health outcomes.

A fourth domain, media health literacy, has been proposed to refer to the ability to interpret health information delivered through mediated means, including through social media (Manganello, 2008). Internet searching is a strategy used by health consumers to find information. Khoo et al. (2008) reported 52% of Australian parents had searched online for child health information. In a study of 214 parents of children receiving surgery, Hand et al. (2013) found that nearly 40% had conducted an Internet search regarding their child's surgical issue.

Low levels of health literacy and/or numeracy have been linked to poor health outcomes. Based on a substantial literature review of 35 studies, O'Neill et al. (2014) concluded that low health literacy in adults is associated with worse health outcomes. Fleary et al. reviewed 17 studies on HL in adolescents and found that adolescents with lower HL were more likely to use emergency services, less likely to engage in preventative health measures, and more likely to engage in unhealthy behaviors, particularly smoking and binge-drinking (Fleary et al., 2018). Moon et al. (2015) analyzed results from the UK Skills for Life Survey of over 4000 adults aged 16–65 years. The authors found that those whose general literacy and numeracy were "below the standard thresholds" were significantly more likely to assess their own health as poor and to experience chronic health conditions (Moon et al., 2015 p. 188). Kakinami et al. (2016) found that parents who demonstrated an ability to comprehend food labels had lower cholesterol levels and their children had lower body mass indexes.

There has been some interest in investigating the relationship between the home literacy environment (HLE) and health literacy. Driessnack et al. (2014) used a single measure from the HLE – the number of children's books in the home – and looked for associations with performance on a health literacy screening test, the Newest Vital Sign (NVS). The authors found that all of the families that had fewer than 10 children's books had very low NVS scores. No assessments were made of reading ability, so this could indicate problems with access to both reading materials and health information, which could in turn lead to a lack of practice in using such materials.

Service Responses and Interventions

Literacy-related barriers to accessing health information and resources have been addressed in two ways. Information and resources can be adapted to the needs of citizens with literacy challenges, and/or educational programs can be developed to assist people to acquire capabilities for seeking and comprehending information, and for communicating with services and practitioners.

An example of resource production is a guidebook on child development and health, designed to be easy to read, that was produced for parents of children enrolled in Head Start and used in conjunction with parent education (Herman & Jackson, 2010). A study of over 9000 parents found that the intervention greatly increased their usage of printed child health information (from 5% to 48%) and reduced visits to doctors and emergency departments. Many parents were still consulting the guidebook up to three years after receiving it (Herman & Jackson, 2010). A series of comic books communicating about early child development were distributed by Rosas-Blum et al. (2018) to 280 US parents of children aged <9 months. Parents' knowledge of developmental milestones increased following use of the comics, as did their willingness to consult a pediatrician. The popularity of the comics was also indicated by parents lending the books to others. However, simplifying health information may not be sufficient for consumers with very low literacy. Indeed, it has been reported that those with "higher reading levels ... benefit most from the provision of plain language materials" (Lin et al., 2007, p. 272).

Assisting health consumers to become critically literate so they can actively seek and assess health information is advocated by Renkert and Nutbeam (2001). Having experienced the difficulty of trying to cover every possible aspect of maternal and child health in antenatal classes, they recommended that instead, health educators support parents to be "empower[ed] ... to make educated choices" (Renkert & Nutbeam, 2001, p. 388). This might involve considering strategies for using online searches and evaluating sources. Empowerment is similarly the emphasis in the parent education program carried out by Carroll et al. (2015). This two-year longitudinal study aimed to promote "interactive and reflective skills" among 103 parent–child dyads consistent with a communicative health literacy approach. Improvements were found on a number of dimensions of maternal health literacy, including use of information and resources, care of children when well and sick, child immunizations, and family planning. The authors found that both health literacy and general literacy improved, as measured by the proportion of mothers with a reading skill level of below sixth grade; however, this decreased from 62% to 37% over the course of the program.

Cultural Responsiveness

Whether promoting early literacy or health literacy, the relevance of programs to the cultures of the communities into which they are inserted is a significant issue. Cultural context, when it is considered, is more likely to influence the selection of resources than the structure of programs or their underlying assumptions. Where there is a significant community whose first language is other than English, resources, such as children's books, can be provided in community languages (Levesque et al., 2018). The Montreal Child's Hospital, which has a suite of literacy promotion activities, has provided books in 26 community languages (Lariviere et al., 2017).

To investigate the impact of changing the language of health resources, Arora et al. (2018) modified a parent health leaflet in two ways. The first modification was simplifying the layout and language while retaining the English language, while the second version was translated into a community language, Arabic. All three versions were presented to a group of Arabic-speaking mothers and their feedback sought. The leaflet translated into Arabic was preferred; however, the mothers also stated the simplified English version was an improvement on the original.

While provision of health resources in community languages can support accessibility and relevance, it does not necessarily involve an engagement on the part of services with the cultural knowledge of communities. A similar point has been made by Anderson et al. (2003) in relation to story reading, which is the centerpiece of ROR and many other primary health interventions into early literacy. Reading books to children as a regular bedtime routine is not a universal cultural practice (Ko & Chan, 2009). Parents' own literacy levels may be barriers to their adopting this practice, and also the content and themes of books may not translate culturally (Janes & Kermant, 2001).

This point is particularly salient when considering Indigenous or First Nations communities in which traditional knowledge and practice systems continue to be important. In a paper on health literacy in the context of Australian Indigenous peoples, the authors identify a significant gap between assumptions of service providers and the worldview of Indigenous peoples regarding health, as well as literacy (Vass et al., 2011). They propose that the domains of *community literacy* and *cultural literacy* are needed to express the distinctive understandings and practices of Indigenous people. In the cultural domain, they explain:

> There is not a word in Yolŋu Matha that easily denotes the English meaning of health. The Yolŋu concept of health, as with many other Indigenous groups, is a comprehensive entity of wellbeing that is linked with land, law and relationships.
>
> *(Vass et al., 2011, p. 36)*

What is required is a dialogue between Western mainstream health (and education) and the cultural knowledge of Indigenous people. Such a dialogue could contribute to the redesign of knowledge systems and resources rather than simply their linguistic simplification and translation.

(Dis)Connections Between the Fields of Literacy and Health

Researchers in the fields of literacy studies and community health share a belief in the importance of literacy for social participation, educational success, and well-being. The extent to which they share understandings of the nature of literacy and how it is learned and practiced is not as certain. Certainly, publications from each of these areas address different audiences and reference different sources. For instance, a literature review commissioned to support the program "Let's Read," which is similar to "Reach Out and Read," cited 49 articles from journals in the fields of pediatrics, psychology, and other health sciences. However, only seven papers from literacy journals and six from education journals were included (Centre for Community Child Health, 2004). This pattern of citation reflects different understandings of the basis on which claims can validly be made.

However, there is also potential for greater dialogue and collaboration. For instance, some interesting similarities can be seen between the Four Resources literacy model (Freebody, 1992; Rush, 2004) and the three-dimensional Health Literacy model (Nutbeam, 2000) in Table 15.1. Both models recognize that a literate citizen needs to be able to do more than operate at the level of basic decoding; they also need to be able to use literacy to communicate and fulfill their purposes. Additionally, they need to be able to deconstruct and evaluate texts. It is true that early literacy promotion delivered as a primary health care strategy has tended to be deliberately narrowly focused on a single strategy, book reading. Even in these programs, however, the communicative domain is integrated through advice about how to share books interactively. We are also seeing broadening of the scope of programs to encompass spoken general language interaction between carers and children.

Critical and cultural dimensions hold great promise for more community-engaged and dialogic approaches to early literacy promotion by health services, as

TABLE 15.1 Four Resources and Health Literacy Comparison

Health Literacy Domains	Four Resources of the Reader
Functional HL	Decoder
Communicative HL	Text Participant
	Text User
Critical HL	Text Analyst

well as health literacy promotion. We are beginning to see a recognition that health literacy is a situated practice and can reflect more diverse values and knowledges than has previously been considered (de Wit et al., 2018; Samerski, 2019). Potential for collaboration between critically informed health promotion advocates and those from literacy studies holds promise for the future.

References

AAP Council on Community Pediatrics. (2016). Poverty and child health in the United States. *Pediatrics, 137*(4), 1–14. https://doi.org/10.1542/peds.2016-0339

Anderson, J., Anderson, A., Lynch, J., & Shapiro, J. (2003). Storybook reading in a multicultural society: Critical perspectives. In A. Van Kleek, S. Stahl, & E. Bauer (Eds.), *On reading books to children: Parents and teachers* (pp. 195–220). Lawrence Erlbaum Associates.

Arora, A., Al-Salti, I., Murad, H., Tran, Q., Itaoui, R., Bhole, S., Ajwani, S., Jones, C., & Manohar, N. (2018). Adaptation of child oral health education leaflets for Arabic migrants in Australia: A qualitative study. *BMC Oral Health, 18*(10), 1–10. https://doi. org/10.1186/s12903-017-0469-z

Bang, J. Y., Adiao, A. S., Marchman, V. A., & Feldman, H. M. (2020). Language nutrition for language health in children with disorders: A scoping review. *Pediatric Research, 87*, 300–308. https://doi.org/10.1038/s41390-019-0551-0

Brandt, D. (1998). Sponsors of literacy. *College Composition and Communication, 49*(1), 165–185. https://doi.org/10.2307/358929

Cates, C. B., Weisleder, A., & Mendelsohn, A. L. (2016). Mitigating the effects of family poverty on early child development through parenting interventions in primary care. *Academic Pediatrics, 16*(3S). https://doi.org/10.1016/j.acap.2015.12.015

Carroll, L. N., Smith, S. A., & Thomson, N. R. (2015). Parents as Teachers Health Literacy Demonstration Project: Integrating an empowerment model of health literacy promotion into home-based parent education. *Health Promotion Practice, 16*(2), 282–290. https://doi.org/10.1177/1524839914538968

Centre for Community Child Health. (2004). "Let's Read": Literature review. Royal Children's Hospital. Retrieved from rch.org.au/ccch/research

de Wit, L., Fenenga, C., Giammarchi, C., di Furia, L., Hutter, I., de Winter, A., & Meijering, L. (2018). Community-based initiatives improving critical health literacy: A systematic review and meta-synthesis of qualitative evidence. *BMC Public Health, 18*(40), 1–11. https://doi.org/10.1186/s12889-017-4570-7

Driessnack, M., Chung, S., Perkhounkova, E., & Hein, M. (2014). Using the "Newest Vital Sign" to assess health literacy in children. *Journal of Pediatric Health Care, 28*(2), 165–171. https://doi.org/10.1016/j.pedhc.2013.05.005

Einboden, R., Rudge, T., & Varcoe, C. (2013). Producing children in the 21st century: A critical discourse analysis of the science and techniques of monitoring early child development. *Health, 17*(6), 549–566. https://doi.org/10.1177/1363459312472081

Fleary, S. A., Joseph, P., & Pappagianopoulos, J. E. (2018). Adolescent health literacy and health behaviors: A systematic review. *Journal of Adolescence, 62*, 116–127. https://doi. org/ 10.1016/j.adolescence.2017.11.010

Freebody, P. (1992). A sociocultural approach: Resourcing four roles as a literacy learner. In A. Watson & A. Badenhop (Eds.), *Prevention of reading failure* (pp. 48–60). Ashton-Scholastic.

Hall, C., & Jones, S. (2016). Making sense in the city: Dolly Parton, early reading and educational policy-making. *Literacy, 50*(1), 40–48. https://doi.org/10.1111/lit.12069

Hand, F., Mc Dowell, D., Glynn, R., Rowley, H., & Mortell, A. (2013). Patterns of internet use by parents of children attending a pediatric surgical service. *Pediatric Surgery International, 29*(7), 729–733. https://doi.org/10.1007/s00383-013-3317-5

Herman, A., & Jackson, P. (2010). Empowering low-income parents with skills to reduce excess pediatric emergency room and clinic visits through a tailored low literacy training intervention. *Journal of Health Communication, 15*(8), 895–910. https://doi.org/10.1080/10810730.2010.522228

Hewer, L. A., & Whyatt, D. (2006). Improving the implementation of an early literacy program by child health nurses through addressing local training and cultural needs. *Contemporary Nurse, 23*(1), 111–119. https://doi.org/10.1080/10810730.2010.522228

High, P., Hopmann, M., LaGasse, L., Sege, R., Moran, J., Guiterrez, C., & Becker, S. (1999). Child-centered literacy orientation: A form of social capital? Pediatrics, *103*(4), 551–557.

High, P. C., LaGasse, L., Becker, S., Ahlgren, I., & Gardner, A. (2000). Literacy promotion in primary care pediatrics: Can we make a difference? *Pediatrics, 105*(4), 927–934.

Janes, H., & Kermant, H. (2001). Caregivers' story reading to young children in family literacy programs: Pleasure or punishment? *Journal of Adolescent and Adult Literacy, 44*(5), 458–465.

Kakinami, L., Houle-Johnson, S., & McGrath, J. J. (2016). Parental nutrition knowledge rather than nutrition label use is associated with adiposity in children. *Journal of Nutrition Education and Behavior, 48*(7), 461–467. https://doi.org/10.1016/j.jneb.2016.04.005

Ko, H. W., & Chan, Y. L. (2009). Family factors and primary students' reading attainment: A Chinese community perspective. *Chinese Education and Society, 42*(3), 33–48. https://doi.org/10.2753/CED1061-1932420302

Khoo, K., Bolt, P., Babl, F. E., Jury, S., & Goldman, R. D. (2008). Health information seeking by parents in the Internet age. *Journal of Paediatrics and Child Health, 44*(7–8), 419–423. https://doi.org/10.1111/j.1440-1754.2008.01322.x

Lariviere, J., Erdos, C., & Ferdinand, J.-M. (2017). Literacy promotion at the Montreal Children's Hospital. *Paediatrics & Child Health, 22*, 92–93. https://doi.org/10.1093/pch/pxx029

Levesque, B. M., Tran, A., Levesque, E., Shrestha, H., Silva, R., Adams, M., Valles, M., Burke, J., Corning-Clark, A. & Ferguson, C. (2018). Implementation of a pilot program of Reach Out and Read® in the neonatal intensive care unit: A quality improvement initiative. *Journal of Perinatology, 38*, 759–766. https://doi.org/10.1038/s41372-018-0060-8

Lin, W., Yang, H., Hang, C., & Pan, W. (2007). Nutrition knowledge, attitude, and behavior of Taiwanese elementary school children. *Asia Pacific Journal of Clinical Nutrition, 16*(S2), 534–546.

Linke, P. 2006. *Right from the start … Loving reading with your baby* (2nd ed.). Parenting SA/Child Youth & Women's Health Services.

Mahoney, A. D., Zauche, L. H., Hallowell, S., Weldon, A., & Stapel-Wax, J. (2017). Leveraging the skills of nurses and the power of language nutrition to ensure a better future for children. *Advances in Neonatal Care, 17*(1), 45–52. https://doi.org/10.1097/ANC.0000000000000373

Manganello, J. (2008). Health literacy and adolescents: A framework and agenda for future research. *Health Education Research, 23*(5), 840–847. DOI: 10.1093/her/cym069

Moon, G., Aitken, G., Roderick, P., Fraser, S., & Rowlands, G. (2015). Towards an understanding of the relationship of functional literacy and numeracy to geographical health inequalities. *Social Science & Medicine, 143*, 185–193. https://doi.org/10.1016/j.socscimed.2015.08.045

Moore, M., & Wade, B. (2003). Bookstart: A qualitative evaluation. *Educational Review, 55*(1), 3–13. https://doi.org/10.1080/00131910303250

Needleman, R., & Silverstein, M. (2004). Pediatric interventions to support reading aloud: How good is the evidence? *Journal of Developmental and Behavioural Pediatrics, 25*(5), 352–363. https://doi.org/10.1097/00004703-200410000-00007

Needleman, R., Toker, K., Dreyer, B., Klass, P., & Mendelsohn, A. (2005). Effectiveness of a primary care intervention to support reading aloud: A multi-center evaluation. *Ambulatory Pediatrics, 4*(5), 209–215.

Nichols, S., Nixon, H., & Rowsell, J. (2009). The "good" parent in relation to early childhood literacy: Symbolic terrain and lived practice. *Literacy, 43*(2), 65–74. https://hdl.handle.net/1959.8/684499915910905001831   https://doi.org/10.1111/j.1741-4369.2009.00519.x

Nichols, S., Rowsell, J., Nixon, H., & Rainbird, S. (2012). *Resourcing early learners: New networks, new actors.* Routledge. https://hdl.handle.net/1959.8/133183915909535601831 https://doi.org/10.4324/9780203112939

Nutbeam, D. (2000). Health literacy as a public health goal: A challenge for contemporary health education and communication strategies into the 21st century. *Health Promotion International, 15*(3), 259–267. https://doi.org/10.1093/heapro/15.3.259

O'Neill, B., Gonçalves, D., Ricci-Cabello, I., Ziebland, S., & Valderas, J. (2014). An overview of self-administered health literacy instruments. *PLoS ONE, 9*(12), 1–14. https://doi.org/10.1371/journal.pone.0109110

Palmer, F. H. (1983). The Harlem Study: Effects by type of training, age of training and social class. In The Consortium for Longitudinal Studies (Ed.), *As the twig is bent … Lasting effects of preschool programs* (pp. 201–236). Lawrence Erlbaum Associates.

Peers, C. (2011). The Australian Early Development Index: Reshaping family–child relationships in early childhood education. *Contemporary Issues in Early Childhood, 12*(2), 134–147. https://doi.org/10.2304/ciec.2011.12.2.134

Puchner, L. D. (1995). Literacy links: Issues in the relationship between early childhood development, health, women, families and literacy. *International Journal of Educational Development, 15*(3), 307. https://doi.org/10.1016/0738-0593(94)00041-M

Renkert, S., & Nutbeam, D. (2001). Opportunities to improve maternal health literacy through antenatal education: An exploratory study. *Health Promotion International, 16*(4), 381–388. https://doi.org/10.1093/heapro/16.4.381

Rikin, S., Glatt, K., Simpson, P., Cao, Y., Anene-Maidoh, O., & Willis, E. (2015). Factors associated with increased reading frequency in children exposed to Reach Out and Read. *Academic Pediatrics, 15*(6), 651–657. https://doi.org/10.1016/j.acap.2015.08.008

Rosas-Blum, E., Granados, H., Mills, B., & Leiner, M. (2018). Comics as a medium for parent health education: Improving understanding of normal 9-month-old developmental milestones. *Frontiers in Pediatrics, 6*, 1–5. https://doi.org/10.3389/fped.2018.00203

Rush, L. S. (2004). First steps toward a full and flexible literacy: Case studies of the four resources model. *Literacy Research and Instruction, 43*(37–55). DOI: 10.1080/19388070509558410

Samerski, S. (2019). Health literacy as a social practice: Social and empirical dimensions of knowledge on health and healthcare. *Social Science & Medicine, 226*, 1–8. https://doi.org/10.1016/j.socscimed.2019.02.024

Smith, H.V. (2019). Inequitable interventions and paradoxical pedagogies: How mothers are "taught" to support their children's literacy development in early childhood. *European Early Childhood Education Research Journal, 27*(5), 693–705. https://doi.org/10.1080/1350293X.2019.1651971

Snow, C. E., Burns, M. S., & Griffin, P. (2000). *Preventing reading difficulties in young children.* National Academy Press. https://doi.org/10.17226/6023

Vass, A., Mitchell, A., & Dhurrkay, Y. (2011). Health literacy and Australian Indigenous peoples: An analysis of the role of language and worldview. *Health Promotion Journal of Australia, 22*, 33–37. https://doi.org/10.1071/HE11033

Vimpani, G. (2003). Theoretical frameworks for promoting children's healthy development in the early years. *Developing Practice* (Autumn), 11–17.

Zauche, L. H., Mahoney, A. E. D., Thul, T. A., Zauche, M. S., Weldon, A. B., & Stapel-Wax, J. L. (2017). The power of language nutrition for children's brain development, health, and future academic achievement. *Journal of Pediatric Health Care, 31*(4), 493–503. https://doi.org/10.1016/j.pedhc.2017.01.007

PART IV
Identity Development and Empowerment

16

IDENTITY MATTERS IN SERVICE-LEARNING LITERACIES

Becoming Authentic and Agentic within Role Affordance

James R. King

UNIVERSITY OF SOUTH FLORIDA

Steven Hart

CALIFORNIA STATE UNIVERSITY – FRESNO

Deborah Kozdras

UNIVERSITY OF SOUTH FLORIDA

Becoming Authentic and Agentic within Literacies' Role Affordances

Adolescents, Identities, and Literacies

Both recent and long-term writing in literacy education have made much of adolescents (Biancarosa & Snow, 2006), their literacies (Moje, 2007), and their identities enacted during what have been called "literacy events" (Alvermann & Wilson, 2007; Barton & Hamilton, 2000; Heath, 1983). However, from our perspectives, too little attention has been directed toward the underlying social transactions within these designated literacy events, even as their performances result in what have been called "adolescent literacies" and "disciplinary literacies."

To begin an examination of literacies and identities, we shift to suggestions by Tierney (2014), who mapped changes in research over recent decades to highlight that literacy is more than a set of skills one learns. Literacy, thusly reconceptualized, is understood as a way of "being" in both personal and social circumstances. Tierney positions literacy as sets of complex processes for "accessing and addressing local and global issues that matter- poverty, shelter, nutrition, health, and general well-being, including hope, possibility, imagination, respect, and self and group determination" (p. 42). In our work, we engage with "being" literate and "doing" literacy when we enact particular literate identities. As such, literacy efforts fashion social roles; articulate appropriate and productive language for enacted role(s); recognize audience and client responses for successful and unsuccessful deployments of selected identity platforms; and perceive activities situated within designed event structures, both within and across specific disciplines. It also means teachers and their students are equal participants in literacy events.

From alternative perspectives, pedagogical literacies have also been refashioned from long-standing content area reading into more recent disciplinary literacies. Wineburg (1991), Moje (2008), as well as Shanahan and Shanahan (2008) have redefined secondary and post-secondary literacies along disciplinary practices, or as disciplinary literacies (DL). However, while we acknowledge the productivity of DL, restructuring literacy practice as a simulation of "real expert literacy" may miss the mark in at least two ways. First, disciplinary literacies reconstructed for classroom use may not sufficiently emulate complex literacy habitus of expert professionals in the real world (Geisler, 1994). That is, reading "like a scientist" in a biology classroom may not sufficiently engage with the habits of literacy practice in field biology (Heller, 2010), a critique we visit later in the chapter. Second, teachers' instantiations of disciplinary literacy may fail to engage students, who perceive their teachers' disciplinary efforts as "school work."

In contrast to specific literacies or unique disciplines, our aim is to demonstrate how literate identities and literacy projects, such as service-learning (S-L), can define, delimit, as well as elaborate each other, across several types of literacy enactments. A starting point for literate identities is found in sociocultural perspectives of learning (Lave & Wenger, 1991; Moll, Amanti, Neff, & Gonzalez, 1990; Rogoff, 1990; Vygotsky, 1978; Wertsch, 1991). Through this lens, learning is a socially situated endeavor; knowledge is a cultural product constructed *through* and constructive *of* interactions, in unique cultural contexts, within/across school and community spheres (Cone & Harris, 1996; Shadduck-Hernandez, 2006; Taylor, 2014).

Within school-based literacies, students position themselves or are positioned by teachers in multiple ways. From van Langenhove and Harrè's (1999) positioning theory model, negotiating these multiple positional stances creates *roles* for the students (Kozdras, 2010). Further, certain of these roles may be recognized as valuable in the completion of task(s) within the literacy contexts, or as roles with social prestige. For example, in a project on diverting green waste for composting, students may use research processes to position themselves as "waste reduction experts." From Gee's (2004) account of "shape shifting portfolio people" where individuals manage selves by building up skills and experiences, enacted in a project, become part of the students' identity kits, different projects may require particular literacy practices, and offer different embedded roles. Continuing with the waste-composting example, students may need to learn disciplinary languages and literacies of sustainability to be effective within community outreach about diverting green waste for composting. Further, if the students in such a project intend to create a green waste reduction program at their school or in their communities, additional literacies perhaps related to marketing and digital media would help enact their plan. Moving outward, the same stances toward literacy practices can be deployed as newsletters for apartment buildings, oral histories of family elders, or travel blogs for trips to Europe. In these scenarios, the rhetorical goal must be the use of particular language and literacies in ways that are validated by the particular audience of experts, avoiding the typical classroom exchange of "good enough" for the teacher. Good-enough contexts outside the classroom may be found in current approaches to S-L.

Service Learning (S-L) and Literate Identities

S-L provides concrete examples of literacies, articulating students' identity work in purposeful learning situations. S-L is distinct in its intentionality to link *academic content* and *social action* to support *community transformation* (Billig & Furco, 2002). S-L is a powerful pedagogical alternative to curriculum-based teaching. S-L promotes competent and effective citizens; combining academic content instruction with opportunities to practice democratic citizenship *while* engaged in service to the community, a real problem (Billig & Furco, 2002; Eyler & Giles, 1999; Kahne & Sporte, 2008; Mendel-Reyes, 1998; Morgan & Streb, 2001; Schine, 1997). S-L pedagogy is premised on establishing reciprocal interactions with(in) school/community, utilizing inquiry to address genuine community needs. S-L inquiry involves phases of investigation and research, deliberation of issues, taking informed action to address the issues, and structured reflection opportunities throughout the process. This is the service half of S-L. One challenge in S-L learning is to broaden the menu of what may count as literacy. It is a conundrum.

Community projects occur in particular fields of inquiry, or disciplines. Students learn specific disciplinary knowledge when S-L creates unique contexts enacted within the school *and* community. As such, S-L might be construed as a narrowing of literacy options for students. However, we suggest that S-L creates third space potential, drawing from literacy practices associated with school and non-school contexts (Moje et al., 2004). But not always. There is a balance between the needs of the project and students' learning. For example, hosting a community poetry-slam event may raise awareness on racial injustice, a potentially productive literacy-learning event. But socially, the production may not interact with the social, economic, and political circumstances that undergird the event, even while creating the desired motivation and practices in literacy.

We argue for the third spaces within S-L that afford hybrid literacies, unique experiences constructed from transformed uses of legacy literacy practices (such as traditional, teacher-controlled reading and writing). These hybrid literacies, constituted from borrowed and repurposed legacy practices, are situated, unique literacy events constructed specifically for and within the service-learning context at hand, like a poetry-slam. Such elaborations for literacy are different from the skill-based, decontextualized borrowing of literacy "strategies" from outside-of-school practices. For example, the results of an S-L inquiry can be reported in the form of a narrative or play about the issue at hand.

Another difference between S-L and traditional classroom work is authentic social engagement. By intersecting community and school contexts, S-L expands upon typical classroom-based peer and student–teacher interactions to also allow youth to negotiate with and within various identities of community members from multiple disciplines (i.e., community leaders, business partners, civic leaders, and pro-youth organizations). For example, students engaged in a water conservation project may need to collaborate with environmental activists and city council members to develop policy initiatives and community awareness materials. Through social action, youth use these experiences as reflexive material in identity development, gaining self-understanding, and a sense of their interrelationships within a broader community (Dworkin et al., 2003; Kahne & Sporte, 2008; Rubin et al., 2009; Youniss & Yates, 1997; Youniss et al., 1999). In developing identity and competence, students acquire literate habits of disciplines, such as sampling and tracking water quality in local rivers, or auditing businesses for their green potential. Sampling requires recording, and patterns in sampling require interpretation, arguably literate practices. However, this uptake does not happen automatically. It is up to a facilitating teacher (whom we have been calling a curator) to name the various literate strategies *as* they emerge within and across disciplinary boundaries. With the curator's naming, the strategy becomes an object/process the students may choose to use again, and intentionally, a transferable strategy.

S-L and Identity Development

Much learning activity within S-L is accomplished within and as a result of students' animation of identity platforms or roles constructed within emerging activity structures. Therefore, understanding identity development in the contexts of S-L is fundamental. Writing presciently on identities occurring within specific cultural groups, Holland, Lachicotte, Skinner, and Cain (1998) offer:

> Significant to our concept is the situatedness of identity in collectively formed activities. The "identities" that concern us are ones that trace our participation, especially our agency, in socially produced, culturally constructed activities – what we call figured worlds.
>
> *(p. 40)*

The richness and fluidity of figured worlds, we argue, is what is needed to create opportunities for students' uptake and use of identities. Holland, et al. (1998) also refer to figured worlds as "as if" contexts: "Figured worlds rest upon people's abilities to form and be formed in collectively realized '*as if*' realms" (p. 49, our emphasis) and subsequently, "A person engaged in a social life, a person involved in an activity or practice, is presumed to have a perspective. One looks at the world in terms of what one is trying to do" (p. 49). And finally:

> These socially-generated, culturally figured worlds, many linguists believe, are necessary for understanding the meaning of words [and other semiotic systems] ... By "figured world," then, we mean a socially and culturally constructed realm of interpretation in which particular characters and actors are recognized, significance is assigned to certain acts, and particular outcomes are valued over others.
>
> *(p. 52, bracketed addition ours)*

This is where Holland et al.'s (1998) "figured worlds" intersect with literacy projects such as S-L, and blend with opportunities for students that imagine new ways of being. As all members involved in a project interact, their individual identities within the project (role affordances) morph to construct a shared sense of identity, which forms the common bonds (or agency) that represent membership in the group.

If the goal in school-based literacy projects is to conjure a simulacrum of "real-world" literacy practices, in an S-L project, what does it mean to realize the efforts expended toward quality products as subordinated to the learning of the students? If these circumstances focus on participant learning, it could mean that project quality suffers, and that is expected. But then how can the curator (most often also the teacher) of the S-L project simultaneously run the project and judge it as non-authentic? This dual role certainly puts the teacher in a bind. Is the work of students only good enough, or does the quality of the work they do not matter because it is "only school, only kids, and nobody will ever see this stuff?" The preceding rationale has occurred in our previous projects, and continues to manifest in ours and others' relationships developed within the projects' social constructs. Our previous relationships with students in project-based literacies, even when all participants were committed to the project, have been inherently problematic. When students become aware of teachers' dual roles (organizer and evaluator), the S-L project may become disingenuous. Students would rightly refuse to participate, or even worse, might continue to participate, but only in order to make their teacher happy. This is the "as if" gone very wrong. A productive focus, one that allows us to stop thinking about the previous, troubling questions, remains on the apprenticing students and quality of project outcomes. These rest on a continuum, with student examples produced later in the apprenticeship hopefully more sophisticated than those at the beginning. In any case, tensions between quality, power, and trust may test limits of the project boundaries.

The social contexts of S-L projects are influenced by differences in positioning and power these different roles offer. In literacy research, identity is increasingly construed as "hybrid, meta-discursive, and spatial" (Lewis & del Valle, 2009). Far from being an essential, or a singular construct, literate identities are seen as multiple, shifting, and connected, such as during the shifting participant roles in a literacy-rich learning project. Gee (2002) discussed this fluidity, within which adolescents negotiate different identities, in terms of "shape shifting portfolio people" (p. 62). Young people (both "competent" and academically "at-risk") increasingly manage their identities as they assemble different literate competencies and deploy strategic aspects of identities (as shifting roles and positions depending on the need within the S-L project). Individuals inhabit and deploy these identities when they participate in a Discourse community (Gee, 1996; 1999), such as a community constructed around and contextualizing an S-L project.

Empowerment, Critical Responses, and Curating within Service-Learning

Comparing the standards for high quality service-learning (National Youth Leadership Council, 2008) with Shor's (1992) characteristics of empowering pedagogy, reveals that by design, service-learning aims to position students for empowerment, for enacting identities denoted by a critical consciousness, and to use reflective problem-posing skills. Ideally, S-L projects begin where students discuss real-world problems, as referenced earlier by Tierney (2014), in the need to address local and global issues. Powerful projects are situated within students' lived experiences and concerns, and lead to mutual benefits for both student learning and community development. Transformative projects allow students to expand their perspective by investigating both local and global problems and creating change through online forums, groups, and social media opportunities. Consider the potential impact of student voice: Greta Thunburg, the Swedish environmental activist, who is creating waves in the realm of climate action. Teachers, students, and community members *should* dialogically influence the direction and activities of the projects. As students present their problems and propose plans for action, teachers facilitate this process through structured debates and through their use of strategic questioning, guiding students to understand alternative views as well as the consequences of various plans of action. Teachers can also solicit parent input when it might enhance students' work. Teachers must also work toward targeting communication strategies, as well as sanctioning certain content. While making space for student voice, teachers can take mentoring or curating stances to help students develop critical democratic skills, such as active listening, civil deliberation/dialogue, and constructive criticism.

As students engage in analyses of social issues through project implementation, learning is a participatory endeavor, and students' constructed identities interact. Hence, through this active participation from positions of power, students can construct and enact identities of problem-solvers, contributors, and empowered change-agents. Analogously, in order for students to work from positions of power, teachers must monitor their needs for situated power within the classroom social context. Teachers' self-awareness is required because their students often first find their voices in critical, even antisocial ways (King et al., 2007). In fact, several studies suggest that the more disenfranchised the students, the more likely they will develop active, critical voices when given the opportunity (Morrell, 2004; Rubin, 2007; Rubin et al., 2009). Therefore, we suggest as teachers "curate" (Potter, 2009) rather than dictate, students can learn awareness, uptake, and use of situated power in S-L classroom discourses. Further, learning this particular kind of self-awareness regarding use of voice is a strategic literacy and life competence. We use curating to mean the selection and negotiation of possible semiotic representations within power-based relationships and contexts. From a language resources perspective, curating certainly involves rhetorical dimensions. The deployment of the various, possible semiotic resources may be driven by teachers' more nuanced understandings of audience, or by perspective taking, or for social consequence purposes when constructing the message. For example, students may practice argumentation regarding a water conservation project intended for a group of town leaders. Within such internal linguistic negotiations, the creative processes of the speakers are tested within the imagined receptive capacities of the audience. Promoting awareness of issues through social media requires literacy skills. Teachers-as-curators create such participation spaces. Likewise, curating may also involve de-briefing such decision making with students after the fact.

Service-Learning Identities and the Projective Stance

An interesting intersection on identity, literacy, and agency can be found in the intrinsically motivating contexts of gaming. To manage self-projection (in contrast with teachers' projective desires), Gee (2007) made the case for gamers' deployment of surrogates, or the person of the player, realized as a virtual character within the games being played. It works like this: First, a view of this virtual world (or a constructed S-L instance of a discipline) is envisioned and set off from the real world by boundaries. Second, a specific agenda is pursued within this game-world opportunity structure to realize certain sets of desires, intentions, and goals (an actor pursues a task within the disciplinary literacy project). Then, players (or S-L participants) try to *become* that imagined actor. Thus, the surrogate embodies the projective stance, a self-constructed, less-intimidating, media-mediated act of becoming.

Moje, Overby, Tysvaer, and Morris (2008) carefully unpack and explain these related constructs related to Gee's concepts within the field of adolescent literacy. To an already complex interplay based on sociocultural accounts of literacy (Lewis et al., 2007), a critical stance including power, identities, and agency is appended. This inclusion by Moje et al. (2008) fits well with Gee's projective stance. Individual's empowerment is based on an effective use of identity, but with a productive ambiguity. Moje's (2015) *4e Heuristic of Disciplinary Literacy* instruction includes the step of Evaluate, which is constituted by meta-level conversations. These conversations bring embedded cultural practices and values to attention. Evaluation provides opportunities to explore specific vocabulary meanings as well as interrogate specific discourse practices. Finally, evaluation necessitates a sense of agency – empowered learners can decide how and when to use what they have learned – when they are aware of the power of literacy practices.

Mastering the projective stance within disciplinary literacies is representative of discourses within particular domains of inquiry (Shanahan & Shanahan, 2008; Wineburg, 1991). These communicative stances and tools are necessary for membership in the group. However, there is a double bind for students. Domain-specific discourse practice often frames disciplines as inaccessibly complex. And the second part of the bind, occurring while the students "master" disciplinary discourses, is the shaping done by the discourse on the individuals who submit to them. From Foucault's (1981) perspective, discourses exert a normalizing influence on the user, to the extent that particular identities may be seen as intersections of the various discourses that create the subjectivity. Or as Holland et al. (1998) suggest:

> … people learn to treat one another and themselves according to categories … Local knowledge is disregarded and replaced by scientific categories imposed by those with power. In this Foucauldian vision, un–reflexive claims to "objectivity" are hollow at best; and at worst they are self-serving means by which science rhetorically claims authority.
>
> *(p. 24)*

Delimited, recursive roles may become comfortable for participants, but may not be the best learning opportunities. Becoming the exclusively "artist" or the "camera person" may constrain a student's literacy flexibility and opportunity structure. The implications for education are immediate. What an actor/student in a situation can say or do is delimited by what the role persona is scripted for, what the actor/student is permitted to say, or what the actor/student can strategically manage to say, given the context, identity expectations, and linguistic resources within a social genre, recognized or not by the player. A strategic move for participating students is to synthesize a role that has expanded, yet structured, communication potential (Gee, 2007). To say the least, this is complex psycho-linguistic work on the part of participating students.

A Summary

Literate identities or platforms students develop within S-L literacy experiences are the standpoints from which they become empowered. Text has powerful influence on the formation of possible identities. Reading and writing particular texts serve as markers for related identities, or what Moje et al. (2008) call "social capital" (p. 138). Likewise, reading and writing are linked to social networks, and, in fact, help to define the social networks. Students' connections between tasks, texts, and identities allow for strong emotional ties to the work and the context. Rich connections between self and the work reinforce standpoints (Harding, 2004; Hartsock, 1998; Spivak, 2009) or identity positionings that embolden critical perspectives on one's work and the work of others. Within these S-L networks, multiple texts function as the media for social transactions that create and maintain affinities. The key here is the use of texts and practices that are authentic, ground the literacy work, and are accessible from the reading repertoires brought to the tasks by students.

Infusing authentic text and practices presents a paradox of sorts. We know youth read with reference to their own social groups outside of the classroom walls, to maintain relationships, and to develop identity(ies). These are arguably very individualistic and personal motivations. So how do texts from different academic disciplines make it into students' S-L reading retinue? Reading out-of-school texts may have established transferable competence that is subsequently tapped when reading school-based texts, but it is also reasonable to suggest that any competence accrued is situationally specific, and tied to specific conditions of motivation (Guthrie et al., 1997).

Further, subject area texts in classrooms seldom provide the meta-discursive information necessary to assume membership in affinity groups. As a solution, Moje et al. (2008) suggest:

> … engineering new types of classroom texts, ones that recognize the need to situate reading and writing within social networks and invite young readers into a relationship with the text and the work of the discipline.
>
> *(p. 148)*

As proposed by Cushman and Emmons (2002), "the reading and writing that emerge from these [literacy] interactions may harmonize with what we know as 'academic' and 'out of school' literacies. And in that harmonizing, these literacies may also help us listen for something new" (p. 231, bracketed elaboration ours). Literacies embedded in service-learning provide a Third Space where multiple Discourses work together to generate new knowledge, new Discourses, and potentially new forms of literacy.

References

Alvermann, D., & Wilson, A. (2007). Redefining adolescent literacy instruction. In B. Guzzetti (Ed.), *Literacy for the new millennium. Vol. 3: Adolescent literacy* (pp. 3–20). Praeger.

Barton, D., & Hamilton, M. (2000). Literacy practices. In D. Barton, M. Hamilton, & R. Ivanic (Eds.), *Situated literacies: Reading and writing in context* (pp. 7–15). Routledge.

Biancarosa, G., & Snow, C. (2006). *Reading next: A vision for action and research in middle and high school literacy – A report to Carnegie Corporation of New York* (2nd ed.). Alliance for Excellent Education. Retrieved from www.all4ed.org/files/ ReadingNext.pdf

Billig, S., & Furco, A. (2002). Research agenda for K-12 service-learning: A proposal to the field. In A. Furco & S. H. Billig (Eds.), *Service-learning: The essence of the pedagogy* (pp. 271–279). Information Age.

Cone, D., & Harris, S. (1996). Service-learning practice: Developing a theoretical framework. *Michigan Journal of Community Service Learning, 3,* 31–43.

Cushman, E., & Emmons, C. (2002). Contact zone made real. In G. Hull & K. Schultz (Eds.), *School's out! Bridging out-of-school literacies with classroom practice* (pp. 203–233). Teachers College Press.

Dworkin, J., Larson, R., & Hansen, D. (2003). Adolescents' accounts of growth experiences in youth activities. *Journal of Youth and Adolescence, 32,* 17–26. https://doi.org/10.1023/ A:1021076222321.

Eyler, J., & Giles, D., Jr. (1999). *Where's the learning in service-learning?* Jossey-Bass.

Foucault, M. (1981). *Untying the text: A post-structural reader.* R. Young (Ed.). Routledge.

Gee, J. (1996). *Social linguistics and literacies: Ideology in discourses* (2nd ed.). Falmer.

Gee, J. (1999). *An introduction to discourse analysis: Theory and method.* Routledge.

Gee, J. (2002). Millennials and bobos, Blues Clues and Sesame Street: A story for our times. In D. Alvermann (Ed.) *Adolescents and literacies in a digital world* (pp. 51–67). Peter Lang.

Gee, J. (2004). *Situated language and learning: A critique of traditional schooling.* Psychology Press.

Gee, J. (2007). Pleasure, learning, video games, and life: The projective stance. In M. Knobel & C. Lankshear (Eds.), *The new literacies sampler* (pp. 95–113). Peter Lang.

Geisler, C. (1994). *Academic literacy and the nature of expertise: Reading, writing and knowing in academic philosophy.* Lawrence Erlbaum Associates.

Guthrie, J., Alao, S., & Rinehart, J. (1997). Engagements in literacy for young adolescents. *Journal of Adolescent and Adult Literacy, 40,* 438–447. www.jstor.org/stable/40015517

Harding, S. (2004). Introduction: Standpoint theory as a site of political, philosophic, and scientific debate. In S. Harding (Ed.), *The feminist standpoint theory reader: Intellectual and political controversies* (pp. 1–16). Routledge.

Hartsock, N. (1998). *The feminist standpoint revisited and other essays.* Westview Press.

Heath, S.B. (1983). *Ways with words: Language, life, and work in communities and classrooms.* Cambridge University Press. https://doi.org/10.1017/CBO9780511841057

Heller, R. (2010). In praise of amateurism: A friendly critique of Moje's "Call for Change" in secondary reading. *Journal of Adolescent and Adult Literacy, 54,* 267–273. https://doi. org/10.1598/JAAL.54.4.4

Holland, D., Lachicotti Jr., W., Skinner, D, & Cain, C. (1998). *Identity and agency in cultural worlds.* Harvard University Press.

Kahne, J., & Sporte, S. (2008). Developing citizens: The impact of civic learning opportunities on students' commitment to civic participation. *American Educational Research Journal, 45*(3), 738–766. https://doi:org/10.1163/9789460910258_010

King, J., Hart, S., & Kozdras, D. (2007). Critical literacy and adolescents. In B. Guzzetti (Ed.). *Literacy for the new millennium, Volume 3: Adolescent literacy* (pp. 173–187). Praeger.

Kozdras, D. (2010). From real to reel: Performances of influential literacies in the creative collaborative processes and products of digital video compositions. Unpublished doctoral dissertation. Tampa, FL: University of South Florida. ProQuest 760087969.

van Langenhove, L., & Harrè, R. (1999). Introducing positioning theory. In R. Harrè & L. van Langenhove (Eds.), *Positioning theory: Moral contexts of intentional action* (pp. 14–31). Blackwell Books.

Lave, J., & Wegner, E. (1991). *Situated learning: Legitimate peripheral participation.* Cambridge University Press. https://doi.org/10.1017/CBO9780511815355

Lewis, C., & del Valle, A. (2009). Literacy and identity: Implications for research and practice. In L. Christenbury, R. Bomer, & P. Smagorinsky (Eds.), *Handbook of adolescent literacy research* (pp. 307–371). Guilford Press.

Lewis, C., Enciso, P., & Moje, E. (2007). *Reframing sociocultural research on literacy: Identity, agency, and power.* Lawrence Erlbaum Associates.

Mendel-Reyes, M. (1998). A pedagogy for citizenship: Service-learning and democratic education. *New Directions for Teaching and Learning, 73,* 31–38. https://doi.org/10.1002/tl.7304

Moje, E. (2007). Developing socially just subject-matter instruction: A review of the literature on disciplinary literacy teaching. *Review of Research in Education, 31*(1), 1–44. https://doi.org/10.3102/0091732X07300046001

Moje, E. (2008). Foregrounding the disciplines in secondary teaching and learning: A call for change. *Journal of Adolescent and Adult Literacy, 52,* 96–107. https://doi.org/10.1598/JAAL.52.2.1

Moje, E. (2015). Doing and teaching disciplinary literacy with adolescent learners: A social and cultural enterprise. *Harvard Educational Review, 85*(2), 254–278. https://doi.org/10.17763/0017-8055.85.2.254

Moje, E., Ciechanowski, K., Kramer, K., Ellis, L., Carillo, R., & Collazo, T. (2004). Working toward third space in content area literacy: An examination of everyday funds of knowledge and discourse. *Reading Research Quarterly, 39*(1), 38–70. https://doi.org/10.5198/RRQ.39.1.4

Moje, E., Overby, M., Tysvaer, N., & Morris, K. (2008). The complex world of adolescent literacy: Myths, motivations, and mysteries. *Harvard Educational Review, 78,* 107–153. doi.org/10.17763/haer.78.1.54468j6204x24157

Moll, L., Amanti, C., Neff, D., & Gonzalez, N. (1990). Funds of knowledge for teaching: Using a qualitative approach to connect homes and classrooms. *Theory Into Practice, 31,* 132–141. https://doi.org/1080/00405849209543534

Morgan, W., & Streb, M. (2001). Building citizenship: How student voice in service-learning develops civic values. *Social Science Quarterly, 82,* 154–169. https://doi.org/10.1111/0038-4941.00014

Morrell, E. (2004). *Becoming critical researchers: Literacy and empowerment for urban youth.* Peter Lang.

National Youth Leadership Council. (2008). K-12 service-learning standards for quality practice. Available at: www.nylc.org/sites/nylc.org/files/files/Standards_Oct2009-web.pdf

Potter, J. (2009) Curating the self: Media literacy and identity in digital video production by young learners. PhD thesis, Institute of Education, University of London.

Rogoff, B. (1990). *Apprenticeship in thinking: Cognitive development in social context.* Oxford University Press.

Rubin, B. (2007). "There's still not justice": Youth civic identity development amid distinct school and community contexts. *Teachers College Record, 109*(2), 449–481.

Rubin, B., Hayes, B., & Benson, K. (2009) "It's the worst place to live": Urban youth and the challenge of school-based civic learning. *Theory Into Practice, 48,* 213–221. https://doi.org/10.1080/00405840902997436

Schine, J. (1997). Looking ahead: Issues and challenges. In K. Rehage & J. Schine (Eds.), *Ninety-sixth Yearbook of the National Society for the Study of Education: Vol. I. Service-learning* (pp. 186–199). National Society for the Study of Education.

Shadduck-Hernandez, J. (2006). "Here I am now!" Critical ethnography and community service-learning with immigrant and refugee undergraduate students and youth. *Ethnography and Education, 1*(1), 67–86. https://doi.org/10.1080/17457820500512804

Shanahan, T., & Shanahan, C. (2008). Teaching disciplinary literacy to adolescents: Rethinking content-area literacy. *Harvard Educational Review, 78*(1), 40–59. https://doi.org/10.7763/haer.78.1.v62444321p602101

Shor, I. (1992). *Critical teaching and everyday life.* University of Chicago Press.

Spivak, G. (2009). *Outside in the teaching machine.* Routledge.

Taylor, A. (2014). Community service-learning and cultural–historical activity theory. *Canadian Journal of Higher Education, 44*(1), 95–107.

Tierney, R. J. (2014). Integrative research review: Mapping the challenges and changes to literacy research. In P. Dunston, L. Gambrell, K. Headley, S. Fullerton, & P. Stecker (Eds.), *Sixty-third yearbook of the Literacy Research Association* (pp. 32–47). Literacy Research Association.

Vygotsky, L. (1978). *Mind in society.* Harvard University Press.

Wertsch, J. (1991). A sociocultural approach to socially shared cognition. In L. Resnick, J. Levine, & S. Teasley (Eds.), *Perspectives on socially shared cognition* (pp. 85–100). American Psychological Association. https://doi.org/10.1037/10096-004

Wineburg, S. S. (1991). On the reading of historical texts: Notes on the breach between school and the academy. *American Journal of Educational Research, 28*, 495–519. https://doi.org/10.3102/00028312028003495

Youniss, J., McLellan, J., & Yates, M. (1999). The role of community service in identity development: Normative, unconventional, and deviant orientations. *Journal of Adolescent Research, 14*, 248–261. https://doi.org/10.1177/0743558499142006

Youniss, J., & Yates, J. (1997). *Community service and social responsibility in youth.* University of Chicago Press.

17

EMPOWERMENT IN DIGITAL LITERACY ACQUISITION PROGRAMS

Learners Who Become Tutors

Jill Castek

UNIVERSITY OF ARIZONA

Gloria E. Jacobs

PORTLAND STATE UNIVERSITY

Introduction

Carmen (all names used are pseudonyms) was in her fifties when her husband unexpectedly died. This life change led Carmen to enter a digital literacy acquisition program in order to learn how to apply for jobs online. She shared that her husband's death left her with no choice – she had to learn. One year after participating as a learner, Carmen became a tutor in the same program. Carmen's pathway to acquiring digital literacy and becoming a tutor was by no means an easy one. In an interview, she and her tutor, Jim, described how she entered the program afraid she would break the computer. Jim told her, and his other learners,

> No one was born knowing anything. And the position that we're all in today is simply because someone took the time [to help us learn] so we were exposed to it. It's just a matter of exposure and application.
>
> *(Jim, personal communication, June, 2014)*

Jim's advice and encouragement helped Carmen gain confidence in her ability to learn, and to continue to build on and apply what she had learned by becoming a tutor.

In our research into the digital literacy acquisition of underserved adults (Castek et al., 2015) we learned that Carmen's self-perception and life experiences were not unusual. Participants often entered learning situations fearful and unsure of their abilities. With the encouragement and support of tutors, along with well-curated online learning plans, learners were able to develop learning persistence along with a flexible set of skills, strategies, mindsets, and sustainable relationships that help them envision new possibilities for themselves.

Carmen and others found what they may have lacked in technical skill on the computer was counterbalanced by their ability to connect with other learners. In fact, all interviewees in this study told us repeatedly that a good tutor was someone with patience, empathy, and the ability to instill confidence. Learners who become tutors were especially adept at demonstrating these qualities given the relationships they built. They were able to encourage new learners in fundamental ways that others with more technical expertise might not have been able to do (Castek et al., 2015).

In this chapter, we explore what learners who became tutors had to say about their experiences and how community-based adult literacy organizations can draw on those experiences to strengthen their program design and volunteer opportunities. We draw from the conceptual framework of community of learners (Rogoff, 1994) coupled with empowerment theory to describe the participation and collaboration between individuals within an organizing structure who focus their shared efforts on a common goal. We focus on participation and collaboration because working together increases access to resources and models processes for problem solving. Within a community of learners, everyone actively contributes to a shared sociocultural activity, but do so in ways that may be asymmetrical. For example, a learning dyad might consist of a "more knowledgeable other" (Vygotsky, 1978) who guides a novice toward greater engagement in the community of learners. Adding empowerment theory to analysis reveals how over time, and through situational collaboration, each member of the partnership gains the ability to achieve personal and collective goals (Rappaport, 1995). A premise of empowerment theory is the emphasis on an individual's strengths or competencies, identified as they develop, as opposed to corrections that can be seen as pointing out deficits (Perkins & Zimmerman, 1995). Empowerment is both process and outcome based (Swift & Levin, 1987). Processes involve an individual's actions and engagement within a particular context, and outcomes include a greater desire to engage in the activity, increases in self-confidence, and feelings of accomplishment.

In the sections that follow, we discuss the importance of volunteer tutors in community-based literacy programs followed by a brief description of our research methodology. We then turn to what learners who became tutors had to say about their experiences. Finally, we conclude with a discussion of ways that volunteer tutoring can help sustain involvement in the community while deepening both learner and program impacts.

The Importance of Volunteer Tutors in Community-Based Literacy Programs

Volunteer tutoring is common in institutions of higher education, professional programs, and library literacy programs (Comings & Cuban, 2000). It also is frequently used in public education in various class settings such as writing workshops, science, mathematics, and special education. These efforts have been well studied and documented in the literature (Fisher & Frey, 2019). Although a common practice, less is written about volunteer or peer-tutoring within adult education settings or community-based programs for adults.

Adult educators tend to be paid tutors who have degrees in adult education or related fields, and their efforts are often supported by volunteers from the community who may also have some level of advanced education. Sandlin and St. Clair (2005) synthesized the little research that has been done on the quality of instruction when volunteers tutor adult literacy learners. However, volunteer tutoring has been recognized by public libraries and professional organizations across the nation as a low-cost option for serving many learners (Beltzer, 2006), which suggests that volunteer tutoring should be part of leadership programs in adult literacy and adult education. Advocates for volunteer tutoring suggest that "to teach is to learn twice," suggesting that tutoring can offer a pathway to extended learning opportunities. As learners share their acquired skills and knowledge with others, sharing that knowledge reinforces what they have learned and helps them to internalize new knowledge as they apply it in new contexts (Fisher & Frey, 2019).

The stages of our digital literacy acquisition research connected us to programs in six states that were implemented in community-based organizations, workforce centers, libraries, community colleges, and re-entry programs. In almost every site we visited, we found tutors who had started their participation as learners. By taking a closer look at the experiences of these adult learners who became tutors we are able to explore short- and long-term impacts on individuals and programs and examine the personal and institutional relationships that surround extended participation as individuals transition from learner to tutor and beyond.

An analysis of interviews with learners who went on to become tutors indicated that they became volunteers because they themselves had been helped to gain new skills. Consistent with the perspective provided by the community of learners framework, the volunteers' service to others was driven by reciprocity, a desire to give back, and the chance to make a significant difference in the lives of others who needed support. They described feeling connected to the community and noted that their service commitment was an outgrowth of a sense of belonging to a system that facilitated both giving and getting services. Donna told us she became a tutor because she had gone through the program as a learner first. She now works primarily with seniors and describes tutoring as a real blessing.

Such personal stories illustrate the sense of community that arose along with the personal rewards of giving back.

About the Study

Data were collected as part of a multi-state Broadband Technology Opportunities Program (BTOP; Jacobs et al., 2015) made up of local networks of community organizations that provided adults opportunities to learn to use computers and the Internet. While each of the programs varied in their implementation strategies and ways they served learners' needs, all shared key features: they used the same online platform designed specifically for adult learners, digital literacy material was available in English and Spanish, learners had the ability to toggle freely between the English and Spanish materials, and learners were able to work at their own pace and identify their own learning goals. Although the digital literacy materials were all online, each program provided in-person tutor support by either paid or volunteer tutors.

The programs in our study varied in the tutor-to-learner ratio. Some programs implemented a classroom-like model with whole-group instructor modeling while some programs were set up as a computer laboratory where tutors would move around helping different learners as needed as learners worked through online materials. Others used a triad model where a tutor sat between two learners and pivoted between two learners at once, and some programs offered one-to-one tutoring. The majority of tutors were volunteers recruited from the community; only a few were paid employees. All tutors were provided some level of training using tutor-training materials curated by a coordinator, which were then customized by local groups to address the unique needs of their program participants.

Participants

Of the 29 tutors we interviewed nationally, five began the program as learners, and one of those (Carmen) participated in three interview sessions spaced roughly nine months apart. Of the five participant learners who became tutors we interviewed, one lived in the mid-west, two were in the southern United States, and two were on the west coast. Three of the individuals were women and two were men. None had experience with computers and the Internet before participating in the digital literacy acquisition project, and none had prior tutoring experience.

In the following sections, we focus on three of the learners who became tutors because they came from different geographic locations and life circumstances. They are not meant to represent all learners who become tutors. Instead, we look to their words to understand some of what it means to make the shift from being a learner to a tutor.

Carmen

Carmen, introduced in the opening vignette, was originally from Costa Rica. She was a native Spanish speaker but fluent in English. She was in her mid-fifties and recently widowed. She had been in the United States for over 40 years and lived on the west coast. She did not hold a high school diploma. She was part of an adult literacy library program.

Reggie

Reggie is between the ages of 25 and 44 and is African American. He had been incarcerated in a prison in the southern United States. He held a high school diploma or GED. As he was approaching re-entry, Reggie participated in a unique digital literacy acquisition program that was part of the larger re-entry effort offered by the prison system where he was held. See Jacobs et al. (2016) and Withers et al. (2015) for more details about the digital literacy re-entry program.

Donna

Donna lived in the rural mid-western United States and participated in a digital literacy acquisition program at a community center that designed programming for seniors. Donna had recently lost her job of 17 years and volunteered a few days a week offering one-on-one tutoring.

Analysis

Interviews were transcribed and analyzed using inductive coding consistent with grounded theory, thus allowing the findings to arise from the data. Development of the findings around learners who became tutors was initially developed during the qualitative analysis phase of the project, and further refinements were made during a post-hoc analysis of the coded interviews.

Becoming a Tutor

Our data indicate that there is no clear path to making the transition from learner to tutor, but we did see several commonalities. Specifically, the interviewees said they were encouraged and inspired to become a tutor by someone (a more knowledgeable other) within the program. Shifting from learner to tutor was part of a transition in how they saw themselves – they had to see themselves as confident and capable, and this shift occurred with the help of their tutor. As their sense of empowerment grew, the individuals all came to understand that they did not have to have all the answers, but needed to be patient, encouraging, and willing to continue learning.

Encouragement

Carmen's experienced tutor, Jim, came to know her as he worked with her in a laboratory setting with a number of other learners. Carmen was especially influenced by Jim's encouragement and the personal connection he made with her. For example, he helped Carmen buy her own computer and helped her set it up at home. Jim said that although Carmen was initially "completely afraid of computers" (Jim, personal interview, June, 2014), he helped her overcome that fear by telling her that "I wasn't born knowing how to use a computer. I had to learn." At some point, Jim saw Carmen's growing confidence and came to the conclusion that "she acquired a lot of skills" (Jim, personal interview, June, 2014), and could be a tutor in the program, particularly because she was friendly, encouraging, and could support learners who spoke both Spanish and English.

Donna's situation was different in that she was learning her skills at a senior center rather than in a library or a program, but she too was identified as a potential tutor by someone in the program – in her case the laboratory coordinator. Donna said that the laboratory coordinator "kept bugging me (laughter), and I thought one day, oh I'll fill [the application] out just to see" (Donna, personal interview, April, 2013).

Reggie became a tutor (called mentors in the re-entry program) through a different and more formal process than Carmen and Debbie. Reggie was drawn from the pool of incarcerated men who were already participating in the prison's mentor program. As Reggie described it, to be a mentor you had to "have good conduct, be laid back, and be willing to help people" (Reggie, personal interview, March, 2013).

In each case, the person who identified the learner as a potential tutor differed, but the basic process was the same. A more knowledgeable other (such as a tutor, laboratory coordinator, or administrator) was able to see what the learner had to offer and worked with that learner to help them see their own potential. As a result, the individual developed their sense of empowerment, which allowed them to take on the role of a more knowledgeable other.

Self-Perception and Goals

Carmen was initially hesitant to take the step from being a learner to becoming a tutor; however, Jim pushed her to see herself in a new light. She told us,

> He keep telling me you're learning, you're doing good. It would be nice if you teach the computer. And I said I don't think I am a teacher. I don't feel confident like that. And he said, yes you do. And he work on that, too. And the program work on your confidence because I didn't have it. And then … that's what he worked on too, on my confidence.
>
> *(Carmen, personal interview, May, 2014)*

As Carmen's comments make clear, Jim taught her more than digital literacy. He helped her develop her confidence and in turn inspired her to work with other learners who were like her.

Like Carmen, Donna was hesitant to make the transition because she felt she did not know enough, but the laboratory coordinator encouraged her by showing her she did. Donna was discouraged because she had been told numerous times that she lacked qualifications, but it was this very experience that helped her be an effective tutor. She said,

> I lost my job after 17 years … so I understand what they're feeling. Their emotions. A lot of them are trying, the same as I am. That kind of stuff … You gotta put yourself in their position. They're frustrated and after having a job and now all of a sudden you don't have a job and myself, I felt like was almost nothing. And you kind of gotta put yourself in their shoes, basically. Cause after applying for jobs and you get told you don't have enough experience, or not enough qualifications, or you're overqualified. And then you don't have enough experience. You may be qualified but. I'm still getting that right now.
>
> *(Donna, personal interview, April, 2013)*

The opportunity to be a tutor may have helped Donna build an image of herself as competent. When working with learners, Donna was able to act as the patient expert and provide encouragement. As she noted, "No matter how many times I had to erase what she was typing in, I'd say ok, let's try it again" (Donna, personal interview, April, 2013).

Reggie (personal interview, March, 2013) said he was drawn to mentoring because he liked helping people, and "I always liked to put people up on what's going on now. You know, modern times … Stop being stuck in the Flintstone era." For Reggie, being a mentor allowed him to continue gaining skills on using the computers. But beyond the technical aspects of digital literacy, Reggie liked having "people call you and talk their problems over with you." He added that he was already doing that type of thing in his personal life, so being a mentor allowed him to "try it out" in a more formal setting.

Carmen and Reggie were similar in that learning how to use computers and becoming a tutor or mentor was part of a life transition. Both individuals were moving toward greater independence and involvement in the world. Reggie's life transition was triggered by release from prison, and Carmen's was triggered by the death of her husband. Donna was also in the midst of a transition and was looking for work. Learning computers and transitioning to being a tutor provided a sense of empowerment to each of the individuals.

Continuing to Learn

Carmen, Donna, and Reggie all spoke about how being a tutor helped them to keep learning and that they came to understand that they didn't have to necessarily know the answers to questions learners asked, but they did have to know how to find out the answers. Donna (personal interview, April, 2013) said that working with learners reminds her "that you've got to keep on top of things. Otherwise you forget." Donna also recognized that learners often knew things she did not know. She said,

> they teach me as much as I teach them, so you're constantly learning … Like depending on what they're working on, show me a shortcut on something. I'm trying to think what else they taught me. Maybe a website that I didn't know about.

Donna also spoke about not always knowing the answer but being persistent and willing to find an answer. She said,

> I went through all my books, and I couldn't remember. I felt bad because I didn't think I really helped her. But then the next time I came in, cause I had tried to figure it out, and the next time I came in, I redid the Excel and then I found it … If there is someone else I can ask I usually, you know, but like if there's no one else, then there's not much, like I told the one lady, I told her, I said, I promise the next time you come we'll get this to work, I promise.
>
> *(Donna, personal interview, April, 2013)*

In sum, Donna's advice was "just do the best you can. I mean, no one knows everything." Within the community of learners at Donna's tutoring site, it was an acceptable social practice to acknowledge lack of knowledge and to allow for shifting roles in who was more knowledgeable at any given moment. This social practice empowered the volunteers to be open to learning as they developed as tutors.

Carmen also learned that because she could not always remember something, she had to be willing to experiment or engage in a trial and error process when working with digital resources. She said,

> When you don't know something [laughter] even when you been through the course, you don't have it all in your head. And sometime oh how is it that I did this? …You start thinking, brainstorming, and then start touching buttons. Maybe this will lead me to this.

The sense that she was part of a community of learners empowered Carmen to explore and experiment. Through this she learned confidence, which she saw as life-changing. She said,

> It help build my confidence. And I'm happy for that, too. Cause when you don't have confidence, it's like you don't know how to do nothing well. Now even if I don't know, I know I'm gonna find a way to learn it, to get there. So my life has changed.
>
> *(Carmen, personal interview, June, 2014)*

Reggie (personal interview, March, 2013) also said that acting as a tutor helped him learn more technical knowledge "cause I don't know everything," but the most of the learning Reggie spoke about was learning how to work with people. He said,

> [The] hardest thing about being a mentor ... is for the people who don't know and you trying your best to explain to how they understand. Because you can't speak to everybody in the same way. They don't pick up the same way. It gave me insight on how to deal with different people most of all, just from dealing with [those in] the program.

For these three individuals, being a tutor provided an opportunity to learn technical skills that would help them find a job, but it also helped them develop the communication skills and confidence that would help them transition to a new phase of their lives. For Donna and Carmen, the goal was to find long-term employment and independence. For Reggie, it was to be prepared for the world outside the prison through the development of skills with digital resources, and also the development of interpersonal management. For all three individuals, by becoming tutors within a community of learners, they were able to see themselves as learners but also as people capable of helping other people.

Impact

Becoming a tutor made a personal impact on the participants, and that impact was felt well beyond their work with learners. Carmen, whom we interviewed several times, shared how her life changed as a result of her learning and tutoring digital skills. For example, in addition to becoming a tutor, Carmen began studying for the GED, a decision she directly attributed to having had the chance to learn to use computers and see what was available online. In her words, by tutoring Spanish speakers, she was able to "refresh her knowledge of Spanish" (Carmen, personal interview, June, 2014). This was especially meaningful because she was able to help women like herself.

In describing her reasons for becoming a tutor, Carmen (personal interview, June, 2014) credited Jim and the fact that he donated his time. She said, "if you know something you know and pass it on, It's like pay back I say." She added that this sense of giving back also motivated her to continue her work. She said, "You wanna give it back and also the fact that you feel very gratifying. You feel happy when you do something for free to others that someone needs. It's gratifying, so you feel happy." She later added, "And by saying thank you, you can do it to others, too. And it's a lot of Spanish speaking ladies at home that they can be more independent by doing this, not just depending on someone else." Thus for Carmen, the ability to use computers gave her a sense of independence and provided her with the opportunity to support women like her.

Reggie revealed that being a tutor/mentor helped him develop interpersonal skills that would help him outside of prison. He noted that "attitudes" were a challenge he faced as a tutor. He shared,

> Fourteen people, fourteen different attitudes. Everybody different. Some people more patient than others … Some just ready to leave cause they frustrated that they can't do it. They don't believe they can do it. Bad attitudes. You know, you got the people with the good attitude, but they seem like they real confused when there's … really not that hard. It's kind of simple, but they, one of the people who get frustrated too. So, you know, there's a lot of attitudes that you're dealing with … Because it can get you frustrated. Dealing with all these different attitudes in a short period of time. And a lot of people, eighty percent might not know anything about what they're doing … I do give up sometimes. But gotta be willing to learn. I can't force anything … you think simple, that might be simple to you but complicated to others.
>
> *(Reggie, personal interview, March, 2013)*

Although we do not know what Reggie's life was like once he was released from prison, we find his understanding of the challenges of working with people with a range of abilities and experiences to be promising.

Conclusions and Implications

Sustaining community-based literacy programs can be challenging due to a number of issues ranging from funding to staffing. One tangible and low-cost way programs can sustain their work is through nurturing volunteerism. In our work with underserved adults engaged in digital literacy acquisition, we found that recruiting learners to become volunteer tutors contributed to a vital community and strengthened programs by providing learners with tutors who had an innate sense of what learners in their community need. A reciprocal relationship was created – learners who became tutors became members of a community of learners and gave back to programs that served them. In turn, the opportunity to tutor contributed to a sense of empowerment and allowed them to continue their personal and professional growth.

Data from the learners who became tutors suggested these individuals were able to build confidence and skills around the use of technology in novel ways that were not accessible to them solely as learners. By taking on the role of more knowledgeable other, they continued to amplify their own learning by helping others learn what they had learned and apply that new knowledge in a range of new contexts. Often, the learners were hesitant to become tutors because they felt they did not know enough about computers or technology to teach others. However, when they reflected on their experiences, these learners who became tutors often spoke of how they encouraged learners, illustrated patience, and sought to build relationships with learners, just as their tutor had done for them. It was this willingness to offer assistance rather than technical expertise that made them good candidates for becoming tutors.

This chapter suggests that tutors and the coordinators that support programs and tutors can help grow and sustain volunteer literacy programs by encouraging learners to become tutors and to provide pathways in support of these transitions. When recruiting new tutors, program coordinators should be encouraged to tap into the rich personal experience and unique perspectives of their learners and draw them in as volunteers. In doing so, tutor coordinators should assure learners that they do, in fact, have the skills to become tutors as long as they are willing to be patient and supportive.

References

Beltzer, A. (2006). Less may be more: Rethinking adult literacy volunteer tutor training *Journal of Literacy Research, 38*(2), 111–140. DOI: 10.1207/s15548430jlr3802_1

Castek, J., Jacobs, G., Pendell, K., Pizzolato, D., Reder S., & Withers, E. (2015). Tutors: The tutor–learner relationship. http://archives.pdx.edu/ds/psu/16200

Comings, J. T., & Cuban, S. (2000). So I made up my mind: Introducing a study of adult learner persistence in library literacy programs. Available from www.wallacefoundation.org/knowledge-center/Documents/Study-of-Adult-Learner-Persistence-in-Library-Literacy-Programs.pdf

Fisher, D. & Frey, N. (2019). Peer tutoring: "To teach is to learn twice." *Journal of Adolescent and Adult Literacy, 62*(5), 583–586. https://doi.org/10.1002/jaal.922

Jacobs, G., Castek, J., Pizzolato, D., Pendell, K., Withers, E., & Reder, S. (2015). Executive Summary: Tutor-facilitated digital literacy acquisition in hard-to-serve populations, a research project. http://archives.pdx.edu/ds/psu/16698 https://doi.org/10.15760/dla.2

Jacobs, G., Withers, E., & Castek, J. (2016). Exiting the pipeline: The role of a digital literacy acquisition program within the Orleans Parish Prison reentry process. In K. Fashing-Varner, L. Martin, R. Mitchell, K. Bennett-Haron, & A. Daneshzadeh (Eds.),

Understanding, dismantling, and disrupting the prison-to-school pipeline (pp. 167–177). Lexington Books.

Perkins, D. D., & Zimmerman, M. A. (1995). Empowerment theory, research, and application. *American Journal of Community Psychology, 23,* 569–578. https://doi.org/10.1007/BF02506982

Rappaport, J. (1995). Empowerment meets narrative: Listening to stories and creating settings. *American Journal of Community Psychology, 23,* 795–807. https://doi.org/10.1007/BF02506992

Rogoff, B (1994). Developing understanding of the idea of communities of learners, *Mind, Culture, and Activity, 1*(4), 209–229. https://doi.org/10.1080/10749039409524673

Sandlin, J., & St. Clair, R. (2005). Volunteers in adult literacy education. In J. Coming, B. Garner, & C. Smith (Eds.), *Review of adult learning and literacy* (Vol. 5, pp. 125–154). Lawrence Erlbaum Associates.

Swift, C., & Levin, G. (1987). Empowerment: An emerging mental health technology. *Journal of Primary Prevention, 8,* 71–94.

Vygotsky, L. S. (1978). *Mind in society: The development of higher psychological processes.* Harvard University Press.

Withers, E., Jacobs, G., Castek, J., Pizzolato, D., Pendell, K., & Reder S. (2015). Corrections and reentry. Digital literacy acquisition case study. http://archives.pdx.edu/ds/psu/16519

18

ART MUSEUMS, LITERACY, AND INTRINSIC MOTIVATION

Mike Deetsch and Kate Blake

THE TOLEDO MUSEUM OF ART

Introduction

Children learn through play, exploration, material manipulation, and kinesthetic movement using not only their eyes and ears, which is where the primary focus on developing literacy skills tends to be, but also through their attention, engagement, and desire to repeat the activity, which increases when the activity is fun and meaningful to them. Museums specialize in engaging learning experiences, and as such, are well-suited to work with school systems to help address the deficit in literacy.

Most museums offer school tours as part of their program catalogue. The Toledo Museum of Art (TMA) welcomes approximately 30,000 school visitors each year. With recent trends showing a decrease in funding in school districts for arts and field trip opportunities (Reeves & Rodrigue, 2016), it is becoming more important than ever to highlight the value of museum-based experiences by measuring the impact field trips and museum learning have on school-based learning. Recent research suggests that field trips to art museums positively affect a child's growth in critical thinking (Greene, 2014; RK&A, 2018), but there is still more research to be done on the transference of a museum experience to classroom learning.

Since 1901, TMA has been dedicated to its purpose of art education. The museum has consistently cultivated innovative programs and curriculum; since its creation, the institution has offered some form of classes and hands-on instruction. The popularity of the museum's art classes for children reached new heights in the years following World War II and have remained a cornerstone of the museum's offerings ever since. The Studio Glass Movement, originating at TMA in the 1960s, and the Museum's Family Center, established in the 1990s, also served as important milestones in the institution's educational journey.

As they entered into the new millennium, museums struggled to become more relevant and sustainable within their communities. In this context, TMA adopted teaching visual literacy as one of five strategic objectives in 2011, aiming to position the museum as an educational leader locally and globally. In the years that followed, TMA developed a variety of visual literacy-specific initiatives, including a comprehensive curriculum that was adapted for schools and adult learners alike.

This chapter will detail the TMA's approach to supporting preK-8 literacy instruction through a pedagogy and curriculum defined as visual literacy. Using case studies drawn from school field trips, teacher professional development, and in-classroom resource development, we will demonstrate our pedagogical approach to teaching visual literacy, its impact on traditional literacy, and outputs from related empirical studies.

What Is Visual Literacy and How Does It Support Textual Literacy?

At TMA, visual literacy is defined as the ability to read, comprehend, and write visual language. Reading visual language is fundamentally concerned with vision. Comprehending visual language is fundamentally concerned with cognition; in other words, the interpretation of what is seen. And writing visual language is fundamentally concerned with action. Visual literacy is more than what we see, it also investigates the biases and preconceptions that color our individual interpretations of images, and in that way, can be thought of as a form of metacognition.

As an institution, TMA teaches visual literacy through a framework which includes: the Language of Art and the Art of Seeing Art: Learning to Look. The first and most closely tied to textual literacy is the Language of Art, which is the development of visual vocabulary as a means of objectively describing an image. Drawing on the established visual vocabulary, the Elements of Art and Principles of Design to describe images, allows an observer to work toward an impartial and subjective description of what is being seen.

The second component, a thinking routine called the Art of Seeing Art: Learning to Look, provides an individual with the tools necessary to comprehend an image. The first three steps – Look, Observe, and See – are the steps by which one "reads" visual language. Looking is akin to skimming. In this step, the viewer quickly surveys the image and takes in visual information. Observation is an active process, requiring both time and attention. Seeing uses the observations to create a mental inventory of all of the image's visual elements.

The second three steps – Describe, Analyze, and Interpret – are the steps by which one "comprehends" visual language. "Describe" is used to articulate the Elements of Art and Principles of Design in relation to the catalogue of identified visual elements. During analysis the viewer begins to make meaning of the objects/entities that are present within the image. Ultimately, the viewer arrives at an interpretation after following the analytical process. It is important to note that "Learning to Look" is a cycle; a viewer returns to looking after he or she is done interpreting.

Taken together, the Language of Art and the Art of Seeing: Learning to Look process are the Visual Literacy framework used at TMA to teach Visual Literacy skills. The components of the framework are interrelated; for example, a strong command of visual vocabulary is an essential tool for describing, step four in the Art of Seeing process. The framework is also scaffolded in structure. By this we mean that although all audiences, to a degree, engage with analysis and interpretation, lessons for younger viewers focus on the Language of Art and Art of Seeing process, while more sophisticated viewers are challenged to engage more deeply with analysis and interpretation.

TMA Teaching Pedagogy and Design Principles

Museums have the power to provide rich and meaningful informal learning experiences for a wide range of audiences. To maximize the effectiveness of these educational experiences, museum teaching should be steered by a clearly defined set of pedagogical practices. At TMA, five key pedagogical principles guide the development and delivery of curriculum: activity-based instruction, multimodal engagement, gamification, audience-focused design, and content agnostic curriculum.

Activity-Based Instruction

At TMA, we are lucky enough to have over 350,000 square feet of gallery space and approximately 30,000 to use as classrooms. Building on Dewey's (1934) conception of "art as experience," programs at TMA are designed to engage participants in learning through doing by actively engaging with our objects and spaces.

Multimodal Engagement

All programs at TMA use a multimodal, multisensory approach. Accepting both the need for a multimodal understanding of visual texts and the theory of Multiple Intelligences suggests that gallery teaching should engage multiple learning styles in order for a diverse audience of students to best attain deep learning (Gardner, 1983; Kress, 2010).

Gamification

Defined as the "use of game design elements in non-game contexts," gamification is employed in the curriculum as both an engagement and learning strategy (Deterding et al., 2011). Specifically, the TMA programs employ three of James Paul Gee's (2005) principles of good learning: well-ordered problems, pleasantly frustrating challenges, and "just in time" information. These strategies are useful for designing activities which are fun and engaging while simultaneously promoting deep learning.

Audience-Focused Design

The participant, not the educator, is at the center of the experience. Building on Vygotsky's (1978) theory of the zone of proximal development and accounting for the diversity in the cognitive development and visual fluency of student visitors, instruction aims to engage participants by producing learning environments which "permit pupils to learn as agents with their peers' collaboration" (Yvon et al., 2013, p. 34). This is achieved through emphasis on peer-to-peer sharing and by incorporating student choice within activity design.

Content Agnostic Curriculum

The goal of visual literacy instruction at TMA is not to teach students facts and anecdotes about the paintings and sculptures in the museum collection (although improved comfort viewing and interpreting works of art is an expected outcome), but rather to use works of art to support classroom literacy goals and develop confidence and enthusiasm. The curriculum is therefore skills-based and not beholden to any specific subject matter. We commonly use the term "content agnostic" to refer to the curriculum's non-dependence on a specific subject area.

Pre-Literacy Skill Development: A Preschool Pilot

In the autumn of 2014, TMA and Toledo Public Schools (TPS) collaborated on the first of two studies to assess the impact of visual literacy experiences on pre-literacy development, specifically on the acquisition of tier two vocabulary (Deetsch et al., 2018). Tier two vocabulary "are of high utility for mature language users" (Beck et al., 2013, p. 20). These "words in the second tier can have a powerful impact on verbal functioning" (Beck et al., 2013, p. 29) and are an important component of language development and reading comprehension.

During the study, participating children were introduced to works of art from the TMA collection and tier two vocabulary through field trips to the museum and in-classroom lesson plans. These museum field trips included gallery visits and art making in the studio and were supported by related classroom lessons to reinforce vocabulary introduced during the visit. The kinds of experiences used in these museum visits ranged from drawing to tactile and kinesthetic experiences. These multimodal experiences were used as opportunities to reinforce targeted descriptive vocabulary.

The research team focused on multimodal pedagogy because the brain is developing at a rapid pace and "early experiences and environments in which children develop in their earliest years can have lasting impact on later success in school and life" (Harvard University, 2016, p. 150). Results of the pilot demonstrated that museum-led visual literacy experiences led to tier two vocabulary acquisition for participating students. (For more on this see Deetsch et al., 2018.)

After the success of the pilot study, the museum and TPS agreed to run an expanded study with the full school (over 275 students). Like the pilot, visits to the museum included gallery visits, a studio art project, and multimodal learning strategies. During the gallery visit, students gathered around a work of art while a docent guided close looking and introduced tier two vocabulary. Included in the gallery experience were a variety of other learning strategies, including guided questions, word repetition, story-book reading, hands-on manipulatives, and gross motor movements.

As a continuation of the museum curriculum, the classroom teachers repeated the vocabulary exposure and multimodal learning strategies in their classrooms daily for the next two weeks. The classroom teachers also facilitated TPS-designed extensions related to museum curriculum. These extensions took the form of facilitated and self-guided classroom activities that reinforced learned vocabulary.

Works of art for the study were chosen based on criteria for early childhood art preferences, including works with bright and contrasting colors, simple compositions, familiar objects or images, representational imagery, and abstraction (Feeney & Moravcik, 1987). Full-color, poster-size reproductions of each work of art were also created and distributed to each teacher for in-classroom use.

As a means of capturing data, teachers kept a daily log of students' uses of the tier two vocabulary. At the end of the study, data analysis demonstrated vocabulary growth consistent with the pilot study. These results show that the learning outcomes for both the pilot and expanded study were attributable to the visual literacy curriculum with a very high degree of certainty. As indicated by the results, the connection between what children see, the words they hear as they interact with supportive adults, and the variety of materials available in the environment to manipulate are key to meaningful learning.

From this research, TMA has developed a series of professional development workshops for early childhood educators to provide teachers with training on techniques for using visual literacy and multimodal pedagogy to support vocabulary development. This curriculum was piloted in the 2019/2020 school year.

Art Museums Supporting English Language Arts

As many teachers know, the key to developing good elementary-age student writers is not just the amount of time spent practicing, but also the relevance of the writing assignments to the student's lives and interests. In this way, visual art, like the works of art in the TMA collection, provide great tools for motivating students and engaging them in the writing process.

The benefits to arts-integrated approaches to writing are not limited to motivation; research has shown cognitive benefits of linking the arts with other academic subjects (Housen, 2002; Silverstein & Layne, 2010). For young writers, writing is a mentally demanding task. It requires the developing author to apply technical skills (grammar, spelling, sentence structure) while performing complex tasks such as idea generation and narrative development. For students, integrating visual media into the writing process facilitates the activation of schema and minimizes the cognitive load (Randal, 2008). Pre-writing art experiences can be effective scaffolds for helping emerging writers express their ideas and opinions, lead to the use of more precise and vivid vocabulary, and foster critical thinking, including metaphor creation and evidence-based reasoning (Tranin et al., 2006).

WordShop: An Elementary School Museum Field Trip

In 2012, the Women's Initiative of the United Way of Greater Toledo launched a creative writing program, *WordShop*, designed to engage area students in creative writing through field trip experiences. In 2016, to take the program to the next level, the team at the Women's Initiative approached TMA about transferring management and operation of the program to the museum. Among the goals identified for TMA adopting *WordShop* were realigning the program curriculum with the Museum's Visual Literacy Framework and pedagogical principles as well as using the visits to empower teachers to use works of art in their classrooms.

Ultimately, the museum developed a 90-minute field-trip program for third–fifth-grade students supported by classroom resources and a teacher professional development workshop. The program aims to support students' visual literacy and writing skills through explorations of the TMA collection and writing activities. During the *WordShop* visit, museum docents engage students in a series of gallery-based literacy activities designed to help them develop descriptive language and become excited about writing. The three activities include:

- *Warm-up activity*: introduces the students to the *WordShop* experience and helps to activate and develop their descriptive vocabulary while looking at works of art.
- *Evidence-based writing activity*: this writing activity provides students with an opportunity to practice close looking, description, and analysis by writing a response to a work of art.
- *Extended writing activity*: a writing activity designed to provide students with an opportunity to expand their close looking, critical thinking, and descriptive writing skills through an extended writing experience.

To support the field trip experience, participating teachers are provided with pre- and post-visit classroom extension activities. A teacher professional development workshop is offered to participating educators to encourage integration of the classroom materials.

Over the course of the pilot year (2016), TMA delivered the *WordShop* program to 740 single-visit students, and 101 multi-visit students. Evaluators collected pre- and post-program student writing samples, observed the tour sessions, and surveyed participating teachers pre- and post-program attitudes and beliefs. The observations supported teachers' perceptions of the docents as knowledgeable and engaging. During the observed tours, evaluators found that the docents demonstrated a high level of knowledge about the museum and the museum collection. The docents also demonstrated knowledge about the goals and activities of the *WordShop* program, and often encouraged students to practice skills, such as close looking, using descriptive vocabulary, and providing visual evidence for their arguments. These observations of the quality of the program were supported by the teacher's survey responses, which indicated that they:

- believed the *pre- and post-visit lessons were valuable and effective* extensions of the TMA visit; and
- believed the program was a *valuable and enjoyable learning experience*, facilitated by a *knowledgeable and engaging docent*, during which students were actively engaged.

According to the teachers who completed the surveys, students enjoyed the *WordShop* program and were actively engaged during the TMA visits. The observations supported this result as well. For the most part, students freely engaged in the writing tasks at the TMA and most volunteered to share their ideas without being prompted to do so.

The high level of student participation observed by the evaluators during the *WordShop* visits was also observed by teachers, whose comments on the teacher survey indicated that they were often surprised by their students' level of engagement. Two teachers wrote:

- A student who is not all that interested in presenting in front of the class, offered to read her response to the group.
- My students were very hesitant at first sharing ideas with the docent, but quickly began participating more readily. I loved some of their responses! A few usually quiet ones were excited to participate.

In addition to the student outcomes, after participating in the program, every teacher who completed the survey agreed that museum programming was relevant to his or her language arts curriculum. Teachers also reported an increase in their confidence to use works of art to facilitate student writing and promote students' interpretation of images, objects, or symbols.

The Case for Teacher Education

Teacher Leaders

Supported by a grant from the Martha Holden Jennings (MHJ) foundation, *Teacher Leaders* is a one-year professional development program that provides cohorts of teachers the tools and confidence to use Museum collections to support classroom English Language Arts (ELA) and social studies learning standards. In the pilot year, the program served 12 area middle school educators drawn from regional public schools. The program began with a week-long summer institute during which participating teachers learned from museum curators about the objects in the collections and worked with museum educators to develop object-based teaching skills. At the end of the week, participating teachers committed to developing and implementing two lesson plans, which would use the museum and its collections to support classroom content standards. The museum supported the classroom implementation through quarterly coaching sessions and by providing transportation subsidies for classroom field trips. The resultant lesson plans were digitized and published on the TMA website to be available for other interested educators. The program maintained a 100% retention rate of participating teachers and generated 26 lesson plans relating museum collections to classroom learning.

Looking Forward, Thinking Back Program

Looking Forward, Thinking Back (LFTB) was the follow up to the Teacher Leader program implemented in year two by the TMA, and again funded by MHJ. *LFTB* was based on best practices for museum/teacher partnerships established during the 2016 *Teacher Leaders* program and expanded on the project-based approach from the pilot year, selecting and updating one of TMA's middle school programs. The 16-member cohort in the *LFTB* program consisted of an array of ELA, social studies, and visual arts educators all actively teaching in middle school classrooms. Their learning activities included:

- *Visual Literacy Workshop*: An intensive two-day experience held at TMA during which participants learned about TMA's approach to building critical thinking, problem solving, and empathy through visual literacy. They received training on TMA's Visual Literacy Framework and coaching on teaching with objects. Subject matter experts from the museum worked with participants to demonstrate the application of visual literacy to content areas relevant to social studies, ELA and visual arts.

- *Assessment of Current Program*: Participating educators applied their understanding of object-based teaching through the lens of visual literacy to critique the TMA program for strengths and weaknesses.
- *Seminars*: Using an applied learning model and guided by teacher-established goals and learning objectives, participating educators met monthly for a series of seminars. During these seminars, educators received additional training on teaching with objects and worked collaboratively to develop lesson plans for the program. These resources developed during the workshops were compiled, digitized, and made available via a digital resource-bank on toledomuseum. org.
- *Reflection workshop*: In late spring of 2018, participating teachers reconvened at TMA for a final workshop to reflect on their experience, provide feedback and constructive criticism on the program, and consider potential next steps.

The program evaluation sought to determine the impact of the program activities on teachers' beliefs and practices regarding the museum and the use of art in their classrooms as well as provide information about the quality of the program from the teachers' point of view. The evaluation consisted of a teacher survey, teacher written reflections, and an observation of the reflection workshop. The teachers completed the paper-and-pencil survey on the first and last days of the workshop. The survey consisted of three main sections that asked teachers about: (1) their awareness and perceptions of TMA programming, (2) their use of art in their curricula, and (3) their use of project-based learning strategies. Teacher reflections were written at the end of the program and were meant to provide a picture of teachers' thoughts about and experiences during the program.

Impact of the Program

LFTB sought to improve teachers' use of artwork in the classroom (including the frequency of using artwork as well as their confidence to use artwork). Teachers reported improvements related to student writing about art and helping other teachers use art in the classroom. Teacher leadership within their schools and the integration of language arts and visual arts were two other outcomes of the program.

The survey results revealed that teachers not only increased their use of art-related practices in the classroom, but they also increased their confidence to use these practices. Confidence (sometimes referred to as self-efficacy, a belief in one's own capabilities) is an important aspect of teacher effectiveness (Bray-Clark & Bate, 2003), so observing changes in both use and confidence is important. Like the increases in teachers' use of artwork, the increases in teachers' confidence to use artwork was statistically significant for all five art-related practices. For most practices, 50% or less of the teachers reported feeling *Somewhat Confident* or *Very*

Confident before the program. After the program, however, more than 80% of teachers reported feeling *Somewhat* or *Very Confident*.

Conclusion

The various school programs offered at TMA demonstrate that visual literacy and arts integration can have a positive effect on student learning and teacher pedagogy, as seen through quantitative and qualitative results. Whether demonstrating increases in student vocabulary or teacher's confidence in leveraging art in the classroom, museum- and arts-based learning provide a myriad of ways to impact school-based learning. In the current educational climate, many school districts are focused on Common Core State Standards, particularly those in ELA; the work at TMA suggests that an art museum can support learning in the field of reading and writing, making a strong argument for the value of the art museum for area students and teachers. Leveraging art cannot only help improve tangible applications of literacy (such as writing), but can also improve one's confidence and interest in diving deeper into the subject.

References

Beck, I. L., McKeown, M. G., & Kucan, L. (2013). *Bringing words to life: Robust vocabulary instruction* (2nd ed.). Guilford Press.

Bray-Clark, N., & Bates, R. (2003). Self-efficacy beliefs and teacher effectiveness: Implication for professional development. *The Professional Educator, 26*(1), 13–22.

Deetsch, M., Glass, R., Jankowski, R., Mylander, E., Roth, P., & Wharton, E. (2018). Visual literacy and its impact on pre-literacy development. *Journal of Museum Education, 43*(2), 148–158. https://doi.org/10.1080/10598650.2018.1426332

Deterding, S., Dixon, D., Khaled, R., & Nacke, L. (2011). From game design elements to gamefulness: Defining "gamification." *MindTrek, 11*, 9–15. https://doi.org/10.1145/2181037.2181040

Dewey, J. (1934). *Art as experience*. Minton, Balch & Company.

Feeney, S., & Moravcik, E. (1987). A thing of beauty: Aesthetic development in young children. *Young Children, 42*(4), 7–15.

Gardner, H. (1983). *Frames of mind: The theory of multiple intelligences*. Basic Books.

Gee, J. P. (2005). Learning by design: Good video games as learning machines. *E-learning, 2*(1), 5–16. https://doi.org/10.2304/elea.2005.2.1.5

Greene, J. P. (2014). The educational value of field trips. *Education Next, 14*, 78–86.

Harvard University. (2016). *Five numbers to remember about early childhood development*. http://developingchild.harvard.edu/resources/five-numbers-to-remember-about-early-childhood-development/.

Housen, A. (2002). Aesthetic thought, critical thinking and transfer. *Arts and Learning Research Journal, 18*(1), 99–132.

Kress, G. (2010) *Multimodality: A social semiotic approach to contemporary communication*. Taylor and Francis. https://doi.org/10.4324/9780203970034

Randal, K. (2008). *Visual arts: Effective means to enhance creative writing quality, master.* State University of New York College at Cortland. www2.cortland.edu/dotAsset/122273. pdf

RK&A Learn with Us. (2018). *Impact study: The effects of facilitated single-visit art museum programs on students grades 4–6.* Available at www.columbusmuseum.org/wp-content/uploads/2020/06/2018_RKA_NAEA_AAMD_ImpactStudy_SingleVisitArtMuseumPrograms_ColumbusMuse.._.pdf

Reeves, R., & Rodrigue, E. (2016). *Fewer field trips mean some students miss more than a day at the museum.* Brookings Institution. www.brookings.edu/blog/social-mobility-memos/2016/06/08/fewer-field-trips-mean-some-students-miss-more-than-a-day-at-the-museum/

Silverstein, L., & Layne, S. (2010). *Defining arts integration.* The John F. Kennedy Center for the Performing Arts.

Tranin, G., Andrzejcazk, N., & Poldberg, M. (2006). Visual arts and writing a mutually beneficial relationship. *Research and Evaluation in Literacy and Technology, 5.* http://digitalcommons.unl.edu/cgi/viewcontent.cgi?article=1004&context=cehsgpirw

Vygotsky, L. S. (1978). *Mind in society: The development of higher psychological processes.* Harvard University Press.

Yvon, F., Chiaguerova, L. A., & Newham, D. S. (2013). Vygotsky under debate: Two points of view on school learning. *Psychology in Russia: State of the Art, 6*(2), https://doi.org/10.11621/pir.2013.0203

19

PLUGGEDINVA

Harnessing the Transformative Power of a Learner-centered Workforce Development Program

Kate Rolander and Susan L. Watson

VIRGINIA COMMONWEALTH UNIVERSITY

Introduction

This chapter explores the transformative impacts of PluggedInVA (PIVA), an adult education workforce development initiative in Virginia, on the individuals who participate and on the communities where they live and work. The model was initially developed in 2008 in response to a need to upskill adult learners for new information technology (IT) jobs in a rural part of the state. In collaboration with an invested employer, a team of educators, occupational trainers, and instructional designers, PIVA was developed as a model of co-enrollment between an adult literacy program and a local community college to prepare students to simultaneously strengthen their basic academic skills while they earn a high school credential and participate in occupational training.

The PIVA developers also sought to disrupt and condense the traditional linear educational career path for lower-skilled adults who had not achieved a high school credential. Typically, this path would begin with basic literacy education and GED® preparation, then move on to post-secondary academic instruction, and finally arrive at occupational training. However, as Merriam and Baumgartner (2020) note, this traditional progression often takes years and does not adequately respond to the immediate employment needs and other life obligations that pose barriers to participation. Additionally, evidence demonstrates that adult learners tend to drop in and out of programs as the demands of their lives shift, which further complicates their opportunities for success in linear educational pathways (Reder, 2008; Rutschow, 2020).

PIVA developers mitigated some of these challenges by simultaneously offering education and training through co-enrollment within a condensed time frame, utilizing a supportive cohort structure to keep students engaged. These design elements are more closely aligned to adult learning principles, originally posited by Knowles (1980), that suggest timely and practical applications of learning are better suited to adults' needs and intrinsic motivations. With a model more in sync with adult learners' needs, PIVA developers were ready to test the framework with students. The pilot PIVA cohort ran in 2009, credentialing and preparing nine adult students for further occupational training and careers in IT (Leander, 2009). Since then, the model has been successfully adopted by programs around the state for a wide range of industries and learner populations. After operating for more than a decade and in more than 200 learner cohorts, we find value in re-examining the PIVA design and its impact on students, educators, and community stakeholders.

Background

In 2008, PIVA developers set out to design a program that would expedite the process that an adult must undergo to simultaneously achieve a high school credential, prepare for the workforce, and earn industry-recognized credentials for high-demand employment opportunities. Prior to the PIVA initiative in 2009, in many of the communities impacted by the need to upskill workers for new industries, adult education programs acted in isolation from higher education and training providers. Basic literacy skills were decontextualized from practice and taught as isolated skills, an approach that Street (1984) describes as the autonomous model wherein reading and writing are treated as discrete knowledge or "neutral technology" (p. 1), presumably transferable from one environment to another. However, without an intentional connection to literacy practice beyond the classroom, the purpose for reading and writing skills practice was, ostensibly, to pass the class and move on to the next one in sequence. Adult education activities designed in such a stand-alone, linear model reinforce gaps in career pathways for adult students, and learners were not developing the kind of literacy practices they needed to further their employment or increase their participation in higher education and occupational training.

By re-envisioning the existing adult education design, the PIVA model grounds literacy instruction within a particular occupational cluster (IT, healthcare, food service), thereby teaching students a literacy practice in which they use reading and writing skills in a purposeful way (i.e., writing reports, reading technical specifications, responding to customers). Reder's (2012) findings supported this theoretical underpinning, showing that starting a new job had a positive impact on adults' reading practices. Also directly relevant to the PIVA model, Nicolay (2017) found that adults were motivated to engage in literacy activities when it became a means to upskill their work qualifications. Additionally, PIVA's grounding in an occupational context works to offset societal and identity-laden barriers to literacy participation in that the model provides an extrinsic rationale for participation in literacy activities when many adults would not otherwise identify themselves as in need of remedial academic work or as having weak literacy skills (Windisch, 2020). As a model that aims to support learners' elevation to desired workforce and training environments, a PIVA program of instruction begins to resemble those of learners' target spaces, particularly their target work spaces.

The pilot program ran during the 2009 recession, and by its completion, the invested employer partner was under a job freeze and was unable to participate as fully in the program. State financial support also dried up; however, the model continued in its rural Virginia location with the support of the participating community college and the local workforce development board without state funding. In 2013, PIVA was added as a line item to the Virginia state budget, and this allowed adult education programs around the state to implement their own regionally responsive PIVA models in the manufacturing; healthcare; heating, ventilation, and air conditioning; machining; education; construction and weatherization; and hospitality industries. Since then, PIVA has run in rural and urban sites across the state serving over 2000 students and has been incorporated into federal, state, and local funding streams, ensuring sustainability through its incorporation into the state's workforce development system (Commonwealth of Virginia, 2016).

The PIVA Model

The model is built within a flexible framework that contextualizes academic skills, soft skills, twenty-first-century skills, digital skills, job readiness, and occupational training, all within a condensed time frame. Merriam and Baumgartner (2020) point out that clear, job-related outcomes are a motivating factor in participation. Likewise, the condensed time frame allows students to find or return to employment much sooner. At the time of the pilot, cohorts ran for close to six months; now they have a range of time spans, from as short as two or three months, depending on the industry's credentialing requirements. It is important to note that PIVA enrolls students in cohorts, which means that all learners attend their adult education and occupational training courses together so they become a supportive network for each other, providing a higher level of accountability to one another and increasing motivation to continue.

Learners also participate in a capstone project, an intensive, community-driven project done in teams that centers on developing a solution to an identified need in the community. This project exemplifies the contextualized, community-driven approach to workforce education that the PIVA model strives to realize. The projects are designed to integrate adult literacy activities, post-secondary readiness, and occupational skill sets. A particularly memorable example was a construction–weatherization project. In this case, the cohort identified a need to weatherize a local homeless shelter. In teams, the group developed project plans and budgets, including labor and materials. They presented the plans to an audience of local stakeholders, and their plans were accepted, allowing their weatherization project to be implemented. They were then able to showcase their accomplishments – and the enhanced shelter – during a public event where they presented their projects and highlighted the new features of the improved shelter. The capstone project not only acts as an opportunity to strengthen critical thinking and problem-solving skills, but also provides an authentic project-based learning experience to integrate the numeracy, literacy, and soft skills that learners have practiced throughout the PIVA program. Additionally, it provides an opportunity for learners to take on leadership roles in their communities, identifying and analyzing local needs and then proposing their solutions to a larger audience of stakeholders.

Conceptual Framework and Methodology

To examine the impacts of the PIVA model on learners, educational practitioners, and the larger workforce development community, we utilize a transformative learning framework influenced by the work of Lave and Wenger (1991). With this framework, learning is primarily a social process, and communities of practice (COPs) are an essential piece of that learning (Lave & Wenger, 1991; Wenger, 1998). A COP is used to signify a context for situated learning wherein "old-timers" work with "newcomers" to pass down the skills, nuances, community-specific language, and special understandings of a specific craft. Wenger (1998) adds that several indicators exist to signal the formation of a COP, among them "sustained mutual relationships, ... shared ways of engaging and doing things together," and "mutually defining identities" (p. 125). He writes that "in spite of curriculum, discipline, and exhortation, the learning that is most personally transformative turns out to be the learning that involves membership in these communities of practice" (1998, p. 6).

In keeping with the PIVA model's treatment of literacy as a practice, we find Lave and Wenger's (1991) framework well suited for explaining the transformative impacts of PIVA as learning via participation in mutually supporting COPs in the communities in which the PIVA cohorts are run. Wenger (1998) posits that we define ourselves both through our participation and our non-participation, our community membership, and by what is familiar or unfamiliar to us. As we shall see, adult learners began to see themselves as something new – a college student or an IT professional, and educators began to change the way they designed their educational programs.

Wenger (1998) writes that a focus on participation as a way to understand and support learning has different implications for individuals and for communities. For individuals, he claims it means that learning becomes "an issue of engaging in and contributing to the practices in their communities"; and for communities, it means "refining their practice and ensuring new generations of members" (p. 7). We use this framework to examine new and existing data and to focus on how participating in PIVA offers a new and creative way to explore this community literacy model. We ask: How have students, educators, and employers been transformed by their participation in the PIVA model?

For this chapter, we review existing qualitative data from four previous external evaluations of PIVA. The initial study of the PIVA pilot (Leander, 2009), a mixed-methods evaluation that accompanied the pilot, emphasized the identity-shifting effects of the cohort structure and of the model's capstone project. Subsequent external evaluations were done on PIVA programs through grants procured through the community college system (Munn et al., 2015; Styers et al., 2016a, 2016b), and these evaluations relied on similar methodologies to the pilot evaluation, each yielding findings consistent with those identified by Leander in 2009. However, little has been done to examine the transformative impacts of PIVA programs since then. To better gauge how the PIVA model transforms people and communities over time, we interviewed two expert educators: one from a rural area where the pilot was implemented in 2009 and another from an urban region who has run multiple PIVA cohorts since 2016. We then analyzed the data through the lens of transformative learning (Lave & Wenger, 1991; Wenger, 1998) to illustrate the transformative nature that PIVA programs have on students, educators, and community stakeholders.

Findings and Analysis

Qualitative findings in all of the evaluations focused on the perspectives of students and instructors regarding the value of the program and its potential to transform lives. The 2015 Trade Adjustment Assistance Community College and Career Training study summarized the researchers' observations, reporting that they saw important changes in academic performance and self-efficacy and that participants felt the program provided "hope and a path forward" (Munn et al., 2015, p. 11). Evaluators found the program to be rigorous and connected to "students' aspirations and needs" (Munn et al., 2015, p. 11). Students across the three external evaluations reported an increased sense of confidence, self-efficacy, and knowledge about career planning. Students in all studies also reported an increased interest and confidence in pursuing higher education, and many continued on to study at their participating community colleges. They reported that their experiences in PIVA were meaningful and tied to their own lives, goals, and needs. Educational staff also reported observing changes in behaviors, confidence, and students' interests in pursuing their goals and regulating their behaviors to achieve those goals. Across the studies, there were, however, lower levels of engagement in the adult education courses (i.e., academic skills, digital literacy, soft skills) than were observed in the occupational training courses, suggesting that students perceived occupational training to be more valuable to them than building academic and soft skills.

Learner Transformations

In all of the external evaluations and in both of the program manager interviews, the instructors, managers, and invested community members commented on the changes they witnessed in the adults who went through PIVA. Speaking about one of their primary recruitment tools, the rural program manager described her program's efforts to harness the transformative power of PIVA by publicizing the successes that learners experience through short articles in six weekly local newspapers. Through this medium, the learners' peers see someone they know achieving a goal they may not have previously envisioned for themselves. "It's really what it takes – seeing themselves differently" (Program Manager interview, 2019). The practitioners in this rural PIVA program acknowledge that many lower-skilled adults in their region may be anxious or intimidated by enrolling at a community college, especially if their past educational experiences were not strong or if their past training and occupational experiences left them feeling unsure about their abilities to learn or succeed in a career. When the pilot program began, for example, professional opportunities in IT were new to that region, so a supportive model like PIVA was needed to attract learners who may not have considered an IT job an option otherwise. "They had not considered a job in that [IT] career field" (Program Manager interview, 2019). She commented that since this experience, helping adults transform perceptions of themselves and of what they are capable of doing has remained at the heart of what her adult education program strives to do.

Learners' Self-Esteem and Self-Efficacy

The opportunities offered by PIVA begin to have transformative effects on learners even before they enter the program. During the PIVA program intake interview, for example, one woman shared with the rural adult education program manager, "this is my time; it's time to do something for me. This is my last chance." The PIVA program afforded her a chance to change her own self-identity and invest in herself. Another woman commented, "I need this in my life." These comments are not uncommon during the PIVA intake processes, and they reveal the program to be a potentially identity-shifting opportunity, one that learners perceive as a vehicle to a new way of being and participating in their own lives.

Another woman in the rural community commented, "you know, it's time for me to do my bit." During the intake interview she shared that her husband had worked so hard, both in a job and on their farm, that she felt she wanted to be able to contribute more to their household by enhancing her earning potential. For her, PIVA was a chance to transform her own personal role from someone who was supported by her husband's work to someone who could work in order to contribute financially to her family – a more equal partner in the home.

Once enrolled in a PIVA cohort, learners commented on how their self-perceptions shifted throughout the experience. Some reflected on the pride they felt about the skills they had learned:

> I still don't know a great deal about computers. But it surprised me, because I'd go home and feel like, 'Oh my god, I did it!' I told my husband all this stuff … My girls are proud of me – I tell them, 'Look what mom can do now.'

Others talked about the impacts of the program on their own outlook on life and their potential to change: "this program helped me with my self-esteem and made me want to continue with my education" (Reflections from a 2012–2013 PIVA cohort). Learners often reported that they gained a new level of self-confidence and self-efficacy as people who were able to learn new skills and who could continue onto higher levels of education, shifting their self-perceptions from that of being unsuccessful at learning to being capable of learning new things and continuing on to higher levels of education.

Participation as Transformation

As a recipient of state innovation funds, the rural adult education program that ran the pilot PIVA project received attention from both local community members and state legislators, and the manager was asked to hold a kick-off event only two weeks after students had begun the cohort. In our interview for this chapter, the rural community program manager recalled that they practiced with the learners to help them present to the large group of people who were expected to attend (including a state senator) about their experiences in the program. One woman in the cohort, reflecting on her position within that space at that moment, commented, "never in my lifetime did I think I would be speaking in front of a group of people like this, but, more importantly, that I would have anything to say that you'd be interested in hearing." The learner-centered nature of not only the program, but of this event, provided this learner, in particular, the platform to share her narrative, her goals, and her reflections about how she perceived herself and how she perceived her place in her community. In this instance, her identity was dismantled from her self-perception of someone who had nothing worthwhile to say; in this moment, she became a public speaker, a storyteller, and a representative for an innovative project.

Learners as Part of a COP

The cohort structure of the PIVA model was repeatedly identified as an essential characteristic of the program that supports students' success in a number of ways.

In the pilot cohort, one learner commented that "the people were helpful in class; a lot of one-on-one has been with the others in the class … we have learned to be interdependent." As the program has continued to grow, the cohorts have continued to provide each other with motivation and an additional level of mutual accountability. As a practice, learners would text or call each other if someone is missing from class; they help each other with transportation and even, on occasion, with financial and personal emergencies. In addition to the occupational and academic skills they are learning, their PIVA COPs focus heavily on learning to support oneself and one's group through mutual care, attention, teamwork, and goal setting. In this sense, the cohorts become COPs where they teach each other to self-regulate and to identify ways to sustain their engagement to transform their career prospects and their personal lives.

Educator Transformations

The adult education program managers and instructors who worked in PIVA programs also spoke about how their participation transformed them as practitioners. One program manager whose program has run more than 45 PIVA cohorts reflected:

> It has raised my expectations of what I should do as a program manager, that just getting by is not good enough. That we have to go the extra mile with our students and being afforded the opportunity to provide training programs changes people's lives, and, therefore, it changes my life, too.

The two program managers with whom we spoke shared that their roles had expanded to include more than the oversight of their programs; they have become partner conveners, problem solvers, workforce development experts, and community leaders.

Within the workforce development system, the PIVA model has effected changes within the structures and processes of adult education programs. For example, one rural program was able to use funds to build their own certified nursing assistant (CNA) laboratory and become their own training provider, increasing access to training for lower-skilled adult learners and strengthening the connection between adult education and occupational training. The program's student recruitment and intake process changed, as well, to become more "intensive and purposeful," including a new interview process and a signed letter of commitment to gauge a candidate's openness and readiness to commit. One program manager stated that the rationale for developing a more personal and intentional intake process was simply that "if we were going to believe in them, they had to believe in the program." The intake process mirrors the program itself as a collaborative and responsive program that centers on the learner experience.

Program Manager Transformations

The role of the program manager has expanded as well to include that of a partner convener and community problem solver. A program manager in an urban area referred to the process of developing responsive programming as "building the plane as we fly it" and emphasized the need for flexibility in design and staffing. Her role in the community now necessitates that she remains infused in partner activities so they can be part of the opportunities to provide solutions to community issues. Along the same vein, in the program that ran the pilot, when state funding disappeared, the manager changed her focus: "What I decided to do was to see if I could build local partnerships." She shifted her work to build local relationships in the community to sustain the program, and it was this effort that helped secure the program's sustainability for the decade to come.

A theme common to all of the evaluation studies and the interviews was the increasingly innovative nature of program planning. Rather than thinking of educational design as a linear process, both of the program managers we interviewed emphasized the need to continuously network, establish strong relationships, and build community–employer partnerships. Both also spoke about the importance of hiring and training a cadre of qualified teachers who, even if they were not placed immediately, would be ready to step into an instructional role when new opportunities arose. The manager of the urban program commented, "You have to hire good staff … and everybody needs to be willing to step up even if it's not in their comfort zone." This process represented a marked difference in the educational program design and hiring practices of the pre-PIVA years when teachers were hired to teach specific courses on a pre-existing and static course schedule. Now, program staff are ready to learn new skills, work at off-site locations, and be flexible with non-traditional course design and schedules that may run at varying times of the day or during non-traditional times of the year.

Community Impacts

PIVA also changed how the adult education programs were perceived as members of a larger community. Before PIVA, one manager described her relationship with the local rural community college as consisting primarily of shared student referrals; but with PIVA, they became partners who planned and worked together. She commented on their participation through PIVA: "It defines who we are … it helped cement a new kind of relationship." She worked hard to maintain their relationship and build programs that saw positive outcomes for students, the adult education program, and for the college, and when the college received funding from external sources to deliver innovative projects to support lower-skilled adults in achieving life-sustaining careers, the college looked to them and the PIVA model: "The community college saw the value in partnering with us … so they asked about writing us into their grants."

A new role for adult education in the workforce development community for these two programs was as identified experts in adult literacy and as reliable partners. "Our partners know that we do what we say we'll do, that they can depend on us." In both regions, the adult education programs were written into partner grants to deliver literacy and basic skills services as part of a larger workforce project; staff from adult education were then co-located at partner offices, a new practice for the field. In the urban program, they were written into plans to apply for large grants to revitalize neighborhoods as part of a larger city plan.

Government agencies, federal workforce initiatives, colleges, and non-profit organizations began to incorporate adult literacy services into their plans and into their grant applications. In these two regions of the state, literacy services and basic skills instruction have been incorporated into a number of new initiatives, including vocational rehabilitation for individuals with disabilities, veterans' occupational training programs, re-entry services for ex-offenders, and trade adjustment activities for outsourced careers. In this sense, PIVA continues to transform the field of adult education by expanding its involvement with outside agencies and breaking down dichotomies between adult learning and occupational training.

Implications

We find that PIVA is a replicable and sustainable adult literacy model that has the potential to transform educators, adult learners, and the communities in which they live. Toward that end, findings suggest two essential factors make the program transformative: educators must continuously work on building and strengthening relationships with community partners, and the learner must be at the center of programmatic and instructional design. The program managers we interviewed emphasized the need to establish and build strong relationships with local community colleges, employers, potential students, and other state agencies serving adults *prior* to designing and launching the PIVA cohort. In so doing, all stakeholders had input into the success of the cohort, and all partners were invested in student outcomes (i.e., increased academic skills, credentials earned, employment, wages). As the rural program manager reflected, "we all need each other." Relationships must precede the program design in order to make it relevant to students' and funders' needs, as well as to garner community investment.

PIVA programs also require innovative design that is learner-centered and grounded in these community relationships. The adult education program must be able to recruit, interest, and build relationships with adult students to keep them engaged and to help them see themselves as capable of having a career in a new field or succeeding in higher levels of education and training, things they may not have envisioned for themselves. Students need to see themselves in success stories, because PIVA could be in a new career area (such as IT) that was not previously something they had considered. One program manager commented that, "they need to be able to see themselves in that job." Likewise, becoming college students was often not a way of identifying themselves or a goal that they had envisioned for themselves. "It's really what it takes – seeing themselves differently."

Documentation from past evaluations and the interviews we conducted in 2019 revealed that the relationships between instructors and the learners had to shift, too, and become one of mutual commitment and trust. The recruitment and intake processes for PIVA are more intensive than traditional adult education programming or training at the community college; they are personal, and they are intentional, honing the needs and the challenges faced by the learners. "Trust us, and we will help you," was how one program manager summarized the message they aim to convey during their learner intake processes.

Conclusion

The aim of PIVA is to expand access to training and career opportunities for adults who may otherwise not be admitted into or who may not succeed in traditional training programs due either to the length of time required to earn a credential or because the program represented an opportunity that the student could not see for themselves. For these learners and the communities where they live, the PIVA program offers hope of something new when economies change and jobs are lost. After the pilot PIVA cohort in 2009, the rural program manager reflected, "Just doing that one cohort showed us how this could transform our program ... could better serve our community, our students, and benefit all of us." Both managers we interviewed shared that, through PIVA, they have witnessed transformations in their learners, in their instructors, in their programs as a whole, and in the larger communities where PIVA happens.

Data show that the PIVA model not only altered how adult education staff structured their programs, but it also engineered a shift in how educators perceive adult learners, as well as how the communities where these programs thrive respond to adult learning initiatives. The employer-driven and learner-centered nature of the design, along with the community-service aspect of the capstone projects, provided space for equal participation with those in their community with whom students may have previously been unable to identify. Additionally, the essential features of the model changed how adult education teachers approach instruction, explicitly relating academic skills to their learners' short- and long-term goals, which continuously shifted along with their "developing identities and knowledge" (Leander, 2009). Indeed, as the rural program manager said in the 2019 interview, "We are onto something special with PIVA." As the program continues to expand across the state and adapts to an increasing number of demands within the workforce development system, it transforms how adult education programs do business and, most importantly, how adult learners perceive their own power to change their lives.

References

Commonwealth of Virginia. (2016). *Workforce Innovation and Opportunity Act Combined State Plan*. Richmond, VA. Available from www2.ed.gov/about/offices/list/osers/rsa/wioa/state-plans/index.html

Knowles, M. S. (1980). *The modern practice of adult education* (revised and updated). Associated Press.

Lave, J., & Wenger, E. (1991). *Situated learning: Legitimate peripheral participation*. Cambridge University Press. https://doi.org/10.1017/CBO9780511815355

Leander, K. (2009). *PIVA evaluation*. Flat World Learning Resources.

Merriam, S. A., & Baumgartner, L. M. (2020). *Learning in adulthood: A comprehensive guide* (4th ed.). Jossey-Bass.

Munn, W., Bor, E., Clery, S., & Sheram, L. (2015). *Evaluation of Southwest Virginia Community College's TAACCCT initiative, first interim report*. JBL Associates.

Nicolay, K. (2017, March 13). Trader certificate prevents workers from falling out of the workforce in Norway. *European Platform for Adult Learning in Europe*. Available from https://epale.ec.europa.eu/en/blog/trade-certificate-prevents-workers-falling-out-workforce-norway

Reder, S. (2008). The development of literacy and numeracy in adult life. In S. Reder & J. Bynner (Eds.), *Tracking adult literacy and numeracy: Findings from longitudinal research* (pp. 59–84). Routledge. https://doi.org/10.4324/9780203888889

Reder, S. (2012). *The longitudinal study of adult learning: Challenging assumptions*. Center for Literacy for Quebec.

Rutschow, E. Z. (2020). Transitioning adult literacy students to postsecondary education. In D. Perin (Ed.), *The Wiley handbook of adult literacy* (pp. 517–540). John Wiley & Sons, Inc. http://doi.org/10.1002/9781119261407

Street, B. V. (1984). *Literacy in theory and practice*. Cambridge University Press. https://doi.org/10.1017/S0142716400007402

Styers, M., Haden, C., Cosby, A., & Peery, E. (2016a). *PluggedIn and ready to work at Southwest Virginia Community College: 2015 interim formative report*. Magnolia Consulting, LLC.

Styers, M., Haden, C., Cosby, A., & Peery, E. (2016b). *PluggedIn and ready to work at Southwest Virginia Community College: 2016 interim formative report*. Magnolia Consulting, LLC.

Wenger, E. (1998). *Communities of practice: Learning, meaning, and identity*. Cambridge University Press. https://doi.org/10.1017/CBO9780511803932

Windisch, H. C. (2020). Making the most of learning contexts. In D. Perin (Ed.), *The Wiley handbook of adult literacy* (pp. 381–406). John Wiley & Sons, Inc. http://doi.org/10.1002/9781119261407

20

WOMEN TUTORING WOMEN

A Community of Learners

Heidi R. Bacon

SOUTHERN ILLINOIS UNIVERSITY CARBONDALE

Patricia L. Anders and Nadia R. Granados

UNIVERSITY OF ARIZONA

Kelly L. Murphy

TOWSON UNIVERSITY

Introduction

The majority of adult education instructors in the United States and Canada, approximately 60% (Ziegler et al., 2009), are volunteers, a legacy that began in the early 1900s when Cora Wilson Stewart established the "Moonlight Schools" (Tabler, 2011). Wilson organized volunteers to teach adult basic literacy at the local one-room school on nights when the moon was full so learners could see to do their work.

Despite the legacy of volunteers in adult literacy, research is sparse. One set of studies focused on procedures for managing volunteers, training, communications, and coordination between program staff, tutors, and students (i.e., Belzer, 2006; Lynch, 2013; Ziegler et al., 2009). Counter to procedural studies, a smaller body of existing literature investigated the relationship between tutors and literacy learners. Lynch (2013; see also Roderick, 2013) proposed a conceptual framework centered on tutor–learner relationships. Her study affirmed a "social practice view of literacy learning" based on "social relationships" (p. 304) between volunteers and learners. She recommended that relationships between volunteers and tutors include "personal sharing activities" to learn about each other as "whole person[s]" (p. 322) and argued relationship building is key to volunteer preparation.

Belzer (2006) and Sandman-Hurley (2008) investigated how tutors tutored. Findings from these case studies underscored the importance of positive tutor–learner relationships, with Sandman-Hurley emphasizing that tutors needed guidance to develop interpersonal skills. These studies also reported that volunteers sometimes deviated from their preparation, returning to familiar practices from personal experience and rejecting approaches they had been taught because they did not fit the paradigm of what they believed learners needed.

As Perry and Luk (2018) discuss, few studies are theoretically grounded. They cite Ilsley's (1985) analysis of volunteerism showing that research "was mostly based on conventional wisdom and experiential insights, with little emphasis on theory" (p. 22). Using a Marxist theoretical frame, Perry and Luk (2018) investigated whether tutoring was an experience that changed a tutor's social justice perspectives and impacted social relationships. Their findings were qualified in that tutors' perspectives shifted but fell short of acknowledging the role of institutionalized inequity, power, and privilege in their relationships with students.

In contrast to most of the volunteer literature, this chapter reports on a theoretically grounded project designed to prepare women to tutor women working toward their GEDs, the Women's Literacy Network (WLN). A literacy organization with whom we partnered, Literacy Connects, provides tutors for children and adults, but few tutors are willing to volunteer in the community where we worked. The need for volunteers to tutor women working to achieve their GEDs was a central challenge identified by community stakeholders, members of a neighborhood "Literacy Council," who advised and helped create opportunities to enhance literacy across the lifespan. Based on an author conducted asset inventory, the Literacy Council designed and developed projects to build on strengths and address literacy challenges identified by the community. The WLN emerged from this process. This chapter reports the program, activities, and project outcomes with implications for future practice and research.

Theoretical Perspectives

Two foundational theories frame the WLN project: communities of practice (Lave & Wenger, 1991) and Goodman et al.'s (2016) comprehensive model of reading. These theories support an ideological model of literacy (Street, 1984) and views reading as the construction of meaning.

Communities of practice (Lave & Wenger, 1991; Wenger, 1998) situate learning in a network of relations involving joint enterprise (i.e., mutual engagement, negotiation, and accountability). Participants use their shared knowledge to engage in thinking and reasoning, and learning is mediated and distributed through the activities and discourses of community members. Lave and Wenger (1991) argue that activity happens both in and with the world; thus, agent, activity, and world are mutually constitutive. As individuals become intensively involved in the practices of the community, they become empowered, gaining understanding through their growing involvement. In a community of practice, these understandings and activities co-exist within a larger system of relationships, uniting members and practice (Garrett & Baquedano-López, 2002).

Goodman's comprehensive theory of reading (Goodman et al., 2016) describes reading as a cognitive, linguistic, and social process that supports proficient reading. Readers draw from semantic, syntactic, and graphophonic language cues to engage in cognitive reading strategies (e.g., initiating, sampling, predicting, confirming/disconfirming, inferencing, integrating, and terminating) in a social context. Miscues, as conceptualized by K. Goodman (2014), are deviations from print that differ from the expected response. When a reader reads something other than what is written, it is often evaluated as wrong and in need of correction. Goodman challenged this evaluation, maintaining that miscues provide a window into the reader's reading process and developed miscue analysis to reveal the strategies a reader is employing to construct meaning.

Retrospective miscue analysis (RMA) was adapted from miscue analysis to develop a pedagogical tool for teachers to help readers reflect on and evaluate their miscues (Goodman et al., 2014). Y. Goodman (2014) reasoned that as readers analyze their miscues retrospectively, they begin to revalue themselves as readers and to renegotiate their reading identities. Evidence from RMA studies suggests that readers become metacognitively and metalinguistically aware of their reading.

These theoretical perspectives framed the conduct, observations, and interpretations of WLN outcomes. We are mindful that "volunteer tutors, like any other educators, must be conscious of their work and their actions and ensure that their thinking and practice are aligned to bring about true and meaningful transformation to the lives of learners" (Perry & Luk, 2018, p. 20). We maintain that a community of practice framework combined with the concepts of RMA aligned thinking and practice.

Description of the WLN Project

In this section, we describe the WLN project: the neighborhood and literacy zone, recruitment of tutors, the tutor preparation curriculum, tutor mentoring, the types of data collected, and methods of analysis. The WLN began in 2010 and ended in 2013; a majority of tutors, however, remained in contact with WLN coordinators and Literacy Connects.

The WLN grew out of a city-wide collaborative establishing "literacy zones" in selected neighborhoods. A literacy zone is a geographically bounded area where community members worked together on a "literacy council" to enhance a culture of literacy in the community. Partners included people from government, non-profits, business, and educational organizations. The literacy zone neighborhood was a tightly knit working-class, predominantly Latinx neighborhood with multigenerational families. Home ownership was relatively high with over 60% of homes owner-occupied. At the inception of the WLN, the neighborhood was home to 18,000 people with 32% of families living below the 2010 federal poverty level (US Census Bureau, 2010) headed by women. Less than half of women age 25 and older had a high school diploma or GED (46.7%), 4.5% of women had an associate degree, and 4.2% had a bachelor's degree or higher.

The project was funded for three years by a local women's foundation. We hired, prepared, and mentored neighborhood women with GEDs to tutor women studying for the GED. Grant funds paid tutors for tutoring, provided tutors and students with transportation and childcare subsidies, and covered GED test fees. Two additional foundations provided $250 community college scholarships for WLN participants.

Tutors were recruited through the neighborhood adult learning center and a local caregiver certification organization, a literacy zone partner. Adult learning center staff telephoned possible recruits, women who had recently graduated with their GEDs, explained the program, and invited them to apply. The caregiver certification organization mailed letters and flyers to graduates of their program who lived in the neighborhood. Interested women completed the application, which included a personal essay about their desire to be part of the WLN, their future goals, and three professional references. Applicants were interviewed by a panel of WLN coordinators and adult learning center staff. The WLN recruited, hired, and prepared 10 tutors per program year.

A tutor preparation curriculum and handbook were developed (Bacon & Lantz-Leppert, 2010).[1] The 20-hour preparation took place over five weeks in four-hour blocks, a departure from the typical 12–15 hours pre-service preparation of most volunteer programs (Belzer, 2006). The curriculum employed a constructivist model of teaching and learning. Each workshop module included specific learning goals, objectives, and related activities. Learners examined their beliefs about literacy and learning, studied the characteristics of adult learners and principles of adult learning, engaged concepts of RMA, became familiar with reading and writing strategies, practiced planning a tutoring session, and discussed the importance of mentoring.

The term "concepts of RMA" differentiated the informal practice of RMA, which we used, from formalized procedures (Goodman et al., 2014). Concepts of RMA as practiced in the WLN included: (1) reading is a language process; (2) reading is constructing meaning; (3) reading is a social transaction; (4) a reader's language and linguistic resources are valued and validated; and (5) miscues are normal, all readers miscue, and miscues help to understand the reading process. Our approach to reading was focused on meaning-making. The idea was for tutors to listen carefully to students' reading and to provide strategies to build on learners' strengths. As such, the WLN broke new ground by deinstitutionalizing RMA and making concepts of RMA accessible to community-based volunteer tutors.

After 20 hours of preparation, tutors were matched with students who met for two hours per week for 10 weeks. At the end of 10 weeks, tutors and students were given the option to continue for another 10 weeks. Tutors whose students

---

[1] A copy of the Handbook is available from Heidi Bacon, hrbacon@siu.edu.

were ready to take the GED or whose students chose not to continue tutoring were matched with a new student. In fall 2010, the WLN added two facilitators who were former tutors. The facilitators helped with mentoring and provided additional instructional support for tutors.

The WLN implemented 90-minute biweekly mentoring sessions. Coordinators and facilitators provided coaching and scaffolding for tutors. The theme for each session grew out of tutors' experiences and interests, and throughout the sessions, coordinators emphasized the importance of tutors forming positive relationships with their students. The women shared deeply and reflected on their practice. They came with questions and discussed situations that arose with their students.

Program evaluation data were collected per Literacy Connects (the WLN's fiscal agent) and the women's foundation. Evaluation data included questionnaires, tutor logs, and stories captured in field notes taken by coordinators during tutor preparation and mentoring. Questionnaires were administered after tutor preparation and at the end of each 10-week cycle. Participants responded to the following questions in writing: (1) What learning has been the most valuable for you? (2) What do you consider to be your most important accomplishment since joining the WLN? (3) Has the way you think about yourself and your literacy changed since you joined the WLN? If so, how? Tutors also submitted biweekly tutor logs. The logs consisted of a checklist of literacy practices (e.g., reading to children, obtaining a library card, checking out library books, registering to vote/voting, and completing job applications) and several open-ended reflective questions about their tutoring. Stories captured in field notes were included in the women's foundation semi-annual reports.

Research data were obtained from a narrative inquiry conducted with five tutors who volunteered to take part in the study during the second year of the WLN (Bacon, 2014). Each tutor participated in a series of four in-depth, unstructured interviews. Interview topics concentrated on the women's reading and writing beliefs and practices, personal school histories, and WLN experiences. Interviews took place at participants' homes, restaurants, and the local branch library, lasting 60–90 minutes each, which Bacon transcribed verbatim. Data were analyzed by first conducting a narrative analysis to construct each tutor's narrative and then thematically (see Ayers, 2008; Saldaña, 2016) to ascertain themes within and across the narratives.

These interviews were the primary data source; however, three years of evaluation data were used to triangulate the interview data. Program evaluation data were organized by source and by date. Evaluation data were also analyzed thematically to identify patterns within and across data sources.

Learning from Women Tutoring Women

Overarching themes consistent with both data sources included: building relationships and community; women and mentoring matter; the impact of learning and practicing concepts of RMA; and local ways of knowing. These themes suggest the design of the WLN fostered interactions enhancing tutors' practices and helped the women fulfill their desire to belong and contribute to what they perceived as important work (e.g., Bacon, 2014; Bacon et al., 2019; Bacon & Kaya, 2018). We elaborate on these themes in the following sections.

Building Relationships and Community

WLN tutors built strong relationships and established close ties that kept them connected to the program, the coordinators, and each other. Relationships formed the glue that kept the community intact. The women likened the WLN to a "circle of women holding hands," "a team," and "a family." Melissa explained that the WLN community created a sense of comfort. When asked to elaborate, she responded:

> We were a group working together and not apart. I felt really good about that. It was like a family the way we were all connected. One of us might have been stronger in reading. One of us might have been stronger in math. One of us might have been stronger in writing, but yet we pulled all this together and it made us strong. It gave us a good foundation.

The WLN learning community closely attended to the "circulation of knowledge-able skill" (Lave & Wenger, 1991, p. 55), and created a space where understandings and activities were used to create community (Wenger, 1998). Tutors expressed feeling a sense of unity in strength and purpose.

Women and Mentoring Matter

Mentoring sessions offered a space to talk about painful reading and writing memories and to heal feelings of failure and shame. Dutro (2019) reminds us that stories are examples of testimony and witnessing that pull us together in moments of close connection. Marla explained: "We all talk about our experiences. I like mentoring. I get together with everybody and talk about everything, like if we have a problem with something." The women engaged in joint problem solving to support and encourage one another. They discussed what worked and collectively brainstormed ideas to address tutoring issues.

Participants underscored the need to support each other as women. One tutor stated, "Children get support at school, but mothers need to learn, too." Participants stressed the importance of women helping women. They frequently noted that "women understand women." For Sally, belonging to a women's network meant she could "relax and be herself" without being "hit on." She explained: "These are women. They understand where I'm coming from." Marla further articulated that mothers have common goals: "We know the goal we want and almost all women who have a family want the same goal." The women saw themselves as resources for each other. They viewed themselves as a community of women helping women. As Sally declared: "Oh my gosh, things are so much more difficult when you're trying to do them on your own. So much more difficult."

The Impact of Learning and Practicing Concepts of RMA

This closely knit community practiced concepts of RMA. The women found the notion of miscues liberating and validating. Practicing concepts of RMA freed them from shame associated with making mistakes or mispronouncing words and enabled them to take control of their own reading. This was powerful learning for Diana, who had been labeled with a learning disability. Diana came to understand: "You can make miscues, but those miscues don't mean you're ignorant and your intelligence is below standards." Diana actively practiced concepts of RMA with her GED students, fiancé, and children. In a similar vein, the WLN community helped Melissa feel more comfortable with the notion of a miscue: "Miscues are great. They are an ear opener or an awareness. Now I'm a better listener." Sally, too, credited her knowledge of miscues with helping her become a better and more patient listener.

WLN tutors reflected on how reading instruction during tutor preparation shifted their perceptions of what counts as reading. Gwen confessed:

> Now I realize they're not mistakes. There's a difference between telling your student that's a mistake and that's a miscue. Let them keep reading because once you tell someone you made a mistake that breaks their confidence. That's like telling them you can't do it.

Amelia offered insight into the reason for encouraging readers to take responsibility for their own reading:

> What really impacted me was when they [coordinators] said that we shouldn't jump in when they [students] are reading. We do that. We think she's having a problem. Just say the word for them. But I never realized that when we do that, we take away their power to try to figure out the word.

Incorporating concepts of RMA in the tutor preparation curriculum was not only novel, it helped the women reframe deficit orientations and work out their own understandings without worrying whether they were doing something wrong or making a mistake. They not only reported changes in the way they listened to readers, they employed wait time before attempting to correct or fix their reading. They learned how to accommodate instruction to meet their students' needs in ways consistent with their preparation. Decontextualized skills instruction is deeply embedded in adult education contexts (Rogers, 2004), but tutors embraced the concepts of RMA and offered unique insights into how they practiced and revalued reading. Their beliefs about reading shifted from accurate oral reading toward a meaning-entered view of reading.

Local Ways of Knowing

In addition to revaluing themselves as readers, the women drew on the experiences and knowledge they brought with them to the WLN (e.g., Larrotta & Serrano, 2012) to generate and produce new knowledge. This was especially impactful for mothers, who told of the adapting strategies they learned and practicing them with their children. For example, Marla's special needs son had not shown progress toward meeting his Individualized Education Program goals. Six months after joining the WLN, he showed 50% growth. She described the reading routine she used with him:

> I tell him to get his picture book and tell me what he thinks the story is going to be about. He goes through every page and tells me what is happening. Then he tries to read. He only reads the words he knows and understands. Then both of us read it. I say the word and he has to say it after me. I really know how to help him learn.

Sally reported making weekly visits to the library. She and her son checked out seven books per week, one for every day of the week. Reading was fun for Sally and her family, as they took turns reading and mimicking the voices of the characters. Another tutor, Mariana, received her GED as a WLN student and returned to tutor. She used her tutoring insights when reading with her son. She reflected, "I've learned good readers don't read as fast as they can. Reading is about understanding." Mariana contrasted her new knowledge with prior strategies she had used with her son such as saying: "That's not how you pronounce it." The women shared stories of families reading together, transforming homework time into family literacy time. They reported feeling better prepared to help their children with homework and more comfortable talking with their children's teachers.

Research and evaluation data also indicated that tutors engaged in self-directed learning, checking out study guides from the library and forming study groups to help tutor more effectively. This activity, generated by the women themselves, is further evidence of changes in local ways of knowing and knowledge production.

Implications and Conclusion

The WLN project substantially adds to the literature on adult literacy volunteer tutors, specifically women tutors. Over a three-year span, 27 WLN tutors successfully tutored 15 students to GED completion and 18 women received scholarships to continue their education. Bacon's (2014) research and the program evaluation data suggest the design of the WLN project fostered close ties through frequent and intense interactions, which emphasized the importance of tutor/student relationships. Tutors reframed their perceptions of reading and revalued themselves as literate and capable of teaching others, which supported local ways of knowing and contributed to their growing sense of agency. The women of the WLN were invested in women tutoring women. They believed the women-only context created a transformative community of practice and expressed feeling safe, cared for, valued, and respected.

Although others have researched the nature of tutor–student relationships, these findings raise questions for further research. For example, what is the nature of same-gender relationships, a male-only network, and how do relationships change if tutors and students are different genders? The nature of mentoring sessions also needs to be unpacked. What conditions are necessary for successful mentoring sessions?

Perry and Luk (2018) maintain that "the ongoing dynamic nature of the relationship between tutors and learners presents an opening through which revolutionary social transformation could emerge" (p. 31). WLN data lend support to the impact of volunteerism. The WLN and its community partners fostered volunteerism. Coordinators modeled effective communication practices during tutor preparation and mentoring, and the women's growing confidence enabled them to take on leadership roles and expand their social networks. The women volunteered with Literacy Connects, the neighborhood Literacy Council, and a disability rights group. Notably, three tutors were employed by WLN partners, and Marla became the Head Start parent liaison for the local school district. In giving back, volunteer literacy tutors advanced positive changes not only in themselves, but also in the broader community. These findings raise another issue that could greatly impact the design of literacy programs. We wonder how literacy programs can plan for and connect with the learners and communities they serve. How might this look in different in- and-out-of-school spaces?

These opportunities influenced practice engagements and built social capital, e.g., "supportive relationships with educators and community members who have access to resources and opportunities" (Compton-Lilly & Delbridge, 2019, p. 533). This was essential because, as Compton-Lilly and Delbridge assert, "The amount of social capital held by an individual depends on the size of his or her network and the amount of capital held by the members of that network" (p. 533). As such, the WLN unlocked opportunities for women to activate their existing capacities and resources into affordances for personal growth. It is a potentially transformative model for women's literacies by investing in families and communities.

Sustainability of projects like the WLN is problematic. The WLN was resource- and time-intensive, making it unattractive to funders who sought scalable projects that measured and reported short-term gains. It was not designed or intended to produce short-term change. The WLN was designed as a "learning support system" (Reder, 2012), an investment in women, families, and community for the long term. Asset-based programs and resources, like the WLN, are crucial to actualize long-term outcomes and require imagination, planning, and preparation, to effect a more hopeful future (see Gee, 2017). Sustainability raises implications regarding current accountability measures and the need for adult literacy programs to challenge rather than reproduce the status quo.

A dearth of literature exists to inform current practice in the field. The WLN featured women tutoring women, which contributes to literature on adult, family, and community literacies. Contrary to Perry and Luk's (2018) study, WLN tutors became agents of change in their homes and communities. They came from the neighborhood, and having walked the walk of their students, they demonstrated a critical consciousness grounded in a shared lived experience of what it means to be a woman adult literacy learner.

Implications for literacy programs from the WLN project might include: (1) reflecting on the program's theoretical framing and aligning preparation accordingly; (2) drawing on adult learners' knowledge and ways of knowing; (3) fostering relationships that enhance social capital; (4) creating partnerships and involving stakeholders; and (5) providing opportunities for tutors and students to engage with local community, perhaps through volunteerism.

In sum, the WLN illustrates how a network of women (coordinators, facilitators, tutors, and students in partnership with community) moved beyond literacy-as-skills to support women characterized by low self-esteem, enhance communication, enhance literacy practices, and promote self-advocacy and activism. The project was theoretically grounded in a pedagogy of situated learning and concepts of RMA with access to intellectual, social, and financial capital. Relatively under-prepared women revalued themselves as literate and became producers of local knowledge. These are worthwhile outcomes. Given today's challenges, we invite adult educators and researchers to improve upon this work and look forward to continuing the conversation.

References

Ayers, L. (2008). Thematic coding and analysis. In L. Given (Ed.), *The SAGE encyclopedia of qualitative research methods* (pp. 867–868). SAGE.

Bacon, H. R. (2014). Constructing literacy identities within communities: Women' stories of transformation. Doctoral dissertation, The University of Arizona. UA Theses and Dissertations. https://repository.arizona.edu/handle/10150/325232

Bacon, H. R., Byfield, L., Kaya, J., & Humaidan, A. (2019). Counter-storying lives and literacies: Narratives of transformational resistance. *Journal of Latinos and Education*. https://doi.org/10.1080/15348431.2019.1685527

Bacon, H. R., & Kaya, J. (2018). Imagined communities and identities: A spatio-temporal discourse analysis of one woman's literacy journey. *Linguistics and Education, 46*, 82–90. https://doi.org/10.1016/j.linged.2018.05.007

Bacon, H. R., & Lantz-Leppert, E. (2010). *Handbook for tutors* (unpublished manual). University of Arizona.

Belzer, A. (2006). What are they doing in there? Case studies of volunteer tutors and adult literacy learners. *Journal of Adolescent & Adult Literacy, 49*(7), 560–572. https://doi.org/10.1598/JAAL.49.7.2

Compton-Lilly, C., & Delbridge, A. (2019). What can parents tell us about poverty and literacy learning? Listening to parents over time. *Journal of Adolescent and Adult Literacy, 62*(5), 531–539. https://doi.org/10.1002/jaal.923

Dutro, E. (2019). *The vulnerable heart.* Teachers College Press.

Garrett, P. B., & Baquedano-López, P. (2002). Language socialization: Reproduction and continuity, transformation and change. *Annual Review of Anthropology, 31*, 339–361. https://doi.org/10.1146/annurev.anthro.31.040402.085352

Gee, J. P. (2017). *Teaching, learning, literacy in our high-risk high-tech world: A framework for becoming human.* Teachers College Press.

Goodman, K. (2014). Reading: A psycholinguistic guessing game. In K. Goodman & Y. Goodman (Eds.), *Making sense of learners making sense of written language: The selected works of Kenneth S. Goodman and Yetta M. Goodman* (pp. 103–112). Routledge. https://doi.org/10.4324/9780203366929

Goodman, K., Fries, P., & Strauss, S. (2016). *Reading the grand illusion: How and why people make sense of print.* Routledge. https://doi.org/10.4324/9781315658421

Goodman, Y. (2014). Retrospective miscue analysis: Illuminating the voice of the reader. In K. Goodman & Y. Goodman (Eds.), *Making sense of learners making sense of written language: The selected works of Kenneth S. Goodman and Yetta M. Goodman* (pp. 205–221). Routledge. https://doi.org/10.4324/9780203366929

Goodman, Y. M., Martens, P., & Flurkey, A. D. (2014). *The essential RMA: A window into reader's thinking.* Richard C. Owen.

Ilsley, P. (1985). *Adult literacy volunteers: Issues and ideas* (Information Series No. 301. National Center Publications, National Center for Research in Vocational Education.

Larrotta, C., & Serrano, A. (2012). Adult learners' funds of knowledge: The case of an English class for adults. *Journal of Adolescent & Adult Literacy, 55*(4), 316–325. https://doi.org/10.1002/JAAL.00038

Lave, J., & Wenger, E. (1991). *Situated learning: Legitimate peripheral participation.* Cambridge University Press. https://doi.org/10.1017/CBO9780511815355

Lynch, J. (2013). A case study of a volunteer-based literacy class with adults with developmental disabilities. *Australian Journal of Adult Learning, 53*(2), 94–103.

Perry, J., & Luk, A. (2018). Volunteer tutors: Agents of change or reproduction? An examination of consciousness, ideology and praxis. *The Canadian Journal for the Study of Adult Education, 30*(1), 19–32. https://cjsae.library.dal.ca/index.php/cjsae/article/view/5397

Reder, S. (2012). The longitudinal study of adult learning: Challenging assumptions. Research Brief. The Centre for Literacy. http://centreforliteracy.qc.ca/sites/default/files/ CFLRsrchBrief_Chllngng_Assmptns.pdf

Roderick, R. (2013). Constructing adult literacies at a local adult literacy tutor-training program. *Community Literacy Journal, 7*(2), 53–75. https://doi.org/10.1353/clj.2013.0010

Rogers, R. (2004). Storied selves: A critical discourse analysis of adult learners' literate lives. *Reading Research Quarterly, 39*(3), 272–305. https://doi.org/10.1598/RRQ.39.3.2

Saldaña, J. (2016). *The coding manual for qualitative researchers* (3rd ed.). SAGE.

Sandman-Hurley, K. (2008). Volunteers tutoring reading-disabled adult literacy learners: A case study. *Adult Basic Education and Literacy Journal, 2*(2), 94–103.

Street, B. (1984). *Literacy in theory and practice.* Cambridge University Press.

Tabler, D. (2011). *Kentucky's moonlight schools. Appalachian history stories, quotes, and anecdotes.* www.appalachianhistory.net/2011/12/kentuckys-moonlight-schools.

US Census Bureau. (2010). 2005–2009 American community survey. www.census.gov/acs/www/data documentation/2009 release/

Wenger, E. (1998). *Communities of practice: Learning, meaning, and identity.* Cambridge University Press. https://doi.org/10.1017/CBO9780511803932

Ziegler, M., McCallum, S. R., & Bell, S. M. (2009). Volunteer instructors in adult literacy. *Adult Basic Education & Literacy Journal, 3*(3), 131–139.

PART V
Partnership Programs

21

LITERACY DEMANDS OF HANDBOOKS OF THREE NATIONAL YOUTH ORGANIZATIONS

Corrine M. Wickens and Donna E. Werderich

DEPARTMENT OF CURRICULUM & INSTRUCTION, NORTHERN ILLINOIS UNIVERSITY

Carol S. Walther

DEPARTMENT OF SOCIOLOGY, NORTHERN ILLINOIS UNIVERSITY

Introduction

Differences in engagement in literacy practices among youth within in- and out-of-school contexts have been well-documented in the literature. Although a great deal of research has investigated literacy engagement in out-of-school settings (Hull & Schulz, 2001), often in various after-school book clubs (Alvermann et al., 1999), youth centers (Morrell, 2015), and community theaters (Winn, 2010), these clubs and youth groups are generally small and community-based. Little research, however, has been conducted regarding the facilitation of literate practices among youth in large national youth organizations.

In recent decades, large national youth organizations have played important roles for youth by integrating important life skills, including literacy, numeracy, decision making, and critical thinking into routine activities and skill development within projects, merit badges, and rank advancement (e.g., Boy Scouts; Heath, 2010). The nature of such literacy expectations has hitherto not been explored. Thus, in this chapter, we examine literacy expectations within handbooks produced by three prominent youth organizations known for their widespread cultural recognition and their historical longevity: Girl Scouts of America, Scouts BSA (formerly Boy Scouts of America), and 4-H. We specifically analyze general measures of text complexity, text features and organization, and language used within these texts (Fairclough, 2003). To do so, we begin first by defining literacy in the next section.

Literacy

Literacy has traditionally indicated an ability to read and write. Through this lens, literacy is a discrete, generalized set of skills to be mastered – skills needed to learn to decode, comprehend, and compose texts (Cope & Kalantzis, 2000; Walsh, 2010). "[It is] a synthesis of language, context, and thinking that shapes meaning" (Winch et al., 2010, p. 697). The International Literacy Association (ILA) expands this definition, situating literacy within varied contexts and for diverse purposes:

> the ability to identify, understand, interpret, create, compute, and communicate using visual, audible, and digital materials across disciplines and in any context. The ability to read, write, and communicate connects people to one another and empowers them to achieve things they never thought possible. Communication and connection are the basis of who we are and how we live together and interact with the world.
>
> *("Why literacy," 2019, paras. 1 & 2)*

Within this frame, literacy denotes social practices that are multifaceted, dynamic, and fluid (Gourlay & Oliver, 2012). Furthermore, because people engage in multiple forms of communication, we speak of literacy not as a singular activity, but as a plurality: literacies.

These literacies include multiple modalities and linguistic forms: written communication (reading and writing), oral communication (speaking and listening), and digital literacies (viewing and representing). Such literacies are all important for youth participation in the three youth organizations, e.g., reading project guidelines, brainstorming with peers and adults regarding possible service projects for different awards (e.g., Bronze, Silver, or Gold in Girl Scouting, or Eagle rank in Scouts BSA), researching information, or viewing how-to videos online to complete a specific task.

Methodology

To investigate the literacy demands of the three youth organizations, we employed interpretivist case study methodology and textual analysis. Case study methodology involves the investigation into phenomenon that is bounded by time, space, or organization (Merriam, 1998). It focuses upon singularity of experiences and uniqueness of context that makes the cases rich for study and analysis (Tellis, 1997). In this study, our cases are defined by the three distinct youth organizations and the primary texts (handbooks, merit badge workbooks, and project manuals) produced for participation within these organizations. While recognizing the variety of formats within this sample of texts, we will use the term "handbooks" to encompass all formats. Then, within the three cases, we engaged in textual analysis, in which texts are understood as socially situated cultural artifacts and social events

TABLE 21.1 Overview of Organizations, Handbooks/Project Manuals

Youth Organization	Handbook/Manual	Grades
Girl Scouting of USA	Brownies	2–3
	Juniors	4–5
	Cadettes	6–8
	Seniors	9–10
Scouts BSA	Tiger	1
	Bear	3
	Webelo 1 & 2	4 & 5
	Scouts	6–12
4-H	Cooking 101, 201, 301	3–12
	Robotics	3–12
	Junk Drawer Robotics	3–12
	Exploring Your Environment: Earth's Capacity	6–8

(Fairclough, 2003). Through this lens, we examined the different text features that would most influence participation in the youth organizations, including text readability, language demands, and literacy supports.

Text Selection

We focused our research on three national youth organizations: Girl Scouts of the USA, Scouts BSA, and 4-H. We chose these three organizations based upon their enduring and widespread recognition. Within these organizations, we evaluated at least one handbook per grade-level band: primary (1–3), intermediate (4–5), middle (6–8), and secondary (9–12). We excluded handbooks for kindergarteners as most are still developing early foundational reading skills. We also excluded specialized affinity groups in Boy Scouting – Sea Scouts, Venturers, and Explorers – as well as Ambassadors, the oldest age group in Girl Scouting, given that the Gold Award, the highest award in Girl Scouting, could be earned either by Seniors (9th–10th grades) or by Ambassadors (11th–12th grades). Table 21.1 reports the handbooks analyzed and their respective age groups.

Methods

We ground our textual analysis within the work of Fairclough (2003). Like socio-cultural understandings of literacy, text for Fairclough represents moments of social relationships constituted within inequitable social structures and dynamics. As instantiations of social interactions, textual analysis attends to different linguistic features within the texts, i.e., semantics, grammar, vocabulary, and phonology

(Fairclough, 2003). For our study, such features also include organizational features of texts (e.g., headings and images) as meaning-making resources for youth.

Readability

To analyze literacy demands of these texts, we needed to first measure text readability. A text readability score, or index, is a general estimation of how difficult a text is to read. We used the online readability tool, Readability Analyzer (https://datayze.com/readability-analyzer.php), to facilitate the computation of text readability, as it estimates readability of text using multiple measures. Given its wide popularity and clear connections to grade levels, we focused upon Fry's (1968) readability scale for readability comparisons. While we use the terminology "grade level"; empirically, grade levels actually refer to "grade estimates." Following typical protocols, we inputted a minimum of 100 words within at least three sections per handbook into the online tool. Figure 21.1 illustrates sample results using the Readability Analyzer.

One challenge in making text readability comparisons is that all the handbooks, except for Tigers and Bears in Cub Scouting, are meant for a grade range (e.g., 6–8). Thus, when analyzing the text readability scores, we based our comparisons against the youngest grades within that grade band. For instance, Webelos spans across grades 4 and 5, so we based our comparisons for fourth graders – the youngest within that grade range expected to use that handbook.

Analysis of Literacy Demands

We next engaged in critical textual analysis of literacy demands within these handbooks. Literacy demands refers to expectations placed upon the reader that might facilitate or hinder comprehension. While measures of text readability serve as a basis for determining literacy expectations, we also paid attention to three other primary components: text features, language function, and language activities. Text features include text organization, headings and subheadings, blocked texts, inset photos and other images, glossaries, and sidebars. Textual features also involved vocabulary, sentence structure, and voice. By literacy supports, we referenced any tool explicitly incorporated in the text meant to support critical thinking, planning, or reflecting. Language function indicates what readers are to *do* with language. These functions "represent the active use of language for a specific purpose ... to express ideas, communicate with others, and show understanding of content" (University of California, 2017, para. 1). As such, we examined task requirements for different projects, merit badges, and rank advancements, to determine whether they reinforced lower level comprehension skills, e.g., explain or recall, or higher-level comprehension skills, e.g., compare/contrast, justify, apply,

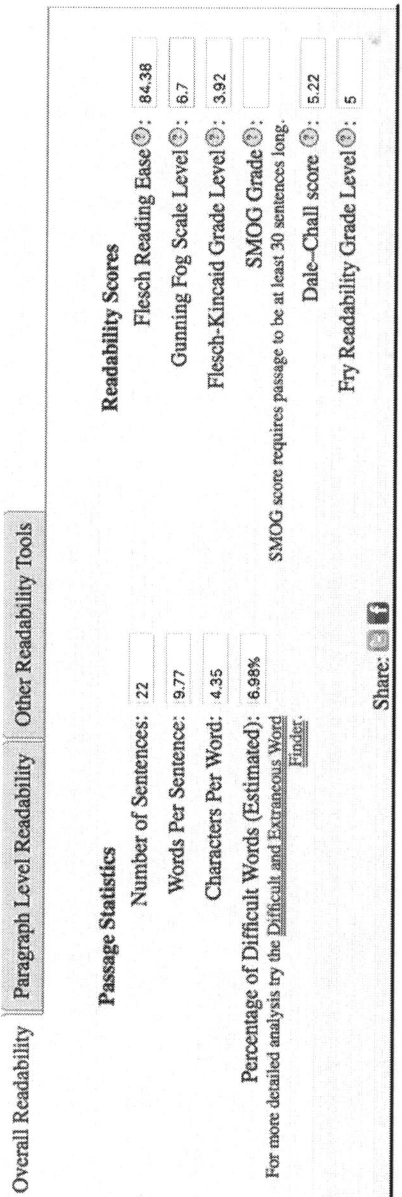

| Overall Readability | Paragraph Level Readability | Other Readability Tools |

Passage Statistics

Number of Sentences:	22
Words Per Sentence:	9.77
Characters Per Word:	4.35
Percentage of Difficult Words (Estimated):	6.98%

For more detailed analysis try the Difficult and Extraneous Word Finder.

Share:

Readability Scores

Flesch Reading Base ⓘ:	84.38
Gunning Fog Scale Level ⓘ:	6.7
Flesch-Kincaid Grade Level ⓘ:	3.92
SMOG Grade ⓘ:	
Dale–Chall score ⓘ:	5.22
Fry Readability Grade Level ⓘ:	5

SMOG score requires passage to be at least 30 sentences long.

FIGURE 21.1 Sample Results from Online Readability Analyzer Tool

create. Finally, we documented different language activities required, involving oral, written, or digital modes of communication.

Youth Organization Cases

All three national youth organizations emphasize skill, character, and leadership development. However, an understanding of the literacy demands expected of the youth and literacy tools to support such demands has largely been lacking. In the following three cases, we provide brief synopses of the organizations, descriptions of the handbooks, and then an analysis of text readability and other literacy demands.

Girl Scouts of the USA

Juliette Gordon Low founded Girl Scouting in 1912 in her hometown of Savannah, Georgia. After meeting Robert Baden-Powell, the founder of Boy Scouts, Low wanted to create a similar organization specifically for girls that would promote self-reliance and resourcefulness in young women (High-Pippert, 2015). Likewise, Girl Scouting's oath and law are fashioned after Boy Scouts, and both organizations share the same motto "Be Prepared." Although organization of levels, ranks, and units differ, both promote acquisition of new skills and service-oriented leadership.

Handbook Description

The Girl Scout handbooks were all designed as enclosed three-ring "Trapper Keeper"-style binders that locked in front and were divided into three primary sections: (1) Handbook, (2) Badges, and (3) My Girl Scouts (see Figure 21.2). The handbook section introduced the young girl to the Girl Scout Promise and Law, origins of Girl Scouting, ceremonies, uniform, and insignia. The handbook section also included two maps, one locating all the other Girl Scout councils in the United States and the wider international association of Girl Guides and Girl Scouts. The other depicted a metaphorical map, illustrating the journey and adventures awaiting the Girl Scout. Finally, each of the handbooks, except for Brownies, provided a description and planning guide for each of the three Girl Scout awards: Bronze Award for Juniors, Silver Award for Cadettes, and Gold Award for Seniors (or Ambassadors).

After the handbook, each guidebook included mini badge manuals and a "My Girl Scouts" section. Badge topics ranged from traditional (or legacy) badge categories in Girl Scouting, including cooking, citizenship, and nature, to more contemporary topics, such as financial literacy and entrepreneurship. The third section, "My Girl Scouts," personalized the Girl Scouting experience for individual girls

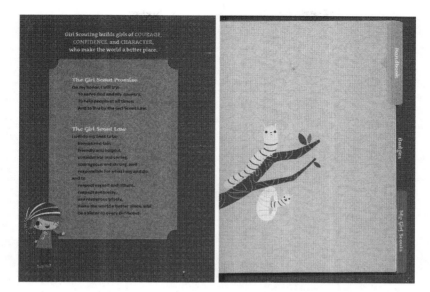

FIGURE 21.2 Brownie "Trapper-Keeper" Style Three-Ring Binder and Handbook

with a Brownie Elf cut-out paper doll (for Brownies), stickers for Brownies and Juniors, and spaces for drawing or writing about their experiences in Girl Scouting.

Readability and Other Literacy Demands

We derived the readability for Girl Scout handbooks from multiple points in each of the handbook sections, exemplar merit badges, and award guidelines. Figure 21.3 demonstrates the average readability for the different age groups from these respective sections. Notably, the handbook for Brownies shows the greatest disparity of nearly five grades. Readability for the Senior handbook was the only one easier on average for the corresponding age group.

Although sentence structure and text organization in the Girl Scout guidebooks were very clear and easy to follow, the cooking and robotics merit badge denoted challenging or specialized vocabulary at every level analyzed. For example, in the Brownie cooking merit badge guide, "Snacks" on one page alone included such multisyllabic terms as appliances, ingredients, and scavenger. The Junior guidebook "Simple Meals" incorporated unique cooking methods as "braised" or "sautéed" or food products, such as quinoa and couscous. The Robotics handbooks comprised even more specialized and technical vocabulary. As such, each handbook included a glossary ranging from 10 to nearly 30 "words to know" within the first few pages. Although one might expect highly specialized vocabulary in the STEM field of Robotics, the vocabulary in Girl Scout cooking merit badges also demonstrated a

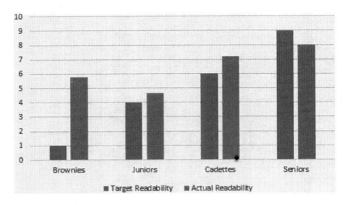

FIGURE 21.3 Analysis of Text Readability for Sample Girl Scout Texts

high number of likely unfamiliar terms and concepts that are undefined in context, which would produce higher demands of the girls reading the handbooks.

Essential to completing various tasks for different merit badges and Girl Scout awards was comprehension of the varied task requirements involved. In this way, girls would apply a range of comprehension literacy and language skills to discuss, research, create, map, and design different performance-based tasks. Girl Scouting includes a unique attribute at the conclusion of each merit badge, regardless of age, connecting skill development and service. Using first-person language, the merit badge states "Now that I've earned this badge, I can give service by …" and presents three bulleted suggestions. Afterwards, girls are encouraged to consider how they are going to provide such service by writing a response to the following prompt, "I'm inspired to …"

In addition to these writing prompts at the conclusion of each merit badge, we noted the greatest number of literacy supports for the service-oriented awards, i.e., Bronze for Juniors, Silver for Cadettes, and Gold for Seniors/Ambassadors. Most take the form of multicolumn planning charts. For instance, an "Observation List" for Juniors and the "Issue Chart" for Cadettes assist with the brainstorming process (see Figure 21.4). Such charts help young people visually organize their ideas for easy and clear reference.

Scouts BSA

The Boy Scouts of America was founded in 1910 by Robert Baden-Powell. The Scouting program is divided into two major divisions according to age and activities, i.e., Cub Scouts and Scouts BSA. Cub Scouts range from kindergarten to fifth grade and Scouts BSA 11–17 years. In 2019, the official name was changed from Boys Scouts of America to Scouts BSA to include girls in Scouting. The Scouting

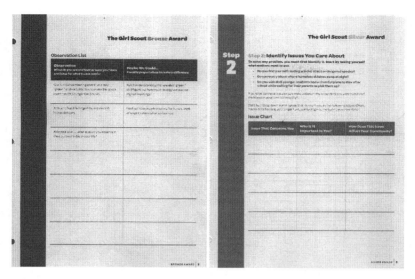

FIGURE 21.4 Observation and Issue Charts from Junior and Cadette Handbooks, Respectively

program teaches values consistent with good citizenship, character development, personal fitness, and leadership – values found in the Scout Oath and Scout Law.

Handbook Description

Each level of the Scouting program has an official handbook, which is a guide that provides all of the information a Scout needs to complete program requirements and achieve the relevant rank (i.e., Tiger Cub). Currently, all Scouting handbooks are spiral-bound with dimensions measured to be roughly 8 inches by 5 inches, include approximately 400 pages, and are consistent in their organization and formulaic formatting. After the booklet, each handbook is then organized into three main sections: (1) Welcome, (2) Program Requirements, and (3) Elective Requirements. The welcome section introduces the youth to Scouting, origins of Scouting, organization and structure, and other important traditions and routines in Scouting. The program and elective requirement sections in all Scouting handbooks underscore enjoying adventures that lead to completion of achievement rank and ultimate pathway to becoming a person of good character.

Readability and Literacy Demands

Similar to Girl Scouting, the readability for the handbooks for younger Scouts all exceeded the corresponding grade levels of the youth (see Figure 21.5). Also,

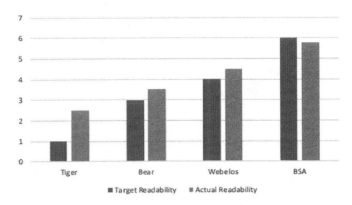

FIGURE 21.5 Analysis of Text Readability for Cub Scouting and Scouts BSA Sample Texts

similar to Girl Scouting, the greatest variance appears with the youngest age group included in this sample, Tigers, while the readability for Scouts BSA handbooks (both for boys and girls) is actually slightly less than target.

For qualitative analysis, we again looked at elements such as text features, language function, and tasks. With respect to text organization, required and elective adventures included a title, picture, and numbered list with information on how the Scout completes the requirements. Common text features found across the handbooks included titles, headings, sidebars, inset photos, and pictures. Text features tended to be simple and merely supplementary to the meaning of text (e.g., images of cooking tools, Scouts participating in adventure/task). The handbooks regularly used simple sentence structure, easy vocabulary, and second-person voice to interact more directly with the Scout. Bear, Webelos, and Scout BSA handbooks increasingly incorporated more academic or technical vocabulary, which were often defined in context (e.g., "the lines on weather maps, called isobars, show the movement of weather systems," bold font removed by authors) and supported with text features such as bold print, pictures and labeled diagrams.

We observed a varied use of context-dependent language functions, but a more limited range of language tasks. For example, the first few requirements often included words such as "list, identify, describe, tell, discuss," and as the requirements progressed in complexity so did the language function (e.g., show, complete, make, demonstrate, plan, and create). Furthermore, we also noted strong progression throughout the levels of advancement in the Scouting handbooks. Then regarding language tasks, the Scout handbooks strongly favored the use of oral communication over written or visual modes of communication. Tasks often involved Scouts talking, sharing, and demonstrating their newly acquired knowledge and skills with others with limited opportunities for Scouts to write, draw, or illustrate. The few instances represented listing and recording, rather than higher-order critical thinking and reflection.

4-H

4-H, which stands for the four central components of the organization's creed "head, heart, hands, and health,"[1] is actually the oldest of the three organizations. A.B. Graham began the organization in 1902 as a youth program in Clark County, Ohio, and was called "The Tomato Club" or "The Corn Growing Club"[2] (4-H, 2020a). Around the beginning of World War I, food and agriculture extension offices began sponsoring and partnering with local clubs to provide curriculum and resources. Unlike Scouts BSA (formerly Boy Scouts of America) and Girl Scouts of America, 4-H has traditionally been a co-educational youth organization that encourages children ages 8–18 to become leaders through hands-on projects in areas like science, agriculture, healthy living, and civic engagement.

Handbook Description

Unlike Girls Scouts and Scouts BSA, 4-H does not produce organizational handbooks per se, but rather topic-specific project handbooks that resemble activities and lessons found in educational workbooks. In fact, 4-H suggests that the organization has a "national curriculum" developed by over 100 public universities. The handbooks are typically printed on standard 8.5 inch by 11 inch paper, average between 30 and 120 pages, and are spiral- or staple-bound. Common organizational features include a brief introduction to the topic and project guide, table of contents, note to the project helper, and glossary. Beyond the basic organization, however, the handbooks vary widely, likely due to differential funding sources. In fact, two of the four sets of handbooks reviewed denoted additional external sponsors.

Readability and Literacy Demands

Similar to Girl Scouts and Scouts BSA, 4-H handbooks demonstrated text readabilities above target level. The results (see Figure 21.6) indicated an average disparity between target readability and actual readability of two grades.

As mentioned, text features varied widely in the 4-H handbooks. For instance, light-colored borders with different pictures of foods and cooking implements lined the edges of each page in the cooking handbooks. Text

---

[1] The 4-H pledge is "I pledge my head to clearer thinking, my heart to greater loyalty, my hands to larger service, and my health to better living, for my club, my community, my country and my world" (4-H Pledge, 2020b).

[2] The website does not explain the variance of original names.

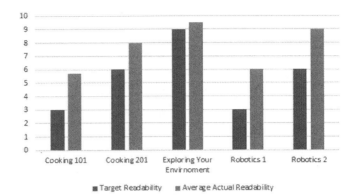

FIGURE 21.6 Analysis of Text Readability for Sample Texts from 4-H Project Manuals

was consistently written in a recipe format that included a list of ingredients, equipment needed, and steps for preparing the recipe. Bullet points, lists of numbers, and bold print were used throughout as common text features for recipes. Other common texts features included headings and black and white pictures related to cooking.

Handbooks for robotics and environmental stewardship, on the other hand, involved varied text features such as pictures, inset photos, shaded text boxes, sidebars, labeled diagrams, charts, and graphs. The Junk Drawer Robotics handbook, for instance, included images of different architectural engineering tools and structures and asked project participants to observe design and material shapes in the real world. Although the environmental stewardship handbook incorporated fewer text features, the page layout was rich with blues, greens, and browns, appropriate for a handbook about caring for the earth and environmental stewardship.

Similar to Girl Scouts and Scouts BSA, sentence structure in 4-H handbooks was largely simple and straightforward. The handbooks also tended to use second-person language, as in "The data operations palette gives you a whole new set of tools that you can use to make your programs more powerful and useful." We noted the use of highly specialized and technical vocabulary across all 4-H handbooks, often defined in context or within small sidebars. The texts demonstrated clear developmental progression for strong knowledge and skill acquisition. Also like Girl Scouts and Scouts BSA, ideas were presented in an objective and performance-based manner, requiring youth to apply higher-order thinking skills.

Language function and language tasks promoted the use of a variety of reading comprehension skills, such as activating background knowledge, summarizing, predicting, drawing conclusions, comparing and contrasting, and problem-solving. Junk Drawer Robotics specifically identified and organized the progression of

TABLE 21.2 Sample Portion of Anticipation Guide in Cooking 201

I know ...	Before	After
The cause of food-borne illnesses	1 2 3	1 2 3
How to prevent food-borne illnesses	1 2 3	1 2 3
How to use food thermometers	1 2 3	1 2 3

activities based upon increasingly challenging skills in its headings: Experiencing, Sharing and Processing, and Generalizing and Applying.

Notably, 4-H handbooks incorporated numerous literacy supports to facilitate youths' comprehension and engagement in these higher-order cognitive tasks. For instance, each cooking handbook included a "What Do You Know?" Anticipation Guide Project; participants are asked to perform a self-assessment of their knowledge of various skills before and after completion of all requirements (Kozen et al., 2006). Table 21.2 represents the first three of 25 concepts or skills in the anticipation/reaction guide from Cooking 201.

To activate background knowledge about what is and is not a robot, the Robotics 1 handbook with EV3 included a visually supported checklist for different everyday objects (see Figure 21.7). Other literacy supports include short-answer comprehension checks, graphic organizers, and discussion protocols.

Additionally, the EV3 Robotics handbooks and environmental steward-ship integrated frequent "writing-to-learn" opportunities with dedicated spaces for taking notes and reflecting upon what was learned in the activities (see Figure 21.8). Finally, many of the 4-H texts also provided technological supports with links to videos and websites for additional information.

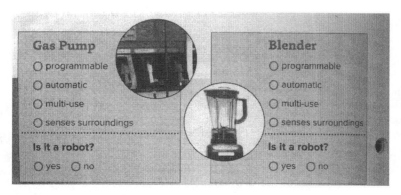

FIGURE 21.7 Robot Checklist from Robotics 1 with EV3

FIGURE 21.8 Writing and Reflection Sample from Environmental Science Handbook

Discussion and Conclusion

All three youth organizations profess strong commitments to leadership, civic participation, and character development. Each of them produces multiple handbooks that enable full participation within these organizations. However, there has been little investigation into the nature of the literacy and language demands expected within these texts. Following Fairclough's (2003) focus on linguistic text features as meaning-making resources, we analyzed multiple text features, literacy supports, language functions and tasks. We found important patterns within text readability, vocabulary, and use of literacy tools for comprehension support.

In regard to readability, we found that a significant majority of the exemplar texts from the three youth organizations were written above target readability. Grade disparities between target and actual readability ranged from one to five grade levels for elementary-aged youth. For high school-aged youth in Girl Scouts and Scouts BSA, text readability demonstrates the opposite trend with text readability largely easier than target grade levels. The majority of the exemplar handbooks in 4-H, however, identified grade levels 3–12, documenting readability trends more difficult. The environmental stewardship handbook demonstrated only a half grade difference between target and actual text readability.

In the case of literacy demands, we noted a wide range of language functions, (e.g., show, complete, make, demonstrate, plan, and create), which demonstrated strong developmental progression. These language demands positively supported performance-based outcomes in each organization. However, we also observed expectations for youth to comprehend a significant number of challenging technical vocabulary. In many cases, youth would not encounter such specialized vocabulary in regular school or home settings, increasing the challenge to independently read the handbooks.

The limited number of literacy supports within the handbooks presented another challenge. Both Girl Scouts and Scouts BSA primarily incorporated literacy supports in preparation and reporting stages for their major awards. 4-H demonstrated the widest use of literacy supports to activate background knowledge, organize information, and apply ideas to new situations. Likewise, 4-H provided more frequent opportunities for writing, as quick comprehension assessments and reflection, as well as collaborative discussions, even including discussion protocols in one set of handbooks sampled. Girl Scouts similarly encouraged collaborative brainstorming and problem-solving, but appeared to prioritize personalized, reflective writing. Scouts BSA handbooks, however, portrayed communication skills as means for reporting information with prompts like: "arrange to talk to your facilitator" or "discuss, describe, and explain." The handbooks incorporated limited opportunities for written communication other than occasional written reports.

Finally, as we discuss the differences in literacy demands within these texts, we must acknowledge issues raised in such visually laden texts, the roles of the adult leaders to support literacy, and differential funding sources. Visual compositional elements provide important scaffolding for understanding, which warrant future considerations. These findings also raise important questions around adult leaders and their role in supporting youths' literacy practices, specifically independent reading and communicating using visual, audible, and digital materials. As such, we advocate for support for adult leaders for literacy learning within such youth organizations. To do so, they might consider partnering with local P12 school districts to provide professional development training for adult leaders in the following ways:

- Providing workshops that can lend academic support in literacy practices
- Developing training modules and resources
- Identifying additional resources for adult leadership

How successful youth are in these organizations depends on their adult leaders' understanding of and their role in supporting the literacy demands of the programs.

References

4-H. (2020a). 4-H History. Retrieved from https://4-h.org/about/history/

4-H. (2020b). 4-H Pledge. Retrieved from https://4-h.org/about/what-is-4-h/4-h-pledge/

Alvermann, D. E., Young, J. P., Green, C., & Wisenbaker, J. M. (1999). Adolescents' perceptions and negotiations of literacy practices in after-school read and talk clubs. *American Educational Research Journal, 36*(2), 221–264. https://doi.org/10.2307/1163539

Cope, B., & Kalantzis, M. (Eds.). (2000). *Multiliteracies: Literacy learning and the design of social futures.* Psychology Press.

Fairclough, N. (2003). *Analysing discourse: Textual analysis for social research*. Routledge. https://doi.org/10.4324/9780203697078

Fry, E. (1968). A readability formula that saves time. *Journal of Reading, 11*(7), 513–578.

Gourlay, L., & Oliver, M. (2012). Beyond "the social": Digital literacies as sociomaterial practice. In R. Goodfellow & M. R. Lea (Eds.), *Literacy in the digital university: Critical perspectives on learning, scholarship, and technology* (pp. 93–108). Routledge.

Heath, S. B. (2010). Family literacy or community learning? Some critical questions on perspective. In K. Dunsmore & D. Fisher (Eds.), *Bringing literacy home* (pp. 15–41). International Reading Association. https://doi.org/10.1598/0711.01

High-Pippert, A. (2015). Girltopia: Girl Scouts and the leadership development of girls. *Girlhood Studies, 8*(2), 137–152. https://doi.org/10.3167/ghs.2015.080210

Hull, G., & Schultz, K. (2001). Literacy and learning out of school: A review of theory and research. *Review of Educational Research, 71*(4), 575–611. https://doi.org/10.3102/00346543071004575

International Literacy Association. "Why literacy?" Retrieved August 8, 2019 from https://literacyworldwide.org/about-us/why-literacy

Kozen, A. A., Murray, R. K., & Windell, I. (2006). Increasing all students' chance to achieve: Using and adapting anticipation guides with middle school learners. *Intervention in School and Clinic, 41*(4), 195–200. https://doi.org/10.1177/10534512060410040101

Merriam, S. B. (1998). *Qualitative research and case study applications in education*. Jossey-Bass.

Morrell, E. (2015). *Critical literacy and urban youth: Pedagogies of access, dissent, and liberation*. Routledge. https://doi.org/10.4324/9780203937914

Tellis, W. M. (1997). Introduction to case study. *The Qualitative Report, 3*(2), 1–14. Retrieved from https://nsuworks.nova.edu/tqr/vol3/iss2/4 https://doi.org/10.1108/10650749710187617

Walsh, M. (2010). Multimodal literacy: What does it mean for classroom practice? *The Australian Journal of Language and Literacy, 33*(3), 211–239.

Winch, G., Ross Johnston, R., March, P., Ljungdahl, L., & Holliday, M. (2010). *Literacy: Reading and writing and children's literature* (4th ed.). Oxford University Press.

Winn, M. T. (2010). "Betwixt and between": Literacy, liminality, and the celling of Black girls. *Race Ethnicity and Education, 13*(4), 425–447. https://doi.org/10.1080/13613321003751601

University of California. (2017). Language functions and forms. Retrieved October 28, 2019 from http://prodev.elpa21.org/module2/module2/resources/LanguageFunctionsForms.pdf

22

BEHIND THE FENCE

A Reading Partnership with the Department of Juvenile Justice

Mary E. Styslinger

UNIVERSITY OF SOUTH CAROLINA

The United States has the highest prison rate in the world (Walmsley, 2018). Despite the fact that this country has less than 5% of the world's inhabitants, we house almost 25% of the total prison population (Lee, 2015). There are more than 2.1 million prisoners in the United States compared to 1.65 million in China, 583,000 in the Russian Federation, 230,000 in Iran, and 204,000 in Mexico (Walmsley, 2018). Our incarceration rate is about 6 times that of Canada, between 6 and 9 times that of Western European countries, and between 2 and 10 times that of Northern European countries (Lee, 2015). About 1 in 37 adults in the United States was under some form of correctional supervision at the end of 2015 (Kaeble & Glaze, 2016), and on any given day, nearly 60,000 youth under age 18 are incarcerated in juvenile jails and prisons in the United States (American Civil Liberties Union, 2020).

As educators, administrators, and community members, we need not only be aware that we are living in the "age of incarceration" (Hill, 2013), but also recognize the need to develop constructive responses to it. Until an alternative to imprisonment is supported, we have a social responsibility to design curriculum and pedagogy that expands instruction in correctional facilities.

Drawing upon social justice theory and pedagogy, this chapter begins with a review of literature revealing the interrelationships between literacy and incarceration. Next, a university–school partnership in which pre-service English teacher candidates read with incarcerated youth is detailed. Research which determined the effects of the reading partnership on teacher candidates and students is shared. The chapter concludes with a discussion of the partnership sustainability and challenges that could impact future collaborations.

Review of Literature

There can be no denying the relationship between literacy, graduation, and incarceration. Hernandez (2011) compared reading scores and graduation results of almost 4000 students and determined that a student who cannot read on grade level by third grade is four times less likely to graduate by age 19 than a child who does read proficiently at that time. If the student who cannot read on grade level lives in poverty, then that same student is 13 times less likely to graduate on time. Couple these facts with a study by researchers at Northeastern University who found that about 1 in every 10 young male high school dropouts is in jail or juvenile detention centers as compared to one in 35 young male high school graduates (Sum et al., 2009), then the connection between a lack of literacy and the nation's growing prison population can be made. The picture is even bleaker for students of color. In 2015, black children were five times more likely than white children to be incarcerated (Olivares, 2017).

The need for expanded literacy instruction in juvenile detention centers has been widely documented and supported (Christle & Yell, 2008; Krezmien & Mulcahy, 2008; Vacca, 2008). Whereas the perceived goal of juvenile detention centers is to rehabilitate youthful offenders, recidivism, or the repeated illegal behavior resulting in additional jail time, is generally viewed as the gauge by which the success of the rehabilitation can be determined. Decreasing illiteracy rates among juveniles is a key factor in reducing recidivism rates in the United States (Music, 2012). Records collected from penal institutions indicate inmates have a 16% chance of returning to prison if they receive literacy help as opposed to 70% chance for those who receive no such help (O'Cummings et al., 2010).

However, conventional teaching methods are not always successful for youth who may not have had positive experiences with traditional schooling (Jacobi, 2008; Snyder & Sickmund, 2006). Instead, alternative literacy practices (Jacobi, 2008) are encouraged. Because the national average length of confinement for youth is 106 days in public juvenile detention centers (Sickmund & Puzzanchera, 2014), such alternative literacy instruction also needs to be implemented in a short amount of time.

Inspired by a need for action, a small-scale response to the call for short-term, alternative literacy curriculum and pedagogy that expands instruction in correctional facilities, the reading partnership described in this chapter attempts to serve the interests of incarcerated youth and larger community through a collaboration between a state university and Department of Juvenile Justice (DJJ).

Theory Underlying Partnership

This partnership is grounded in a commitment to social justice theory and practice. Teachers for social justice structure learning experiences which develop critical awareness, fostering in students a sense of agency and capacity to interrupt and change oppressive patterns in themselves and in the world, which surrounds them. In short, they teach by raising student consciousness and then trusting that students "will feel increasingly challenged and obliged to respond" to the inequities and injustices they come to recognize and realize (Freire, 2000/1970, p. 81). Social justice informed learning experiences help students develop their critical awareness and support an ethical approach toward social action and change. As Freire (2000/1970) advocated, students need to be engaged in consciousness-raising problem solving. Agency and engagement are intrinsic to social justice teaching in a democracy because as learners challenge individual and systemic forms of injustice, they also learn how to be active and engaged citizens.

In order to support and develop teachers for social justice, college and university programs can offer opportunities for collaboration and critical engagement while also providing authentic opportunities to develop practical knowledge (Carnes, 2019; Kelly, 2018). We know teacher candidates struggle to become teachers for social justice as they enter the classroom (Ajayi, 2017; DeMink-Carthew, 2018; Downing et al., 2018; Goodwin & Darity, 2019; Ra, 2017). We need examples of social justice practice in higher education which concurrently raise critical consciousness and improve pedagogical knowledge.

Whenever a social justice framework is applied to teaching, we should always have the goal to act (Stachowiak, 2017). The purpose of this reading partnership is to help teacher candidates use the tools of literacy and provide opportunities to take action as a way of using the word to transform the world (Freire, 2000/1970). Providing teacher candidates with an opportunity for collaborative social action through literacy teaching allows them to demonstrate the knowledge they have gained through social justice learning experiences and gives them a platform to display their ability to transform knowledge into productive action for the betterment of society (Naiditch, 2010).

Because this partnership involves collaborative planning between DJJ and the university, between teacher candidates and DJJ students, it can be considered a social action project. It is an attempt to reach beyond community service, which can be wrought with false understandings of need and a lack of planning and collaboration between the "helpers" and the "helped" (Stachowiak, 2017). Lash and Kroeger (2018) outline social action projects as a meaningful component of teacher preparation programs that allow teacher candidates to contextualize teaching for social justice and to demonstrate best practices. In an effort to assist teacher candidates as they transform their conceptual knowledge into practical application, Lash and Kroeger (2018) suggest that social action projects can help teacher candidates conceptualize the basic tenets of teaching for social justice and offer an "inroad" for teacher candidates to understand current issues (p. 706).

Description of Partnership

For more than ten years, I have facilitated reading partnerships between university students and incarcerated youth. This short-term, alternative literacy practice has the potential to serve the interests of incarcerated youth by challenging traditional curricula, pedagogical practices, and culturally irrelevant texts, which often contribute to the alienation and disempowerment of many students (Morrell, 2005). As participating youth have the opportunity to select a book based on their experiences and interests, more culturally responsive text may allow students to learn life lessons as they see themselves and their circumstances reflected in the reading. In addition, as students read one-on-one with a teacher candidate who designs pedagogy according to individual needs and interests, these youth may be exposed to more culturally responsive teaching. As Gay (2010, p. 31) explains, when we see cultural differences as assets, use cultural knowledge to guide curriculum and instruction, challenge racial and cultural stereotypes, and become change agents for social justice and academic equity, then we are teaching in culturally responsive ways.

This university–school partnership also endeavors to meet the needs of teacher candidates through the provision of a diverse teaching experience. Researchers have long argued that teacher education programs need to move beyond traditional course work and include field experiences that allow teacher candidates to work with diverse students in diverse settings (Adams et al., 2005; Cooper, 2007; Keengwe, 2010; Vaughan, 2005). These experiences allow teacher candidates to collaborate with students who are frequently culturally, ethnically, academically, and socioeconomically different from themselves. It needs to be mentioned, however, that difference does not denote deficiency. Experiences such as these can be invaluable in teacher education programs because they can encourage a change in teacher candidates' conceptions about students and their families (Cooper, 2007).

This reading partnership experience is required for secondary English teacher candidates enrolled in a summer intensive adolescent literacy seminar, one of the courses required within a graduate teacher certification program located at a university in the southeastern United States. Participation is voluntary and optional for students enrolled through the DJJ. No funding is necessary for the partnership other than that garnered by the university from tuition which covers the cost of instruction. No costs are associated with the project other than books provided to students.

Prior to meeting with the students, English teacher candidates build their literacy background knowledge, engaging in readings, discussions, and assignments in a typical university setting. We begin by reflecting on personal experiences, critically considering the contextual and cultural experiences that have shaped us as readers, and laying an important foundation in understanding issues of justice and equity. Next, we explore definitions of reading and consider different models of reading instruction. We review data published by the National Assessment of Educational Progress (NAEP) and publications from NCTE's Commission on Reading. In order to gain a window into a reader's processes, we learn how to conduct a miscue analysis and facilitate a retrospective miscue analysis. We read texts (Gallagher, 2009; Mueller, 2001) to gain understanding of why readers may struggle and to learn how to support readers before, during, and after reading (Appleman & Graves, 2011; Beers, 2003; Tovani, 2000). Tatum (2005, 2009) reminds us of the importance of always being culturally responsive, and we review the tenets of culturally relevant pedagogy. We read excerpts from *Literacy behind Bars* (Styslinger et al., 2017), learning from those who are incarcerated and those who teach them. Vital is deepening an understanding of the relationships between incarceration and literacy if we are to educate for any sustainable social change.

Along with reading professional texts related to adolescent literacy research, theory, culture, and pedagogy, teacher candidates are immersed in young adult literature. They scour the YALSA (www.ala.org/yalsa/booklistsawards/booklistsbook) and In the Margins (inthemarginssite.blog/awards-list/) award sites and browse books from the classroom library, knowing they will soon need to select novels to read alongside incarcerated youth. Once a strong literacy foundation has been more firmly established, typically a 20-meeting-hour endeavor, students travel behind the fence, and all future meetings are held on site at a school associated with the DJJ.

At the initial meeting, following a group ice breaker, the students and teacher candidates are partnered randomly. DJJ students, male and female, range in age from 12 to 18 with reading levels from fourth grade to college level. The English teacher candidates are forewarned not to ask questions about why the students are incarcerated; instead, they begin conversations with questions about school, sports, music, movies, video games, and likes and dislikes in an effort to find books of interest. The teacher candidates share information about their own likes and dislikes as well. Eventually they administer and record a reading interview adapted for adolescent readers (Goodman et al., 2005). This interview format helps the teacher candidates discover how students define reading and consider the role of literacy, in all its forms, in their lives. After this first meeting, teacher candidates listen to the recording a number of times and take detailed notes, thinking about this reader. What makes him unique? How did she come to language and reading? What are his interests? Instead of deficits, what funds of knowledge does she bring to literacy? Teacher candidates summarize their thinking in relation to this student and justify book selections.

At the second meeting, teacher candidates talk with students about what they have learned from the interview and share their notes, asking any necessary follow-up questions. Eventually they introduce book choices, explaining the books' relationship to the reading interview and allowing students to select among three works. Each book choice is introduced through a pre-reading strategy designed by the teacher candidate. For example, a teacher candidate creates a list of general statements related to key ideas in Angela Johnson's *The First Part Last* (i.e., Your choices define who you are. It's okay to ask for help when you need it. It's important to take responsibility for your actions. Only mothers know how to take care of children. The best time for learning is during a struggle). Before reading, the reading partners agree or disagree with each statement. Next, they discuss their responses, activating prior knowledge. Once a novel is selected, the reading part-ners collaboratively establish a reading calendar.

Over the next four meetings, teacher candidates frontload, support, and extend the reading processes of students, planning and facilitating pre-reading, during reading, and post-reading strategies in relation to the novels selected. All planning is influenced by the initial reading interview. For example, a teacher candidate and DJJ student who love to draw, sketch/visualize Jonas's colorless world in Lois Lowry's *The Giver*.

In addition, teacher candidates administer and record a miscue analysis (Goodman, 1969) with different genre (i.e., poetry, prose) including an oral and silent retelling in order to better understand the cue systems (i.e., graphophonic, syntactic, and semantic) utilized by individual readers. At a meeting following the administration of the miscue analysis, teacher candidates facilitate a retro-spective miscue analysis (RMA) designed to foster metacognition. During an RMA, teacher candidates prompt students to consider reading miscues through guided questioning. Teacher candidates select miscues for discussion and help students become more reflective about their own reading processes, asking questions (Goodman & Marek, 1996) such as: Does the miscue make sense? Was the miscue corrected? Did that miscue affect your understanding of the text? After each meeting, teacher candidates and students reflect on their experiences through talking and writing and consider what they are learning about reading, readers, teachers, teaching, and each other. The partnership concludes after three weeks with a luncheon and the presentation of a new book by the teacher candidate to the student.

Research on Partnership

In order to determine the effects of this partnership experience on both teacher candidates and incarcerated youth, two studies have been conducted. As we know, teaching and research are reciprocal processes. There is no teaching without research and no research without teaching, Freire (2001) reminds us. The first inquiry (Styslinger et al., 2014), focused on teacher candidates, posed the following question: What are the effects of the reading partnership on teacher candidates' understandings of literacy and its relationship with issues of culture and ability? To answer this question, I engaged in the action research process.

Data were collected from 13 teachers pursuing initial certification in sec-ondary English ranging in age from 21 to 33 years old including eight females and five males; 11 identified as white, one African American, and one biracial. Interviews lasting 30–60 minutes were conducted and transcribed with six teacher candidates. To gather teacher candidates' understandings of literacy, cul-ture, and incarcerated youth, documents from the course, including definitions of reading (pre- and post-field experiences), literacy autobiographies, cultural autobiographies, profiles of incarcerated youth (pre- and post-field experiences), and a variety of free-writes which prompted response to assigned reading, literacy processes, and the importance and impact of culture on literacy (pre- and post-field experiences) were collected. A Demographic Background Questionnaire was adapted from Ritterhouse (2007) and provided to teacher candidates before and after partnership experiences. In addition, open-ended surveys including a Burke Interview and course evaluation (which included open responses) were administered.

Data were divided into pre- and post-reading partnership experience categories and then into subsequent data sets. Data were coded individually by three researchers, myself and two doctoral students, using a content analysis approach. Data were analyzed by set for pre and post understandings of literacy, culture, and incarcerated youth, and analyses were compared. In order to note any effects, findings were organized before and after the DJJ reading partnership.

Overall, findings indicated that reading partnership experiences expanded English teacher candidates' understandings of literacy, including its relationship with issues of culture and ability. By the end of their experiences, these English teacher candidates challenged stereotypes and wanted social justice.

Taking part in the reading partnership contributed to teacher candidates' increased understandings of literacy. Initially, teacher candidates explained reading only in terms of phonics and skills, drawing upon personal experiences with literacy instruction; post-field experiences, these same teachers, drawing upon new experiences with diverse students, emphasized "meaning" and "understanding." Whereas initial definitions of reading stressed the individual experience, after reading experiences with DJJ students, teacher candidates explained reading as a "collaborative" process which is "shared among participants," one that involves "teamwork" and "strategies." Later explanations of reading included references to culture as teachers noted the importance of choice in text, suggesting titles far beyond the canonical and classical works included prior to partnership experiences. Teacher candidates noted the importance of access to text, realizing its relationship to literacy growth. Teacher candidates also reflected on the perceptions students had of themselves as readers, recognizing the role this could play in perceived ability.

Reading partnership experiences contributed to the expanded understandings of the relationship between culture and literacy for teacher candidates. Prior to reading with incarcerated youth, these teacher candidates described the relationship as transactional (i.e., culture affects a transaction with text), textual (i.e., culture affects a teacher's choice of text), and impedimental (i.e., culture negatively affects a student's experience with literacy). After reading with diverse students, these teacher candidates still acknowledged the roles culture plays in reader transaction and text selection; however, they also included dialectical considerations, suggesting that *what* students read or say matters more than *how* they say. Notably absent was understanding culture as impediment, and in its place were questions, pondering literacy as a civil right.

Reading partnership experiences also altered perspectives of incarcerated youth. English teacher candidates were initially quick to characterize youth they would be reading alongside, describing them personally and academically in stereotypical ways. After working one-on-one with students, teacher candidates were resistant to characterize, categorize, or classify students, now seeing individuals. After reading partnership experiences, teacher candidates recognized incarcerated youth as capable and literate. They offered multifaceted descriptions, refusing to stereotype. An incarcerated youth is:

> … black, white and every shade in between. He is talkative and quiet. He reads and doesn't read. Some are beyond proficient, and some are still working readers. Some enjoy allusions to Greek mythology and some enjoy that, at least, the "Ball Don't Lie." They have complex thoughts and are filled with the same emotions that we all experience daily. They've made crucial mistakes, but so have we. They have a troubled past; but like everyone, they look to the future. They still smile, still enjoy being told that their opinions are valuable. And deep down, there is still some that want to do good work, make that valid point, and impress the teacher. Ultimately, an "incarcerated young person" is a phrase with only two words that are relevant to who they are.

A second action research study (Styslinger & Bunch, 2017) revealed the effects of the literacy partnership on students. After each session, students were asked to reflect on daily learning by answering the following questions: What did you learn about reading today? What did you learn about teachers and/or teaching today? Through a content analysis of a total of 70 exit slips completed by students after five meetings during the summer of 2015, I hoped to answer the following question: What are these youth learning about reading, teachers, and teaching from this literacy collaboration? Five prevalent themes were evident across student responses: reading is about meaning; reading is an active process; reading relates to life; teachers and readers are individuals; and teaching is hard work.

Throughout the collaboration, students at DJJ discovered and reiterated that reading is more about the process of meaning-making and less about reading words. They indicated that reading is "more than what's on the page." You have to "think about what you are reading" and you "gotta think outside the box." Students recognized that "sometimes you have to read between the lines and actually try to figure out what it is the writer [is] really talking about." Reading is a process through which to gain knowledge, and more than a few students realized they read too quickly and need to slow down in order to better understand.

DJJ students recognized that in order to understand, a reader has to be a practicing participant in the process. Reading is an active process that requires work to understand. As one student details, "A real reader will question, evaluate, predict, and respond to the material he reads." Another recalls his own process and proficiency:

> When we went back and went over my miscues, I saw that I will also read in my own words and put some of my own meanings into the book instead of just reading word for word. ... I am a better reader then I thought I was.

DJJ students realized their responsibility in becoming more literate, acknowledging they need to find their "likes and dislikes" in order to locate books and genre of interest. A few also declared that reading is a lifelong process, and even proficient readers can improve their reading strategies.

DJJ students connected reading to experience, conveying that "reading can make you look at things in much more detail." Students made personal connections: "If you pay attention to what you're reading, some situations in the book can relate to the situation in your life." One student even went so far as to acknowledge, "This experience has taught me not to hide what has happened in the past, but to reflect and elaborate on paper about them."

This collaborative endeavor helped students recognize and value the individual teacher. As DJJ students summarize: "All teachers are not the same"; "Some teachers take the time to understand you"; and "Teachers have their own unique and genuine style." They come to realize "teachers don't plan to make a subject lame" and many are "concerned about us" and are "dedicated."

And last, students became more aware of the hard work involved in teaching. DJJ students realized the preparation involved, gaining insight into daily planning and instruction. As one DJJ student admits, "teachers go through a lot of hard work to prepare things for us."

Sustainability of Partnership

Reading partnerships rooted in social justice theory and pedagogy offer rich resources for teacher education programs. I have evidenced a change in teacher candidates' understandings of literacy, culture, and ability, likely due to opportunities to read with diverse students in diverse settings. It is hoped that such experiences meet the needs of all involved, in this case, serving the interests of teacher candidates, incarcerated youth, and the larger community. Further research is needed to determine the effects of such experiences on students (especially in relation to rates of recidivism) and community, but I can attest to increased understandings of literacy, its relationship to culture and ability, and offer that such experiences may inform future efforts to teach for social justice.

Of course, there are logistical challenges along the way: student absences, scheduling difficulties, administrative changes, and time/space constraints, to name a few. There is also the underlying paradox of mandatory teacher candidate participation in social justice projects, but the potential of a partnership between a university and DJJ, among future teachers and incarcerated youth, should prevail over any difficulty. We can make efforts to teach for justice, knowing incarcerated youth and teacher candidates will walk away with greater understandings of reading, teaching, and each other. There is much to be learned from reading behind the fence.

References

Adams, A., Bondy, E., & Kuhel, K. (2005). Preservice teacher learning in an unfamiliar setting. *Teacher Education Quarterly, 32*(2), 41–62. Retrieved from www.teqjournal.org/TEQ%20 Website/Back%20Issues/Volume%2032/Volume%2032%20Number%202.html

Ajayi, L. (2017). Preservice teachers' perspectives on their preparation for social justice teaching. *Educational Forum, 81*(1), 52–67. https://doi.org/10.1080/00131725.2016.1242677

American Civil Liberties Union. (2020). *America's addiction to juvenile incarceration: State by state.* www.aclu.org/issues/juvenile-justice/youth-incarceration/americas-addiction-juvenile-incarceration-state-state

Appleman, D., & Graves, M. F. (2011). *Reading better, reading smarter: Designing literature lessons for adolescents.* Heinemann.

Beers, K. (2003). *When kids can't read, what teachers can do.* Heinemann.

Carnes, N. (2019). Supporting middle grades teacher candidates in becoming culturally competent. *Current Issues in Middle Level Education, 24*(1), 7–13. https://doi.org/10.20429/cimle.2019.240103

Christle, C. A., & Yell, M. L. (2008). Preventing youth incarceration through reading remediation: Issues and solutions. *Reading & Writing Quarterly, 24*, 148–176. https://doi.org/10.1080/10573560701808437

Cooper, J. E. (2007). Strengthening the case for community-based learning in teacher education. *Journal of Teacher Education, 58*(3), 1–11. https://doi.org.2F10.1177%2F0022487107299979

DeMink-Carthew, J. (2018). Learning to teach in a "world not yet finished": Social justice education in the middle level preservice teacher classroom. *Middle School Journal, 49*(4), 24–34. https://doi.org/10.1080/00940771.2018.1488471

Downing, G. A., Black, B., & Smith, E. L. (2018). Preservice teachers' views on social justice topics in the mathematics classroom. Paper presented at the Annual Meeting of the American Educational Research Association, New York City, NY, April 13.

Freire, P. (2000/1970). *Pedagogy of the oppressed* (M. B. Ramos, Trans.). The Continuum International. (Original work published 1970.)

Freire, P. (2001). *Pedagogy of freedom: Ethics, democracy, and civic courage* (P. Clarke, Trans.). Rowman & Littlefield.

Gallagher, K. (2009). *Readicide: How schools are killing reading and what you can do about it.* Stenhouse.

Gay, G. (2010). *Culturally responsive teaching: Theory, research, & practice* (2nd ed.). Teachers College Press.

Goodman, K. S. (1969). Analysis of oral reading miscues: Applied psycholinguists. *Reading Research Quarterly, 5*(1), 9–30.

Goodman, Y., & Marek, A. (1996). *Retrospective miscue analysis.* Richard C. Owen.

Goodman, Y., Watson, D., & Burke, C. (2005). *Reading miscue inventory: Alternative procedures.* Richard C. Owen.

Goodwin, A. L., & Darity, K. (2019). Social justice teacher educators: What kind of knowing is needed? *Journal of Education for Teaching: International Research and Pedagogy, 45*(1), 63–81. https://doi.org/10.1080/02607476.2019.1550606

Hernandez, D. J. (2011). *Double jeopardy: How third grade reading skills and poverty influence high school graduation.* Retrieved from https://files.eric.ed.gov/fulltext/ED518818.pdf

Hill, M. L. (2013) Teaching English in the age of incarceration. *English Journal, 102*(4), 16–18.

Jacobi, T. (2008). Writing for change: Engaging juveniles through alternative literacy education. *Journal of Correctional Education, 59*(2), 71–93. www.ncjrs.gov/pdffiles1/ojjdp/grants/251118.pdf

Kaeble, D., & Glaze, L. (2016). Correctional populations in the United States, 2015. Available from www.bjs.gov/content/pub/pdf/cypus15.pdf

Keengwe, J. (2010). Fostering cross cultural competence in preservice teachers through multicultural education experiences. *Early Childhood Education Journal, 38*, 197–204. https://doi.org/10.1007/s10643-010-0401-5.

Kelly, M. R. (2018). Stop, collaborate and listen: Co-designing social justice teacher education programs with preservice teachers. Doctoral dissertation, University of Colorado-Boulder. ProQuest LLC.

Krezmien, M. P., & Mulcahy, C. A. (2008). Literacy and delinquency: Current status of reading interventions with detained and incarcerated youth. *Reading & Writing Quarterly, 24*, 219–238. https://doi.org/10.1080/10573560701808601

Lash, M. J., & Kroeger, J. (2018). Seeking justice through social action projects: Preparing teachers to be social actors in local and global problems. *Policy Futures in Education, 16*(6), 691–708. https://doi.org/10.1177%2F1478210317751272

Lee, M.Y. H. (2015, July 7). Yes the U.S. locks people up at a higher rate than any other country. The Washington Post. Retrieved from www.washingtonpost.com/news/fact-checker/wp/2015/07/07/yes-u-s-locks-people-up-at-a-higher-rate-than-any-other-country/

Morrell, E. (2005). Critical English education. *English Education, 37*(4), 312–321.

Mueller, P. N. (2001). *Lifers: Learning from at-risk adolescent readers.* Heinemann.

Music, E. (2012). Teaching literacy in order to turn the page on recidivism. *Journal of Law & Education, 41*(4), 723–730.

Naiditch, F. (2010). Critical pedagogy and the teaching of reading for social action. *Critical Questions in Education, 1*(2), 94–107. https://files.eric.ed.gov/fulltext/EJ1047717.pdf

O'Cummings, M. O., Bardack, S., & Gonsoulin, S. (2010). The importance of literacy for youth involved in the juvenile justice system. Retrieved from https://neglected-delinquent.ed.gov/resource/ndtac-issue-brief-importance-literacy-youth-involved-juvenile-justice-system

Olivares, J. (2017). Fewer youths incarcerated, but gap between blacks and whites worsens. Retrieved from www.npr.org/2017/09/27/551864016/fewer-youths-incarcerated-but-gap-between-blacks-and-whites-worsens

Ra, S. (2017). Preservice teachers' entering beliefs and preconceptions about teaching for social justice. Doctoral dissertation, George Mason University. ProQuest LLC.

Ritterhouse, G. E. (2007). Perceptions of beginning teachers' preparation for culturally responsive teaching: Voices from the field. Doctoral dissertation, Wichita State University. ProQuest LLC.

Sickmund, M., & Puzzanchera, C. (2014). *Juvenile offenders and victims: 2014 national report.* National Center for Juvenile Justice.

Snyder, H., & Sickmund, M. (2006). *Juvenile offenders and victims: 2006 national report.* US Department of Justice, Office of Justice Programs, Office of Juvenile Justice and Delinquency Prevention.

Stachowiak, D. M. (2017). Social action and social justice: A path to critical consciousness for engagement. *Voices in the Middle, 24*(3), 29–32.

Styslinger, M. E., & Bunch, T. R. (2017). Reading buddies: A school–university partnership. In M. E. Styslinger, K. Gavigan, & K. Albright (Eds.), *Literacy behind bars* (pp. 71–77). Rowman & Littlefield.

Styslinger, M. E., Gavigan, K., & Albright, K. (Eds.). (2017). *Literacy behind bars: Successful reading and writing strategies for use with incarcerated youth and adults.* Rowman & Littlefield.

Styslinger, M. E., Walker, N., & Eberlin, E. L. (2014). Teaching in third space: Understanding pre-service teachers' reading with incarcerated teens. *Journal of Reading Education, 39*(2), 23–29.

Sum, A., Khatiwada, I., McLaughlin, J., & Palma, S. (2009). The consequences of dropping out of high school: Joblessness and jailing for high school dropouts and the high cost for taxpayers. Retrieved from www.northeastern.edu/clms/wp-content/uploads/The_Consequences_of_Dropping_Out_of_High_School.pdf

Tatum, A. W. (2005). *Teaching reading to black adolescent males: Closing the achievement gap.* Stenhouse.

Tatum, A. W. (2009). *Reading for their life: (Re)Building the textual lineages of African American adolescent males.* Heinemann.

Tovani, C. (2000). *I read it, but I don't get it: Comprehension strategies for adolescent readers.* Stenhouse.

Vacca, J. S. (2008). Crime can be prevented if schools teach juvenile offenders to read. *Children and Youth Services Review, 30*, 1055–1062. www.researchgate.net/deref/http%3A%2F%2Fdx.doi.org%2F10.1016%2Fj.childy outh.2008.01.013 https://doi.org/10.1088/1475–7516/2008/01/013

Vaughan, W. (2005). Educating for diversity, social responsibility and action: Preservice teachers engage in immersion experiences. *Journal of Cultural Diversity, 12*(1), 26–30.

Walmsley, R. (2018). *World prison population list* (12th ed.). Institute for Criminal Policy Research. Retrieved from www.prisonstudies.org/sites/default/files/resources/downloads/wppl_12.pdf

23

THE EVOLUTION OF THE MILE READING MENTORING PROGRAM

The Role of Collaboration in a Teacher Education–Juvenile Corrections Partnership

Joanna C. Weaver, Timothy J. Murnen,
Meggan K. Hartzog, and Cynthia Bertelsen

BOWLING GREEN STATE UNIVERSITY

Historical Background

The Catalyst for the JRC Literacy Project

Teaching health education in a juvenile detention center (JDC) transformed my thinking regarding literacy. Literacy is a vital set of skills for youth to develop, and an important aspect of health education. A one-on-one reading mentoring program was in place in the JDC where I taught in Ohio. This program assisted students reading below a sixth-grade level by pairing them with a college student who taught fluency and comprehension from a scripted lesson. As students were pulled from my health class once a week to work with college students, I saw the value of literacy. Students returned to class volunteering to read aloud, writing more during our weekly journal assignments, and answering higher-order thinking questions relating to my health lessons. Foundational literacy skills empowered these students to begin obtaining necessary health literacy skills. The importance of a one-on-one reading mentoring program that focused on students' literacy needs influenced my decision to initiate a conversation about having a similar reading mentoring program in a JDC and juvenile residential center (JRC) near my current university community. To accomplish this, I needed to facilitate a collaborative partnership between a university and a JRC. In addition, this partnership would eventually need university student mentors and the student residents as integral to this collaboration.

(Meggan Hartzog, third author)

Theoretical Perspective

The Value of Collaboration

In the last ten years, there have been repeated calls for teacher education programs to reinvent themselves, to shift their focus toward a more field-centric model – where field experiences for pre-service teachers are central to the program rather than add-ons or peripheral experiences – and to develop collaborative partnerships between universities and school and community partners (Cochran-Smith & Villegas, 2014; Darling-Hammond et al., 2005; NCATE, 2010; Zeichner, 2010). Educational leaders continue to call on teacher education programs to develop more systematic approaches to these partnerships and to integrate them throughout the program from the first year to the last (AACTE, 2018). Zeichner's research in particular has explored various partnership configurations (Professional Development Schools, in-residence programs, etc.), noting that most descriptions of collaboration focus on the relationship between the pre-service teacher and the classroom mentor teacher rather than the institutions themselves (Zeichner, 1996, 2010). While large, grant-driven literacy intervention programs exist, such as *America Reads* (Worthy et al., 2003) and *Project MORE* (Putnam County ESC, 2020), limited evidence exists of collaborative efforts between university teacher education programs, schools, and community partners that focus on developing a sustained reading mentoring model.

While some research spotlights the benefits of collaborative approaches to reading instruction with "at-risk" youth (Allen & Swearingen, 2002; Styslinger, 2019; Styslinger et al., 2014; Williamson et al., 2013), we wanted to explore the role collaboration played in shaping the structure of a reading program at a local juvenile residential center (JRC), and the impact of such a collaborative model on all of the stakeholders involved.

Research on Literacy Among Students in Juvenile Correctional Facilities

The low level of literacy among youth who are incarcerated is well documented and widely discussed in research (Brunner, 1993; Guerra, 2012; Krezmien & Mulcahy, 2008; Krezmien et al., 2013; Malmgren & Leone, 2000; Williamson et al., 2013). Literacy's impact is captured in Jacobs' (2006) assertion that

> early reading and learning failures are precursors to unemployment (Bureau of Labor Statistics, 1999), crime (Ayers, 1999; Davis et al., 1999), drug addiction (National Institute on Drug Abuse, 1997), homelessness (National Law Center on Homelessness and Poverty, 1997), and prison sentences (Bureau of Justice Statistics, 1991).

(p. 112)

While several research studies suggest that reading instruction can be an effective tool in reducing recidivism (Center on Crime, Communities, and Culture, 1997; Guerra, 2012; Krezmien & Mulcahy, 2008; Krezmien et al., 2013; Malmgren & Leone, 2000), there is limited scholarship on the structure and function of any sustained reading programs for youth who are incarcerated. Most studies are brief research projects rather than long-term programs (Malmgren & Leone, 2000; Snowling et al., 2000), and few explore the development and structure of a sustained reading program grounded in collaboration (Styslinger et al., 2014).

In response to the limited scholarship on university undergraduate programs that provide reading mentorship to youth in correctional facilities, this chapter focuses on the evolution of a reading mentoring program designed for a local JRC through a collaboration of university faculty, JRC administrators, and undergraduate pre-service teacher education majors serving as mentors to the youth. While we touch on the impact on the JRC students, our primary focus in this piece is to describe the design of the collaboration and explore its value for all stakeholders.

Methodology

Our strong track record of successful mentor training and school partnerships at our university laid the foundation for the JRC mentoring partnership (Murnen et al., 2018). Driven by our desire to create a reading mentoring program that is sustained, systematic, and responsive to the diverse learning needs of the students at the JRC, we developed a study to examine the evolution of the *Mentoring in Literacy Enhancement* (*MILE*) program and the central role collaboration played in this process. The following research questions frame this study: How did the collaboration of the participants shape the development of the organizational structure of the *MILE* reading mentoring program? How did the collaboration impact planning, instructional decision-making, and reflective practice?

Participants

Participants included four interconnected groups: JRC administrators, university researchers, mentors (i.e., pre-service teachers), and JRC residents. The mentors, residents, and juvenile facility administrators are addressed by pseudonyms. The mentors in the fall semester – Gabby and Sandy – were recruited from a larger pool of reading mentors, based on their competence and interest. For ten weeks, the mentors each worked with a resident at the JRC every Tuesday and Thursday. In the following spring semester, this team was expanded to four mentors – Gabby, Carly, Shelby, and Callie – who mentored on Saturday mornings for ten weeks. The mentors and residents are integral to the development and evolution of the MILE program. Facility administrators included Tom, the county Juvenile Court

Executive Director, and Barb, the JRC Director. The roles of all of the participants are elaborated more fully in the program evolution description.

Data

For this study, data sources included mentors' reflection journals, researchers' notes from weekly conferences with the mentors, field notes from site observations, mentors' lesson plans, SOAP notes (Lenert, 2016; Many & Many, 2014), and facility administrators' reflections.

Method of Analysis

The primary tool for data analysis was the constant comparative method used in grounded theory (Kolb, 2012; Strauss & Corbin, 2008). During the pilot study (i.e., the first semester of our reading mentoring program at the JRC), researchers analyzed mentors' reflective journal entries along with field notes collected during site visits and weekly conferences with mentors, focusing on signature events and emerging themes in the learning experiences of the residents. The mentors' insights during reflection were particularly central to this process. Researchers gauged mentors' reflections against their own observations during site visits. From this first wave of analysis, we made strategic adjustments to the structure of the reading mentoring program and to the tools for data collection and analysis.

SOAP Notes and Reflective Dialogue as Reflective Practice

Two key tools in our data collection and analysis are the use of SOAP notes and reflective dialogue. Both are central to our conceptualization of reflective practice. For our purposes, we use Kovacs and Corrie's (2017) definition: "reflective practice refers to how insights and understandings can be gained from learning through experience … This in turn relies upon the practitioner being both self-aware and able to critically evaluate their decisions and reactions in practice-based contexts" (p. 2).

SOAP notes (Dye, 2005; Lenert, 2016; Many & Many, 2014; Mills et al., 2020) support reflective practice by functioning as a structured tool for capturing reflection while the mentor is in the act of mentoring the reader. As Many and Many (2014) explain, "The SOAP noting process provides teachers with a consistent method of compiling relevant information about how students are progressing through the curriculum" (p. 1). Using four categories – Subjective, Observation, Assessment, and Planning – SOAP notes help mentors record their observations while teaching or shortly after, so mentors can improve their instruction. In this way, the mentors' SOAP notes served both as *reflection-in-action* and *reflection-on-action*

(Beck & Kosnik, 2001; Kovacs & Corrie, 2017; Mills et al., 2020; Schön, 1983; Weaver et al., 2019).

In addition to SOAP notes, mentors (along with university researchers) engaged in reflective dialogue. Reflective dialogue (Weaver et al., 2019) often occurs after instruction and promotes conversations among colleagues (Dearman & Alber, 2005; Rarieya, 2005; Schön, 1983). This promotes thoughts and reflections about students' learning, engagement, or lesson foci, where mentors can comment on each other's responses (Maher & Jacob, 2006) while receiving collaborative feedback from their colleagues (Gut et al., 2016; Maher & Jacob, 2006; Many & Many, 2014; Rarieya, 2005).

In the pilot study, reflective dialogue took place each week in debriefing sessions after mentors had taught and had time to begin reflecting on SOAP notes. These debriefing sessions – integrating reflective SOAP notes and reflective dialogue – were instrumental in shaping the structure of the MILE program. Thus, the collaborative feedback functioned as reflection-on-action.

The Evolution of the Reading Partnership

A one-on-one reading mentoring program in Olson County (a pseudonym) Juvenile Detention Center (JDC) inspired literacy researchers from a Northwest Ohio university to discuss the feasibility of a reading mentoring program for student residents in a nearby JRC. The university already facilitated a reading mentor training program to prepare undergraduate students to mentor in area schools (Murnen et al., 2018), so the addition of a JRC would be an incremental evolution of this existing program. We toured the Olson County JDC, discussed with the administrators the pros and cons of their reading mentoring program, and then examined their reading materials. The evolution of the MILE mentor reading program can be seen in Figure 23.1.

The Olson County JDC implemented a scripted reading mentoring program, Mentoring For Reading Achievement (M4RA; Mentoring 4 Reading Achievement, 2020), that employed cold, warm, and hot reads and charts of student reading growth, using leveled reading texts from the Reading A–Z program (Reading A–Z, 2020). A *cold read* takes place when a text is selected at the reader's independent reading level. The mentor records the words per minute. A *warm read* happens when the resident reads the same passage over (and over again), but the errors are not documented, and a *hot read* is the final reading when, again, words per minute are recorded and compared against the cold read. The Reading A–Z materials were designed for students who read up to a fifth-grade reading level. These materials appeared to meet the needs of students in the Olson County JDC. A JDC staff member oversaw the program and helped organize the reading materials each week for the residents' mentoring folders.

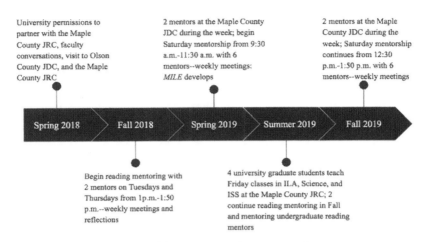

University permissions to partner with the Maple County JRC, faculty conversations, visit to Olson County JDC, and the Maple County JRC

2 mentors at the Maple County JDC during the week; begin Saturday mentorship from 9:30 a.m.-11:30 a.m. with 6 mentors--weekly meetings; *MILE* develops

2 mentors at the Maple County JDC during the week; Saturday mentorship continues from 12:30 p.m.-1:50 p.m. with 6 mentors--weekly meetings

Spring 2018   Fall 2018   Spring 2019   Summer 2019   Fall 2019

Begin reading mentoring with 2 mentors on Tuesdays and Thursdays from 1p.m.-1:50 p.m.--weekly meetings and reflections

4 university graduate students teach Friday classes in ILA, Science, and ISS at the Maple County JRC; 2 continue reading mentoring in Fall and mentoring undergraduate reading mentors

FIGURE 23.1   The Evolution of the MILE Reading Mentor Program

After observing the Olson County JDC reading mentoring program, we set up initial meetings with our own local JRC in Maple County, knowing that the success of this program would rely on collaboration to meet the needs of all stakeholders. Like other mentoring programs administered with university teacher education candidates, it would need to address the needs of the students and administrators at the facility but would also need to serve in preparing university pre-service teachers to be educators.

After preliminary meetings, including opportunities for the Maple County JRC to consult with Olson County JDC, Maple County was enthusiastic to implement the reading program and agreed to host two undergraduate mentors the first semester. The JRC also designated an administrator to supervise the program and be the liaison between the university and the JRC. Based on the rec-ommendation from the Olson County JDC reading mentoring program, the team implemented the same M4RA program using the Reading A–Z materials, and the Maple County JRC administrators and university researchers agreed that the researchers would develop the packets of materials for the mentors to implement.

The Evolution of the MILE Reading Program: Fall Semester

Our work training undergraduates to be reading mentors is grounded in a debate over two approaches – a structured approach designed to match student reading levels with text readability using scripted materials and a more dynamic approach grounded in selecting materials around student interest. Traditional approaches favor the structured leveled reader strategy (Engelmann, 1999; Fountas & Pinnell,

2006; Johns & Elish-Piper, 2016; Roe & Burns, 2011); more recent models favor beginning with student interest to guide and challenge students to higher levels of literacy (Miller, 2009; Tatum, 2008).

Because the mentors chosen for the MILE reading program would be implementing the Mentoring for Reading Achievement (M4RA) model which employs the Reading A–Z materials, they would need additional training in these particular tutoring strategies. As a result, the university researchers and JRC administrators invited the facilitator of the M4RA model, who had provided similar guidance, to the reading program at the Olson County JDC. Through collaboration with the JRC administrators and mentors, we adapted the afore-mentioned approaches to include cold, warm, and hot reads, resident interests, and reflective practice. In addition to using this structured, scripted model, we developed an interest survey to help mentors assess the interests and strengths of the students they would be mentoring at the JRC, which in turn served to guide subsequent instruction.

During the first semester of the partnership, two university undergraduate mentors, Gabby and Sandy, worked with two JRC residents for 10 one-hour sessions on Tuesday and Thursday afternoons. Mentors used the informal reading inventory (IRI; Roe & Burns, 2011) and interest survey to assess residents' reading levels and interests, and then began to select appropriate reading materials from the Reading A–Z website. They worked with residents on fluency and compre-hension and tracked fluency using the fluency chart. In addition, they also kept a reflective journal of their insights and findings after each session with their JRC resident. Finally, mentors participated in weekly reflective dialogue sessions with research faculty members to reflect on and debrief their experiences. The breakdown of the mentors' activities, reflections, and journal entries helped the partnership team identify and develop materials to be utilized by future mentors, including the reflective SOAP notes.

Reflections from the Pilot Semester

During this reflective process, Gabby voiced a concern regarding the mismatch of materials to the student's reading level and interest. She said: "More work needed to be done to match residents' interests with authentic texts, such as novels, short mystery stories, and fiction texts that address current events and interests of the residents" (Reflective Dialogue, Session 1). Up to that point, we had been focused on finding the best texts within the Reading A–Z materials to match to students' reading levels. Gabby's insight during the reflective dialogue illustrates how her thinking on student interest and the selection of materials was evolving and how it shaped the way we structured the program for future semesters. She clearly saw a need to engage the personal interests of the residents that the Reading A–Z materials alone did not provide. Jacobs' (2006) research supports Gabby's revelation when he argues that "adolescent males who can discover literature that speaks to their interests may become more involved and interested readers" (p. 113).

In response to Gabby's reflection, the researchers and mentors identified strengths and weaknesses of the existing model and designed the pedagogical model for ongoing semesters. Mentor reflective journals and notes from those meetings illustrated two key components: while much of the deliberate structure of the program (the IRI, the M4RA cold–warm–hot fluency charting, the comprehension questions, and vocabulary games and exercises) was valuable and needed to be continued, the actual texts from the Reading A–Z materials were not the most appropriate for all students, in terms of readability level and student interest. As a result, all future mentors received additional training and orientation using other reading resources such as Newsela.com and Rewordify.com.

Evolution of the MILE Reading Program: Spring Semester

Grounded in observations and discussions from the first semester of mentoring, the researchers reset several key features of the pedagogical model, including the addition of SOAP notes (Lenert, 2016; Many & Many, 2014) to structure the reflection-in-action and reflection-on-action. As a result, the mentoring program evolved into the following six-step framework: (1) an eight-hour IRI and readability training; (2) pre-assessment of the resident using the interest survey and the informal reading inventory; (3) creation of high-interest lesson plans each week, grounded in texts of interest and appropriate challenge for the residents; (4) a meeting to discuss the plans with researchers before mentoring; (5) implementation of the plan with the resident; and (6) reflection on the effectiveness of the plan using SOAP notes, reflective journaling, and collaborative discussion – focusing on student engagement and reading growth.

Findings

To understand more clearly how the collaboration shaped our organizational structure and impacted instructional decision-making, we examined our research questions. These questions serve as a framework for discussion of the findings.

The Development of the Organizational Structure of the MILE Program

The reading program evolved from a collaborative effort with interconnected participant groups, including faculty from the university, administrators from both juvenile centers, and the director of the M4RA reading program. Our opportunity to view the Olson County JDC reading mentoring program laid the foundation for the program we implemented in Maple County. The value of this collaborative dialogue is reflected in Tom's (the Juvenile Court Executive Director) response to this research question:

> The organizational structure evolved from a collaborative assessment of the needs and resources of the agency, a consensus on the desired outcomes of the program, the cooperative and equitable use of each agency's resources, and a team approach to problem solving when difficulties were encountered.

Barb, the Maple County JRC Director, focused on the impact of the collaborative program on the residents at the JRC. Her response helped shape how the program grew into the second semester. She wrote:

> The collaboration between JRC and the reading mentoring program has directly impacted the residents who we work with. They experienced improved reading performance, which boosted their self-confidence with their reading ability. The program helped the residents become avid readers and reinforced life-long reading goals. The residents were respectful and appreciative of their tutors.

Barb also responded to challenges in the collaboration process: "Challenges of the program include the varied levels and capabilities of participants, material availability, and time spent with students, due to other facility obligations." For example, additional mentoring times were established, such as the Saturday schedule to fit within the facility routines and obligations and doubling the number of mentors and residents during the second semester. Another addition to the structure of the program was the development of the program name by the administrators – *Mentoring In Literacy Enhancement (MILE)*.

Furthermore, a key aspect of the partnership was the input of the first two mentors. As a result, faculty and the second wave of mentors met to develop a plan for extending and supplementing text materials and comprehension strategies, focusing first on the reading needs and interests of the next round of residents. Finally, the addition of a colleague from our graduate reading faculty to the research team brought the implementation of SOAP notes that she had used extensively with graduate mentors in the reading center. Teaching our undergraduates to utilize SOAP notes reinforced the importance of reflection and the impact on instructional practice and student learning.

Impact of Collaboration on Planning and Instruction, and Reflective Practice

Collaborative Reflection Informed Planning and Instructional Practice

During the pilot semester, a mentor, Gabby, followed the structured M4RA model, using the Reading A–Z reading materials while engaging the resident in cold–warm–hot reads with growth charts to assess fluency and comprehension. However, this approach evolved in the reflective collaboration with the faculty researchers. As Gabby continued to work with her resident, she learned he had a stronger interest in fiction texts. In reflection meetings, Gabby stated, "I thought I would have to work harder to get his interest. He seems to have a natural interest in reading, but it may have had to do with the selections. He definitely likes fiction more than non-fiction" (Session 5). This led Gabby to select passages and texts beyond the Reading A–Z texts that were grade-level appropriate and were better suited for the resident's interests, such as the mythology texts that he expressed interest in reading.

In the reflective, collaborative process, mentors noted that student interest was an integral component to motivating students to be engaged in this reading mentoring program. Also, they expressed that implementing texts without the scripted M4RA lesson created some initial struggle. For example, Gabby shared, "I struggled to figure out what changes I could make to recreate the article at his level." As she continued to learn about her resident's interests, she continued selecting and adapting texts and passages that were developmentally appropriate, while maintaining the structure of the cold–warm–hot reads and fluency charting.

SOAP Notes Reflection Informed Debriefing Sessions and Instructional Planning

Mentors who joined the MILE project in the second semester were introduced to SOAP notes (Lenert, 2016; Many & Many, 2014) that were intended for reflection following each lesson they taught. In this program, SOAP notes included a one-page template. This structure supported a reflective process that guided the debriefing sessions and the dialogue with colleagues that informed the pedagogical decision-making process the mentors used in designing each week's lesson plans. For example, Carly's SOAP notes illustrate how her resident's needs and interests shaped the decision-making process.

Carly included that her resident needed to "work on vocabulary and reading with expression – focus on vocab and more in-depth comprehension questions to make sure he is retaining and comprehending" (Carly, SOAP note, Week 2). In addition, she stated that her resident "was very interested in sports articles," something she had learned from his interest survey (Carly, SOAP note, Week 2). As a result, during the debriefing session, other mentors suggested finding articles about March Madness. In Week 3, Carly brought in an article about March

Madness, based on the collaboration in the debriefing session and her resident's interest in basketball.

Conclusion and Implications

The findings suggest that a dynamic, collaborative partnership mentoring model exists across three core constituents – the researchers, the facility administrators, and the mentors. This model was effective in implementing a reading mentoring program in a juvenile correctional facility as illustrated in Figure 23.2.

The first collaborative partnership involved university researchers and facility administrators collaborating to develop the initial structure and to address programmatic and logistical needs as they emerged. The collaborative dialogue and reflection helped operationalize the framework that would be utilized to meet the needs of the residents and address the logistical challenges.

The second collaborative partnership involved university faculty and undergraduate mentors engaging in the reflective dialogue process with SOAP notes, weekly meetings, reflective journals, and field observations. These processes enabled the partners to continually address the learning needs of the JRC residents and the pedagogical decision-making of the undergraduate mentors. Within this model, undergraduate mentors had the unique opportunity to engage in collaborative discussions with their peers, university researchers, and at times even with the JRC administrators. Weekly reflective conversations and written reflections between university researchers and the undergraduate mentors throughout the program shaped the evolution of the reading program significantly. Their reflections on their experiences fostered growth in the program.

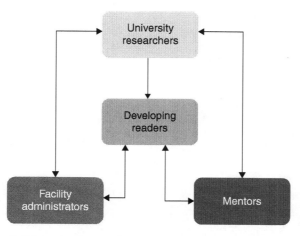

FIGURE 23.2   Collaborative Partnership Mentoring Model

The key to all of these collaborative efforts was our shared focus on creating a sustainable partnership. This collaborative partnership mentoring model created a vibrant and responsive structure that can serve as a model for future undergraduate and graduate reading mentoring programs, as well as for future university and community partnerships.

Because of these collaborations, a strong and sustained partnership provided additional growth in the MILE program in Maple County: (a) increased the number of mentors each semester; (b) initiated the MILE program at the JDC; (c) implemented a graduate summer reading program at the JRC; and (d) began a teaching experience every Friday across content areas during the summer at the JRC. Moreover, we anticipate the potential for continued upscaling of this mentoring program by implementing it on a larger scale across multidisciplinary education programs.

References

Allen, D. D., & Swearingen, R. A. (2002). Development of pedagogical knowledge related to teaching at-risk students: How do inservice teachers and preservice teachers compare? *Reading Horizons, 43*(1), 49–60.

American Association of Colleges for Teacher Education (AACTE). (2018). *A pivot toward clinical practice, it's lexicon, and the renewal of educator preparation: A report of the AACTE Clinical Practice Commission.* AACTE.

Beck, C., & Kosnik, C. (2001). Reflection-in-action: In defence of thoughtful teaching. *Curriculum Inquiry, 31*(2), 217–227. https://doi.org/10.1111/0362-6784.00193

Brunner, M. S. (1993). *Reduced recidivism and increased employment opportunity through research-based reading instruction.* NCJ Publication No. 141324. Department of Justice, Office of Juvenile Justice and Delinquency Prevention. https://doi.org/10.1080/10573560701808460

Center on Crime, Communities, and Culture. (1997). *Abandoned in the back row: New lessons in education and delinquency prevention.* Author. https://www.njjn.org/uploads/digital-library/Executive-Summary--Abandoned%20in%20the%20Back%20Row_CJJ_1-11-13.pdf

Cochran-Smith, M., & Villegas, A. M. (2014). Framing teacher preparation research: An overview of the field, part 1. *Journal of Teacher Education, 65*(4), 1–15. https://doi.org/10.1177/0022487114549071

Darling-Hammond, L., Hammerness, K., Grossman, P., Rust, F., & Shulman, L. (2005). The design of teacher education programs. In L. Darling-Hammond, & J. Bransford (Eds.), *Preparing teachers for a changing world* (pp. 390–441). Jossey Bass.

Dearman, C. C., & Alber, S. R. (2005). The changing face of education: Teachers cope with challenges through collaboration and reflective study. *The Reading Teacher, 58*(7), 634–640. https://doi.org/10.1598/RT.58.7.4

Dye, D. (2005). Enhancing critical reflection of students during a clinical internship using the self-S.O.A.P. note. *The International Journal of Allied Health Sciences and Practice, 3*(4), 1–6.

Engelmann, S. (1999). *Corrective reading series guide* (3rd ed.). McGraw-Hill.

Fountas, I., & Pinnell, G. (2006). *Teaching for comprehension and fluency: Thinking, talking, and writing about reading, K-8.* Heinemann.

Guerra, S. F. (2012). Using urban fiction to engage at-risk youths in literacy instruction. *Journal of Adolescent & Adult Literacy, 55*, 385–394. https://doi.org/10.1002/JAAL.00047

Gut, D. M., Wan, G., Beam, P. C., & Burgess, L. (2016). Reflective dialog journals: A tool for developing professional competence in novice teachers. *School–University Partnerships, 9*(2), 60–70.

Jacobs, S. (2006). Listening, writing, drawing; The artistic response of incarcerated youth to young-adult literature. *Educational Horizons, 84*(2), 112–120.

Johns, J., & Elish-Piper, L. (2016). *Basic reading inventory: Kindergarten through grade twelve and early literacy assessments* (12th ed.). Kendall-Hunt.

Kolb, S. (2012). Grounded theory and the constant comparative method: Valid research strategies for educators. *Journal of Emerging Trends in Educational Research and Policy Studies, 3*(1), 83–86.

Kovacs, L., & Corrie, S. (2017). Building reflective capability to enhance coaching practice. *The Coaching Psychologist, 13*(1), 4–12.

Krezmien, M., & Mulcahy, C. (2008). Literacy and delinquency: Current status of reading interventions with detained and incarcerated youth. *Reading & Writing Quarterly, 24*(2), 219–238. https://doi.org/:10.1080/10573560701808601

Krezmien, M., Mulcahy, C., Travers, J., Wilson, M., & Wells, C. (2013). Reading performance of incarcerated youth: Understanding and responding to a unique population of readers. *Journal of Special Education Leadership, 26*(2), 71–81.

Lenert, L. (2016). Toward medical documentation that enhances situational awareness learning. *AMIA Annual Symposium Proceedings*, 763–771. (Published online February 10, 2017.)

Maher, M., & Jacob, E. (2006). Peer computer conferencing to support teachers' reflection during action research. *Journal of Technology and Teacher Evaluation, 14*(1), 127–150.

Malmgren, K., & Leone, P. (2000). Effects of a short-term auxiliary reading program on the reading skills of incarcerated youth. *Education and Treatment of Children, 23*(3), 239–247.

Many, T. W., & Many, B. T. (2014). SOAP notes: A tool to promote reflective dialogue about student learning. *TEPSA News, 71*(2), 1–2.

Mentoring 4 Reading Achievement. (n.d.) Welcome to M4RA.org! Retrieved February 20, 2020 from www.m4ra.org

Miller, D. (2009). *The book whisperer: Awakening the inner reader in every child.* Jossey-Bass.

Mills, A., Weaver, J. C., Bertelsen, C., & Dziak, E. (2020). Take pause in quiet moments: Engaging in reflection to guide instruction. *The Reading Teacher, 74*(1), 71–78.

Murnen, T. J., Bostic, J., Fordham, N., & Weaver, J. C. (2018). Adopt-an-apprentice teacher: Re-inventing early field experiences. In T. Hodges, & A. Baum (Eds.), *Handbook of research on field-based teacher education* (pp. 367–394). IGI Global. https://doi.org/10.4018/978-1-5225-6249-8.ch016

NCATE. (2010). *Transforming Teacher Education through Clinical Practice: A national strategy to prepare effective teachers.* Report of the Blue Ribbon Panel on clinical preparation and partnerships for improved student learning. National Council for Accreditation of Teacher Education.

Putnam County ESC. (2020). Project MORE: Mentoring in Ohio for reading excellence. Retrieved February 24, 2020 from www.ohioprojectmore.org/

Rarieya, J. (2005). Reflective dialogue: What's in it for teachers? A Pakistan case. *Journal of In-service Education, 31*(2), 313–335. https://doi.org/10.1080/13674580500200281

Reading A–Z. (2020). Retrieved February 20, 2020 from www.readinga-z.com

Roe, B., & Burns, P. (2011). *Informal reading inventory: Preprimer to twelfth grade* (8th ed.). Cengage.

Schön, D. (1983). *The reflective practitioner: How professionals think in action.* Temple Smith.

Snowling, M. J., Adams, J. W., Bowyer-Crane, C., & Tobin, V. (2000). Levels of literacy among juvenile offenders: The incidence of specific reading difficulties. *Criminal Behaviour and Mental Health, 10,* 229–241. https://doi.org/10.1002/cbm.362

Strauss, A., & Corbin, J. (2008). *Basics of qualitative research: Grounded theory procedures and techniques* (3rd ed.). SAGE.

Styslinger, M. E. (2019). Just listen: Reading conversations with incarcerated youth. *English Journal, 109*(2), 23–31.

Styslinger, M. E., Walker, N., & Eberlin, E. L. (2014). Teaching in "third space": Understanding pre-service teachers' reading with incarcerated teens. *The Journal of Reading Education, 39*(2), 23–29.

Tatum, A. (2008). Toward a more anatomically complete model of literacy instruction: A focus on African American male adolescents and texts. *Harvard Educational Review, 78*(1), 155–180. https://doi.org/10.17763/haer.78.1.6852t5065w30h449

Weaver, J., Lavery, M., & Heineken, S. (2019). Reflective practice: The impact of self-identified learning gaps on professional development. *Journal on Empowering Teaching Excellence, 3*(2), 54–74.

Williamson, P., Mercurio, M., & Walker, C. (2013). Songs of the caged birds: Literacy and learning with incarcerated youth. *The English Journal, 102*(4), 31–37.

Worthy, J., Prater, K., & Pennington, J. (2003). "It's a program that looks great on paper": The challenge of America reads. *Journal of Literacy Research, 35*(3), 879–910. https://doi.org/10.1207/s15548430jlr3503_4

Zeichner, K. (1996). Designing educative practicum experiences for prospective teachers. In K. Zeichner, S. Melnick, & M. L. Gomez (Eds.), *Currents of reform in preservice teacher education* (pp. 215–234). Teachers College Press.

Zeichner, K. (2010). Rethinking the connections between campus courses and field experiences in college- and university-based teacher education. *Journal of Teacher Education, 61*(1–2), 89–99. https://doi.org/10.1177/0022487109347671

24

STEM STORIES

Connecting STEM and Literacy in an Afterschool Program

Mary-Kate Sableski, Margaret Pinnell, Shannon Driskell, and Todd Smith

UNIVERSITY OF DAYTON

Suzanne Franco

WRIGHT STATE UNIVERSITY

Introduction

The study described in this chapter addresses the intersection of the pressing needs for enhanced literacy rates and improved science, technology, engineering, and mathematics (STEM) skills, particularly among underserved youth. Specifically, this chapter examines how pedagogies of literacy and design can be applied within a community-based afterschool program in an urban context to raise both literacy achievement and STEM interest. Results are discussed from the first year of a three-year study focused on an afterschool program that implemented STEM lessons enhanced with literacy content in one underserved, urban elementary school. The lessons incorporated research-based best practices for attracting underrepresented students to engineering, were mapped to the state content standards, were infused with diverse or culturally relevant literature, and included literacy activities. The lessons also reflected the needs and interests of the local community in which the program was situated through the literature selections and design activities. This study explored the following research questions using both qualitative and quantitative methods:

> What is the relationship between the use of integrated literacy and STEM lessons in an afterschool program and students' end-of-year standardized literacy performance?

What is the difference in students' self-described interest and skills before and after attending an afterschool program that uses integrated literacy and STEM lessons?

Review of Literature

Of all fourth-grade students who took the 2017 National Assessment of Education Progress (NAEP) reading assessment, 63% failed to reach the *Proficient* level, with 32% below the *Basic* level (NAEP Reading Report Card, 2017). Given that a child's ability to read by the end of third grade is a critical predictor of their future success, these statistics are alarming (Annie E. Casey Foundation, 2010). Additionally, the next generation of scientists and engineers must be inspired to pursue STEM fields at an early age (Bagiati et al., 2010). Not only is there a demand for STEM proficiency, but there is also a need for a more diverse STEM workforce (McSherry, 2005; National Science Foundation, 2015; Page, 2007; US Bureau of Labor Statistics, 2015). A diverse STEM workforce is essential to achieving innovative solutions to the world's most challenging problems (Bagchi-Sen, 2001; Van Horne et al., 2006). Therefore, communities need to enhance the literacy skills and exposure to STEM education for all children beginning at a very young age.

Research suggests that integrating STEM and literacy can be a very effective strategy for helping students achieve in both areas (Cervetti et al., 2006, 2012; Cotabush et al., 2013; Guthrie & Ozgungor, 2002; Padilla et al., 1991; Palincsar & Magnusson, 2001; Romance & Vitale, 2001; Sterling, 2014; Wyss et al., 2012). The enhanced literacy performance when integrated with STEM is believed to be due to several factors, including common intellectual processes and advanced comprehension skills required in both disciplines (Baines, 2015; Cox, 2012; National Research Council, 2011; Padilla et al., 1991). Further, embedding STEM and literacy content within culturally responsive teaching approaches holds promise for keeping students engaged in STEM fields (Ingen et al., 2018).

The use of literature as a "hook" for STEM projects can help increase students' motivation and interest in STEM (Cervetti et al., 2006, 2012). Given the goal of attracting underrepresented groups to STEM fields, consideration of the diversity represented in the selected literature is critical. Seminal research points to the need for all children to see windows, mirrors, and sliding glass doors (Bishop, 1990) in the literature they read. When children see themselves in literature, they can imagine possibilities for their futures. However, it is well documented that books representing diversity are challenging to find (Cooperative Children's Book Center, 2019). In recent years, movements such as We Need Diverse Books helped to increase diversity among the books published, including books that represent both STEM content and diversity. However, the children's book market still does not include enough literature representing STEM content and diversity (Kelly,

2019). Programs such as the one described in this chapter have the potential to increase awareness for literature that represents both diversity and STEM content. Further, selecting literature that not only reflects diverse groups, but also the cultural reality of the local community, can help children to see both windows and mirrors as they participate in programming in their communities.

Methods

Context for the Study

The STEM Stories after-school program leverages the success of a pilot study (Pinnell et al., 2018) in which previously developed Engineering Outreach Modules were modified to include literacy activities, while also developing new integrated literacy and STEM lessons. The STEM Stories development team consisted of four university faculty members from different disciplines: School of Engineering, Department of Mathematics, Department of Physics, and Department of Teacher Education. Additionally, a faculty member from another university served as the external evaluator for this project.

The university partnered with a local school that is one of five underserved urban elementary schools in the Dayton Public Schools Neighborhood School Center (NSC). These schools are centered on their neighborhoods, serving as healthy places of learning for children and families. The university has a long-standing relationship with this NSC and its NSC site coordinator. One of the faculty team members worked with this school on previous STEM-related grants, and the Department of Teacher Education places student teachers in this school for its Urban Teacher Academy. The Urban Teacher Academy is a specialized program for pre-service teachers who have an interest in working with high-poverty and high-needs student populations. This long-standing relationship among the university and the NSC, NSC site coordinator, and Urban Teacher Academy, along with the pilot study (Pinnell et al., 2018), demonstrates the partnership that helped develop trustworthiness among the teachers and faculty involved in this study. Furthermore, the STEM Stories development team met several times during the planning stage to discuss the afterschool program logistics and activities with the school principal, NSC site coordinator, two classroom teachers, and two undergraduate students who helped support the after-school program. Throughout the after-school program, weekly communication continued among the development team and the classroom teachers, undergraduate students, and NSC site coordinator.

The after-school STEM Stories program included components to increase participation from students and families. First, the program met at the school twice a week from 4:00 p.m. to 5:30 p.m. from September through April. Each session included a snack, often tied to the lesson content. The program also included two family engagement events. One occurred mid-way through the program and one at the end. Both engagement events included dinner for participants, opportunities for families to engage in the lessons, opportunities for students to share their literacy and STEM projects with their families, and take-home activities.

During the after-school sessions, one STEM Stories lesson was generally facilitated over four 90-minute sessions that spanned two weeks. A typical lesson engaged the student participants in reading during the first week, including read aloud and relevant vocabulary and comprehension building activities; the second week involved the students in the Engineering Design Process of defining the problem, planning, creating a prototype or design, testing the design, improving the design, and engaging in redesign based on the outcome of the testing.

The STEM Stories development team created kits for each lesson that included three copies of the picture book, presentations that introduced the scenario, a lesson plan that included the design challenge and how the designs should be tested, and consumable materials required for the program participants to build and test their designs. The literature for each lesson was selected by the development team based on the connection it presented to the STEM topic of the lesson, as well as the cultural relevancy or diversity offered in the book and its connection to the community. A rubric was developed to evaluate the literature selections for the lessons (see Figure 24.1).

When developing the lessons, the team focused on culturally relevant pedagogy (Ladson-Billings, 1995) to connect to students, families, and the community. Lessons began with a literature selection that reflected the STEM content, but also incorporated culturally relevant and/or diverse characters so that students could see themselves in the STEM challenge. Further, the STEM lessons aimed to both build upon students' background knowledge and expand it beyond their local community. For example, one of the lessons begins with *The Airport Book* (Brown, 2016), to build background knowledge about a conveyor belt for the STEM challenge. In our local community, the history of air travel is a familiar topic, as the Wright Brothers were born and raised in our city. During the introductory discussion to the book, the teacher discovered that the students did not know the meaning of the word *luggage*. Most of the students had never been on an airplane trip; thus, this was an unfamiliar word to them. Through the use of culturally relevant and diverse literature, the STEM Stories lessons helped to build on and create background knowledge based on the community-based needs students' brought to the after-school program.

Participants

The STEM Stories program was facilitated at an urban pre-kindergarten through sixth grade school with 54% of the students from underrepresented populations and 90% of the students qualifying for free or reduced lunch. Fifty-five second- and third-grade students registered for the after-school program with six of these students attending between 66% and 100% of the time, four students attending

	0	1	2
Literary Quality	This book is of low literary quality, receiving low reviews from the Horn Book or other review sources. The story is not rich and nuanced, and the text does not draw the reader in to the book.	The book is of average literary quality, reflected in low to average reviews from outside sources. The text is engaging but does not contain complex characters or textual elements.	The book is of high literary quality, receiving consistently high reviews and/or multiple awards. The text is complex, nuanced, and engaging, drawing readers in through rich language and storytelling.
Illustrations	The illustrations are bland and do not match the text.	The illustrations are engaging and somewhat align with the text.	The illustrations are rich and engaging and align well with the text. The illustrations are an integral part of the story.
STEM Connections	STEM connections are either absent or too forced into the story. The STEM connections are not a natural component of the story.	STEM connections are present, but there are missed opportunities in the story to highlight or discuss them. The connections are vague and under-developed.	STEM connections are an integral, natural component to the story. The STEM connections are not overly stated but are woven into the story.
Literary Skills/Strategies	The book does not present any opportunities to teach literacy skills or strategies because of its limited text and scope.	The book presents some opportunities to teach literacy skills or strategies, but they are forced and not an integral, natural part of the story.	The book is rich in opportunities to teach key literacy skills and strategies because of its complex structure and meaningful use of language.
Interest/Appeal	The book is not interesting or appealing to the students it will be presented to because of its topic, presentation, or format.	The book will be somewhat engaging to the students it will be presented to but will not stand on its own as a hook into the STEM lesson.	The book is interesting and engaging because of its topic, presentation, or format and will stand on its own as a hook into the STEM lesson.
Diversity and Cultural Relevancy	The book does not represent diverse groups of people in relevant or authentic contexts or does so nominally or inappropriately.	The book represents diverse groups of people in somewhat relevant and authentic contexts. The diversity is represented through "changing the color of the crayon".	The book represents diverse groups of people in relevant and authentic contexts. The representation goes beyond "changing the color of the crayon".

FIGURE 24.1 STEM Literature Rubric

between 51% and 65% of the time, eight students attending between 31% and 50% of the time, and 37 students attending between 0 and 30% of the time. Student transportation issues, competing after-school programs, and illness impacted the students' ability to participate in the program on a regular basis. The STEM Stories team relied on the school, the NCS site coordinator – who is well connected with the students, their families, and the community – two classroom teachers, and two undergraduate students to reach out to students and families to encourage attendance. In addition, the family engagement sessions, as well as incentives such as snacks and attendance rewards, reflected attempts to increase attendance and connections with families.

Data Sources

The data sources for this study included pre/post STEM interest survey responses, literacy assessment scores, and journal entries. Student participants responded to a pre- and post-activity using a modified AWE (Assessing Women and Men in Engineering) survey (Lower-Elementary Pre- and Post-Activity) that was validated for the Women and Men in Engineering Project (www. engr.psu.edu/awe/secured/director/precollege/pre_college.aspx). The AWE is a survey used to assess students' interest in STEM. AWE survey responses were used to determine if the STEM Stories lessons contributed to the participants' self-reported attitudes, interests, and awareness toward STEM. Qualitative data were coded using themes predetermined (a priori) according to project objectives and specific feedback purposes as well as themes that emerged during the analyses.

MAP (Measures of Academic Progress) assessments were administered at the site during the school year, and the state standardized reading test was administered at the end of the school year. The literacy scores were used to determine if the STEM Stories lessons contributed to the literacy skills of the participants.

Journal entries were analyzed to explore whether and how student literacy developed from the integration of writing activities into the lessons. Journal entry prompts were given with each lesson, and students were encouraged to focus on ideas, not mechanics, in their entries. Student journals were collected and catalogued for qualitative analysis to characterize the literacy activities.

Data Analysis

The program was evaluated qualitatively and quantitatively to ensure the objectives of the study were met and to provide feedback during the program period so that modifications could be made as needed. AWE STEM Interest survey (2017) data were collected at the beginning and the end of the after-school program. The student responses for each question were tallied, and the two drawings were labeled for analyses. Changes in the student interests and attitudes from pre- to post-survey were calculated using a *t* test or a Wilcoxon Test depending on the sample size.

Student literacy scores for the state literacy assessments were compared using a *t* test. The MAP assessment was administered in early fall, early spring, and late spring before the final administration. The early fall and late spring test scores were used to determine levels of growth. The state literacy scores were compared to a state minimum proficient score to determine if the student was reading on grade level. The previous grade-level state testing data were used to compare to the current score, if available.

Journal entries were analyzed using thematic coding to determine patterns in the responses. Two of the researchers read the journal entries, applying open coding (Strauss & Corbin, 1990) to identify themes across the responses. The researchers then compared their codes and grouped similar codes to identify themes. Additionally, the researchers tallied the number of lines for each journal response and compared them within and across individual students. From these data, three case-study students were identified based on their consistent attendance and participation in the program.

Results

STEM Interest Survey

A majority of the 24 students that participated in the post survey agreed with all but two statements (see 1c and 3b in Table 24.1). The average of the responses to statements 3a and 3b revealed that approximately 54% of the students agreed and only 29% disagreed with wanting to pursue STEM careers. Although responses to statement 1c, *I am good at engineering*, reflected that approximately 17% disagreed; 79% of the responses to statements that described characteristics of engineers (i.e., 1d, 1e, 3c, 3d, 3e) reflected that students rated themselves interested in or good in those characteristics. Statement 1d is the best example of students' strong interest in characteristics of engineers.

Literacy Assessment Scores

The school administered the MAP assessment (NWEA, 2018) to the third grade students in the fall, winter, and spring. The three MAP reading test scores, including the subcategories of vocabulary, informational text skills, and literature skills, were studied for each student who attended the STEM Stories program at least 40% of the time (15 students). Five students scored higher in the spring than projected on the fall assessment. Examining the MAP subcategories, one student scored higher than projected in the understanding of literature, one student scored higher than

TABLE 24.1 2017–2018 AWE Post Survey Student Results

Statements	Agree	Not sure	Disagree	Missing
1a. I am good at science.	16	5	2	1
1b. I am good at math.	19	1	3	1
1c. I am good at engineering.	10	7	4	3
1d. I like learning how things work.	22	2	0	0
1e. I am creative.	19	2	3	0
3a. I would like to be a scientist.	16	2	6	0
3b. I would like to be an engineer.	10	6	8	0
3c. I would like a job where I invent things.	16	3	5	0
3d. I would like to design machines that help people walk.	20	2	2	0
3e. I would enjoy a job helping to make new medicines.	18	3	3	0
3f. I would enjoy a job helping to protect the environment.	18	5	1	0
3g. Scientists help make people's lives better.	17	4	3	0
3h. Engineers help make people's lives better.	17	4	3	0
3i. I know what scientists do for their jobs.	18	2	4	0
3j. I know what engineers do for their jobs.	15	7	2	0

projected regarding understanding of informational text, and one student scored higher than projected regarding vocabulary acquisition. The STEM Stories lessons included content which addressed these subcategories; therefore, it is possible that the lessons may have contributed to the higher than expected scores. The end-of-year state reading test scores were also examined for those who attended at least 40% of the time, and 14 of the 15 students (93%) passed. This is compared to students district-wide, where 34% passed the state reading test (Ohio Department of Education, 2017).

Journal Entries

Analysis of the journal entries revealed a dominant theme of increased writing volume. Figure 24.2 provides examples of beginning and end-of-year responses from one student who demonstrated significant change.

Students typically wrote more when they were asked to connect the STEM content to their personal lives. For example, analysis of the entries demonstrated that students responded to the prompt "Describe your dream house" at the beginning of the program year with an average of three lines of text. By the end of the year, the students responded to the prompt "Describe your favorite room in your house" with an average of 30 lines of text. One student responded

October 12, 2017   March 20, 2018

FIGURE 24.2 Example of Increase in Writing Volume in Journal Entries

with two lines of text at the beginning of the year and responded with 46 lines of text by the end of the year. Throughout the year, there were opportunities to respond to journal prompts, and those that invited richer responses connected with students' personal lives.

Three case-study students were selected following an analysis of the journals. The students were selected because they attended more than 50% of the time, over the course of the entire program. Thus, they participated in journal entries across the program period. Other students were not chosen because their attendance did not persist across the entire program, or they did not participate in journal entries on a consistent basis. See Figure 24.3 for a comparison of the writing volume of three case-study students who attended over 50% of the time. This chart represents the entries the students did complete for the days they attended. See Appendix 24.1 for a list of the corresponding journal prompts.

Students' writing volume varied across the 39 weeks. One trend in the data for three students that attended at least 21 of the sessions is that their writing volume increased when comparing the first ten weeks (weeks 1–10) of the program to the last ten weeks (weeks 30–39) of the program. During the first ten weeks, on average Student A wrote 4.6 lines, Student B wrote 5.4 lines, and Student C wrote 4.1 lines. During the last ten weeks, on average Student A wrote 13.7 lines, Student B wrote 17.7 lines, and Student C wrote 17.1 lines. Thus, a combination of regular attendance and participation, along with journal entries that connected to students' personal lives, led to increased writing volume in the three case-study students.

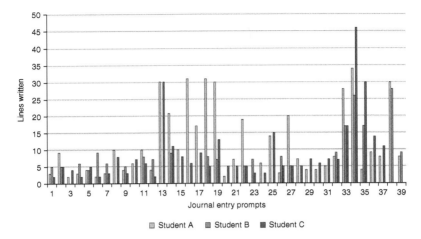

FIGURE 24.3 Number of Lines Written per Journal Entry for Three Case Study Students

Discussion

Preliminary data suggest that the STEM Stories program may have been helpful in literacy skill development but may not have sufficiently inspired students to explore engineering as the STEM interest data were inconclusive. The STEM Stories lessons developed during the first year of the project are shared on a website for widespread distribution and use (https://udayton.edu/engineering/k-12-programs/stem-stories-for-third-grade-students/index.php). During the second year of the project (2018–2019), the STEM Stories program was expanded to two additional schools in the same district. Each of these three schools has a diverse student population that reflects the school's neighborhood.

At the beginning of the third year, the development team held a professional development session for any teacher or after-school director interested in facilitating the lessons in their programs. The session was attended by 25 participants, and the response to the session was positive. Participants learned the theoretical foundations of the lessons, as well as the practical components involved in facilitating the lessons. This professional development session was built on the lessons learned from the first year, which demonstrated that the STEM Stories lessons may have impacted literacy achievement and STEM interest for the students. Thus, the development team sought to train more teachers and after-school leaders in using the program with fidelity in their individual contexts.

Purposefully applying literacy-related pedagogies, such as the use of diverse and culturally relevant literature and writing opportunities grounded in out of school experiences, has the potential to contribute to student literacy across domains. Students from underserved backgrounds with limited exposure to vocabulary and language and who encounter fewer opportunities to develop higher-level comprehension skills can benefit from participation in these activities. Using literacy-related pedagogies across domains may have contributed to closing the opportunity and achievement gap in both literacy and STEM areas and connecting to the students' out of school lives through culturally relevant literature and pedagogy infused throughout the lessons.

Implications

The results of this study provide implications for the integration of STEM and literacy content, as well as the potential of after-school programs to develop participants' literacy skills and STEM awareness. This study is limited in its generalizability due to its focus on one school; however, the results of the study informed the development of the after-school program in two additional sites in the second year, indicating the program can be replicated when delivered with fidelity.

Literature Selections

The literature selected for the lessons point to several implications and opportunities for future research. Table 24.2 displays the results of the content analysis of the literature selections using the researcher-developed rubric as a tool. Each of the books selected were of high literary quality, included rich illustrations, and provided strong STEM connections and opportunities for teaching literacy skills and strategies. Five of the books did not represent any diversity, four displayed moderate diversity, and four displayed strong diversity. Given the publishing trends for culturally relevant children's literature, which demonstrate that 50% of the available books represent only white characters (Cooperative Children's Book Center, 2019), this distribution demonstrates the books selected for the STEM Stories program represented a greater percentage of diversity (62%) than is available in the market.

The literature selected for each lesson presented opportunities for building background knowledge, vocabulary, and comprehension skills, in addition to the opportunities for connecting to STEM content. Pairing interactive read-alouds of an engaging, diverse, rich picture book with active, hands-on literacy and STEM lessons has the potential to engage students across domains in developing both STEM interest and literacy skills. However, this study is an example of the challenges in locating literature that represents both diversity and STEM content, and the need for more such books in the market.

The study described in this chapter provides a model for other after-school programs seeking to bring literacy, along with STEM awareness, to the community.

TABLE 24.2 Analysis of Literature Selections using the STEM Literature Rubric

Book title	Rubric categories				
	Literary quality	Illustrations	STEM connections	Literacy skills/ strategies	Diversity/ cultural relevancy
If I Built a House (Van Dusen, 2012)	2	2	2	2	0
Two Bobbies (Larson & Nethery, 2008)	2	2	1	2	0
All the Water in the World (Lyon, 2011)	2	2	2	1	1
The Airport Book (Brown, 2016)	2	2	1	2	2
Emmanuel's Dream (Thompson, 2015)	2	2	2	2	2
Stanley at Sea (Bailey, 2008)	2	2	1	2	0
The Knights Before Christmas (Holub, 2015)	1	2	1	2	0
Tiny Stitches (Hooks, 2016)	2	2	2	2	2
Volcano Rising (Rusch, 2013)	2	2	2	2	1
Twenty-One Elephants and Still Standing (Prince, 2005)	2	2	2	2	0
Iggy Peck, Architect (Beaty, 2007)	2	2	2	2	1
The Most Magnificent Thing (Spires, 2014)	2	2	2	2	1
Galimoto (Williams, 1990)	2	2	2	2	2

After-school programs fill a critical role in the promotion of literacy in the communities they serve, and the STEM Stories program described in this chapter is one way to accomplish this goal.

References

Annie E. Casey Foundation. (2010, January 1). Early warning! Why reading by the end of third grade matters: A KIDS COUNT special report by the Annie E. Casey Foundation. Retrieved from www.aecf.org/resources/early-warning-why-reading-by-the-end-of-third-grade-matters/

Bagchi-Sen, S. (2001). Product innovation and competitive advantage in an area of industrial decline: The Niagara region of Canada. *Technovation, 21*(1), 45–54. https://doi.org/10.1016/S0166-4972(00)00016-X

Bagiati, A., Yoon, S. Y., Evangelou, D., & Ngambeki, I. (2010). Engineering curricula in early education: Describing the landscape of open resources. *Early Childhood Research & Practice, 12*(2). https://ecrp.illinois.edu/v12n2/bagiati.html

Baines, L. (2015). The language arts as foundational for science, technology, engineering, art, and mathematics. In X. Ge, D. Ifenthaler, & J. M. Spector (Eds.), *Emerging technologies for STEAM education: Full STEAM ahead* (pp. 247–258). Springer. https://doi.org/10.1007/978-3-319-02573-5_13

Bailey, L. (2008). *Stanley at sea.* Kids Can Press.

Beaty, A. (2007). *Iggy Peck, architect.* Abrams Books for Young Readers.

Bishop, R. S. (1990). Walk tall in the world: African American literature for today's children. *The Journal of Negro Education, 59*(4), 556–565. https://doi.org/10.2307/2295312

Brown, L. (2016). *The airport book.* Roaring Brook Press.

Cervetti, G. N., Pearson, P. D., Bravo, M. A., & Barber, J. (2006). Reading and writing in the service of inquiry-based science. In R. Douglas, M. Klentschy, & K. Worth (Eds.), *Linking science and literacy in the K-8 classroom* (pp. 221–244). NSTA Press.

Cervetti, G. N., Barber, J., Dorph, R., Pearson, P. D., & Goldschmidt, P. G. (2012). The impact of an integrated approach to science and literacy in elementary school classrooms. *Journal of Research in Science Teaching, 49*(5), 631–658. https://doi.org/10.1002/tea.21015

Cooperative Children's Book Center. (2019). Retrieved August 26, 2019, from https://ccbc.education.wisc.edu/default.asp

Cotabush, A., Dailey, D., Robinson, A., & Hughes, G. (2013). The effects of a STEM intervention on elementary students' science knowledge and skills. *School Science and Mathematics, 113*, 215–226. https://doi.org/10.1111/ssm.12023

Cox, A. M. (2012). An exploration of the practice approach and its place in information science. *Journal of Information Science, 38*(2), 176–188. https://doi.org/10.1177/0165551511435881

Guthrie, J. T., & Ozgungor, S. (2002). Instructional contexts for reading engagement. In C. C. Block, & M. Pressley (Eds.), *Comprehension instruction: Research-based best practices* (pp. 275–288). Guilford Press.

Ingen, S., Davis, J., & Arndt, K. (2018). The synergy between integrated STEM lessons and culturally responsive teaching in elementary classrooms. *Research in the Schools, 25*(1), 1–19.

Kelly, L. (2019). An analysis of award-winning science trade books for children: Who are the scientists, and what is science? *Journal of Research in Science Teaching, 55*(8), 1188–1210. https://doi.org/10.1002/tea.21447

Holub, J. (2015). *The knights before Christmas.* Henry Holt and Company.

Hooks, G. (2016). *Tiny stitches.* Lee & Low Books.

Ladson-Billings, G. (1995). But that's just good teaching! The case for culturally relevant pedagogy. *Theory into Practice, 34*(3), 159–165. https://doi.org/10.1080/00405849509543675

Larson, K., & Nethery, M. (2008). *Two bobbies.* Walker and Company.

Lyon, G. E. (2011). *All the water in the world.* Atheneum/Richard Jackson Books.

McSherry, J. (2005). Challenges persist for minorities and women. *Electronic Design, 53*(23), 59–62.

The Nation's Report Card. (2017). NAEP Reading Report Card. Retrieved from www.nationsreportcard.gov/reading_2017/nation/achievement?grade=4

National Research Council. (2011). *Successful K12 STEM education: Identifying effective approaches in science, technology, engineering and mathematics.* The National Academies. https://doi:10.17226/13158

National Science Foundation. (2015). National Center for Science and Engineering Statistics. Retrieved May 13, 2020 from www.nsf.gov/statistics/

NWEA. (2018). MAP reading fluency. Author. Retrieved from www.nwea.org/map-reading-fluency/

Ohio Department of Education. (2017, December 12). Results for Ohio's State Tests. Retrieved from http://education.ohio.gov/Topics/Testing/Testing-Results/Results-for-Ohios-State-Tests

Padilla, M. J., Muth, K. D., & Padilla, R. K. (1991). Science and reading: Many process skills in common. In C. M. Santa, & D. E. Alvermann (Eds.), *Science learning: Processes and applications* (pp. 14–19). International Reading Association.

Page, S. (2007, January 26). Diversity powers innovation. Center for American Progress. www.americanprogress.org/issues/economy/news/2007/01/26/2523/diversitypowers-innovation

Palincsar, A. S., & Magnusson, S. J. (2001). The interplay of first-hand and second-hand investigations to model and support the development of scientific knowledge and reasoning. In S. M. Carver, & D. Klahr (Eds.), *Cognition and instruction: Twenty-five years of progress* (pp. 151–193). Lawrence Erlbaum Associates.

Pinnell, M., Kurup, R., Stock, R., Turney, V., & Wendell, T. (2018). Using engineering design to increase literacy among third graders: A pilot study. *Research in the Schools, 25*(1), 47–58.

Prince, A. J. (2005). *Twenty-one elephants and still standing.* Houghton Mifflin.

Romance, N. R., & Vitale, M. R. (2001). Implementing an in-depth expanded science model in elementary schools: Multi-year findings, research issues, and policy implications. *International Journal of Science Education, 23*(4), 373–404. https://doi.org/10.1080/09500690116738

Rusch, E. (2013). *Volcano rising.* Charlesbridge.

Sterling, S. (2014, November 8). *Incorporating literacy in your STEM classroom.* Learning Sciences International. http://blog.learningsciences.com/2014/11/18/incorporating-literacy-in-your-stem-classroom

Spires, A. (2014). *The most magnificent thing.* Kids Can Press.

Strauss, A., & Corbin, J. (1990). *Basics of qualitative research.* SAGE.

Thompson, L. (2015). *Emmanuel's dream.* Schwartz & Wade.

US Bureau of Labor Statistics. (2015, Sept. 12). STEM occupations: Past, present, and future. US Department of Labor. Retrieved from www.bls.gov/spotlight/2017/science-technology-engineering-and-mathematics-stem-occupations-past-present-and-future/home.htm

Van Horne, C., Frayret, J. M., & Poulin, D. (2006). Creating value with innovation: From centre of expertise to the forest products industry. *Forest Policy and Economics, 8*(7), 751–761. https://doi.org/10.1016/j.forpol.2005.06.003

Van Dusen, C. (2012). *If I built a house.* Dial Books.

Williams, K. L. (1990). *Galimoto.* Lee and Shepard Books.

Wyss, V. L., Heulskamp, D., & Siebert, C. J. (2012). Increasing middle school student interest in STEM careers with videos of scientists. *International Journal of Environmental and Science Education, 7*(4), 501–522.

Appendix 24.1

Journal Entry Prompts

---

1. What would your dream house look like?
2. Will your house survive the rain, wind, or hail? What would you do differently if you had more time to build your house?
3. What is the strongest part of your house?
4. When is your birthday? Or describe yourself?
5. How did the community help the dog and the cat find a permanent home?
6. What do you know about water?
7. The best day of my life was …
8. How will you improve your filtration system?
9. What is your favorite drink?
10. What is your favorite part about STEM?
11. If I could fly, I would …
12. Write about a time when you tried your hardest at something.
13. What makes me unique?
14. What are you thankful for?
15. How would you change your design?
16. What is your favorite animal?
17. What do I want to do when I grow up?
18. What did you do over Thanksgiving?
19. How do you make a cake?
20. What does school mean to you?
21. What would you like to be when you grow up?
22. What are you thankful for?
23. What did you do over the holidays?
24. What would you do if you were President?
25. Who is your favorite superhero?
26. What is your favorite food?
27. Would you rather be famous or rich?
28. What would you do if someone gave you one million dollars?
29. What is your favorite TV show or movie?
30. What would you do if you were a principal?
31. What is your favorite animal?
32. If I could eat anything for dinner it would be …
33. Why do we need bridges?
34. My favorite room in my house is …
35. What do engineers do?
36. If you could be anyone in the world, who would you be?
37. Describe how you would build a robot.
38. What does the saying "it's raining cats and dogs" mean?
39. If you could invent anything in the world, what would you invent?

25

A SUSTAINED PROGRAM OF COMMUNITY ENGAGEMENT IN AFTER-SCHOOL LITERACY ACTIVITIES

Kristen L. White and Judith Puncochar

NORTHERN MICHIGAN UNIVERSITY

In the current era of high-stakes testing, standardization, and accountability, teacher education is under intense scrutiny regarding how well prospective teachers (PTs) are prepared to teach an increasingly diverse US student population. Widespread use of value-added methods (VAMs) are used to rate a teacher's ability to effectively teach all students (Darling-Hammond, 2015). A controversial element of VAMs is linking student test scores to a teacher's perceived effectiveness. Tools like VAMs that purport to estimate a teacher's contribution to student learning also plague teacher education because VAMS can be used to rate teacher preparation programs (TPPs) (Lincove et al., 2014). As a result, some teacher educators are implementing a core set of high-leverage teaching practices (Ball & Forzani, 2011; Forzani, 2014; McDonald et al., 2013; Windschitl et al., 2012). At the same time, literacy teacher preparation reform has argued for expanded notions of the goals of TPPs asserting that teacher educators have a responsibility to introduce and transform teaching practices so that they are more responsive to the "changing forms of literacy in our society" (International Literacy Association, 2018, p. 2).

These issues are compounded by the fact that a disproportionate number of white, middle-class, female PTs (Cross, 2005; Sleeter, 2001; Snyder, 2014) learn to teach from white, female teacher educators in predominantly white institutions (Merryfield, 2000). As white teacher educators ourselves, we are keenly aware that we prepare mostly white, female PTs to teach within a rural context where these issues are reflected in these demographics. At the same time, we continuously seek ways to improve our understanding of a set of "core teaching practices" recently mandated by the department of education in the state in which we teach, while also expanding our own notions of literacy. Taking heed of Sleeter's (2008) call to teacher education, we seek to prepare teachers who are confident in their abilities to teach in the "most diverse and challenging contexts" (p. 1954). We view these newly introduced core practices through the lens of culturally relevant teaching. In turn, we are continuously expanding our knowledge of culturally relevant teaching and the dynamic ways that children and youth use literacy to communicate. Geographic and demographic constraints pose challenges to the ways our TPP promotes equity and democracy with transformative teaching practices (Sleeter, 2008).

Standards documents, such as the International Literacy Association Standards for Reading Professionals – revised 2017 (International Literacy Association, 2018b), outline what teachers should know and be able to do. The organization also recently published a position statement advocating for transformative literacy teacher preparation (International Literacy Association, 2018a). These documents help guide revisions of course design, instruction, and consideration of field experiences across our program. Additionally, as teacher educators, we are inspired by our different areas of study to work together to transform our teaching practices. In spite of the ever-changing landscape of teacher education, the surveillance of TPPs, and the changing forms of literacy, we are encouraged by feedback accumulated over a decade from PTs who report positive learning outcomes in a pre-methods course with an early field experience in the form of academic service learning in our program.

The inclusion of field experiences often occurs in teacher education research. These experiences are particularly beneficial early in Teacher Preparation Programs (LaMaster, 2001; Lasley et al., 1986; Sleeter, 2008). An after-school community center experience provides PTs with a neighborhood context to bridge theory and practice (Coffey, 2010; Zeichner, 2010). A field experience is typically defined as an off-campus teaching experience with a specified number of hours where the PT spends time in a school with a classroom teacher learning to do the work of teaching (LaMaster, 2001). In contrast, service-learning is defined as a "successful teacher education practice that has been identified to provide students with field experiences in the community and to expose them to diverse settings" (Coffey, 2010, p. 336). The field experience we describe in this chapter is service-learning conceptualized as an early field experience in our program. At the university where we teach, the number of field experience hours varies across the required coursework but are assigned according to the state's Teacher Preparation Program standards.

Overview of a University–Community Partnership

Sociocultural theory posits that PTs' understandings are influenced by context (Gee, 2004; Grossman et al., 2000). Likewise, knowledge is constructed in situ. We believe that the context we create and how we model equity and democracy in our program is taken up by PTs. In this chapter, we explore how we are in dialogue with schools in the community that our PTs and we work in. We discuss how this partnership is related to three areas of literacy. First, we describe how

PTs' community experiences have affected our teacher education program. Next, we explain the impact an ongoing 15-year partnership between the university and local housing development has had on the community. Last, we end with a discussion about how interacting with children and youth has affected our PTs' evolving views of themselves as educators.

We have established and maintained an ongoing 15-year partnership between a local housing development based on income, the Huron River Youth and Family Center (HFC),[1] and a rural university in the Upper Midwest of the USA. The TPP where we teach services both undergraduate and graduate students. HFC is a high-density housing area that is home to about 115 families in a four-block area of the city. HFC families are predominantly female head-of-household family structures. Some HFC caretakers are university students and many have two or three part-time jobs. The HFC community center provides learning activities and supervised time for children while HFC caregivers run errands, study, participate at HFC, or work.

Initially, HFC was grant-funded by the Kellogg Foundation in 1996 as a model for delinquency prevention to provide youth with a safe, fun, supervised place to learn and socialize. When grants were no longer available, the YMCA oversaw HFC operations for about 10 years, after which the city's Housing Commission has managed HFC. This organic relationship grew out of mutual need and resulted in an example of the many ways that our program interacts with the community and the local schools (Sleeter, 2008). We posit that this longstanding collaboration with its continuous improvement serves as a model for other teacher education programs with an interest in preparing PTs for transformative teaching.

Teacher Education Program in Dialogue with the Community

As a new faculty member with a commitment to preparing PTs to teach in diverse classrooms, Judy, the second author, was the instructor for an entry-level educational foundations course that students take before the reading method courses that Kristen (the first author) teaches. Revising the course syllabus for academic service learning in 2005, Judy reimagined the course with its field experience hours to serve a community agency with PTs' support of K-12 student learning in an after-school setting. HFC provided a valued venue for pre-methods PTs to apply their knowledge of teaching for learning under the direction of HFC directors in settings beyond traditional classrooms. This course qualifies as a credit-bearing service-learning course within the university. To maintain the service-learning designator, the course must have PTs successfully engaged in three criteria. First, the participation in an organized service activity must meet an identified community need. Second, students who engage in service-learning activities must reflect on their activities in such a way as to gain further understanding of course

---

[1]   All names are pseudonyms.

content, a broader appreciation of the discipline, and an enhanced sense of personal values and civic responsibility (Bringle & Hatcher, 1995). Third, student-learning outcomes are assessed for effectiveness using rubrics and a capstone field report.

The university started the ongoing HFC collaboration in January 2005 with 50 teacher candidates at the request for lessons in conflict resolution and for after-school homework help. At the end of the first semester, four PTs questioned the value of the HFC experience on their course evaluations. The next semester, PT comments about HFC were consistently positive. One PT suggested reducing the required number from 10 hours. The student wrote, "not so many hours at HFC. Just don't make it mandatory." Since 2005, the PT comments have been positive and focused on learning. One PT wrote, "Service Learning has provided a place to link the course concepts to real-world actions." Providing field experiences early in the PTT program allows PTs an opportunity to apply their learning in real world settings. Our teacher preparation programs have intentionally increased the number and kinds of field experiences throughout our courses. We reduced the number of participation hours at HFC from ten to seven to make room for time at a bilingual immersion school and for engagement in a Poverty Simulation experience (www.povertysimulation.net/contact/).

Community Impact of a 15-Year Partnership

HFC is open for after-school activities from 3:00 p.m. to 6:00 p.m. on full school days and closed on half-days and Professional Development school days. Ideally, two to four PTs are available every hour to participate in a variety of after-school programming. PTs and the HFC Director use an online HFC calendar to sign up for hours of service. Over the course of a semester, 50–60 PTs have accumulated a total of 350–450 hours of service at HFC. Some PTs continue with their service at the HFC after the semester is over (e.g., one PT provided 2.5 years of mentoring with an individual HFC student). A consistent mentoring relationship with a K-12 student is not always possible. PTs determine their participation depending upon their class and work schedules. Sign-up is on a first-come basis. In a class of 60 PTs, the distribution of PTs on site at any given day has remained remarkably even. PTs occasionally conducted their required hours during a single week. This flexibility is important because many of PTs work full- or part-time, commute long distances, and have other life responsibilities.

HFC serves about 40 K-12 students each full school day. PTs synchronized their onsite participation during a healthy snack, helping with homework, and music and sports lessons and practice. PTs collectively contributed an average of about six hours of participation at HFC each day. PTs also helped to create HFC programs based on community interests and needs (e.g., music lessons, American Sign Language classes, art projects, football on Thursdays, and math puzzles on Mondays). Some of these programs have continued over several years (e.g., the art program and American Sign Language lessons). HFC directors and teachers at local schools have made positive comments about how the PTs' encouragement and support for homework help had a positive effect on the academic achievement of HFC students in the classroom. PTs have overwhelmingly written positive reflections about their service within the HFC community and hands-on opportunities to apply course concepts and educational theories.

Literacy Activities

Throughout the 15-year collaboration, PTs have worked with children and youth at the HFC to design and implement various activities. These activities were built on students' interests, the local context, and helped to develop literacy by providing students with choices of literacy-based activities. For example, PTs developed an art program that has provided experiences with tessellations, clay making, scratch art, recycled art, and Styrofoam self-portraits. Students wrote about their art projects and orally described their projects to families, peers, and neighbors. A main purpose of art is to communicate, which is at the heart of literacy. Some of the initial artwork remains visible in the HFC art gallery. Students have sharpened their literacy practices with authentic purposes for communication, including conflict resolution strategies, one-on-one tutoring, the Homework Helpers Program, a gardening project, and planning dances.

The PTs have helped HFC students develop literacy and communication skills through the following activities:

- Senior Youth Council Facilitators
- Junior Youth Council Facilitators
- Tutoring
- Planning Valentine's Day Dances
- Homework Helpers Program
- Art Program (with art captions)
    - Tessellations (math fun)
    - Clay Making
    - Scratch Art
    - Styrofoam self-portraits
    - HFC Art Gallery
    - Photography (with photo captions)
- Planting seeds
- Football on Thursdays (football rules and "huddle" communication)
- Earth Day Fair
- Animal Skins Activities
- Recycled Paper Making
- Composting
- Catch and Release Fishing
- Lake Clean-up

- Recycled Art (beauty, message, and sustainability)
- Music Literacy through Lessons
  - Guitar
  - Drum
  - Piano
- Monday Math Puzzle
- American Sign Language tutoring and workshop
- Environmental Activities Program (Animal Tracks in the Snow)
- Friday Night Socials (until 7:30 p.m.) with movies, popcorn, games, and snacks.

PTs' Evolving Views of Becoming Literacy Educators

PTs wrote required critical reflection papers to connect their learning and course content with service-learning community experiences. Reflection questions were necessary to guide PT observations and limit generalizing, stereotyping, and systematic types of social perception inaccuracies (e.g., exhibiting overconfidence in judgments, opinions, and decisions, seeking confirming information without noticing disconfirming information to stereotypes, and making attribution errors; see Puncochar, 2016). Course concepts framed the nature of human biases and the development of language and literacy in children.

Teacher candidate reflections center mainly on their feelings, developing relationships, and understanding of service-learning as real-world, value-added experiences to course objectives. Reflection papers were required to include connections to educational theory and research. Although PTs were adept at observing examples of educational theories in the classroom, they were not as skilled at self-reflection of their personal expectations and activation of stereotypes. In addition, their reflections generally omitted any mention of cultural assets of the neighborhood community. Occasionally, PTs championed their personal role in "helping" HFC students achieve success in various activities and thereby checked off a completed course requirement from the list of field experience activities.

Some PTs participated in classrooms where HFC students went to school. The development of intercultural perspectives appeared to occur when PTs observed HFC students in more than one context. However, whether seven hours of field experiences at HFC is enough to break down stereotypes and hone intercultural competencies and sophistication remains unknown. Even with considerable instructor feedback, PTs probably need more time to reduce systematic types of social perception inaccuracies and increase intercultural sophistication.

PTs wrote extensively on the importance of participating in their community and on the benefits of service learning to their own learning, but they rarely mentioned wanting to use service-learning in their future classrooms. This omission is understandable in an entry-level education course. Coordination between classroom teachers, university instructors, and community members is necessary to achieve a purposeful, productive community-based, service-learning, literacy-rich experience. Service-learning activities must align with the cultural needs of the community, develop within an appropriate educational context, and maintain and improve the community partnership over time.

PT Reflections on HFC

Themes of diversity and application of course concepts were consistently present in PT reflections on their HFC field experiences. The number of diverse cultures represented by HFC students and families caught the attention of PTs. "HFC also has a higher percentage of students from different ethnic backgrounds than the local school districts." PTs wondered whether parents in the neighboring areas did not know the HFC program was free and open to the public or whether parents made a choice to "segregate their children from the HFC children." PTs who grew up near the HFC community expressed surprise at how "wonderful" the program is for the community. They reflected on the HFC current relative obscurity. "Growing up we heard HFC was stereotyped as the 'bad' side of town … HFC is truly a wonderful program and the fact that more people do not know HFC exists is a shame."

PTs have professional responsibilities to engage with students from diverse cultural backgrounds. Their openness to cultural diversity could suggest a possible link between PTs' willingness to support literacy acquisition of HFC students (see Castro, 2010).

> I was disappointed to see how uncomfortable my peers were at HFC. While I was playing pool and coloring with the children, my peers sat on the couches looking around nervously. I am saddened that relating to the lives of people we all work and go to school with is so uncomfortable for the mass majority.

The detachment of PTs within their HFC experiences was subtle:

> HFC was another experience I did not see coming … I noticed younger students with ragged clothes and messy hair, and older students who were too busy to look up from their iPhones. The overall experience was confusing with mixed emotions … In the future, I will be prepared as a future educator to react and make a difference in the lives of these children.

We cannot expect PTs to "be prepared" without providing them with additional opportunities to explore and practice responses within culturally diverse spaces. However, providing additional opportunities must be accompanied by education about the nature of prejudice and bias; otherwise, even children's innate curiosity toward new learning could be associated with a deficit model.

> The experience of teaching the HFC students how to cut pineapple, as well as seeing their reaction to how pineapple tasted, gave me an opportunity to reflect on the importance of community spaces such as HFC to educate the students in instances where they might not receive essential life skills otherwise.

One could argue whether learning how to cut a pineapple is an essential life skill; however, transitioning between socioeconomic classes requires PTs and their students to be open to embracing cultural experiences across socioeconomic divides. Whether PTs are prepared to transverse cultural divides is the subject of further inquiry.

Community partners have potential to create authentic spaces through which teacher candidates are able to develop culturally responsive literacy practices (see Cipollone et al., 2018). From the HFC Director's perspective, PTs benefit the most by seeing how children play and use their imaginations outside classroom settings and by experiencing how children understand and act on directions for activities. We encourage PTs to explore how to engage HFC children in play that promotes literacy through the PTs' content areas (e.g., the application of science through cooking and the identification of animal tracks in snow). Children implicitly construct self-concepts through interactions in social settings such as everyday play (Chafel, 2003).

HFC also provides an opportunity for PTs to observe how some families function beyond school and collaborate with participating adults and children.

> HFC is an important part of the community because the program helps students meet basic needs that could take away from their learning experience. I have seen children as well as their parents eat meals and spend time at HFC.

Collaboration is an important element of a literacy pedagogy for teachers of linguistically and culturally diverse children (Cipollone et al., 2018). The HFC director wrote,

> I am grateful each and every day for the help of your students and program. They truly help the HFC program more than they know. Even just the one-on-one mentoring they give by playing a simple game or coloring a picture means so much to our children, and these children need it most.

PTs frequently reflected on the importance of patience and the need to proceed step-by-step through games and homework. These shared experiences have implications for literacy pedagogy and teachers of culturally and linguistically diverse children. More time is needed for action teaching (Plous, 2000) to challenge PTs to analyze the literacy processes that they are using and to make an effort to implement practiced, improved solutions.

PT reflections encompassed diversity and course topics such as social development of HFC children.

> At HFC, I observed a group of students gossiping about another student who was not present. The students who joined the original group displayed characteristics of morality based on peer opinion (Stage 3; Kohlberg, 1984). The students possibly thought since other students were gossiping that gossiping must be morally acceptable.

Initially, beginning PTs might not have the pedagogical skills to explore the moral reasoning of HFC students through discussion, but opportunities to approach the role of cliques, friendships, and peers and reflect on possible approaches to engaging students in a discussion of ethical behavior are available to PTs during university class time.

Likewise, frequent application of course topics on leadership and problem solving (see Puncochar, 2013) were present in PT reflections.

> The field experience that I am going to run through the Authentic Leadership Model is handling weather-related school cancellations. Every time the schools are canceled, all after-school activities are canceled too, including HFC. The mission is keeping students safe during weather-related conditions.

Traveling to HFC was an issue for some PTs, which could have had an effect on PT attitudes toward participating in field experiences at HFC. In general, teacher education faculty could have better attitudes toward community service than PTs have (Bauer et al., 2007). PT criticisms about HFC participation hours focused primarily on difficulties of scheduling around PT classes, jobs, and athletic responsibilities.

Conclusion

Service-learning activities were organized to meet identified community needs and provide a setting beyond typical classrooms for PTs to apply course content within authentic cultural contexts. A coordinated effort to include HFC outcomes in service-learning experiences helped maintain communication and a sense of reciprocity and equity. Balancing learning outcomes for a community partner and university program was necessary to secure positive outcomes for PTs, program accreditation efforts, and our community partner's success. Striving toward service-learning success with a university and community partner remains an ongoing challenge. Declining enrollments and resources in teacher preparation programs have created challenges and required collaborative work to achieve successful outcomes.

Sharpening a focus on community culture and service-learning goals has helped to maintain a successful 15-year partnership with a university and neighborhood community center. Our continuous cross-cultural service-learning partnership has required attention to equity and articulation of community needs directly linked to university and community learning outcomes. In turn, a shared commitment between teacher education programs and community partners to prepare literacy teachers to "embrace a moral stance in the face of an educational system that is falling short on the promise of providing educational opportunities for all" could help to prepare beginning teachers to teach with transformational practices (International Literacy Association, 2018a, p. 2). Responsive and powerful transformational teaching practices are necessary for successful literacy attainment of learners within their cultural contexts.

Preparing PTs to teach with increasingly diverse student populations remains an ongoing challenge for our rural university. A sustainable collaboration between our university and a local community income-based housing program has been a complex balance of effective learning experiences for PTs and HFC families. A sense of equity has developed over our 15-year partnership. Community needs are linked directly to the university program's Student Learning Outcomes for PTs to enhance the literacies of children and youth within a community. Instructors and PTs learn about the neighborhood culture as supportive of literacy needs of local schoolchildren. Our sustainable 15-year partnership offers evidence that beginning PTs can provide responsive learning to deepen the literacy activities within a community.

References

Ball, D. L., & Forzani, F. M. (2011). Building a common core for learning to teach: And connecting professional learning to practice. *American Educator, 35*(2), 17. https://doi.org/10.1177/0888406415577453

Bauer, E. H., Moskal, B., & Gosink, J. (2007). Faculty and student attitudes toward community service: A comparative analysis. *Journal of Engineering Education, 96*(2), 129–140. https://doi.org/10.1002/j.2168–9830.2007.tb00923.x

Bringle, R., & Hatcher, J. (1995). A service-learning curriculum for faculty. *Michigan Journal of Community Service Learning, 2*, 112–122. http://hdl.handle.net/1805/4591

Castro, A. J. (2010). Challenges in teaching for critical multicultural citizenship: Student teaching in an accountability-driven context. *Action in Teacher Education, 32*(2), 97–109. https://doi.org/10.1080/01626620.2010.10463553

Chafel, J. (2003). Socially constructing concepts of self and other through play. *International Journal of Early Years Education, 11*, 213–222. www.tandf.co.uk/journals/default.html https://doi.org/10.1080/09669760320000147334

Cipollone, K., Zygmunt, E., & Tancock, S. (2018). "A paradigm of possibility": Community mentors and teacher preparation. *Policy Futures in Education, 16*(6), 709–728. https://doi.org/10.1177/1478210317751270

Coffey, H. (2010). "They taught me": The benefits of early community-based field experiences in teacher education. *Teaching and Teacher Education, 26*(2), 335–342. https://doi.org/10.1016/j.tate.2009.09.014

Cross, B. E. (2005). New racism, reformed teacher education, and the same ole' oppression. *Educational Studies, 38*(3), 263–274. https://doi.org/10.3102/0091732X16686949

Darling-Hammond, L. (2015). Can value added add value to teacher evaluation? *Educational Researcher, 44*(2), 132–137. https://doi.org/10.3102/0013189X15575346

Forzani, F. M. (2014). Understanding "core practices" and "practice-based" teacher education learning from the past. *Journal of Teacher Education, 65*(4), 357–368. https://doi.org/10.1177/0022487114533800

Gee, J. (2004). *An introduction to discourse analysis: Theory and method.* Routledge.

Grossman, P. L., Valencia, S. W., Evans, K., Thompson, C., Martin, S., & Place, N. (2000). Transitions into teaching: Learning to teach writing in teacher education and beyond. *Journal of Literacy Research, 32*(4), 631–662. https://doi.org/10.1080/10862960009548098

International Literacy Association. (2018a). *Transforming literacy teacher preparation: Practice makes possible.* [Literacy leadership brief]. Retrieved from https://literacyworldwide.org/docs/default-source/where-we-stand/ila-transforming-literacy-teacher-preparation.pdf

International Literacy Association. (2018b). *Standards for the preparation of literacy professionals 2017.* Author.

Kohlberg, L. (1984). *The psychology of moral development: The nature and validity of moral stages (Essays on Moral Development, Volume 2).* Harper & Row.

LaMaster, K. J. (2001). Enhancing preservice teachers field experiences through the addition of a service-learning component. *Journal of Experiential Education, 24*(1), 27–33. https://doi.org/10.1177/105382590102400107

Lasley, T. J., Applegate, J. H., & Ellison, C. (1986). The expectations and problems of university supervisors of early field experiences. *Journal of Education for Teaching, 12*(2), 127–140. https://doi.org/10.1080/0260747860120202

Lincove, J. A., Osborne, C., Dillon, A., & Mills, N. (2014). The politics and statistics of value-added modeling for accountability of teacher preparation programs. *Journal of Teacher Education, 65*(1), 24–38. https://doi.org/10.1177/0022487113504108

McDonald, M., Kazemi, E., & Kavanagh, S. S. (2013). Core practices and pedagogies of teacher education: A call for a common language and collective activity. *Journal of Teacher Education, 64*(5), 378–386. https://doi.org/10.1177/0022487113493807

Merryfield, M. M. (2000). Why aren't teachers being prepared to teach for diversity, equity, and global interconnectedness? A study of lived experiences in the making of multicultural and global educators. *Teaching and Teacher Education, 16*(4), 429–443. https://doi.org/10.1016/S0742-051X(00)00004-4

Plous, S. (2000). Responding to overt displays of prejudice: A role-playing exercise. *Teaching of Psychology, 27*, 198–200. https://doi.org/10.1207/S15328023TOP2703_07

Puncochar, J. (2013). Observations on leadership, problem solving, and preferred futures of universities. *Education Leadership Review, 14*(1), 29–36. www.ncpeapublications.org

Puncochar, J. (2016). Striving for academic service learning success in a rural K-12 tribal school. In R. Stoecker (Ed.), *The landscape of rural service learning and what it teaches all of us* (Chapter 13, pp. 137–143). Michigan State University Press.

Sleeter, C. (2008). Equity, democracy, and neoliberal assaults on teacher education. *Teaching and Teacher Education, 24*(8), 1947–1957. https://doi.org/10.1016/j.tate.2008.04.003

Sleeter, C. E. (2001). Preparing teachers for culturally diverse schools: Research and the overwhelming presence of whiteness. *Journal of Teacher Education, 52*(2), 94–106. https://doi.org/10.1177/0022487101052002002

Snyder, T. D. (2014). *Mobile digest of education statistics 2013* (NCES 2014–085). National Center for Education Statistics, US Department of Education.

Windschitl, M., Thompson, J., Braaten, M., & Stroupe, D. (2012). Proposing a core set of instructional practices and tools for teachers of science. *Science Education, 96*(5), 878–903. https://doi.org/10.1002/sce.21027

Zeichner, K. (2010). Rethinking the connections between campus courses and field experiences in college- and university-based teacher education. *Journal of Teacher Education, 61*(1–2), 89–99. https://doi.org/10.1177/0022487109347671

26

THE POWER OF LITERACY FOR COMMUNITY ENGAGEMENT

Partnering with Youth Community-Based Organizations*

Crystal Chen Lee, Jose A. Picart, Nina Schoonover, and Kelsey Virginia Dufresne

NORTH CAROLINA STATE UNIVERSITY

Recent research has highlighted the benefit of community-based organization (CBO) environments for student learning outcomes – these contexts center students' perspectives – and aim to empower students through writing that taps into out-of-school literacy practices (Cammarota, 2011; Green, 2013; Watson & Bemeyer, 2019; Wright & Mahiri, 2012). With these literacy practices, CBOs function as important spaces for students to find "restorative" (Winn, 2010) potential outside of traditional English education, and to make connections across home, school, and community. CBOs seek not to replace traditional schools, but rather to build partnerships between teachers and their communities to share pedagogical practices in mutually beneficial ways (Brooks & Smith, 2013; Gardner, 2011; Warren, 2005). However, empowering pedagogies in CBOs are often disconnected from universities that prepare aspiring teachers or support in-service learning, thus fueling the home–school divide.

The Literacy and Community Initiative (LCI) is an interdisciplinary project examining youth literacies that address the need for increased partnerships among universities, schools, and communities (Campano, Ghiso, & Welch, 2016; Harris & Kiyama, 2013; McMillon, 2016). The LCI is a partnership between North Carolina State University, the Friday Institute for Educational Innovation, and three local youth-serving CBOs (Bull City YouthBuild, Juntos NC, and CORRAL Riding Academy). The project investigates and promotes literacy as a means of increasing advocacy, developing leadership skills, and enhancing social and emotional well-being among traditionally underserved students.

* Research for this chapter was supported by the North Carolina State University Catalyst Grant and Outreach and Engagement Incentive Grant.

The mission of the collaborative partnership is to explore what happens when youth *write* their stories, *engage* with educational stakeholders, and *lead* in their communities.

This interdisciplinary project is unique in its collaborative mission. University researchers and CBO leaders co-develop the literacy curriculum implemented in the three organizations to help students develop their literacy skills through writing and publishing texts, such as personal narratives, poetry, and advocacy letters. An important aspect of the curriculum comes in the end when youth participate in community dialogues through public readings of their work. These acts allow them to lead in their communities by sharing their perspective on how others can advocate for underserved youth.

In the developing second phase, the project aims to measure the degree to which engaging in these literacy activities: (a) increases the participants' abilities to advocate for themselves and their communities, (b) enhances participants' specific leadership skills (self-efficacy and goal-setting), and (c) promotes the participants' social and emotional well-being (self-compassion, self-esteem, and self-determination). In this second phase, the project seeks to integrate three distinct threads of research on youth development: (1) critical literacy, (2) community-embedded learning that inspires and supports youth advocacy development, and (3) psychology research related to the social/emotional development of self-determination, self-esteem, and self-compassion.

The Literacy and Community Initiative seeks to answer the following three research questions designed through a model of *Write, Engage,* and *Lead*:

1. *Write.* What are the narratives and literacy experiences of underserved youth in CBOs?
2. *Engage.* How does the narrative writing process empower underserved youth to improve literacy learning and engage with multiple stakeholders in their community?
3. *Lead.* How does publishing their narratives enable youth to lead and advocate for themselves and their communities? In turn, how does the reading, writing, and sharing of narratives inspire the community to act and advocate for underserved youth? To what degree does participating in the project activities contribute to enhancing the participants' self-compassion, self-determination, and self-esteem?

This chapter will focus on *Phase 1* of LCI research, which sought to answer the first two questions: *Write* and *Engage.* Meanwhile, we continue to build and develop measures for the third set of research question related to the *Lead* component of our model. In this chapter, we present the experiences and research that has emerged from two of LCI's CBO partnerships: Juntos NC and Bull City YouthBuild of Triangle Literacy Council.

Theoretical Framework

The Literacy and Community Initiative is structured within a critical literacy framework (Comber, 2015; Morrell, 2008). This theoretical framework guides both the research as well as the relationships built between the university and the community-based organizations. Both of the organizations at the focus of this chapter, Juntos NC and Bull City YouthBuild, serve traditionally marginalized and underserved students of color as well as immigrant or first-generation students. Therefore, we brought a critical literacy lens specifically to these populations as we centered our work.

Critical Literacy and Community Literacy Practices

As community-based organizations exist outside of traditional schools, they allow students to explore positions of power within themselves, their communities, and their worlds in transformative ways (Comber, 2015; Morrell, 2008). More specifically, literacy practices, such as reading, writing, and speaking, can center and amplify the experiences of students underserved due to systemic racial, ethnic, and social inequities. Our definition of critical literacy is rooted in Freire's (1985) views on the liberating nature of participatory literacy practices. CBOs are uniquely centered within the communities they serve, offering potentially authentic and reflexive literacy development for the youth.

Writing and speaking about their experiences alongside peers at community-based organizations can help students position and see themselves within their communities (Camangian, 2008; Campano, Ghiso, Rusoja, et al., 2016; Johnson, 2017). These acts allow underserved youth to move past any external labels or stereotypes (Watson & Beymeyer, 2019; Winn, 2010) that deny them an individually defined sense of self. As students are encouraged to explore their own selves, they can develop identities "not limited to generalizations and stereotypes that have negatively impacted their self-image, as well as the images other people have imposed on them" (Fisher, 2003, p. 387). Youth-serving CBOs can also enable students to find academic potential outside of traditional schools, particularly for students who have already struggled or have been unsuccessful in those environments. More specifically, this in turn helps to build the university–school–community partnership (Gardner, 2011; McMillon, 2016; Warren, 2005) as students develop critical literacy skills that push them to question and explore system-wide educational structures. For these traditionally underserved students, we see freedom in community-based organizations to promote critical literacy that engages students with centering themselves in their communities.

Critical Literacy and Marginalized Students

Critical literacy and written expression have power in the hands of marginalized youth. Winn (2010) found that through writing with the adolescent incarcerated black girls at the center of her study revealed a collective use of literacy "to move away from physical and symbolic imprisonment and toward imagining possibilities beyond incarceration" (p. 426). These young women looked to writing as a way to navigate away from marginalization and the confines of structures that have traditionally held them in. In another piece, Winn (2013) called for "restorative English education," a curriculum and pedagogy framed around healing, transformation, and empowerment as it begins and is structured around the voices of youth.

Expression, both written and verbal, can foster belonging among students as they build communal literacy practices, particularly ones where they reflect on their pasts and look toward their futures. In their study of a theater-based program for incarcerated youth, authors Vasudevan et al. (2010) saw that participation in this program gave students "a chance to re-author themselves outside of the (sometimes limiting) expectations of their home and community affiliations, as well as those of school and the criminal justice system" (p. 64). Through these critical reflections of self, community, and world, students developed critical consciousness and notions of positioning themselves against a tradition of silencing.

Critical Literacy and Immigrant Students

As immigration is increasingly and negatively publicized in political spheres, immigrant and first-generation students face additional challenges that accompany them to the classroom. In her work with the diversity found within the immigrant journey and experience, Suárez-Orozco (2017) stated: "When large swaths of a society begin to loudly and unabashedly proclaim exclusionary messages toward its immigrants, it creates a climate of national hatred and xenophobia" (p. 527). Thus, traditional education environments in America are often inaccessible for immigrant students due to numerous inhibitory factors that do not affect "mainstream populations" (Stewart, 2013) and that teachers are often unaware of.

Furthermore, scholars and educators are finding that an equity framework is fundamental (Comber, 2015) for immigrant students. As Rodríguez-Valls (2016) wrote, "Education in an era of diaspora calls for the full inclusion, participation and presence of all students and their families in the teaching and learning occurring in schools" (p. 47). Through using critical and culturally relevant pedagogies in her coordinating role in with PODER-YES program, Kelly (2012) found that such critical literacy practice not only better reaches immigrant students where they are, but also aids in fostering collaboration and empowerment in the classroom as a whole. Kelly (2012) also argued for this practice as it relies upon and benefits from the experiences and memories of immigrant students as a resource in the classroom.

Toward a Theory of Change for Youth Literacy and Leadership

The LCI project expands upon this critical literacy framework for marginalized youth and immigrant students through a theory of change. The mission of LCI is to build university and youth community-based partnerships by amplifying student voices through student publication, advocacy, and leadership. We believe that literacy can be a force for educational equity, a vehicle for community engagement, and a form of leadership. With the creation of LCI, the team developed a theory of change/logic model to better measure the effectiveness of our work. LCI assumes tenets of critical literacy that argue that reading and writing investigates positions of power within self, community, and world that offers transformative outcomes for youth (Morrell, 2008). We assume that critical literacy practices are liberating for marginalized youth, and youth-serving CBOs enable students to realize their potential outside of traditional school environments. Grounded in these assumptions, we developed a theory of change (Figure 26.1) that encourages youth to "Write, Engage, and Lead" as a pathway to increased self and community advocacy, increased leadership potential, and increased educational equity.

Methodology

Multiphase Mixed-Methods Design

The research component of LCI is a multiphase mixed-methods design that was built on an exploratory sequential design (Creswell, 2012) in which we generate insights from qualitative data to inform the quantitative phases of this project. In all phases of the project, the research design will advance three project goals: (1) to increase student literacy (reading, writing, and speaking); (2) to promote student social/emotional development; and (3) to enhance student advocacy and leadership skills. Below is the project's five-year framework:

- Phase I (Years 1–2) PILOT & PROTOTYPE: Co-develop the key components of the literacy curriculum and document the collaborative process of university–CBO partnerships. (*Phase I is the focus of this chapter.*)
- Phase II (Years 2–4) SUSTAIN & EXPAND: Improve and enhance the literacy curriculum to increase its effectiveness in CBOs.
- Phase III (Years 4–5) CO-EVOLVE & BUILD CAPACITY: Modify, innovate, and adapt the literacy curriculum in ways that shift ownership and implementation of the project to community partners.

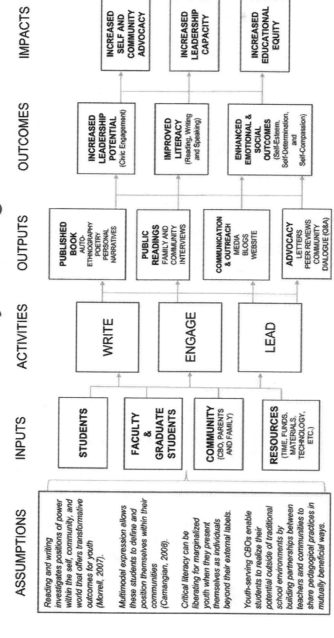

FIGURE 26.1 LCI Logic Model

For this report, we focus on Phase I of the project through the qualitative case-study methodology and findings. However, we include elements of Phases II and III in order to shed light of the overall project for the community-based purposes of this handbook.

Qualitative Case-Study Design for Juntos NC and Bull City YouthBuild

In this book chapter, we present the two CBOs, Juntos NC and Bull City Youthbuild, as a bound case within a qualitative case study. During Phase I, we collected only qualitative data for the purposes of illuminating the literacy practices and narratives of students' writing and engagement in their programs. The case study was designed to investigate "the meaning people make of their lives in very particular contexts" (Dyson & Genishi, 2005, p. 35). Aligned with our critical literacy framework, the personal narratives of underserved youth were historicized, contextualized, and analyzed for context-specific meaning-making.

This study generated four types of qualitative data: document reviews which included the writing drafts and published books, pre- and post- semi-structured interviews, and qualitative surveys with students and staff (Bogdan & Biklen, 2007; LeCompte & Schensul, 2010), ethnographic observation and researcher memos of the writing process (Angrosino & Mays de Perez, 2000) in each organization, and a public reading attendee survey. Multiple data collection methods allowed for triangulation across data sets.

At the public readings in the CBO's corresponding communities, the students would share their stories with their peers, family members, friends, and the public. The significance of this was that their stories were documented, shared, and explored in a setting beyond the classroom. Thus, we found the students centered in the study when the focus was drawn to their own stories and experiences (Kelly, 2012). Furthermore, the families and communities of these authors also felt empowered through their students' voices.

The largest data set was the students' writing from the published books as well as participant observations of this process. From these data, we drew themes of the students' meaning-making, literacy learning, and community engagement. In addition, field notes and thematic memos were generated at the two CBOs and interviews were transcribed concurrent with document reviews and observations. The pre and post interviews and qualitative surveys of the students and staff were used to assess the students' writing progress, self-esteem, and leadership develop-ment. Through an iterative process, we analyzed the qualitative data inductively and deductively and subscribe to the notion of transferability from this work. Our data revealed youth experiences with writing and publishing that we believe carry over (i.e., are transferable) to other CBOs and communities.

In Phases II and III of this project, quantitative data will be used to help inform the qualitative data (Creswell, 2012), and we will use descriptive and inferential statistics to compare findings across the CBOs and subgroups of students. More specifically, we believe that quantitative measures of student motivation and social emotional development (self-efficacy, self-compassion, and self-determination) may serve as intervening variables that help explain the themes that emerge from the youth narratives and writing. During all phases, design-based research (DBR) will "improve educational practices ... based on collaborations among researchers and practitioners" (Wang & Hannafin, 2005, p. 6) through contextually sensitive design principles.

Context and Participants

Through this multi-phase approach to data collection and analysis, this interdisciplinary work leveraged intersections among universities, CBOs, and communities to develop educational practices that were relevant and meaningful to youth's lives. By foregrounding youth voices and leadership, we contribute to research on university–community partnerships that recognize the full humanity of youth. Based on established university–community partnerships, we studied the literacy experiences of a purposeful and convenient sample of 10–15 students (ages 14–21) in each of the two CBOs (total of 20–25). Each CBO's missions are detailed below.

Triangle Literacy Council's Bull City YouthBuild

The Triangle Literacy Council seeks to provide youth, adults, and families with literacy skills, and Bull City YouthBuild (BCYB), is an organization within this council. BCYB is a 9-month education and leadership program that serves low-income youth who are not enrolled in school and are unemployed. As a part of YouthBuild's national network funded by the Department of Labor, BCYB youth gain academic and leadership skills through receiving their high school equivalency and working with Habitat for Humanity. The program is centered on community service, academic success, job training, and leadership development. Through the partnership between Literacy and Community Initiative and Bull City YouthBuild that started in 2017, the students have published three books: *Blueprints: Rebuilding Lives and Redesigning Futures*, *Strong and Unbroken*, and *See Unbroken Pieces Through the Shadows*.

Juntos, NC

Juntos NC works to unite community partners and families to help Latinx secondary students complete and succeed in high school and attend higher education. Juntos NC aims to provide a safe space of community for Latinx students while making education accessible to families and students through 4-H clubs, mentoring and success coaching, family and community event nights, and workshops. The

LCI has worked with Juntos NC and the Juntos Hispanic Literacy Group's student authors, all at their high school, to meet biweekly after school to practice writing, reading, and performing their pieces, and ultimately sharing their stories. Together the students have published two books: *The Roots of Our People: From One World to Another – Juntos* and *The Voices of Our People: Nuestras Verdades.*

Collectively, the students from these two organizations authored and published the five books shown in Figure 26.2. The two Juntos HLG book covers were created and designed by student, Briza, who wanted to demonstrate the group's Latin roots. Briza expressed in "A Note on the Art" at the beginning of the book that these roots, like those for plants and trees, are essential for growth, which further encapsulates the students' explorations of the dualities of their identities. The LCI students have also taken creative ownership for each book they have published by generating the book titles and designing all the book covers.

Findings

Significant findings emerging from the data are informed by our review of the relevant literature and strongly suggest that student and youth empowerment are rooted in the opportunity for the discussion, analysis, and sharing of their own experiences and stories. Deductive coding of the first two books published by our student authors revealed how participants positioned themselves through their language, as well as how they advocated for others and their communities. While both the writing and research projects were framed within the LCI curriculum, the words of the students and the themes that emerged from their writing are unique to their respective community-based organizations.

Bull City YouthBuild Findings

Through our analysis of the first book published by Bull City YouthBuild students, *Blueprints: Rebuilding Lives and Redesigning Futures*, we found these students renegotiating and repositioning their past, rebuilding their community, and redesigning their futures. As many of these students have faced past hardships, in their poetry and memoirs, we saw them weighing their past decisions as they saw YouthBuild helping them build their future. In her poem, "What was, What is, What will be" (see Figure 26.3), YouthBuild student Jane balanced the hardships from her past with her current strength and resilience. She concluded her poem with, "I am from the highs and lows and / the moments in between / From where you are now and where you'll be." Here, we saw her considering the pieces of her life that have both shaped who she is, but also pushed her toward her future.

As we coded this language throughout students' poems, we looked to the ways the students redefined themselves and reflected positively on "who they are, where they live, and how they might bring changes to the world around them" (Cammarota, 2011, p. 829), revealing shifting modes of critical literacy practices.

FIGURE 26.2   Book Covers of Five Published Books (Blueprints: Rebuilding Lives and Redesigning Futures; The Roots of Our People: From One World to Another – Juntos; Strong and Unbroken; The Voices of Our People: Nuestras Verdades; and See Unbroken Pieces Through the Shadows)

What was, What is, What will be.

Jane Rodriguez

I am from a belief in God.
From the hard-working to helping hands.
I am from "*I can do anything*".
I am from a broken home and a busy parent,
Where hands are busy through the day, and tired,
But keep going.
I am from where no one taught me what's right from
wrong,
But still living life to the *fullest*.
I am from the highs and lows and
the moments in between
From where you are now and where you'll be.

FIGURE 26.3 "What was, What is, What will be" by Bull City YouthBuild Student, Jane Rodriguez

Alternative literacy spaces can open the door for students to redefine themselves during their participation in the program, and we found this in the narratives of YouthBuild students as they wrote "clear goals for myself" in redesigning their futures.

Another theme that emerged from their book was a sense of rebuilding community and the strength that came from working together. In their collective poem, the students wrote about the power of teamwork at YouthBuild: "we're a family and will always bring a pleasing and welcoming comfort to the cohort. We won't deny or be malicious to anyone; we're eager to help the ones that need it." In this work, they showcased their desire to not only help themselves succeed, but also build up the people around them. For example, a student wrote about her dream of becoming a "therapist and help people with their problems. I'm a very good listener, and I give great advice because I have my own story to tell." We found her considering her own strengths in focusing on how she might give back to her community. Students' narratives revealed how they recognized their potential value, not failure, for supporting themselves and those around them.

As they wrote about rebuilding the community, both through constructing a Habitat for Humanity home as well as fostering relationships between one another, the students also wrote about moves for the future and ways of redesigning their lives. Their words reflected how they saw potential within themselves as strong individuals in their communities. Students shared their goals that lay out the steps ahead in their narratives; "I want to try to be better so I can say that I did it by myself." This consideration for the characteristics of success revealed that these students aimed for independence and accountability in their future lives. One student wrote that at YouthBuild, "instead of getting mad or frustrated, we would just fix anything that need to be fixed," highlighting how he wrote about strength in their perseverance and responsibility.

For some, Bull City Youthbuild was more than a chance to recreate stability in their lives, but as they wrote: YouthBuild "made me a better person," and "What Youthbuild means to me is guiding me to the right path of success." For these students, it was their involvement in the community-based organization that fostered this support system that they felt they needed to lift them up toward the future. These findings from our analysis of *Blueprints: Rebuilding Lives and Redesigning Futures* demonstrate how the narrative writing process fostered student engagement in their community-based organization as they reflected upon the qualities of leadership, education, and service.

Juntos, NC Findings

The Juntos Hispanic Literacy Group created a safe space for identity exploration as the participants explored their positionality as immigrant students with friends and peers who could relate to or understand their experiences. As Briza wrote in her letter to the educational stakeholders of her school district: "We are the next generation of the United States. We are the children of immigrants who left everything behind for us to have this opportunity. We are also some of the students most persecuted for the most minimal mistakes." Here, Briza employed the pronoun "we" to unify the Latino youth of this writing group, but also the voice of all immigrant youth. While the immigrant experience is very diverse and unique for all, Briza pointedly positions and frames these stances with "we" to highlight the generalizing stereotyping and blanketing maltreatment of immigrant and first-generation youth in America. A similar usage of "we" is seen throughout these texts, including Andrea's poem on the American dream (see Figure 26.4).

After the publication of their first book, the student authors then used their printed narratives to advocate for the immigrant community. When asked to write a poem about her relationship to language (see Figure 26.4), Andrea wrote: "We need to be more than just sounds, / We need to be the difference in the community." Thus, the student authors of HLG performed readings and wrote pieces responding to the political climate and the topic of immigration, as well as the realities of discrimination, inequality, and the threat of deportation. In doing so, they advocated for better educational standards and equity in the classroom and increased accessibility to the American dream for all. As Kevin stated in his autoethnography regarding immigration and the American government: "I still hold hope because if this country's short history has taught me anything it's that no matter what challenges we face, eventually the power and voice of the people shine through."

We all come with one dream,
We want anything but being separated from parents or loved ones.
We all have the desire of a better future,
More opportunities.
Even when we are put down or to the side in our hearts we still have the same dream.
With or without an accent we should speak up with no fear.
We need to be more than just sounds,
We need to be the difference in the community.
We need to do what feels right in order to make an impact, to open eyes.
We are to fight, keep our heads up, be united and be strong.
We will come together and deliver the message we want.

FIGURE 26.4 "Dreams and Desire" by Juntos, NC Student Andrea Zavala-Cervantes

As the authors revealed through their writing and advocating: together their voices are effecting change, and *juntos sus voces están haciendo transformaciones.*

In sharing their narratives with community members through book readings at local bookstores, schools, and university settings, Juntos NC students received powerful responses from their audiences. One attendee wrote that after listening to the students read from their book they "learned that high school students can be serious writers," highlighting a need for promoting more transformative and restorative writing practices with youth. Some attendees connected personally with the Juntos NC students and wrote that "this reading made me feel proud to be a Latino," which revealed how impactful it can be to have texts that mirror one's experience. Finally, audience members also wrote directly to the students calling for them to "keep finding your own voice even when all others are shouting at you" and "You are enough … You are our future," offering praise and empowerment to the Juntos NC students to continue creating and writing their stories.

Conclusion

This project succeeded in expanding its critical literacy framework (Comber, 2015; Freire, 1985; Morrell, 2008) through a theory of change for youth literacy and leadership. Our findings show how a logic model structured around theoretical assumptions helped us to use critical literacy theories to achieve youth literacy and leadership goals in the context of community-based organizations. Our logic model translates the underlying assumptions of the critical literacy framework into relationships among the required resources, the activities the youth will experience, student deliverables (outputs) over the duration of the project, as well as projected outcomes and impacts. The results of our project are consistent with previous research findings and provide further evidence that student and youth empowerment is enabled when they have the opportunity for the discussion, analysis, and sharing of their own experiences and stories in a community-based setting.

Rooted in critical literacy theory, our findings reveal that when youth express themselves in writing alongside their peers at community-based organizations, it helps them position and see themselves within their communities (Camangian, 2008; Campano, Ghiso, Rusoja, et al., 2016; Johnson, 2017). By doing so, they move past external labels or stereotypes (Watson & Beymeyer, 2019; Winn, 2010) and develop a stronger sense of self. The findings also show that as youth are encouraged to explore their own lives, they develop more positive self-identities (Fisher, 2003). Our findings also show that literacy programs embedded in youth-serving CBOs enable students to find academic potential outside of traditional schools and push them to question and explore system-wide educational structures.

The results of this project may also have important implications for how we continue to build our university–school–community partnerships. As students in this project developed critical literacy skills they began to increasingly question and explore system-wide educational structures. Their questions and explorations may ultimately provide educators with valuable insights into how these partnerships can better serve traditionally marginalized and underserved students of color as well as immigrant and first-generation students.

References

Angrosino, M. V., & Mays de Pérez, K. A. (2000). Rethinking observation: From method to context. In N. K. Denzin & Y. S. Lincoln, *Handbook of qualitative research* (pp. 673–702). SAGE.

Bogdan, R. C., & Biklen, S. K. (2007). *Qualitative research for education: An introduction to theories and methods.* Laureate Education, Inc.

Brooks, W., & Smith, M. W. (2013). Documenting instructional practices in a literacy-infused arts program: Respecting pedagogues from the community. *Journal of Adolescent and Adult Literacy, 57*(1), 51–59. Retrieved February 18, 2020 from www.jstor.org/stable/24034327.

Camangian, P. (2008). Untempered tongues: Teaching performance poetry for social justice. *English Teaching: Practice and Critique, 7*(2), 35–55.

Cammarota, J. (2011). From hopelessness to hope: Social justice pedagogy in urban education and youth development. *Urban Education, 46*(4), 828–844.

Campano, G., Ghiso, M. P., Rusoja, A., Player, G. D., & Schwab, E. R. (2016). "Education without boundaries": Literacy pedagogies and human rights. *Language Arts, 94*(1), 43–53.

Campano, G., Ghiso, M. P., & Welch, B. J. (2016). *Partnering with immigrant communities: Action through literacy.* Teachers College Press.

Comber, B. (2015). Critical literacy and social justice. *Journal of Adolescent & Adult Literacy, 58*(5), 362–367.

Creswell, J. W. (2012). *Qualitative inquiry and research design: Choosing among five approaches* (3rd ed.). SAGE.

Dyson, A. H., & Genishi, C. (2005). *On the case* (Vol. 76). Teachers College Press.

Fisher, M. (2003). Open mics and open minds: Spoken word poetry in African diaspora participatory literacy communities. *Harvard Educational Review, 73*(3), 362–389.

Freire, P. (1985). *The pedagogy of the oppressed.* Continuum.

Gardner, J. (2011). Placed blame: Narratives of youth culpability. *Urban Education, 46*(4), 588–610.

Green, K. L. (2013). "The way we hear ourselves is different from the way others hear us": Exploring the literate identities of a black radio youth collective. *Equity & Excellence in Education, 46*(3), 315–326.

Harris, D. H., & Kiyama, J. M. (2013). The role of school and community-based programs in aiding Latina/o high school persistence. *Education and Urban Society, 47*(2), 182–206.

Johnson, L. P. (2017). Writing the self: Black queer youth challenge heteronormative ways of being in an after-school writing club. *Research in the Teaching of English, 52*(1), 13–33.

Kelly, C. (2012). Recognizing the "social" in literacy as a social practice: Building on the resources of nonmainstream students. *Journal of Adolescent & Adult Literacy, 55*(7), 608–618.

LeCompte, M., & Schensul, J. (2010). *Designing and conducting ethnographic research.* AltaMira.

McMillon, G. T. (2016). School–university–community collaboration: Building bridges at the water's edge. *Journal of Adolescent and Adult Literacy, 60*(4), 375–381.

Morrell, E. (2008). *Critical literacy and urban youth: Pedagogies of access, dissent, and liberation.* Routledge.

Rodríguez-Valls, F. (2016). Pedagogy of the immigrant: A journey towards inclusive classrooms. *Teachers and Curriculum, 16*(1), 41–48.

Stewart, M. A. (2013). Giving voice to Valeria's story: Support, value, and agency for immigrant adolescents. *Journal of Adolescent & Adult Literacy, 57*(1), 42–50.

Suárez-Orozco, C. (2017) The diverse immigrant student experience: What does it mean for teaching? *Educational Studies, 53*(5), 522–534. https://doi.org/10.1080/00131946.2017.1355796

Vasudevan, L., Stageman, D., Jay, J, Rodriguez, K., Fernandez, E., & Dattatreyan, E. G. (2010). Authoring new narratives with youth at the intersection of the arts and justice. *Perspectives on Urban Education, 7*(1), 54–65.

Wang, F., & Hannafin, M. J. (2005). Design-based research and technology-enhanced learning environments. *Educational Technology Research and Development, 53*(4), 5–23.

Warren, M. (2005) Communities and schools: A new view of urban education reform. *Harvard Educational Review, 75*(2), 133–173.

Watson, V. & Beymeyer, A. (2019). Praisesongs of place: Youth envisioning space and place in a literacy and songwriting initiative. *Research in the Teaching of English, 53*(4), 297–319.

Winn, M. T. (2010). "Betwixt and between": Literacy, liminality, and the ceiling of Black girls. *Race, Ethnicity and Education, 13*(4), 425–447.

Winn, M. T. (2013). Toward a restorative English education. *Research in the Teaching of English, 48*(1), 126–135.

Wright, D. E., & Mahiri, J. (2012). Literacy learning within community action projects for social change. *Journal of Adolescent and Adult Literacy, 56*(2), 123–131.

INDEX

Abas, S., 193
adolescent literacy, 29, 60–61; identity
  and, 91; identity and disciplinary
  literacies and, 211–12; *See also* FIU
  MS in Reading/Literacy Education;
  GSU student teachers and homeless
  youth tutoring; *Mentoring in Literary
  Enhancement (MILE)*
adult education and literacy, 6, 47,
  224–26, 246–47; reduced recidivism and,
  114–15; volunteers and, 258–59; *See also*
  Broadband Technology Opportunities
  Program (BTOP); Language Partners
  (LP); PluggedInVA (PIVA); Women's
  Literacy Network (WLN)
after-school STEM programs. *See* STEM
  in afterschool programs
Airport Book, The (Brown), 318
Alarcón, Francisco, 16, 18
American Academy of Pediatrics
  (AAP), 198
Anderson, M.T., 180–81
anti-racism, 37. *See also* culturally relevant
  pedagogy; culturally sustaining pedagogy
Assassination of Brangwain Spurge, The
  (Anderson and Yelchin), 180–81
assessment of literacy, 62–63, **64**, 197; Basic
  Reading Inventory (BRI), **64**; Florida
  Standardized Assessment and, 67, **68**, 69;
  Measure of Academic Progress (MAP),
  320–21; miscue analysis, 260–61,
  263–65, 267, 292, 294; National

Assessment of Educational Progress
  (NAEP), 292, 316
at-home literacy, 3, 40–44, 163–64, 172–73
Au, K.H., 60

baby boomers, 128
Baker, C., 44
Basic Interpersonal Communication Skills
  (BICS), 38–39, 42–44
Basic Reading Inventory (BRI), **64**
Baumgartner, L.M., 246, 248
Bears on Wheels (Berenstain), 41
Becker, Aaron, **177**, 180
Belzer, A., 258
Berry, Wendell, 147–48
Between the Lines program (Blanton
  Museum of Art, Austin, TX), *174*, 175,
  177–79, *179*
bilanguaging, 121. *See also* bilingualism
bilingual education, 3, 35; bilingual
  family learning case study, 37, 39–44;
  bilingualism, 11, 18–19, 36, 44, 124;
  graphic organizers and, *18*, 18–20,
  20; language mapping and, 20–21, *22*;
  mixed-level and intergenerational, 47;
  reasons for lack of enthusiasm for,
  36–37; two-way bilingual education
  models and, 36. *See also* Cabrini
  ESOL Center
Bilingual Superheroes / Superhéroes Bilingües,
  18, 18–20, *20*
bilingualism, 11, 18–19, 36, 44, 124

Blanton Museum of Art (Austin, TX): *Art of the Book* event (BookPeople book store) and, 180–82; *Between the Lines* program, *174*, 175, 177–79, **179**, *179*; *Tales & Trails (Cuentos and Caminos)*, 172–75, *174*, **176–77**; *See also* museum-based programs

BookPeople (independent bookstore), 180

Books in Motion, 157–59, 160–67, **161**; list of books covered by, **158**; as model of intergenerational literacy, 159–60. *See also* public library programs

Bowlby, J., 40

Broadband Technology Opportunities Program (BTOP): study details, 226; tutor participants and experiences, 226–33

Bronfenbrenner, U., 60–61, 69

Bull City YouthBuild, 342–44, 348–53, *352*

Cabrini ESOL Center, 47–48; community building and, 52; ESOL curriculum building and, 51–52; history and context, 48–49; intergenerational class formation, 49–50; methodology and participants, 50–51; normalizing vulnerability with creativity, 55–58, *56*; parent-child relationships as classroom resource and, 52–53, *53–54*; peer relationships and, 54–55

Calling the Doves/El Canto de Las Palomas (Herrera), 14

Cambiaso, Luca, *179*

CANDLES Holocaust museum, 184, 190–93; background of and Holocaust, 185; Eva Kor's life lesson storytelling, 187–90; literacy and critical practices at, 186, **194**, *194*; participatory action research (PAR) at, 187–90, *188–89*, *191*; picture of Holocaust timeline, *188*; walking interview methodology and, 186–87, 193. *See also* museum-based programs

Chair for My Mother, A (Williams), 102, 107–8

Chan, A.H., 129

Chen, K., 129

Chinen, K., 29

Chinese heritage language schools, 24–26, 29

citizenship, 44, 61

Cognitive Academic Language Proficiency (CALP), 38–40, 42–44

collaboration, 31, 303, 310–12, *311*, 337–39; in reading instruction to "at-risk" youth, 302. *See also Mentoring in Literary Enhancement (MILE)*

collectivity, 78

communities of practice (COP) framework, 249, 252–53; Women's Literacy Network (WLN) and, 259

community literacy, 2, 12, 78, 160–61, 163, 166–67, 203, 344

community-engaged methodologies, 12–13

context: defined, 5

creativity and community, 47–49, 52, 55–58, *56*, 119–21, *120*, 180. *See also* Cabrini ESOL Center; museum-based programs

critical literacy, 186–87, 348, 352, 354–55; immigrant students and, 345–46; Literacy and Community Initiative and, 343–44; marginalized students and, 345

Crossing Borders with Bilingual Poetry workshop, 16–18, *17*

cultural literacy, 75, 203

culturally relevant pedagogy, 4, 60, 75, 203–5, 331, 338; assessment of literacy and, **77**, 83; restorative English education, 345; STEM and, 315–20, *319*; teacher education and, 336–39. *See also* FIU MS in Reading/Literacy Education

culturally sustaining pedagogy (CSP), 60, 73–75, **76–77**, 77; collectivity and, 78, 83–86. *See also* Fijian community literacy for young children

Cummins, Jim, 38–39, 44

Curdt-Christiansen, X.L., 29

Cushman, E., 219

Dawn's Presence - Two Columns (Nevelson), 174

demonstration as literacy component, 182

Dew/El rocío (bilingual poem, Alarcón), 16

Dewey, John, 61, 147

differentiation: FIU MS in Reading/Literacy Education and, 60, 63, **64–66**

digital divide, 129–30

digital literacies. *See* technology literacies

disciplinary literacies (DL), 211–12

Discourse community, 216, 219

discussion as literacy component, 102–3, 106, 108–10, 182

Dreamers (Morales), 55–56

drug rehab programs, 103, 105. *See also* fathers and trauma informed literacy; Healthy Transformations Rehabilitation Facility (HTRF)

dual-immersion bilingual schools, 3, 36, 333; two-way bilingual education models and, 36

early childhood literacy, 238–39; STEM programs and, 315–16

East Asian community-based writing programs, 24–25; history of, 25–26; language socialization and maintenance and, 31

educational workforce development initiatives, 6. *See also* PluggedInVa

elderly population. *See* gerontechnology and iPads

emergent bilinguals: translanguaging framework for, 11–13

Emmons, C., 219

empowerment theory, 202, 216–17, 224, 345, 350, 354–55; adult volunteer tutors in digital literacies program and, 227–31, 233; identity development and, 5–6

English: in Fiji, 73–74; as focus of second-language learning in U.S., 35

English as a Second Language . *See also* Cabrini ESOL Center

English Language Arts: museum programs supporting, 239–42

ESOL curriculum, 3, 47, 51–52

Esther and Ahasuerus (painting, Cambiaso), *179*

ethics, **77**, 81–83, 291

ethnic identity, 29–30

Fagan, W., 160–61

faith-based programs, 2–3, 47–48, 145, 148. *See also* Cabrini ESOL Center

family literacy, 102; bilingual family learning case study, 37, 39–44; shared reading and, 104–5; trauma-informed approaches to, 110–11. *See also* Cabrini ESOL Center; fathers and trauma informed literacy

fathers and trauma informed literacy, 102, 107–11; theoretical perspectives and related research and, 103–4; trauma defined, 103–4. *See also* family literacy

field experiences: GSU student teachers and homeless youth tutoring and, 92–98

Fijian community literacy for young children, 4, 73–74; culturally sustaining pedagogy (CSP) and, 75, **76–77**, 77, 83–86, *85*; *Mandir* (trilingual picture book, The Temple) and, 78–81, *79*, 83; multilingual books created, 73–74, **76**, 77–79, 83–86, *85*, 86; strategies developed with communities, 78–79, *79*

FIU MS in Reading/Literacy Education, 59, 65; course content, 62–63; design of program, 59–62; differentiation and class assignments, 63, **64–66**; FSA score case study, 67–69, **68**

Florida Standardized Assessment (FSA), 67, **68**, 69

Four 4-H handbook 7, 273, 283–87, *284–86*

Freebody, P., 84–85

Freire, P., 6, 185, 187, 291, 294, 344

gamification, 217–18, 237–38

Gaon Mei Saal Ke Karikaran (A Year in Our Community), 83

García, O., 44, 91, 117

Gee, J.P., 38, 119, 212, 216–17, 238

gerontechnology and iPads, 4, 130; case study of at senior living center, 131–39. *See also* technology literacies

Girl Scouts of America, 7, 273, 278–80, *279–81*

Go, Dog, Go! (Eastman), 41

Goodman, K.S., 259–60

graphic organizers, *18*, 18–20, *20*

Green State University, 89–91. *See also* GSU student teachers and homeless youth tutoring

GSU student teachers and homeless youth tutoring, 91–92, 98–99; community-based field experiences, 92–98; Family Partnership model, 89–91

Haitian communities, 3, 59–60, **68**

health literacy, 197, 201–2, **204**

health services-based programs, 5, 197; culturally relevant pedagogy and, 203–5; early literacy promotion and interventions and, 198–200, 204–5; language nutrition and Talk With Me Baby (TWMB) program and, 200; literacy-related barriers to health info interventions, 202; marketing of literacy services and, 200–201. *See also Reach Out and Read* (ROR)

Healthy Transformations Rehabilitation Facility (HTRF), 105; family literacy program description, 106

Heath, S.B., 75

heritage language programs, 4, 24–27, 30; language maintenance, 24, 31; language socialization and, 27; traditional value inculcation and, 27–29; transnationalism and, 26. *See also* East Asian community-based writing programs; Fijian community literacy for young children

Herrera, Juan Felipe, 14

Holland, D., 214–15, 218

Holocaust, 5, 185, *188*, 193. *See also* CANDLES Holocaust Museum

homeless youth, 4. *See also* GSU student teachers and homeless youth tutoring

Hoot (Hiassen), 158, 167

Hull, Glynda, 1

Huron River Youth and Family Center (HFC) partnership, 332–39

identity development, 211–12; empowerment theory and, 5–6; heritage language schools and, 27, 29–30; service-learning projects and, 214–16

Ilsley, P., 259

immigrant youths, 7, 11, 20, 37, 39, 48–49, 114, 121–22, *123*, 260; critical literacy and, 345–46. *See also* Cabrini ESOL Center; Haitian communities; heritage language programs

In My Family / En Mi Familia (Garza), 107

incarceration rates, 289

Indigenous peoples, 75–76, 203–4

information literacy, 131. *See also* metaliteracy

interactive theatre, 5, 121–22, *123*

intergenerational literacy programs, 5, 47, 49–50, 159–60. *See also* Books in Motion; Cabrini ESOL Center; gerontechnology and iPads

International Literary Association Standards for Reading Professionals, 331

iPad technology in elder populations. *See* gerontechnology and iPads

IT jobs. *See* PluggedInVA (PIVA)

Janks, H., 119

Japanese heritage language schools, 24–26, 29

Journey (Becker), **176–77**, 180

Juntos NC, 342–44, 348–54, *351*, *353*

juvenile detention/residential center programs, 7, 289–98, 302; literacy research and youth literacy rates, 302–3. *See also Mentoring in Literary Enhancement (MILE)*

Kahne, J., 61

Kim, J., 28, 152

Kim, J.-I., 29

Kim, S.J., 28

Knapczyk, Jillian J., 148

Kor, Eva and Miriam Mozes, 185, 188, 192–93. *See also* CANDLES Holocaust museum

Korean heritage language schools, 24, 26, 28–29

Kularski, C.M., 129

Ladson-Billings, G., 60, 75

language development, 2–3; language nutrition and Talk With Me Baby (TWMB) program and, 200

language ideologies, challenging, 119–21, *120*

language maintenance, 24, 31

language mapping, 20–21, *22*

Language Partners (LP): challenging language ideologies and, 119–21, *120*, 124–25; data analysis and participatory action research, 117; history of, 115–16; as minoritizing or liberatory space, 116, 123–25; monoglossic language ideologies and, 115, 117–19, *118*, 121–22, 124. *See also* prison-based programs

language socialization: heritage language schools and, 27

Latinx community, 11, 20, 37, 39, 48–49, 114, 260

Lave, J., 249, 259

Li Wei, 12

literacy: defined, 12, 274

Literacy and Community Initiative (LCI), 342–43; critical literacy framework, 344; immigrant students and, 345–46; marginalized students and, 345; *Write, Engage,* and *Lead* model and, 343; youth leadership and literacy, 346–47, *347*. *See also* Bull City YouthBuild; Juntos NC

literacy expectations within youth organization handbooks, 7, 273–75,

286–87. *See also* Four 4-H; Girl Scouts of America; Scouts BSA; text readability
Little Free Libraries, 150–51
low-income housing and reading access, 148–50
Luk, A., 259, 266–67
Luke, A., 84–85, 124

Maguire, M.H., 29
Mandir (trilingual picture book, The Temple), 78–81, *79*, 83
McGuffey Readers, 145–46
Measure of Academic Progress (MAP), 320–21
Medina, Jane, 16
Mentoring in Literary Enhancement (MILE), 303–4; collaboration and, 303, 310–12, *311*; evolution of, 305–9, *306*; SOAP notes and reflective dialogue and, 304–5, 307–11
Merriam, S.B., 246, 248
metaliteracy, 131
miscue analysis, 260, 292, 294
Moje, E., 212, 217–19
Moll, Luis, 60, 75
Moller, S., 129
monoglossic language ideologies, 16, 22, 115, 117–19, *118*, 121–22, 124
Morales, Yuyi, 55–56
Most Magnificent Thing, The (Spires), 173, *174*, **176**
motivation, 5, 29–30, 40, 121, 139, 163, 177, 213, 219, 240, 247–48, 253, 316, 349
multilingual texts, 73–74, **76**, 77–79, 83–86, *85*, 86
multiliteracies, 91
museum-based programs, 5–6, 171–72, 182–83, 193, 235; English Language Arts programs, 239–42; social transformation and, 184, 186; story telling and, 187–90. *See also* Blanton Museum of Art (Austin, TX); CANDLES Holocaust Museum; Toledo Museum of Art visual literacy program

National Assessment of Educational Progress (NAEP), 292, 316
national youth organizations and literacy, 273, **275**. *See also* Four 4-H; Girl Scouts of America; Scouts BSA
Neuman, Susan, 148
Nevelson, Louise, 174

Nichols, S., 198, 200
Nimrod, G., 130
No Child Left Behind Act of 2001, 59

Orpheus Charming the Beasts (painting, Scorza), 179–80, *181*

parent-child relationships: as classroom resource, 52–53, *53–54*
Parker, Frances, 146–47
participatory action research (PAR), 4, 74, 115–17, 125; at CANDLES Holocaust museum, 187–90, *188–89*, *191*
partnership literacy programs, 6. *See also* 4-H; Girl Scouts of America; Scouts BSA
Patton, M.Q., 131
peer instruction, 4, 6, 54–55, 124–25, 214, 225, 238, 311, 334, 336, 338, 344, 348, 353, 355. *See also* Language Partners (LP)
Perry, J., 259, 266–67
PluggedInVA (PIVA), 246, 250–56; background of, 247–48; communities of practice (COP) framework in, 249; PIVA model, 248–49
poetry, 16–18, *17*
positioning theory model, 212, 215
practitioner inquiry studies, 3, 47–48, 51
prison-based programs, 4, 7, 114–15. *See also* juvenile detention/residential center programs; Language Partners (LP)
public library programs, 5, 157. *See also* Books in Motion

Reach Out and Read (ROR), 199, 203. *See also* health services-based programs
Reading A-Z program, 305–8, 310
Renkert, S., 202
retrospective miscue analysis (RMA), 260–61, 263–65, 267
Rock Bottom (Mitchell), 173, **176**
rural programs, 5, 7; historical and philosophical background and, 145–48; Little Free Libraries and, 150–51; low-income housing and reading access and, 148–50; summer literacy programs, 151–56, **153–54**

Sandman-Hurley, K., 258
School's Out: Bridging Out-of-School Literacies with Classroom Practices (Hull and Schultz), 1
Schultz, Katherine, 1

Scorza, Sinibaldo, 179, *181*

Scouts BSA, 7, 273, **275**, 280–83, *282*

second-language learning: BICS and CALP and, 38–39, 42–44; dual-immersion model and, 36; at elementary level, 35–36; English as focus of in U.S., 35

service-learning projects, 6, 145, 212–14, 218–19, 338–39; citizenship and, 61; empowerment, critical responses and curating within, 216–17; identity development and, 214–16; literate identities and, 219

shared reading, 104–5

Shor, I., 216

Sleeter, C., 330

SOAP notes, 304–5, 307–11

Social Emotional Learning (SEL), 171–72, 177

social justice and transformation, 7, 37, 213; CANDLES Holocaust museum and, 184, 186, 190–93; ethics and, **77**, 81–83, 291; Language Partners (LP) and, 116, 123–25; reading partnerships and, 297–98; teacher education and, 289, 330–31; tutor's perspective of, 259. *See also* GSU student teachers and homeless youth tutoring; service-learning projects; STEM in afterschool programs

social media, 134, 193

social networks, 218–19

sociocultural perspectives, 103

Spangenberg, G., 115

Spanish, 37; as pedagogical tool, 121–22, *123*

Spanish/English bilingual programs, 11–13. *See also* emergent bilingual learners

spatial justice, 3

STEM in afterschool programs, 7, 315–26, 316–26, 317–20; culturally relevant pedagogy and, 315–20, *319*

storytelling, 5, 187–90, 193

summer literacy programs, 7, 151–56, **153–54**

Tales & Trails (Cuentos and Caminos) program (Blanton Museum of Art, Austin, TX), 172–75, *174*; books and artworks used in, **176–77**

Talk With Me Baby (TWMB), 200

teacher education, 7, 242–44, 297–98, 302–3; culturally relevant pedagogy and, 330–31, 336–39; field experiences and, 92–98, 302, 331, 338; juvenile detention/residential center programs and, 7, 289–98, 301–2; lack of diversity in prospective teachers, 330; unofficial teaching spaces and, 98–99; Urban Teacher Academy, 317; value-added methods (VAMs) and, 330. *See also* FIU MS in Reading/Literacy Education; GSU student teachers and homeless youth tutoring; Huron River Youth and Family Center (HFC) partnership; *Mentoring in Literary Enhancement (MILE)*

technology literacies, 128, 193, 223–24; digital divide and, 129–30; metaliteracy and, 131; review of relevant literature and, 129; volunteer tutors and, 232–33. *See also* Broadband Technology Opportunities Program (BTOP); gerontechnology and iPads; PluggedInVA (PIVA)

technophobia, 130

text readability, 276, 286–87; 4-H handbook and, 283, *284–86*; in Girl Scouts of America handbooks, 278–80, *279–80*; Scouts BSA handbook and, 281–83, *282*

Thomas, W.P., 36, 39, 44

Thunberg, Greta, 216

Tierney, R.J., 211, 216

To Kill a Mockingbird (Lee), 158, 162, 165, 167

Toledo Museum of Art visual literacy program, 6, 235–36; pre-literacy tier two vocabulary program with Toledo Public Schools, 238–39; teaching pedagogy and design principles, 237–39; visual literacy and textual literacy, 236–37. *See also* museum-based programs

Tonatiuh, Duncan, 19

translanguaging, 11–15, 20–22

transnationalism, 26; heritage language schools and, 31

trauma-informed approach. *See* fathers and trauma informed literacy

Tucker, G.R., 29

Undocumented: A Worker's Fight (Tonatiuh), 19

unique communities, 3–4

university/community-based partnership programs, 7, 193, 289, 292, 317, 331–32, 342, 355; Cabrini ESOL Center and U of Pennsylvania as, 48–49.

See also FIU MS in Reading/Literacy
Education; GSU student teachers and
homeless youth tutoring; Huron River
Youth and Family Center (HFC)
partnership; Literacy and Community
Initiative (LCI); *Mentoring in Literary
Enhancement (MILE)*
unofficial spaces, 91–92, 98–99. *See also*
Healthy Transformations Rehabilitation
Facility (HTRF)
Urban Teacher Academy, 317

Verdi (Cannon), 173, **176**
visual literacy, 236–37. *See also* Toledo
Museum of Art visual literacy program
volunteer tutoring, 6, 225–26; adult
education and literacy and, 258–59;
empowerment theory and, 229–31;
technology literacies and, 232–33.
See also Broadband Technology
Opportunities Program (BTOP);
*Mentoring in Literary Enhancement
(MILE)*; Women's Literacy
Network (WLN)

walking interview methodology,
186–87, 193
We Need Diverse Books Movement, 316
Wegner, E., 249, 259
Westheimer, J., 61
*What Teachers Can Do When Kids Can't
Read* (Beers), 62
White, T., 152
Winn, M.T., 345
Women's Literacy Network (WLN),
263–67; communities of practice
theory and, 259; description of, 260–62;
retrospective miscue analysis (RMA)
and, 260–61, 263–65, 267
Wright, W.E., 44
Write, Engage, and *Lead* model, 7, 343
writing programs for emergent bilinguals,
13–22; theoretical perspectives and, 26–27;
translanguaging framework for, 11–13

Yelchin, Eugene, 180–81
youth lens, 91

Zeichner, K., 302

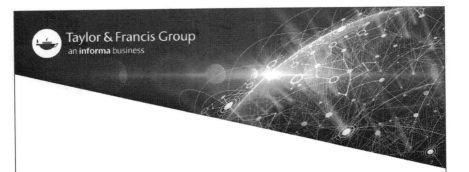